A
PEACEABLE
HOPE

A
PEACEABLE
HOPE

Contesting Violent Eschatology
in New Testament Narratives

David J. Neville

Baker Academic
a division of Baker Publishing Group
Grand Rapids, Michigan

Published by Baker Academic
a division of Baker Publishing Group
P.O. Box 6287, Grand Rapids, MI 49516-6287
www.bakeracademic.com

Printed in the United States of America

Library of Congress Cataloging-in-Publication Data
Neville, David J.
    A peaceable hope : contesting violent eschatology in New Testament narratives / David J.
Neville.
        p.   cm.
    Includes bibliographical references (p.   ) and index.
    ISBN 978-0-8010-4851-7 (pbk.)
    1. Bible. N.T.—Criticism, Narrative. 2. Narration in the Bible. 3. Violence in the Bible.
4. Violence—Biblical teaching. 5. Eschatology—Biblical teaching. I. Title.
BS2361.3.N465 2012
225.6—dc23   2012030498

New Testament Scripture is translated by the author.

13   14   15   16   17   18   19   7   6   5   4   3   2   1

For Sonia,
who shares my hope no less than my life

Contents

Studies in Peace and Scripture
Series Preface

Visions of peace abound in the Bible, whose pages are also filled with the language of violence. In this respect, the Bible is thoroughly at home in the modern world, whether as a literary classic or as a unique sacred text. This is, perhaps, a part of the Bible's realism: bridging the distance between its world and our own is a history filled with visions of peace accompanying the reality of violence and war. That alone would justify study of peace and war in the Bible. However, for those communities in which the Bible is sacred Scripture, the matter is more urgent. For them, it is crucial to understand what the Bible says about peace—and about war. These issues have often divided Christians from one another, and the way Christians have understood them has had terrible consequences for Jews and, indeed, for the world. A series of scholarly investigations cannot hope to resolve these issues, but it can hope, as this one does, to aid our understanding of them.

Over the past century a substantial body of literature has grown up around the topic of the Bible and war. Studies in great abundance have been devoted to historical questions about ancient Israel's conception and conduct of war and about the position of the early church on participation in the Roman Empire and its military. It is not surprising that many of these studies have been motivated by theological and ethical concerns, which may themselves be attributed to the Bible's own seemingly disjunctive preoccupation with peace and, at the same time, with war. If not within the Bible itself, then at least from Aqiba and Tertullian, the question has been raised whether—and if so, then on what basis—those who worship God may legitimately participate in war. With the Reformation, the churches divided on this question. The division was unequal, with the majority of Christendom agreeing that, however regrettable war may be, Christians have biblical warrant for participating in it. A minority countered that, however necessary war may appear, Christians have a biblical mandate to avoid it. Modern historical studies have served to bolster one side of this division or the other.

Meanwhile, it has become clear that a narrow focus on participation in war is not the only way, and likely not the best way, to approach the Bible on the topic of peace. War and peace are not simply two sides of the same coin; each is broader than its contrast with the other. Since the twentieth century and refinement of weapons of mass destruction, the violence of war has been an increasingly urgent concern. Peace, however, is not just the absence of war, but the well-being of all people. In spite of this agreement, the number of studies devoted to the Bible and peace is still quite small, especially in English. Consequently, answers to the most basic questions remain to be settled. Among these questions is that of what the Bible means in speaking of *shalom* or *eirēnē*, the Hebrew and the Greek terms usually translated into English as "peace." By the same token, what the Bible has to say about peace is not limited to its use of these two terms. Questions remain about the relation of peace, in the Bible, to considerations of justice, integrity, and—in the broadest sense—salvation. And of course there still remains the question of the relation between peace and war. In fact, what the Bible says about peace is often framed in the language of war. The Bible very often uses martial imagery to portray God's own action, whether it be in creation, in judgment against or in defense of Israel, or in the cross and resurrection of Jesus Christ—actions aimed at achieving peace.

This close association of peace and war, to which we have already drawn attention, presents serious problems for the contemporary appropriation of the Bible. Are human freedom, justice, and liberation—and the liberation of creation—furthered or hindered by the martial, frequently royal, and pervasively masculine terms in which the Bible speaks of peace? These questions cannot be answered by the rigorous and critical exegesis of the biblical texts alone; they demand serious moral and theological reflection as well. But that reflection will be substantially aided by exegetical studies of the kind included in this series, even as these studies will be illumined by including just that kind of reflection within them.

In the present volume, David Neville investigates passages in the New Testament Gospels, Acts, and Revelation that portray a violent *eschaton*. His concern is that throughout the centuries, Christians have been drawn to the violent eschatology of the first and last books of the New Testament without appreciation for the tension between the moral vision presented in the accounts of Jesus' life and vengeful end-time judgment. Rather, Neville proposes a "*shalom*-oriented canonical trajectory" and offers several "treasure texts" to aid in reading the Gospels, Acts, and Revelation. His work contributes to and expands the purposes of the series.

Studies in Peace and Scripture is sponsored by the Institute of Mennonite Studies, the research agency of the Anabaptist Mennonite Biblical Seminary.

The seminary and the tradition it represents have a particular interest in peace and, even more so, an abiding interest in the Bible. We hope that this ecumenical series will contribute to a deeper understanding of both.

Laura L. Brenneman, New Testament Editor
Ben C. Ollenburger, Old Testament Editor

Preface and Acknowledgments

The theological and moral conundrum explored in this book has been with me for some time, but I began to work on it in earnest in a paper presented at the 2005 International Society of Biblical Literature meeting in Singapore. In 2006 I was granted sabbatical leave for the second half of the year, during which time I prepared for publication two journal articles on moral vision and eschatology in the Gospels according to Matthew and Mark. It was then that I also carefully read Willard Swartley's landmark work on New Testament theology and ethics, *Covenant of Peace*.[1] I remain grateful to Stephen Pickard, then director of St. Mark's National Theological Centre in Canberra, and the Council of St. Mark's for making possible that period of study leave. At that point, this book had not yet been conceived, but preliminary steps toward it had been taken.

In 2008 Rodney Clapp, then editorial director of Brazos Press, was instrumental in accepting my proposal for this book. I underestimated how long it would take for me to make good on the proposal, and he moved on shortly before I submitted the manuscript. I nevertheless acknowledge his generosity and kindness in accepting my book proposal. Since his departure from Brazos Press, my book has been carefully shepherded toward publication by Robert Hosack, executive editor of Baker Academic, and my editor, Lisa Ann Cockrel. To both Bob and Lisa, as well as to others at Baker who have worked on this book, I express heartfelt thanks.

To facilitate progress on this book, I was granted a brief period of study leave during the southern summer months of 2009–10. I am grateful to the current director of St. Mark's, Tom Frame, and the St. Mark's Council for relieving me of my administrative responsibilities for a couple of months to

---

1. Swartley, *Covenant of Peace*. My initial response to this book appeared as a review article: Neville, "Second Testament."

enable me to draft the central part of this book. I also acknowledge Heather Thomson's gracious willingness to shoulder the administrative responsibilities I cast aside during that time. In this and other ways, she has supported my work.

While writing this book, I have been encouraged by a number of generous people. Some have made time to look over drafts of chapters and proffered valuable feedback. Peter Llewellyn and Russell Warnken, teaching colleagues within Charles Sturt University's School of Theology, have commented constructively on individual chapters. In response to my work on the Gospels according to Matthew and Mark, Keith Dyer of Whitley College in Melbourne has been a source of encouragement from the outset and given me much upon which to reflect. Willard Swartley kindly read the central chapters on Luke–Acts and offered constructive criticism seasoned by words of encouragement. As chapter 3 makes evident, his work on the peace theme in Luke's Gospel and Acts serves as both stimulus and basis for my treatment of Luke as the evangelist of peace. If Swartley's work has been decisive for my thinking about the Lukan literature, John Painter's scholarship has been crucial for my thinking about the Fourth Gospel. Painter, Foundation Professor of Theology in Charles Sturt University's School of Theology, read an earlier version of my chapter on the Fourth Gospel, peppering its pages with searching questions and perspicacious observations. That chapter is undoubtedly better than it would otherwise have been, but Painter is not responsible for my use of his work. I nevertheless register my gratitude for the character and caliber of his scholarship. Laura Brenneman, visiting lecturer in the department of religion at the University of Illinois at Urbana-Champaign, and Chris Marshall of Victoria University of Wellington, New Zealand, have also expressed encouragement for this project. I am especially grateful to Laura for facilitating the inclusion of this book in the Studies in Peace and Scripture series. While watching this series develop over two decades, I never dared dream that my work might one day find a place alongside authors from whom I have learned so much. I am also grateful to Steven Ogden, principal of St. Francis Theological College in Brisbane, for inviting me to deliver the 2010 Felix Arnott Lecture. His invitation afforded me the opportunity to consider my reading of Revelation in response to John Dominic Crossan's indictment of John the prophet-seer. What any of these people will make of this book upon its publication remains to be seen. They well know, in any case, that however much I might like to shirk responsibility for its shortcomings, such does not rest on them.

In various and sundry ways over the past decade, the library staff of St. Mark's Anglican National Memorial Library has been indispensable to me. In particular, Kaye Malins has tracked down monographs and articles for me via interlibrary loan, and the present library manager, Susan Phillips, has been a continuous source of encouragement. When in need of respite, I invariably conceal myself in our library.

During the writing of this book and indeed for many years, three people have played incalculable roles in my life. One of these is Thorwald Lorenzen, who has broadened my understanding of what theology and biblical interpretation mean for both the church and the wider world. Not only has he read and responded to every chapter of this book as it stuttered toward completion, but his presence and friendship have also helped to keep me sane and hopeful. From afar, Philip Matthews has kept tabs on me, keeping me honest and in more ways than one reminding me of the bigger picture. More than anyone else, however, Sonia has shared this journey with me, tolerating (sometimes even embracing) my idiosyncrasies, and keeping faith with me. Words fail me, so to Sonia I dedicate this book, with thanks for her love and companionship.

Three of the chapters of this book draw from earlier publications, albeit significantly revised in each case. I am grateful to the following publishers for permission to make use of earlier materials:

Chapter 1: "Toward a Teleology of Peace: Contesting Matthew's Violent Eschatology," *Journal for the Study of the New Testament* 30 (2007): 131–61; and "Violating Faith via Eschatological Violence: Reviewing Matthew's Eschatology," in *Validating Violence—Violating Faith? Religion, Scripture and Violence*, ed. William W. Emilsen and John T. Squires (Adelaide: ATF Press, 2008), 95–110.

Chapter 2: "Moral Vision and Eschatology in Mark's Gospel: Coherence or Conflict?" *Journal of Biblical Literature* 127 (2008): 359–84; and "Grace Elicits Correspondences: The Theologian as Peacemaker," in *Embracing Grace—The Theologian's Task: Essays in Honour of Graeme Garrett*, ed. Heather Thomson (Canberra: Barton Books, 2009), 119–34.

Chapter 7: "Faithful, True, and Violent? Christology and 'Divine Vengeance' in the Revelation to John," in *Compassionate Eschatology: The Future as Friend*, ed. Ted Grimsrud and Michael Hardin (Eugene, OR: Cascade Books, 2011), 56–84. Used by permission of Wipf and Stock Publishers. www.wipfandstock.com

Unless otherwise indicated, all translations of New Testament texts are my own. Not every passage discussed is provided in full, however, so it is recommended that readers have a copy of the Bible at hand.

David J. Neville
St. Mark's National Theological Centre
Canberra, November 2011

Introduction

There is a discrepancy at the heart of the New Testament. Briefly stated, the discrepancy is this: although the canonical Gospels present a fairly uniform picture of Jesus as an advocate of peace and practitioner of nonretaliation, certain texts within these same Gospels and in other parts of the New Testament apparently anticipate a future arrival, or *parousia*, of Jesus in the guise of a violent avenger. The same Jesus who blesses peacemakers, teaches nonretaliation, and responds nonviolently to violence directed against himself is nevertheless associated with end-time vengeance. To varying degrees, in fact, the biblical Gospels portray Jesus himself as anticipating a role in end-time judgment, whether of violent vengeance or of a more benign kind.[1] Among the four canonical Gospels, the Gospel according to Matthew accentuates the retributive character of the parousia of Jesus, whereas the other three downplay the prospect of eschatological vengeance. Outside the Gospels, the Acts of the Apostles envisages the judgment of the returning Jesus in relatively benign terms, whereas the Apocalypse of John depicts the returning Jesus in imagery suggestive of retributive vengeance. The emphasis on end-time recompense in the Gospel according to Matthew and the violent imagery employed to depict end-time judgment in the Revelation to John have had a dominant influence on the church's teaching on last things, despite the presentation in both texts of an understanding of Jesus's identity and significance incompatible with an affirmation of divine violence.

Although this book focuses principally on eschatological texts, I am not preoccupied with eschatology for its own sake. Insofar as end-time expectations contribute to shaping moral vision, moral convictions, and moral

---

1. This book is not concerned with Jesus as a historical figure but with a select number of texts in which some of his earliest interpreters witness to his enduring significance. What can be ascertained about the historical Jesus pertains to its argument, however. For example, the dispute over whether or not Jesus was an "apocalyptic prophet" bears on the substance of this study.

commitments, however, eschatological texts in the Gospels, Acts, and Revelation are profoundly important for New Testament theology and ethics.
Moreover, to the extent that the Christian conviction concerning the incarnation discloses who God is and how God relates to the world, New Testament
texts featuring divine or divinely authorized eschatological vengeance provoke
the perturbing question of whether or not Jesus's end-time role conforms to
and coheres with his historic role.

Among people of faith for whom the Gospel accounts of Jesus's mission
and message provide moral orientation, the tension caused by the biblical discrepancy between peaceful incarnation and vengeful return is disorienting no
less than perplexing. This is especially so for Christians who recognize that a
commitment to peace is at the heart of Christian discipleship. What authorizes
that commitment to peace is generally understood to be the peaceable character
and teaching of Jesus. If the returning Jesus is understood to abandon peaceful
confrontation of the powers that diminish life, however, that calls into question
the peacefulness of Jesus's historic mission—in terms of both its efficaciousness and its exemplariness. If the returning Jesus resorts to violent retribution,
must that not invalidate the particular mode of incarnation "fleshed out" by
Jesus? And if the returning Jesus resorts to vengeance, must that not offer an
alternative christologically grounded rationale for the moral life of Christians?

In recent theological discussion of the atonement, concerns have been raised
about the image of God inherent in theories of atonement fixated on propi-
tiation, penal substitution, or satisfaction of divine honor. No less troubling,
however, is the image of God inherent in end-time expectations that feature
violent retribution on the part of God and/or God's agent(s). To anticipate that
ultimately God will resort to vengeance on those who oppose the divine will is
equally likely, if not more likely, to authorize violent attitudes and conduct as
atonement theories predicated on the necessity of divinely willed violence, especially when coupled with the conviction that one (or one's group) is on God's
side and knows God's will. It has been argued that, in certain circumstances,
nonretaliation can be predicated only on the expectation of eschatological
vengeance,[2] but I find this argument troubling for two reasons. First, while
the expectation of eschatological vengeance may restrain violent retaliation
for some here and now, it may also have the opposite effect of authorizing, if
only implicitly, violent retribution for wrongs suffered or threats perceived.
Second, it effectively manufactures God in our image, largely because we find
it difficult to imagine violence being quelled by anything other than greater
violence. There is enough in the biblical narrative of God and God's ways,
especially in the story of Jesus recounted in the Gospels, to encourage people
of Jewish and Christian faith to envisage God as more creative and imaginative than we can conceive. Indeed, to insist on God's prerogative to resort to

---

2. See, e.g., Volf, *Exclusion and Embrace*, 275–306; and Holland, "Gospel of Peace."

vengeance is to call into question the salvific significance of the cross, which in Christian tradition signifies the disarming of evil.

A number of biblical passages discussed in this book might be described as both "eschatological" and "apocalyptic." These terms are sometimes used interchangeably, but to no one's advantage. Although they invariably qualify interrelated ideas found in New Testament (and related) texts, they are nevertheless distinct. For example, on the basis of extensive analysis of primary texts, Christopher Rowland argues that while eschatology features in many apocalyptic texts, it is neither necessarily present in nor determinative for all such texts.[3] For Rowland, then, within the genre of apocalyptic writings, eschatology is but one of a number of possible topics addressed. In the following description by Leander Keck, "eschatology" and "apocalyptic" are related, but not necessarily so, and "apocalyptic" serves to qualify a particular conception of "eschatology":

> Although the Greek *eschatos* means last in a sequence (as in Mk 12:22) or rank (as in Mk 10:31), in theological discourse the "eschatological" refers not to termination (as in "the end of the world") but to telos, the goal or consummation of God's purposes and activities. The expected *eschaton* takes on an "apocalyptic" cast when God's consummating action abruptly intervenes (irrupts, breaks in) in an increasingly rebellious scene, bringing both definitive judgment and salvation.[4]

On the basis of a distinction similar to that made by Keck (above), John Dominic Crossan argues for differentiating between eschatology and apocalyptic along the lines of genus to species. In other words, when conceived in relation to each other, apocalyptic may be considered a subset or particular form of eschatology, of which there are other, nonapocalyptic expressions. The views of Rowland and Crossan, two scholars who have thought long and hard about such matters, may seem the reverse of each other, but they are not mutually exclusive. The crucial point on which they concur is that to varying degrees in relation to certain texts from antiquity, eschatology and apocalyptic overlap but are not synonymous.

Perhaps the most basic distinction between eschatology and apocalyptic is that eschatology relates to a set of beliefs about the end of things, in terms of both their termination and their purpose (*telos*),[5] whereas apocalyptic relates to a perception of reality shaped by an interpretation of the flawed character of the world, especially in view of its divinely ordained origin. Eschatology concerns the realization of the divine purpose, whether by restoration to

---

3. Rowland, *Open Heaven*, 23–48. See also idem, *Christian Origins*, 54–61.

4. Keck, *Who Is Jesus?* 70.

5. In the citation from Keck above, *telos* is separated from termination, but such a separation does not pertain in biblical literature. On different ways in which the term "eschatology" has been used in theological discourse, see Caird, *Language and Imagery*, chap. 14.

original harmony or by renewal to something beyond the imaginable. Eschatological convictions as part of an apocalyptic worldview necessarily address how wrongs will ultimately be righted, how the flawed and fractured features of the world and human interrelationships will finally be fixed. In apocalyptic perspective, what is wrong with the world is beyond remedy by humanity alone; ultimately only the One responsible for the world in the first place can bring it to its intended last place, its goal.

While eschatology and apocalyptic are overlapping rather than synonymous concepts, the eschatologies of the four biblical Gospels, Acts, and the Revelation to John are apocalyptic to varying degrees. Few would contest this, except perhaps in relation to the Fourth Gospel, which is often regarded as nonapocalyptic because of its emphasis on realized eschatology, meaning eschatology that stresses fulfillment already realized in the mission and message of Jesus. The remaining Gospels, however, along with Acts and Revelation, have more future-oriented eschatological perspectives. This differentiation between future-oriented and realized eschatological perspectives demonstrates that eschatology is not a fixed, inflexible set of beliefs. It features different aspects according to other core convictions with which it is combined. In this connection, Crossan has drawn helpful distinctions, albeit focused on pre-Gospel sources for understanding Jesus as a historical figure. I am concerned with the variegated eschatological perspectives of some early Christian writers, but Crossan's distinctions nevertheless apply and in my judgment may be pressed further.

In a significant number of publications spread across four decades, Crossan has been concerned to safeguard the eschatological outlook that he attributes to Jesus from what is commonly associated with apocalyptic eschatology. His descriptions have changed over time, but he has consistently affirmed that Jesus's own eschatological outlook was nonapocalyptic. For this purpose, in his book *In Parables*,[6] Crossan differentiates between prophetic and apocalyptic eschatology; in *The Birth of Christianity*,[7] he distinguishes between ethical and apocalyptic eschatology; and more recently, he favors collaborative as opposed to apocalyptic eschatology.[8] According to Crossan, Jesus repudiated the apocalyptic eschatology of his mentor, John the Baptist, and embraced a prophetic or ethical or collaborative eschatology, each intended by Crossan to characterize Jesus's own stance as a disavowal of eschatological resolution premised on divine violence. For now, however, Crossan's differentiations are the important point. Apocalyptic eschatology is one type or species of eschatology, not the only kind on offer.

For those with access to Crossan's *Birth of Christianity*, a careful reading of chapters 15 and 16 of that book is good medicine. There Crossan discusses

6. Crossan, *In Parables*, 25–27.
7. Crossan, *Birth of Christianity*, esp. chaps. 15–16.
8. See, e.g., Crossan, *God and Empire*, chap. 3; idem, "Jesus and the Challenge"; idem, "Divine Violence."

eschatology as a genus-level term, ever in need of qualification if one is not to be misunderstood. In his view, three species of eschatology can be detected in the earliest sources for understanding the historical Jesus: apocalyptic, ascetical, and ethical. Interestingly, however, Crossan finds it necessary to differentiate further between two subspecies of apocalyptic eschatology: *primary* apocalyptic eschatology, in which the apocalyptic dimension is intrinsic and indispensable; and *secondary* apocalyptic eschatology, in which the apocalyptic perspective is peripheral and subsidiary. "Secondary apocalypticism is like a cosmic sanction—believed in, of course, but added on as one's primary and essential message is refused and rejected."[9] In Crossan's view, one finds primary apocalyptic eschatology in Paul and the Gospel according to Mark, secondary apocalyptic eschatology in Q (understood as a sayings *Gospel*). For my purposes, not only Crossan's distinctions between apocalyptic and nonapocalyptic eschatologies but also his subcategorization of apocalyptic eschatology into two subforms are helpful.

For Crossan, "eschatology is divine radicality. It is a fundamental negation of the present world's normalcy based on some transcendental mandate."[10] Perhaps this evocative definition is rather too removed from the term's etymological roots, but it helps to make sense of Crossan's specific distinctions between apocalyptic eschatology and both ascetical and ethical eschatology. Since my own distinctions between two different subforms of apocalyptic eschatology are indispensable to the argument of this book, I here cite Crossan on apocalyptic eschatology at length:

> Apocalyptic eschatology (or apocalypticism) negates this world by announcing that in the future, and usually the imminent future, God will act to restore justice in an unjust world. Whether the result will be earth in heaven or heaven on earth can remain quite vague and open. Whether the space-time universe of ordinary experience will continue or not can also remain vague and open. But two aspects are not negotiable if apocalypticism is intended. One aspect is that the primary event is an interventional act of God. Human actors may certainly be important in preparation, by their sufferings, in initiation, by their symbolic activities, or even in cooperation, by military action under angelic or divine control. All of those human details may be open for discussion, but what is not debatable is that some intervening act of overwhelming divine power is imagined and invoked. In plain language, we are waiting for God.
>
> The other aspect that is not negotiable is the total absence of evil and injustice after the apocalyptic consummation takes place. It will not be just a case of kinder, gentler injustice but of a perfectly just world. There will be no evil

9. Crossan, *Birth of Christianity*, 265. In debate with Dale Allison, Crossan teases out this distinction between primary and secondary apocalyptic eschatology into five interrelated distinctions: destructive or transformative; material or social; primary or secondary; negative or positive; violent or nonviolent. See Crossan, "Eschatology, Apocalypticism."

10. Crossan, *Birth of Christianity*, 282.

or evildoers in this postapocalyptic world. One could imagine an apocalyptic revelation of God such that all humans thereafter would freely and voluntarily live together in perfect justice, peace, and love. Willingly and without constraint. That is, after all, how theology has always explained human free will in an after-this-life heaven. But that is not the standard apocalyptic scenario for the unjust. There is all too often a transition from justice to revenge, a divine vengeance that results in human slaughter. When those two aspects are combined, apocalyptic eschatology almost inevitably presumes a violent God who establishes the justice of nonviolence through the injustice of violence. That may well be understandable in particular human circumstances. That may well be understandable when a genocide of them from above is invoked to prevent their genocide of us here below. But all too often, be it of pagans by Jews or of Jews by Christians, apocalypticism is perceived as a divine ethnic cleansing whose genocidal heart presumes a violent God of revenge rather than a nonviolent God of justice.[11]

There is little, if anything, to gainsay in these two luminous paragraphs. Note carefully, however, what Crossan himself affirms is indispensable to apocalyptic eschatology and what is negotiable. Observe, too, the way in which Crossan's crucial sentences are constructed following this statement: "But that is not the standard apocalyptic scenario for the unjust." Such a statement accepts that there is a standard apocalyptic scenario but also that there are deviations from the norm, hence the presence of sentences containing the phrases "all too often" and "almost inevitably." My argument in this book is that while the standard apocalyptic scenario is undoubtedly represented in the New Testament, most noticeably in the Gospel according to Matthew and in the Revelation to John, there are also deviations from this standard scenario, most notably in the Gospel according to Mark, the Fourth Gospel, and Acts. Moreover, even in New Testament texts that feature the standard apocalyptic scenario, other prominent features within these texts subvert or destabilize that scenario.

In Crossan's classification, ascetical eschatology is a form of world-negation by means of various forms of withdrawal, and "ethical eschatology . . . negates the world by actively protesting and nonviolently resisting a system judged to be evil, unjust, and violent."[12] The key feature of ethical eschatology is its implacable opposition to systemic or structural evil, but without resorting to the violent means by which such structures are maintained and perpetuated. Moreover, according to Crossan, ethical eschatology is not grounded in transcendent violence, as is apocalyptic eschatology. This is not fully in keeping with the description of apocalyptic eschatology cited in full above, even if true to the "standard apocalyptic scenario."

11. Ibid., 283.
12. Ibid., 283–84.

After presenting two historical illustrations of ethical eschatology (or non-violent resistance) from about the time of Jesus and drawing two corollaries from this kind of eschatology, Crossan reminds readers that these forms of eschatology are but three of a larger number of eschatological types. He also indicates that these three forms can be combined in various ways. Although he sees no difficulty in combining apocalyptic with ascetical eschatology and ascetical with ethical eschatology, he has misgivings about the possibility of combining apocalyptic with ethical eschatology. "Can they be combined?" he asks, and the answer he provides is best heard in his own words:

> As long as apocalypticism involves a God who uses force and violence to end force and violence, they cannot be combined; one has to choose between them. This is implicit in my terminology. Ethicism, short for ethical eschatology, is ethical radicalism with a divine mandate based on the character of God. What makes it radical or eschatological ethics is, above all else, the fact that it is nonviolent resistance to structural violence. It is absolute faith in a nonviolent God and the attempt to live and act in union with such a God. I do not hold that apocalypticism and asceticism are not ethical. Of course they are. It may also be ethical to go to war in the name of an avenging God. But all ethics is not eschatological or divinely radical. Ethical eschatology is, by definition as I see it, nonviolent resistance to systemic violence.[13]

Notice how Crossan's answer begins: "*As long as* apocalypticism involves a God who uses force and violence to end force and violence. . . ." In other words, there is at least a theoretical possibility of *nonviolent* apocalyptic eschatology, which would then qualify that mode of apocalyptic eschatology as ethical in Crossan's sense. It is difficult to know what to make of Crossan's concession that both apocalyptic and ascetical eschatology are ethical in and of themselves, but their disqualification as ethical in his precise sense seems to stem from their nongrounding in the conviction that God is nonviolent. For Crossan, the decisive issue is whether or not any form of eschatology is grounded in, and is an expression of, God as nonviolent. On this we concur. The question between us, then, is whether there are expressions of biblical eschatology that meet the two nonnegotiable criteria for counting as apocalyptic eschatology but do not presume divine vengeance because of an understanding of God as nonviolent.

In *Peace, Violence and the New Testament*, Michel Desjardins discusses the apocalyptic worldview of the New Testament as a whole, contending that this vision of reality is "overtly violent," by which he means that within the apocalyptic worldview of the New Testament writers, "Satan and his forces were determined to inflict horrific violence on earth and on humankind, and in this respect God was no different."[14] In other words, the apocalyptic vision

13. Ibid., 287.
14. Desjardins, *Peace, Violence*, 83–92, esp. 84.

of reality shared among New Testament writers is inherently violent because it is premised on divine or divinely authorized eschatological vengeance. A similar perspective pervades *Knowing Truth, Doing Good*, by Russell Pregeant.[15] The first time one encounters the term "apocalyptic" in this book, it occurs within the phrase "standard apocalyptic expectation."[16] One is reminded of Crossan's "standard apocalyptic scenario." Although Pregeant demurs from Crossan's judgment that Jesus repudiated John's apocalyptic eschatology,[17] the way in which he characterizes this particular mode of eschatology reveals that he, too, regards apocalyptic eschatology as inherently violent.[18]

As much as I have learned from Crossan, Desjardins, and Pregeant on the moral implications of apocalyptic eschatology, I nevertheless see things somewhat differently. I accept that apocalyptic eschatology often, perhaps standardly, anticipates eschatological vengeance on the part of God or God's agent(s), but I also consider that the interpretive creativity clearly evident in so many of the New Testament writings led some of those writers to relativize or even eliminate divine vengeance from the standard apocalyptic scenario to which they were otherwise indebted for expressing their understanding of Jesus's significance, theologically and ethically.

Lest anyone think that I regard New Testament writers as absolute pioneers in this respect, I consider that Jesus and his followers innovated only insofar as they drew, even if selectively, from Jewish tradition. The range of biblical expressions of eschatological vengeance demonstrates that the New Testament, no less than the Old, presents a violent God-image. Even when the theology of New Testament writers subverts or destabilizes such a violent God-image, however, that, too, is grounded in Jewish theological traditions and convictions. Grappling with either the prospect or expressions of divine violence is not a task reserved for scholars of the Hebrew Bible nor one in which stories of Jesus provide only the antidote. Some early apocalyptic texts served a militant purpose or function, but others advocated a nonmilitant stance, as John J. Collins has shown.[19] Analogously, in my view, apocalyptic eschatology may be premised on the radicality of divine peace no less than on divine violence. Indeed, under the impress of the mission and message of Jesus, apocalyptic eschatology was seemingly squeezed toward an alternate grounding in divine peace rather than divine violence. Although some New Testament writers found the impetus for this reorientation in the life, teaching,

15. Pregeant, *Knowing Truth, Doing Good*.
16. Ibid., 31.
17. Ibid., 95.
18. See ibid., 144, 162–63, 318, 325–30. Unfortunately, where Pregeant begins to address the theme of eschatological vengeance hermeneutically (325), he seems to equate eschatology with apocalyptic, thereby confirming the importance of Crossan's efforts at terminological clarification.
19. J. Collins, "From Prophecy to Apocalypticism."

death, and resurrection of Jesus, that does not imply that such a reorientation was not Jewish. Insofar as this shift in orientation was influenced by Jesus, it was first and foremost a shift *within* Judaism or, perhaps better, within one expression of Judaism.

At various points throughout this book, I pause to preclude a potential inference from my larger argument, to wit, that I disavow divine judgment. It is comprehensible why a theological and ethical aversion to eschatological vengeance might lead to the inference that divine judgment is considered inimical. Though Walter Wink may be correct to underscore the ambivalence of the biblical theme of judgment,[20] I nevertheless affirm divine judgment as biblically and theologically meaningful. Judgment is the theological corollary of divine sovereignty, which was the burden of Jesus's message, at least according to three of the Gospel writers. In biblical perspective, judgment is the Creator's prerogative. Moreover, if God is not our judge, humanity and history judge themselves, leading to the conclusion that historical winners, those with wealth and might, are ultimately proved right, irrespective of the means by which they prosper and prevail.

Eschatological judgment is more about reversal than about retribution, however, more about righting than requiting wrongs. This is illustrated by Jesus's eschatological blessings, formulated two different ways in Matthew 5:3–12 and Luke 6:20–26. In their Matthean form, divine judgment is expressed as eschatological reversal impinging on the present, without reference to recompense for wrongdoing. In their Lukan form, promises of eschatological reversal are balanced by corresponding warnings of eschatological woes. Reversal is not only primary, to the point that the woes of Luke 6:24–26 largely emphasize the reversal motif, but even the woes themselves do not belabor the theme of retribution. In other words, anticipation of eschatological judgment is principally and indispensably focused on reversal; the concern with recompense is secondary and peripheral.

In *Who Is Jesus? History in Perfect Tense*, Keck laments the relative absence of attention to eschatological judgment in recent Christian theology and ethics. "This has resulted in a gross impoverishment of discourse about the moral life," in Keck's view, "as well as a serious abbreviation of the role of Jesus in that life and in the discourse about it."[21] Although I affirm the theological and ethical significance of divine judgment, it is my conviction that such judgment should be conceived christologically, in other words, in light of the story of Jesus recounted in the Gospels. In this respect, the Gospel according to Matthew is perhaps the most difficult to read with integrity because Matthew records Jesus himself as warning of eschatological vengeance in redundant fashion. When compared with the other Gospel accounts, however, it becomes

20. Wink, *Human Being*, 179–81.
21. Keck, *Who Is Jesus?* 153.

apparent that Matthew has heightened the theme of eschatological vengeance in Jesus's teaching. In any case, since all four Gospel writers envisage that Jesus mediated divine presence in some sense, Jesus's way of responding to human recalcitrance is presented as God's way of doing the same. As a result, divine judgment construed christologically is unlikely to be purely retributive or vengeful, however much God may be entitled to avenge wrongs.[22]

Various passages discussed in the following chapters feature a Semitic expression represented in Greek as ὁ υἱὸς τοῦ ἀνθρώπου (ho huios tou anthrōpou, lit., "the son of the person"). Where this expression occurs in much of the Old Testament, it generally signifies an individual human being, but Daniel 7:13–14 refers to a heavenly figure described as "one like a son of man." Although this humanlike figure seems to be interpreted as representing "the holy ones of the Most High" (see 7:18, 22, 27), by the first century of the Common Era there is evidence that Daniel's image of "one like a son of man" was conceived in certain circles as a transcendent deliverer with the authority to judge. The biblical Gospels compose a significant part of the textual evidence for this historical judgment, but there is also the evidence of the Parables of Enoch (1 Enoch 37–71) and 2 Esdras (or 4 Ezra).[23]

I am not concerned with whether and, if so, how the historical Jesus made use of Daniel's image of "one like a person." Often enough, however, Gospel passages considered throughout this book attribute to Jesus the use of the phrase "the son of the person," with apparent reference to himself. I have wrestled with how best to translate this linguistically awkward phrase, especially if, as seems likely, it was (in the passages discussed) a pointed allusion to Daniel's humanlike heavenly figure. In The Human Being: Jesus and the Enigma of the Son of the Man, Wink claims to translate this idiom literally, so as to draw attention to the oddity and crudity of the twofold definite article, but the Greek expression he translates as "the son of the man" is more gender-inclusive than he conveys.[24] A more accurate translation option would be "the son of the person." My own preference, wherever one is confident of an allusion to Daniel 7:13–14, is the (or that) humanlike One, not only because this phrase is gender-inclusive but also because it draws attention to the allusive function of the Greek idiom and is faithful to the generic meaning of the original Semitic expression.[25] Perhaps not every "the son of the person" saying alludes to Daniel's heavenly figure, however, and some New Testament

22. On divine judgment in biblical tradition, see Reiser, Jesus and Judgment; Travis, Christ and the Judgement.

23. On the development, by the first century CE, of a Jewish "tradition" of a transcendent deliverer-judge derived from Dan. 7:13–14, see Nickelsburg, "Son of Man"; A. Collins and J. Collins, King and Messiah, chap. 4; J. Collins, Scepter and the Star, chap. 8.

24. Wink, Human Being, 17.

25. For a discussion of the linguistic evidence relating to this expression and various context-sensitive translation options, see A. Collins, Cosmology and Eschatology, 139–58.

scholars have turned to translating this expression as "the Son of humanity." This seems a reasonable compromise, not least because it represents one solecism with another.

None of the canonical Gospels provides us with the name of its author, but in the case of the first three Gospels and Acts there is no reason to depart from the convention dating back to antiquity of referring to their respective authors as Matthew, Mark, and Luke. In retaining these traditional names, however, I make no inferences about the respective identities of these Gospel writers. The Fourth Gospel is traditionally known as the Gospel according to John, but in this book I refer to its author as "the evangelist" or "the Fourth Evangelist" because a certain prophet-seer named John is incontestably the author of the Revelation to John. References to this John are therefore always references to John the prophet-seer, not to the author of the Fourth Gospel.

Some readers may wonder whether the Revelation to John fits within a discussion of narrative texts from the early Christian movement(s). The Gospels and Acts are clearly narrative in form, but can the same be said for Revelation? In certain respects, Revelation fits the genre of apocalypse, although it is not attributed to some figure from the ancient past such as Enoch or Ezra, as are other apocalyptic writings. On the one hand, the book itself seems to be an amalgam of literary types. Revelation 1:3 and numerous references in the final chapter (22:7, 10, 18–19) indicate that John himself understood his work as a prophecy, and Revelation 1:4–7 takes the form of a letter opening. With respect to genre, therefore, the book of Revelation is mixed. On the other hand, insofar as John recounts the content of his vision in narrative form, even if somewhat disjointedly with respect to chronology, his work can be analyzed from a narrative perspective. Indeed, in *Tales of the End*, David Barr opens the prologue to his commentary on Revelation by intimating that the most important point to grasp for making sense of John's Apocalypse is that it is a narrative.[26] Like the Gospels, moreover, Revelation (re)tells the story of Jesus, even if in different mode and perspective. Barr actually discerns three interrelated story lines within Revelation, not a single and unified narrative account, but he acknowledges that how one outlines this book is largely dependent on what one seeks. Barr's three separate story lines are the result of his quest for sequences of causally connected events.[27] Other narrative analyses have also been proposed.

Among New Testament scholars, James Resseguie has done more than most to master narrative analysis as an interpretive method and to apply narrative criticism to New Testament texts. In his introductory *Narrative Criticism of the New Testament*, he devotes at least half of the chapter on plot to discussing what he describes as the "U-shaped plot" of Revelation, U-shaped

---

26. Barr, *Tales of the End*, 1.
27. See ibid., 10–16.

because there is discernible movement from unawareness to insight.[28] Moreover, Resseguie has authored two volumes on Revelation from a narrative-critical orientation.[29] In his narrative commentary on Revelation, Resseguie argues for a linear conception of the literary structure of the book, although not along the lines of strict chronological sequence.[30] Whether this conception of Revelation's literary structure has emerged from Resseguie's narrative analysis of the book or vice versa, the point is that Revelation is susceptible to narrative interpretation as are the Gospels and Acts. In short, the Revelation to John is discussed in this book not only because it would be absurd to omit it from an ethical appraisal of violent eschatology in the New Testament but also because there is a narrative dimension to the Apocalypse of John that makes it fitting to discuss Revelation along with the four canonical Gospels and Acts.[31]

Furthermore, as will become clear in the first and final chapters of the body of this book, Revelation is important for its paradoxical canonical role. Along with the Gospel according to Matthew, the Revelation to John encloses the New Testament with books that feature eschatological vengeance, a theological emphasis that provokes the central moral concern of this study. By contrast, however, along with the vision of creation in Genesis 1:1–2:3, the vision of the new Jerusalem at the end of Revelation serves to enclose the entire biblical canon within visions of divinely intended *shalom*. Against the symbolic tenor of the book, therefore, I advocate a *shalom*-oriented interpretation of Revelation in line with its christological heart.

At the end of a book titled *Christ Is the Question*, Wayne Meeks poses this question about the eschatological Jesus:

> So how ought we to imagine the End of Days—the last chapter of the Jesus story, the ultimate shape of Jesus' identity? Shall we imagine Jesus standing in armor, his foot on the neck of the conquered infidel? Shall we imagine the Jesus of Michelangelo's Sistine ceiling, averting his gaze from the anguished hordes of the pagans and heretics and sinners who are being dragged off to hell? Or shall we imagine a Christ who smiles at the surprise of those sons of Abraham who come from east and west to join him in the kingdom that now is to be handed over to the one inscrutable God, who cannot imagine that they are really here? Can you picture the Son of the Human who, at the last judgment when he sits on his throne, surprises the sheep on his right as much as the goats on the left: "Lord, when did we see you . . . ?"[32]

28. Resseguie, *Narrative Criticism*, 213–40.
29. Resseguie, *Revelation Unsealed*; idem, *Revelation of John*.
30. Resseguie, *Revelation of John*, 54–59.
31. The definition of the genre of apocalypse developed by the Apocalypse Group of the Society of Biblical Literature Genres Project begins as follows: "'Apocalypse' is a genre of revelatory literature with a narrative framework." See J. Collins, "Introduction," 9.
32. Meeks, *Christ Is the Question*, 139; see 130–32 for his discussion of Christ's handing over the kingdom to God, drawing from 1 Cor. 15:24–28.

In Matthew's scenario of final judgment, the enthroned Son of humanity surprises the sheep no less than the goats, but that does not preserve the goats from eternal punishment. On the evidence of the Gospels, Acts, and Revelation, readers might well answer each of Meeks's four final questions in the affirmative. But to do so would be to affirm that the last chapter of the Jesus story is conceivably another story, not the final chapter of the same story. My study of the four canonical Gospels, Acts, and Revelation is premised on the conviction that the *final chapter* of the Jesus story is the final chapter *of the Jesus story* and therefore that "the ultimate shape of Jesus' identity" is already known.

Part 1

THE GOSPELS ACCORDING TO MATTHEW AND MARK

1

Nonretaliation or Vengeance?

Protesting Matthew's Violent Eschatology

In the Gospel according to Matthew, Jesus pronounces a blessing on peace-makers (5:9), commands nonretaliation alongside love for enemies no less than neighbors (5:38–48), and conducts his mission nonviolently. As a series of end-time judgment texts makes clear, however, Matthew envisages that, as the coming Son of humanity, Jesus will return as a violent avenger. This apparent incongruity leads John Riches to ask, "Is the judgment which Jesus will bring inconsistent with the ethic which he teaches?"[1] This perplexing portrait of Jesus as a proponent of nonretaliation who nevertheless anticipates eschatological vengeance puts those who take their moral bearings from Jesus in a profound predicament. How does one resolve the moral tension caused by this deep-seated discrepancy within Matthew's Gospel?

In *The Moral Vision of the New Testament*, Richard Hays concludes his discussion of Matthew's eschatology with a subsection titled "Eschatology as Ethical Warrant." His remarks bring the ethical quandary associated with Matthew's eschatology into sharp relief:

> In Matthew, eschatology becomes a powerful *warrant* for moral behavior. The motivation for obedience to God is repeatedly grounded in the rewards and punishments that await everyone at the final judgment. . . . This is nowhere

1. Riches, *Conflicting Mythologies*, 287.

more evident than in Matthew 24:37–25:46, where he appends to the Markan apocalyptic discourse five units of additional material stressing in various ways the necessity of being prepared for the coming of the Son of Man. . . . The aim of such stories is to instill godly fear in the hearers and to motivate them to do the will of God while they still have opportunity, before the judgment comes upon them.

It would not be correct to say that these stories provide only *warrants* for obedience to God; they also define significant ethical *norms* having to do primarily with just and merciful treatment of others and with responsible use of property. . . . The parable of the sheep and the goats, with its powerful portrayal of care for the needy as the basic criterion for God's eschatological judgment of human deeds, has had a powerful impact on the church's imagination; the story reinforces Matthew's earlier emphasis on mercy as the hallmark of the kingdom of God.[2]

In response to Hays, three points may be made as an overture to this chapter. First, Hays correctly recognizes that "in Matthew, eschatology becomes a powerful warrant for moral behavior." But the moral "warrant" he identifies within Matthew's Gospel is ethically problematic. Promises of reward and threat of punishment are not the best means to a mature, well-integrated morality.[3] Second, for Hays, the parables of judgment in Matthew 24–25 provide not only warrants for obedience to the will of God but also "define significant ethical norms," including just and merciful conduct toward others. This may be so, but what Hays does not detect—or at least acknowledge—is the ultimate validation of violence inherent in the retribution intrinsic to Matthew's eschatology. After all, what greater warrant for violence could there be than divine vengeance?[4] And third, there can be no doubt that the scenario of the sheep and the goats in Matthew 25:31–46 has had a "powerful impact on the church's imagination," perhaps best exemplified in Michelangelo's *Last Judgment*. I am less confident than Hays, however, that this scenario "reinforces Matthew's earlier emphasis on mercy as the hallmark of the kingdom of God." Certainly that is not *all* it reinforces, as Michelangelo's picture attests.

To be fair to Hays, his discussion of Matthew's "eschatology as ethical warrant" occurs within the first part of his work, concerned with New Testament texts at the descriptive or exegetical level. Yet one searches in vain within the remaining parts of his book—concerned with the synthetic, hermeneutical, and pragmatic tasks associated with New Testament ethics—for further discussion

2. Hays, *Moral Vision*, 106–7.
3. For sagacious reflections on promised reward in relation to Christian morality, however, see Keck, *Who Is Jesus?* 175–77.
4. I appreciate that the expectation of divine eschatological vengeance has enabled some to eschew violence, leaving vengeance to God. But for others who have expected God to exact vengeance, the logic of "If they have it coming, why not now?" has proved irresistible, especially among those who regard themselves as on God's side and executors of the divine will.

of the relation between eschatological vengeance and ethics. Discussing the synthetic task, Hays is adamant that tensions *between* New Testament writings be allowed to stand. But he seems to have tuned out certain tensions *within* individual writings, most notably the disturbing discrepancy between Matthew's portrayal of Jesus as a teacher of nonretaliation and Matthew's own violently retributive eschatology. Later, within Hays's discussion of the pragmatic task, his treatment of "Violence in Defense of Justice" (chap. 14) naturally concentrates on Matthew 5:38–48; in the second section of this chapter, he stresses how uniformly the New Testament as a whole disavows violence for Christians. But the issue of eschatological vengeance, its role within the same Gospel as one finds the Sermon on the Mount, and its repercussions for moral vision—Hays passes over these in silence.

In this respect, Hays is not alone. Within a major work of New Testament theology intended to restore the theme of peace to a central place, Willard Swartley concentrates on the Sermon on the Mount in his chapter "Matthew: Emmanuel, Power for Peacemaking."[5] Although he considers the question of consistency between Jesus's nonviolent ethic and his vitriolic invective against the Pharisees, he does not address the tension between the nonviolent teaching and example of Jesus and his foreseen role in executing eschatological vengeance, except to comment in a footnote: "Some apocalyptic scenes (13:41–42; 24:27–31) are consummation-judgments that belong to the divine prerogative. They do not provide warrant for the moral practices of Jesus' disciples."[6] Whether or not divine eschatological vengeance provides legitimate sanction for human conduct, to anticipate divine violence as the means to realize the reign of God in its fullness is corrosive for moral vision and imagination. The moral problem of eschatological vengeance is therefore too pressing to be ignored, as recognized by the Matthean scholar Russell Pregeant, who is both alert to the problem and willing to grapple with it. "The question," he observes, "is whether and how we can reconcile the nonviolent teachings and deeds of Matthew's Jesus with his announcement of the eschatological violence that God will eventually bring not simply on the wicked but [also] on those who have rejected Jesus."[7]

A Matthean Muddle?

Readers with more than a passing acquaintance with the four biblical Gospels are aware that each is concerned to recount the story of Jesus so as to provoke,

5. Swartley, *Covenant of Peace*, chap. 3.
6. Ibid., 90.
7. Pregeant, *Knowing Truth, Doing Good*, 144. Unfortunately, by the time Pregeant addresses eschatological vengeance hermeneutically in the final chapter of his book, he discusses it in broad terms, with little reference to Matthew's Gospel.

promote, and preserve faith in him as God's agent of redemption and, in Matthew's case, "resTorahtion."[8] It is also well understood that each Gospel writer made the Jesus story his own by emphasizing certain features and by minimizing or even omitting others. Indeed, as early as Irenaeus of Lyons, toward the end of the second century CE, when the symbols associated with the four living creatures derived from Ezekiel 1 and Revelation 4 were allocated to the Gospels, it was understood that each evangelist had distinctive theological emphases.[9]

Depending on the sequence of the four Gospels in early codex collections, the allocation of the four symbols varied, especially with respect to the Gospels of Mark and John. According to the so-called Western or Old Latin order—Matthew, John, Luke, Mark—the lion represents John's Gospel, and the eagle represents Mark's. But according to the Eastern or Greek (and now canonical) order, the lion represents Mark's Gospel and the eagle John's. In most witnesses the symbol of a person was allocated to Matthew's Gospel, and the symbol of an ox to Luke's. By the time of Jerome's Latin Vulgate, or "Common version" (ca. 400 CE), the standard pattern was set: Matthew, represented by a person; Mark, a lion; Luke, an ox; and John, an eagle.[10] Nevertheless, Augustine dissented, and his dissent reflected a concern to discriminate meaningfully between the theological emphases of the respective Gospels. In his view, Matthew's Gospel was best represented by the lion, reflecting an emphasis on the regal human nature of Christ; Luke was best represented by the ox, reflecting a concern with the sacerdotal human nature of Christ; Mark was best represented by the person, reflecting an interest in the humanity of Christ; and John was best represented by the eagle, reflecting an emphasis on the divinity of Christ.[11]

Whether one agrees with the majority of patristic writers or with Augustine on which symbol best represents Matthew's Gospel, the point remains that Matthew's portrait of "Jesus Messiah, son of David, son of Abraham" (Matt. 1:1) is distinctive. Among his typical emphases are the following features, each organically related to his christological focus:

1. the fulfillment of Scripture in the story of Jesus
2. Jesus's teaching as fulfillment, not annulment, of Torah and the prophets, hence Christian continuity with Jewish Scripture

8. This wordplay derives from Wengst, "Aspects of the Last Judgment," esp. 235. Wengst uses "the resTorahtion of justice" in connection with Matthew's citations of and allusions to Jewish Scripture. The phrase makes best sense as a distillation of Matt. 5:17–20.

9. See Irenaeus, *Adv. haer.* 3.11.8. In Ezek. 1:10, all four living creatures apparently have faces with composite features of a human being, a lion, an ox, and an eagle, whereas in Rev. 4:7 each of these likenesses distinguishes only one of the living creatures.

10. See Burridge, *Four Gospels*, 25–28. Although occasionally belabored, Burridge's symbolic treatment of the Gospels helpfully identifies their distinctive emphases.

11. See Augustine, *De consensu evangelistarum* 1.6.9. Augustine did not claim originality for his view but referred to earlier dissenting interpreters with whom he agreed. The order Matthew, Luke, Mark, John is the order in which Augustine allocated the symbols from Rev. 4:7 to the four Gospels.

3. an emphasis on moral "righteousness," understood as obedience to the will of God expressed in Torah and interpreted by Jesus
4. the Christian assembly (Matthew is the only evangelist to use the term *ekklēsia*)
5. imminent eschatological expectation (Matthew is the only Gospel writer to use the term *parousia*)
6. judgment, or positive and negative recompense[12]

To a significant extent, the final two themes coalesce in Matthew's Gospel. The expected parousia (arrival) is a time of retributive judgment.

The theme of end-time judgment is widely shared among Jewish and early Christian writers. Paul, the "apostle of grace," affirmed eschatological judgment on the basis of human conduct (see Rom. 2:5–11; 2 Cor. 5:10). In his view, rectification by grace does not preclude judgment of human works.[13] In this respect, Paul and Matthew were of a mind, since Matthew clearly envisaged that those in the church no less than those without would one day answer to the Judge of all. Behind this perspective is the conviction that the God responsible for creating the world is, for that reason, the rightful Judge of the world.[14]

That Matthew looked forward to end-time judgment is not, in itself, ethically problematic. What is problematic is the depiction of divine judgment that Matthew apparently anticipated. As a number of parabolic texts and their interpretations make clear, his end-time expectation is characterized by the threat of divinely authorized retributive violence for those ultimately determined to be unrighteous, wicked, or evil. This eschatological stance is ethically problematic because divine vengeance comprises an ultimate validation of violence. This is not simply a disturbing curiosity in the history of Jewish-Christian thought. As Günther Bornkamm once observed, "No other Gospel is so shaped by the thought of the Church as Matthew's, so constructed for use by the Church; for this reason it has exercised, as no other, a normative influence in the later Church."[15] If for no other reason, the reality that violent eschatology is an integral part of the deeply ingrained moral legacy of this brilliant but baffling Jewish-Christian scribe (Matt. 13:52) must be recognized and addressed—theologically, morally, and pastorally.

In many respects the influence of Matthew's Gospel is cause for celebration. Think, for example, of the moral vision articulated in the Sermon on the Mount, in which Matthew portrays Jesus as the authoritative interpreter of

---

12. On this major Matthean theme, see Marguerat, *Le jugement*; Charette, *Theme of Recompense*; Luz, *Matthew 21–28*, 285–96; Angel, "Inquiring into an *Inclusio*"; Schnelle, *Theology of the New Testament*, 446–49, 458–60; Wilson, *When Will These Things Happen?*

13. See Yinger, *Paul, Judaism*.

14. For Paul, Rom. 3:6 reveals that God's entitlement to judge the world is a theological axiom.

15. Bornkamm, "End-Expectation and Church," 38.

Jewish tradition, indeed, as one who *fulfills* or brings to completion Torah and the prophets (5:17). In the section devoted to Jesus's teaching as the fulfillment of Torah (5:17–48), three of the six so-called "antitheses" relate directly to the prohibition of violence against fellow human beings.[16] The first intensifies the prohibition against homicide so that it prohibits anger, the fifth undoes the principle of (restrained) retaliation by advocating nonretaliation, and the sixth enjoins love of enemies as opposed to loving neighbors, whether kinfolk or resident aliens, but hating enemies.[17] Even the remaining three can be understood as prohibitions against violence either to one's marriage partner, in the sense of violating sexual fidelity, or to linguistic integrity. Moreover, this distillation of Torah-fulfilled culminates with the injunction to emulate the indiscriminate "perfection" of God, who makes the sun rise on both the good and evil alike and who showers rain on both the just and the unjust (5:45–48).[18]

The moral vision of Jesus, as presented in the Beatitudes and Antitheses of Matthew 5, is widely recognized as an ethical high-water mark, even among those who regard it as an impossible ideal. "The *ethical character* of this Gospel is its outstanding feature," asserts Gerd Theissen, largely on the basis of Jesus's teaching in the Sermon on the Mount.[19] As Dale Allison points out, however, Matthew's Gospel is a reservoir of mixed messages.[20] Even within the confines of chapter 5, one detects discomfiting elements. For example, one can accept that someone must be least in the kingdom of heaven (5:19), but the terms of entry into that kingdom are strict (5:20), and several infractions seem to lead inexorably to the smoldering fires of Gehenna. As envisaged by Matthew, discipleship is not for the weak-willed or fainthearted. This is borne out by the complex of sayings that conclude the Sermon on the Mount, the force of which is aptly summed up by Gerhard Barth: "What matters is the doing of God's will; this is all that is enquired about at the judgment; the commandments are the conditions of entrance into the kingdom of God, which the disciples are required to fulfil."[21] But the discrepancy between eschatological

16. They are called "antitheses" because they take the form "You have heard that it was said . . . , but I say. . . ." While the form of the sayings emphasizes Jesus's interpretive authority, they should not be taken as antithetical to Jewish Scripture or tradition. They might better be understood as interpretive intensifications of scriptural obligations.

17. Leviticus 19:17–18, 33–34 enjoins love of neighbor, whether kin or resident alien, but not hate for enemies. Possibly the reference to hating enemies alludes to sectarian Jews who did advocate hate for outsiders, as in the *Community Rule* (1QS 1.1–10) at Qumran.

18. In the parallel version of this saying in Luke 6:36, the terminology of "mercy" replaces that of "perfection." Here Luke's interpretive instinct is unerring: divine "perfection" displays indiscriminate magnanimity and mercy.

19. Theissen, *Gospel Writing*, 48, emphasis original. Throughout his chapter on Matthew's Gospel, Theissen emphasizes Matthew's ethical concerns, which correlate to his depiction of Jesus as a peaceable, humble Messiah.

20. Allison, "Deconstructing Matthew," in *Studies in Matthew*, 237–49.

21. Barth, "Matthew's Understanding of the Law," 60.

vengeance and Jesus's own teaching on nonretaliation and nonviolent conduct is nowhere better illustrated than in parables attributed to Jesus that feature divinely authorized retributive violence.

Eschatological Vengeance in Matthew's Parables

The tension within Matthew's Gospel between Jesus's peaceful moral vision and eschatological vengeance is helpfully explored in Barbara Reid's study "Violent Endings in Matthew's Parables and Christian Nonviolence."[22] Reid not only recognizes but also seeks to resolve the tension between the moral guidance of Jesus in Matthew's Sermon on the Mount and the image of God (or God's agents) ultimately dealing vengefully with various kinds of persons in several Matthean parables. First, Reid surveys references to various forms of violence in Matthew's Gospel. Then she describes how Jesus and his disciples are portrayed as victims of violence, but in this section she also devotes space to the enigmatic sayings in Matthew 11:12 (about the reign of heaven suffering violence) and 10:34–36 ("I came not to bring peace but a sword"). In her third and longest section, Reid discusses responses to violence described by Matthew, with particular reference to Jesus's teaching on nonretaliation and love for enemies in 5:38–48. In a brief fourth section, she explores eight Matthean parables that feature eschatological vengeance. In a penultimate section, Reid evaluates four possible solutions to the moral tension inherent in Matthew's Gospel. Finally, she identifies theological and hermeneutical questions arising from her discussion. Here I revisit Reid's discussion of Matthew's parables featuring end-time vengeance for the purpose of both confirming and building upon her fundamental insight that the violent endings to some of Matthew's parables are not only in tension with other aspects of Jesus's moral guidance but also provoke profound interpretive challenges.

The eight parables discussed briefly by Reid are the twin parables of the tares and the dragnet (Matt. 13:24–30, 40–43, 49–50), the parable of an unforgiving slave (18:23–35), the parable of tenants in a vineyard (21:33–44), the parable of a wedding banquet (22:1–14), the parable of a waiting slave (24:45–51), and the two parables of the talents and final judgment (25:14–46). Of these eight parables, four are unique to Matthew (tares, dragnet, unforgiving slave, final judgment).[23] The four other parables have parallels or partial parallels in Luke's Gospel, but only one, tenants in the vineyard, is found in all three Synoptic Gospels. The picture that emerges from these parables in Matthew's Gospel is that those determined to be wicked, unresponsive, or

22. Reid, "Violent Endings."
23. Other uniquely Matthean parables include hidden treasure and priceless pearl (13:44–45), workers in a vineyard (20:1–16), two sons (21:28–32), and ten bridesmaids (25:1–13), yet another eschatological parable with a disconcerting ending.

irresponsible will ultimately experience the full force of divine retributive violence.

Beginning with the parables unique to Matthew's Gospel, the twin parables of the tares and dragnet are found in the collection of parables relating to the reign of heaven in Matthew 13.[24] The first point to notice about the parable of the tares is that it is one of only two parables within the collection of parables in this chapter to receive an interpretation; the other is the parable of the sower, as it is named in 13:18. Moreover, the parable of the tares is the only one about which the disciples request an explanation of its meaning. In the case of the parable of the sower, the disciples do not explicitly seek an interpretation. Clearly Matthew did not intend for it to be misunderstood. In 13:37–43, the parable of the tares is given a focus-shifting allegorical interpretation,[25] with the tares representing those who belong to the evil one, identified as the devil, and the harvest representing the end of the age. According to Matthew's end-time scenario, angels sent by the Son of humanity will first sort out from the righteous both what causes people to fall away and those persons who behave contrary to Torah, then discard them into a fiery furnace, a place of "wailing and teeth-grinding." This is a favorite Matthean phrase, first used in 8:12 to warn that those who expect to join the patriarchs of Israel at the eschatological banquet may well have their places taken by others from east and west and be thrown into darkness outside the reign of heaven.[26] The phrase "wailing and teeth-grinding" occurs nowhere else in the New Testament except in Luke 13:28, where, unlike its parallel in Matthew 8:12, it "expresses the regret of those who are excluded from the eschatological banquet."[27] For Matthew, however, its meaning is manifestly more grisly, as Blaine Charette observes: "Whatever the origin or tradition history of the declaration, it is quite clear that in Matthew's Gospel it fulfils an important function as a solemn refrain underscoring the distress experienced by the cursed in the place of future punishment."[28] Moreover, Matthew delights in the phrase, using it a further five times in the parables of the tares (13:42), dragnet (13:50), wedding banquet (22:13), waiting slave (24:51), and talents (25:30). This speaks volumes about his mind-set.

The same end-time scenario depicted in the parable of the tares is replayed in the parable of the dragnet. Several phrases are repeated: "This is how things are at the conclusion of the age" (13:40, 49); "They [angels] will cast them [the

24. Although uniquely Matthean, the parables of the tares and dragnet have partial parallels in the *Gospel of Thomas* 57 and 8.

25. See Snodgrass, *Stories with Intent*, 196, 211.

26. Wailing also appears in Matt. 2:18, citing Jer. 31:15, to describe the impact of Herod's slaughter of infants.

27. Allison, *Resurrecting Jesus*, 65.

28. Charette, *Theme of Recompense*, 140. Charette relates this phrase to the misery associated with "the torments of eternal punishment" (141).

unrighteous] into the furnace of fire" (13:42, 50); and "There [in the furnace of fire], there will be wailing and teeth-grinding" (13:42, 50). For those with ears to hear (13:43b), Matthew takes pains to repeat himself. No interpretation is needed this time. Concerning this parable and what it reveals of Matthew's mind-set, Klyne Snodgrass remarks: "All the discourses in Matthew close with a saying on judgment, four of which sayings are parables of judgment, and the dragnet fills this role for the parables discourse."[29]

The parable of the unforgiving slave in Matthew 18:21–35 is also a parable of the reign of heaven. Reid notices that this parable, which she names "Forgiveness Aborted," concludes with the king or master handing over the unforgiving slave to be tortured. But she ignores the force of the concluding exhortation in 18:35, which reads: "So also my heavenly Father will do to you [pl.] unless each of you [pl.] forgives one's brother from your [pl.] hearts." Here Jesus concludes his instruction on forgiving largesse, in response to Peter's question about how often he should forgive an offense-prone brother (18:21). In Matthew's narrative, the parable of the unforgiving slave is intended to reinforce Jesus's instruction to forgive limitlessly—not seven times only, but seventy-seven (or perhaps even seventy times seven) times. But the conclusion to this parable envisages God as dealing with unforgiving persons in a most unforgiving way![30] Perhaps, as Christopher Marshall cautions, one should not overread or "press the logic" of this parable. "The reaction of the king," he insists, "is intended to underline the eschatological seriousness of the demand placed upon the messianic community to practice forgiveness, as well as to clarify that forgiveness is not a matter of cheap grace or eternal leniency."[31] Even so, the image of Jesus's heavenly Father as handing over unforgiving believers to torturers is morally obscene.

The "parable" or scenario of final judgment in 25:31–46 is the finale to Matthew's fifth and final discourse marked by the repeated refrain, "When Jesus had concluded these sayings/instructions/parables . . ." (7:28; 11:1; 13:53; 19:1; 26:1).[32] This scenario of the final judgment of the nations reiterates the notion of discriminating the righteous from the unrighteous, only this time according to the criterion of whether or not the needs of "the least significant" have been attended to. Those deemed not to have served the needs of "the least significant," and hence those of the judging king, are banished to "eternal" fire and punishment. If understood as incessant, "eternal" punishment for temporal misdemeanors, no matter how serious, is morally repugnant. Many

29. Snodgrass, *Stories with Intent*, 485. See also Schnelle, *Theology of the New Testament*, 460.

30. Peter's query in Matt. 18:21 may presuppose remorse on the part of the brother or sister each time that person offends, but that is not made explicit; cf. Luke 17:3–4.

31. C. Marshall, *Beyond Retribution*, 77. Marshall neglects to note that the king hands the unforgiving slave over to tormentors until he repays an unrepayable debt. Even in parable, this reflects a retributive rather than forgiving mind-set.

32. Although partially parabolic, Matt. 25:31–46 is not a parable in the strict sense.

Christian advocates of justice understandably see in this passage their raison
d'être for activism on behalf of the poor and the powerless, but what of the
character of the judging king on whose behalf such activism is conducted?[33]

So much for the four parables belonging to Matthew's special tradition,
commonly designated "M." What, then, of the other four shared with the
Gospels of Luke and (in one instance) Mark? The parable of tenants in a
vineyard not only appears in all three Synoptic Gospels but also in the same
basic context—following Jesus's arrival in Jerusalem, his symbolic disruption
in the temple, and the following question about his authority to do "these
things." Yet distinctively, between the question regarding Jesus's authority
and the parable of the tenants (21:33–46), Matthew interposes another of his
unique parables, the parable of two sons (21:28–32). In other words, despite
the shared context, Matthew's parable of the tenants is the second of two
parables told by Jesus in response to the request by chief priests and elders to
disclose the source of his authority. Both feature work in a vineyard, which
may explain their juxtaposition. Furthermore, both in Jesus's response to the
question about the source of his authority and in the parable of two sons, Jesus
refers to the mission of John the Immerser. The parable concludes with Jesus's
admonition that toll collectors and sex workers "enter the reign of God" (not
"heaven," despite belonging to M) ahead of chief priests and elders because,
unlike the chief priests and elders, toll collectors and sex workers believed
John (and presumably responded appropriately). In short, the parable of two
sons is a parable of reversal.

A distinctive emphasis within the parable of the tenants appears in 21:34a,
41d, and 43, each of which is uniquely Matthean. Matthew 21:34a reads: "But
when the season for *fruit-bearing* drew near. . . ." Also, 21:41 ends with Jesus's
interlocutors asserting that other vinedressers will give to the vineyard owner
fruits in their appointed seasons. Finally, 21:43 records Jesus as saying, "For
this reason I tell you that the reign of God will be withdrawn from you and
given to people groups producing its *fruits*." For Matthew, "bearing fruit"
is code for right conduct in accord with God's will (3:8–10; 7:16–20; 12:33).

According to Reid, "In the parable of the treacherous tenants (21:33–46),
the response of the landowner to the murder of his servants and son is to
put those evil ones . . . to a miserable death, and to lease the vineyard to
other tenants who will give him the produce at the harvest time (21:41)."[34]
She does not observe, however, that "they" (presumably the chief priests and

---

33. Another sting in the tail of this end-time scenario is that the sheep are *unaware* that
what they did for those in need was done also for the judging king. Perhaps the implication of
the question posed by the goats in Matt. 25:44 is that if they had only known the divine equa-
tion—divine presence among or divine association with the insignificant—they would have cared
for the needy. Is advocacy on behalf of those in need judged as "righteous" if done *because one
is aware* of the judging king's identification with such people?

34. Reid, "Violent Endings," 249.

elders of 21:23 or chief priests and Pharisees of 21:45) make this inference in response to Jesus's question, "So, when the master of the vineyard happens to arrive, what will he do to these vinedressers?" (21:40). Though their inference is reasonable, the way in which Jesus responds suggests that they are off the mark. Moreover, while Jesus's statement in 21:43 seems to confirm the inference of leasing the vineyard to other vinedressers, it does not reiterate the notion of ensuring that bad people will come to a bad end. Reid draws attention to the harshness of 21:44, which seemingly grants to the stone of 21:42 destructive prowess, but she ignores its textual uncertainty.[35] So perhaps Matthew's version of the parable of the tenants is a little less vindictive than Reid makes out.

Reid seems to accept that the parable of the wedding banquet in Matthew 22:1–14 is the same as the parable of the great feast in Luke 14:15–24, despite the different literary context and relatively few verbal parallels. Certainly there are similarities, and Reid correctly identifies violent and vindictive elements in Matthew's parable that are absent from Luke's:

> In the parable of the wedding feast (22:1–14), Matthew adds the detail that the king's envoys were seized, treated shamefully, and killed (v. 6). The king in anger sends his troops and destroys those murderers and burns their city (v. 7). Another group of servants is dispatched to go into the streets and gather all whom they find, both evil . . . and good (v. 10). The uniquely Matthean conclusion (vv. 11–14) has the king confront an improperly attired guest, who is then bound hand and foot and cast into the outer darkness, where there is weeping and gnashing of teeth (v. 13).[36]

Matthew 22:1–14 follows closely upon the parables of two sons and tenants in a vineyard (21:28–44), and Matthew seems to link this third parable to the previous two. As in 21:35–36, here 22:6 says that slaves sent out are killed, a seemingly gratuitous detail except that it prepares for the king's retribution in 22:7. Moreover, as in the earlier parables of the tares and dragnet, those gathered at the wedding feast include both the evil and the good. But the parable does not end with anyone separating out the righteous from the unrighteous and consigning the unrighteous to fire, as in the earlier parables. Rather, one guest without a wedding garment is silent when asked how he gained entry without suitable attire, so he is expelled to "the outer darkness," no less a place of wailing and teeth-grinding than fire.[37]

---

35. Matthew 21:44 is closely paralleled by Luke 20:18, but there is no Markan parallel. On balance, however, Matt. 21:44 is probably original. See Charette, *Theme of Recompense*, 138–39; Snodgrass, *Stories with Intent*, 286.

36. Reid, "Violent Endings," 249.

37. "The outer darkness" is a phrase distinctive to Matthew, occurring three times in his Gospel (8:12; 22:13; 25:30) and always in association with wailing and teeth-grinding. It signifies banishment from the light of divine presence. See Charette, *Theme of Recompense*, 142–43.

Although the parable of the wedding banquet in Matthew 22:1–14 is dissimilar from its (alleged) Lukan parallel, the same cannot be said of the parable of the waiting slave in Matthew 24:45–51, which is closely similar to Luke 12:41–46, even if placed in a different context. It is difficult to know whether Matthew envisaged one slave only or two. The introduction of the term "bad," "evil," or perhaps "irresponsible" in 24:48 suggests a second slave, but this may simply be a description based on how he decides to treat fellow slaves after surmising that his master is delayed. Recalling a study by Otto Betz, Snodgrass draws attention to parallels between this parable and Psalm 37, concluding that "Jesus' parable looks like an eschatological version of Psalm 37 applied to disciples through use of the servant imagery."[38] With respect to violent endings, however, there is little to separate this Matthean parable from its Lukan parallel. In both, the slave is diced in two and shares the fate of undesirables ("hypocrites" in Matt. 24:51; "the faithless" in Luke 12:46). The Matthean accent appears in the concluding clause, "There, there will be wailing and teeth-grinding" (24:51).

Like the parable of the wedding banquet, the parable of the talents in Matthew 25:14–30 is significantly different from its alleged Lukan parallel, the seemingly conflated parable of the minas located immediately before Jesus's entry into Jerusalem (Luke 19:11–27). Set within the context of the eschatological discourse of Matthew 24–25,[39] the parable of the talents is the third of four parables seemingly intended to drive home the point of 24:42, "So be watchful, because you do not know on what day your Lord is arriving," and 24:44, "So you also be ready, because the Son of humanity is arriving when you do not expect it." As Reid points out, the slave who did nothing with the talent entrusted to him is consigned to outer darkness, where there is wailing and teeth-grinding (25:30),[40] like the irresponsible slave two parables earlier (24:45–51) and even more like the inappropriately attired guest of the parable of the wedding banquet (22:10–13).[41] Compared with its (alleged) Lukan parallel, however, Matthew's parable is hardly more violent overall since in Luke's parable the nobleman-king orders that his opponents be slaughtered. But, for reasons outlined in chapter 3, the figure of the nobleman-king in Luke's parable is unlikely to represent the returning Son of humanity, as the master in Matthew's parable almost certainly does.

While one can agree with Reid that all these Matthean parables end in violent punishment and therefore envisage God or God's agent(s) as meting

38. Snodgrass, *Stories with Intent*, 502.
39. For a well-argued case in favor of accepting Matt. 23 as part of this discourse, see Hood, "Matthew 23–25."
40. Reid, "Violent Endings," 250.
41. While the irresponsible slave of Matt. 24:45–51 is punished for reprehensible conduct, the same cannot be said for the guest without a wedding garment or the slave entrusted with one talent. Passivity and timidity are punished no less severely than abusive and irresponsible behavior.

out violent retribution at the end of the age, it is not so evident that "in the parables that Matthew takes over from Mark or Q, he intensifies the violent punishments for those who do evil."[42] In the parable that Matthew shares with Mark, the parable of the tenants, Matthew's version is more vindictive than Mark's, especially if Matthew 21:44 is genuinely Matthean. In all four parables shared with Luke, however, not much separates Matthew from Luke on this point, apart from Matthew's repeated phrase, "There, there will be wailing and teeth-grinding." This is not to gainsay Reid's principal point, however, which concerns the discrepancy between, and moral implications of, contrasting images of God in Matthew's Gospel:

> Throwing evildoers into a fiery furnace, binding them hand and foot, casting them into outer darkness where there is weeping and gnashing of teeth, putting them to a miserable death, cutting and breaking them into pieces and crushing them, destroying murderers and burning their city, depriving them of the presence of God, putting them with hypocrites or with the devil and his angels for all eternity stand in clear contrast to the boundless, gratuitous divine love described in the Sermon on the Mount (5:44–48). The punishments meted out in the parabolic endings present a far different picture of how God acts. Is there inconsistency in God's actions? Which path are disciples to take as children who are supposed to imitate the divine ways?[43]

Having set out to resolve the tension in Matthew's Gospel caused by these contrasting portrayals of God's character, Reid offers four possible ways of doing so.[44] One is to acknowledge that in the process of composition, the Gospel writer may have incorporated diverse strands of tradition without trying to reconcile contradictory materials. But in the case of the concluding clause reiterated on five separate occasions, "There, there will be wailing and teeth-grinding," this clearly represents the final redactor or author's perspective. Moreover, as Reid acknowledges, even if this resolution is illuminating at a literary or compositional level, the theological problem for disciples of Jesus remains.

A second resolution of this particular tension in Matthew's narrative is to view the Gospel writer as a teacher addressing disciples at different stages of moral development. In other words, Matthew's parables with violent endings are instructive for those who operate at the level of reward and punishment, whereas the Sermon on the Mount is for those at a higher level of moral development. As Reid recognizes, however, this distinction must be imposed on the narrative; it does not emerge from the Gospel itself, since nowhere is there any indication of which teachings of Jesus are directed toward those at

42. Reid, "Violent Endings," 249.
43. Ibid., 250.
44. Ibid., 250–53. This theological tension within Matthew's Gospel, along with its moral ramifications, is explored further in Reid, "Which God Is with Us?"

a lower or higher level of moral development. One might add that insofar as Matthew's parables of eschatological judgment anticipate the action of God or God's agent(s), one would be entitled to regard vindictive retribution as morally superior to love that seeks to emulate the (supposed) indiscriminate goodness of God. In other words, how God acts ultimately might be considered more morally illuminating than how God acts penultimately.

A third resolution, which Reid finds inadequate, is to deny that the principal characters in the parables of retribution represent God. "Rather, these parables unmask the violence of these characters and the unjust systems they perpetuate. Their purpose is to lead hearers toward action that confronts such injustice."[45] Some of Matthew's eight parables under discussion may be susceptible to such an interpretation, but as Reid points out, it is difficult to argue this for the parables of the tares and unforgiving slave. The same might be said for the parable of the dragnet, which clearly echoes the parable of the tares, and the scenario of final judgment. The context of the parables of the waiting slave and talents also suggests an interpretation along the lines of eschatological vengeance.

Reid's preferred resolution is to demarcate between divine and human violence: "Another explanation is that the kind of nonviolent confrontation of evil that Jesus advocated in the Sermon on the Mount is not applicable to the kind of situation envisioned in these eight parables. All of them can be understood as portraying an end-time setting with a reckoning that is final."[46]

One can agree with Reid's assessment of the likely eschatological dimension of each of the parables examined without accepting her judgment that "this interpretation satisfactorily resolves the tension."[47] Admittedly, for Reid, this implies that disciples are not in a position to emulate eschatological retribution; rather, in the present, disciples of Jesus are bound by his teaching to confront evil, injustice, and violence nonviolently. But Reid makes an assertion that exacerbates the tension she claims to have resolved: "Nonviolent confrontation of evildoers is not pertinent to scenes of end-time judgment."[48] If this is a purely descriptive assessment of Matthew's moral vision, it may be accurate, but in view of alternative perspectives, even within the New Testament, one is entitled to ask why this should be so. After all, if evil can be undone only by greater evil or if violence can be vanquished only by greater violence, has either been overcome? Reid is cognizant of the problem that followers of Jesus may authorize violence against perceived evil here and now by appealing to anticipated eschatological vengeance on God's part.[49] This is undoubtedly a

45. Reid, "Violent Endings," 251 (summarizing a view she disputes).
46. Ibid., 252; cf. Swartley's assessment in the opening section of this chapter.
47. Reid, "Violent Endings," 253.
48. Ibid., 252.
49. Desjardins, *Peace, Violence*, 91, observes that although some believers are willing to leave vengeance to God, others adopt the opposite position: "Since God is our model and he solves his problems through violence, so can we."

significant moral problem. But there is another and arguably more destructive problem, which concerns one's theology (in the precise sense of reasoning about or imagining God) and what follows ethically from that theology. For if one accepts that God's ways are but our ways, only more forceful and potent, that is either idolatry (understood theologically) or projection (understood psychologically).

Alongside other considerations in the final section of her study, Reid raises the question of how we understand the "nature" or "character" of God. "Does God at the end-time set aside compassion and engage in vindictive violence?" she asks.[50] Her answer is that this kind of question cannot be adequately answered exegetically but must be addressed within the context of systematic and constructive theology. I demur. With respect to Matthew's Gospel, the *story of Jesus* itself, even (or perhaps especially) as told by Matthew, undoes the logic of eschatological vengeance. In other words, Matthew's story of Jesus is more morally determinative than stories told by Jesus within his narrative, even the uniquely Matthean parable of workers in a vineyard (Matt. 20:1–16), which is more consonant with Jesus's moral teaching in the Sermon on the Mount.[51]

Reid's study is premised on the proviso that Matthew's parables provide windows into Matthew's theology, showing his conception of God. Given the figurative nature of parables, however, is one entitled to interpret the violent and retributive imagery of Matthew's parables as an accurate index of his eschatology? Perhaps one is better advised to focus on Matthew's record of Jesus's eschatological teaching. Yet eschatological language is often no less figurative than parabolic language. Although it is prudent not to press either parabolic or eschatological language too literally, it nevertheless seems reasonable to accept that, in Matthew's case, both a significant number of his parables and his representation of Jesus's eschatological teaching reveal a retributive apocalyptic mind-set according to which divine judgment is construed as eschatological vengeance. This is especially so in view of the interpretive guideline of *end stress* in relation to parables. As Snodgrass points out, "For most parables what comes at the end is the clinching indicator of intent."[52] This is no doubt why Reid focuses her study on violent *endings* in so many of Matthew's parables.

The interpretive rule of *end stress* also sheds light on the significance of the fact that of the eight parables Reid discusses, three occur at the *culmination* of Jesus's eschatological discourse in Matthew 24–25. Not only is Matthew's version of Jesus's eschatological discourse punctuated by parables toward its end (24:32–44) but the discourse is also given added exclamatory force

50. Reid, "Violent Endings," 253.

51. Framed as this parable of workers in a vineyard is by mirror-image reversal sayings (Matt. 19:30; 20:16), Matthew could not have emphasized more emphatically that the justice of the reign of heaven is different from, but not less than, human conceptions of justice.

52. Snodgrass, *Stories with Intent*, 30.

by the series of four parables that clearly serve to illustrate and reinforce it
(24:45–25:46). As a result, it seems safe to conclude, with Reid, that the violent endings to many of Matthew's parables mirror Matthew's theological
eschatology. Snodgrass concedes that "the harshness of some parables of
judgment (e.g., Matt 18:34 or 24:51) is offensive and troublesome to some, but
these parables are not realistic descriptions of judgment," he avers. "Rather,
they warn about the reality and seriousness of judgment."[53] And its *severity*,
one must surely add!

Even if Matthew's parables reliably mirror his retributive apocalyptic mind-
set, they are not the sum total of his eschatology. Though it is not possible to
give detailed attention to Jesus's eschatological teaching in Matthew 24, along
with its attendant exegetical and interpretive difficulties, a distinctive feature
of this section provides a suitable focus for analysis.

The Parousia of the Son of Humanity

Matthew 24, together with the parallel passages in Mark 13 and Luke 21, is
an interpretive minefield. One important question is whether this block of
teaching on the lips of Jesus relates primarily to his end-time return, to the
destruction of Jerusalem and the temple, or to both (in separate parts of the
discourse). To my mind, both Jerusalem's destruction and Jesus's return as the
eschatological Son of humanity are in view in Matthew 24, but it is difficult to
ascertain whether parts of the discourse relate to one of these events alone and,
if so, which parts relate principally to Jesus's end-time return. This difficulty
has led Vicky Balabanski and Ulrich Luz to recommend reading 24:4–31 as
two parallel sequences (24:6–14, 15–31).[54] For Balabanski, the culmination of
the first sequence (24:13–14) addresses the first part of the disciples' twofold
question in 24:3, and the conclusion to the second sequence (24:29–31) answers
the second part of their question.[55] By contrast, R. T. France, Jeffrey Gibbs,
David Garland, and Alistair Wilson see the entirety of 24:4–35 as concerned
with first-century events, most notably the destruction of Jerusalem.[56] For
France, Garland, and Wilson, moreover, 24:4–35 comprises Jesus's response
to the first part of his disciples' twofold question, with the remainder of the
discourse (24:36–25:46) addressing the second part of their question.

53. Ibid., 31.
54. Balabanski, *Eschatology in the Making*, 153–73; Luz, *Matthew 21–28*, 180–206. Luz
adopts Balabanski's two-sequence interpretation; but for Luz, Matt. 24:29–31 does not parallel
24:13–14, as for Balabanski.
55. See also Balabanski, "Mission in Matthew."
56. France, *Gospel of Matthew*, 889–931; Gibbs, *Jerusalem and Parousia*, esp. chap. 6; Garland, *Reading Matthew*, 239–49; Wilson, *When Will These Things Happen?* 109–61, 224–47.
France has been advocating this viewpoint in relation to Mark 13 and Matt. 24 since his early
work *Jesus and the Old Testament*.

Perhaps the most crucial issue raised by these different interpretive approaches is the meaning of 24:29–31, which anticipates cosmic catastrophe *immediately following* the affliction apparently associated with the lead-up to the destruction of Jerusalem, which in turn gives way to the coming of the Son of humanity and related events. Probably most interpreters see this passage as referring to the end-time return of Jesus as the judging Son of humanity. For France and those influenced by him, however, 24:29–31 (and indeed, 24:32–34) is metaphorical language signifying the exaltation of Jesus as the Son of humanity, of which the destruction of Jerusalem is its primary historical manifestation. In later chapters I explain why I demur from France and others in relation to the parallel passages Mark 13:24–27 and Luke 21:25–28; yet in Matthew 24 the pattern of occurrences of the distinctive Greek term *parousia* gives one pause.[57]

This term *parousia* occurs four times in Matthew 24 but nowhere else in the Gospels, Acts, or Revelation.[58] Its primary meaning is "presence," but in an eschatological context it signifies "arrival." In Matthew 24 it initially appears in the disciples' two-part question, "Tell us, when will these things occur, and what is the sign of your *parousia* and culmination of the age?" (24:3). The "these things" to which they refer picks up on the ambiguous "all these things" of 24:2, which Jesus apparently connects to the impending destruction of the buildings that comprise the temple. One might take the disciples' twofold question to imply that they connect the impending destruction of the temple with Jesus's arrival as eschatological agent. Implicit in their question is the identification of Jesus's arrival with the end of the age.

Until 24:27 much of Jesus's instruction in this discourse comprises a warning about what must occur before his arrival at the end of the age so that his disciples are not led astray. The indeterminate time leading up to (but not necessarily signaling) the end will be characterized by upheaval, persecution, tribulation, and false messianic and prophetic claims. The ambiguity of all such circumstances and events implies that none in itself nor any of them together signals the end precipitated by the parousia. Rather, as 24:27 clarifies, the Son of humanity's parousia will be unmistakable, no less than lightning that comes out of the east and illuminates the west.

In view of the verbal and thematic connections between Matthew 24:30, where the Greek term *parousia* does not occur, and 24:3, 27, 37, and 39, where it does, many interpret the reference to seeing the Son of humanity coming on

57. Although France developed his particular interpretation of Jesus's eschatological discourse in relation to Mark 13, it seems better suited to Matt. 24; cf. France, *Gospel of Matthew*, 891–93. For narratological reasons, Cooper in "Adaptive Eschatological Inference" sees the coming of the Son of humanity as bireferential: realized intratextually within Matthew's Passion Narrative but proleptically of end-time events such as his coming *in glory* for vindication and judgment.

58. Regarding Johannine eschatology, the presence of this term in 1 John 2:28 shows that future-oriented eschatology is not alien to that part of the Johannine tradition represented by the Fourth Gospel and the Johannine Epistles.

the clouds of heaven in 24:30 as signifying his end-time parousia. France accepts 24:27 as a parenthetical reference to Jesus's end-time return, but alongside other considerations the absence of the term *parousia* at 24:30 leads him to deny that anything prior to 24:36 (apart from 24:27–28) relates to the end. If he is correct, the coming of the Son of humanity on the clouds of heaven in 24:30 refers to Jesus's exaltation, confirmed by Jerusalem's destruction and the growth of the church. Matthew 24:29–31 may not be about *end-time* judgment, in France's view, but it nevertheless expresses divine judgment in the form of Jerusalem's destruction, perhaps even as the pattern for eschatological judgment at the parousia.

If, however, 24:30–31 describes the parousia of the Son of humanity without using that specific term,[59] the note of judgment is muted. Following the signs of cosmic collapse described in 24:29, which will immediately follow the earlier tribulation of indeterminate duration, the sign of the Son of humanity will appear in the sky. What comprises this heavenly sign is not specified, but in the absence of all other skylights (24:29), Matthew no doubt envisages a luminous sign of some kind. Perhaps echoing the earlier assurance that the Son of humanity's arrival will be unmistakable (24:27–28), Matthew here has Jesus say that all the tribes of the earth will lament the appearance of the sign even as they see the Son of humanity coming on the clouds of heaven with power and glory. W. D. Davies and Dale Allison support the view that the ambiguous "sign of the Son of humanity" is an ensign (in their view, the cross) raised by the Son of humanity to signal "muster for the eschatological battle."[60] The confluence of evidence they provide in support of this interpretation is impressive, and such an interpretation helps to explain the mournful response of all earthly tribes.

Perhaps surprisingly, however, there is no eschatological battle. Or if one is presumed, it is passed over in silence. The majesty of the coming Son of humanity is emphasized, and 24:31 affirms that he will dispatch his angels with a trumpet blast. All this coheres with an interpretation along the lines of eschatological battle. Rather than engage in battle, however, the mustered angelic host engages in a gathering exercise, bringing together the Son of humanity's chosen ones from the four winds! It is difficult to know whether Matthew envisages everything described in this passage as occurring in the heavens, that is, with the Son of humanity's coming to God (as in Dan. 7:13) and then sending his angels to gather his elect from across the reach of the heavens. What is striking, however, especially in light of the end-time imagery

59. See also Matt. 24:42–44, esp. 24:44, which France accepts as referring to the parousia without using the term; cf. France, *Gospel of Matthew*, 941–43. The remainder of my discussion of the parousia of the Son of humanity accepts this interpretation, but without presuming France's interpretation to be incorrect (even if theologically perturbing).

60. Davies and Allison, *Commentary on Matthew*, 3:359–60; cf. Boring, "Gospel of Matthew," 443–44, who considers the sign of the Son of humanity to be the coming Son of humanity himself, not some preliminary warning sign. So, too, Luz, *Matthew 21–28*, 201–2.

displayed in so many of Matthew's parables, is the absence of any description of violence on the part of the coming Son of humanity or his angels.

If this were all Matthew had to say about the parousia of the Son of humanity, one would have to rethink what is implied by his eschatological parables with violent endings. A little later in the discourse, however, Jesus returns to the theme of the parousia of the Son of humanity to emphasize that its timing is impossible to forecast. Matthew 24:37–39 reads as follows:

> For as the days of Noah were, so will the arrival [*parousia*] of the Son of humanity be. For as, in the days before the cataclysm, they were eating and drinking, marrying and marrying off, until the day Noah entered into the big box, and they were unaware until the cataclysm came and swept them all away, the arrival [*parousia*] of the Son of humanity will occur in the same way.

While the emphasis is on the unpredictability of the Son of humanity's arrival, the effect of that arrival is nevertheless associated with the cataclysmic consequences of the great flood. Indeed, the primary point is already made before one reaches the note about the flood sweeping everyone away. Nevertheless, W. D. Davies and Dale Allison rightly remark:

> Noah's contemporaries . . . were remembered as great sinners who did not foresee God's wrath. . . . Sometimes the flood was a prototype of the last judgment or end of the world. . . . But our saying goes its own way in focusing neither upon the sins of Noah's generation nor his righteousness but upon the unexpected nature of the cataclysm that overtook the world while people went about their daily business unawares.[61]

Matthew's record of Jesus's teaching regarding the parousia of the Son of humanity hardly matches the severe imagery of eschatological vengeance encountered in Matthew's parables of end-time judgment. Only the (secondary) analogy with the cataclysmic flood resonates clearly with Matthew's retributive apocalyptic eschatology. As mentioned earlier, however, this analogy is followed by a series of parables, all of which illustrate and reinforce the eschatological discourse and most of which emphasize eschatological vengeance.

The Construction of Violence in Matthew's Gospel

In a set of studies on violence in the New Testament, Warren Carter addresses "Constructions of Violence and Identities in Matthew's Gospel."[62] This study is largely directed toward undermining the dominant tendency (in the past) to

61. Davies and Allison, *Commentary on Matthew*, 3:380. This is said specifically of Matt. 24:37, but it is true of the entire analogy.
62. Carter, "Constructions of Violence."

attribute much of the violence depicted in Matthew's Gospel to Jews, whether Jewish responsibility for Jesus's violent death or Jewish persecution of Jesus's disciples. Hence his analysis of the "construction of violence" in Matthew's Gospel, with reference to two questions: "How does Matthew construct violence? And how does that construction function?"[63]

Carter first points out that in relation to violence against Jesus's disciples, Matthean scholars have used the ethnic designation "the Jews" when societal status is the more accurate category: "The Gospel does not construct violence around the term *Ioudaioi*."[64] He then provides a table setting out the various agents of violence in Matthew's Gospel, the type of violence perpetrated, and those against whom violence is done. Not surprisingly, various categories of ruling elites feature prominently as agents of violence, such as Herod, Pilate, and religious leaders. So, too, do Jesus and God, however, especially in eschatological contexts. Carter contends that, for Matthew, violence is an ideological construct with both cosmic and theological dimensions. In other words, the violence perpetrated by earthly powers and rulers is an expression of Satan's opposition to God's purpose for the world and involvement in the world, especially in the mission of Jesus. According to Carter, "Violence is constructed [in Matthew's Gospel] as the way of the world. Significantly, it is the gospel that provides the perspective that unmasks the true cosmic and theological nature of the social-political-religious violence."[65]

If violence as displayed by Matthew is "the way of the world," however, what can one say about Jesus's divinely authorized, retributively violent parousia? Carter acknowledges the tension highlighted by Reid between Jesus's exhortations to nonviolence and his anticipated violent retribution at the parousia. "Violence is the activity of God, not disciples," he writes, "and is reserved for the future, not the present."[66] His response to this Matthean construction is that the anticipation of eschatological vengeance functioned sociologically both to establish and to reinforce the identity of the community of disciples as "the minority suffering righteous who live liminally awaiting God's vindication."[67] In short, the expectation of end-time vengeance served to instill hope and assurance in a beleaguered community of faith. Carter also contends that the expectation of divine retribution legitimates nonviolent practices on the part of disciples here and now: "Disciples can 'afford' this nonviolent stance because the apocalyptic worldview affirms the coming triumph of God and of believers. Disciples can endure nonviolently in the meantime because, in the end, God will punish the opponents."[68]

63. Ibid., 82.
64. Ibid., 85.
65. Ibid., 98.
66. Ibid., 98–99.
67. Ibid., 99.
68. Ibid., 100.

Understandable as this may be in historical context,[69] how valid is such an expectation when the writing of a harassed community of faith becomes canonical Scripture at the hands of those with temporal power and in the hands of a religious majority? What remains valid, it seems to me, is the hope of eschatological vindication at various levels, such as the restoration to wholeness of those whose lives have been overwhelmed by suffering and the eschatological verification of (1) Christian epistemology and (2) an ethic grounded in the teaching and example of Jesus. But to expect—and worse, to delight in the prospect of—divine vengeance against oppressors, enemies, and those considered beyond the pale is ultimately self-defeating.

Carter draws attention to a number of sociological studies that show how social groups whose mind-set is similar to Matthew's actually stimulate or provoke violent and repressive behavior. Even if Matthew's Gospel does not endorse violence on the part of disciples of Jesus, one can see how easily its dualistic, retributive-apocalyptic worldview, its stark we/they mentality, and its violent rhetoric against perceived opponents might inculcate vengeful attitudes and violent behavior.[70] Thus, both directly and indirectly, the Gospel according to Matthew leans in the direction of condoning violence. This profoundly problematic possibility finds expression in Carter's devastating, albeit hyperbolic, conclusion: "Given Jesus' rhetorically violent condemnation of the status quo, his physically violent anticipation of judgment in his temple actions, and the violent visions of God's eschatological triumph accomplished through Jesus' *parousia* and eschatological battle, Matthew's gospel finally, but ironically, capitulates to and imitates the imperial violence from which it seeks to save."[71]

Within their respective studies, both Reid and Carter take time to discuss the problem of defining violence. Both select fairly wide definitions, which include psychological violation as well as physical damage, structural as well as interpersonal violence. An arresting feature of Carter's discussion, however, is his appeal to the category of "cultural violence," a description borrowed from Johan Galtung for "the use of 'the symbolic sphere' of human existence such as religion to identify God as an agent of violence."[72] Earlier, in response to Reid, I suggested that to envisage God as acting violently at the *eschaton* is likely a form of idolatry, constructing God in our image. Perhaps a better term for

---

69. I survey some other assessments of the role of violent eschatology within Matthew's sociohistorical context in Neville, "Toward a Teleology of Peace," 135–52. See also Sim, "Rise and Fall of Matthew."

70. Rhetorical violence on the part of Jesus (as in Matt. 23) is historically explicable, even if we have learned that the rhetoric of rage so easily deteriorates into physical violence. See Johnson, "New Testament's Anti-Jewish Slander." There is good reason to regard the vitriolic rhetoric that Matthew attributes to Jesus as reflecting the life-setting of Matthew and those whom he represents. (The same dynamic is also present in the Fourth Gospel.)

71. Carter, "Constructions of Violence," 102.

72. Ibid., 91; cf. Galtung, "Cultural Violence."

this is blasphemy, in the sense of defaming the divine, for what could be more dishonoring than to project onto God our basest and least creative quality?

Protesting Matthew's Violent Eschatology

On the one hand, there can be little doubt that Matthew's eschatology presumes that God or God's agent(s) will ultimately indulge in retributive violence against the unrighteous, irrespective of the criteria used to separate the wicked from the righteous—whether obedience to Torah as interpreted by Jesus or compassion for the "least significant." On the other hand, both in Jesus's moral teaching, especially in the Sermon on the Mount, and in his conduct, violence is eschewed as incompatible with the "nature" or "character" of God. Thus there is a deep-seated tension between Matthew's violent eschatology and his description of the nonviolent moral vision of Jesus, grounded in the indiscriminate "perfection of Providence."

For Matthew, hypocrisy or incongruity between word and deed, teaching and action, was anathema. To label an opponent a hypocrite was, for Matthew, a severe and cutting insult. This is why he liberally applied the term to scribes and Pharisees (Matt. 23:13, 15, 23, 25, 27, 29), who were more likely to have been his own than Jesus's opponents, but ensured that in many and varied ways Jesus acts as he teaches. In "Matthew: A Retrospect," W. D. Davies and Dale Allison detail multiple connections between Jesus's words and deeds before concluding: "One could go on and on in this vein, citing instances of Jesus acting in accord with his speech."[73] Yet what Matthew anticipated on the part of the eschatological judge, the returning Son of humanity, is incongruent with his record of what the selfsame Son of humanity taught about violence and vengeance.

While this incongruity is perturbing, Matthew may not have perceived this tension as inherently contradictory. He may even have failed to perceive the tension. As Allison observes,

> Matthew, understandably enough, did not share the modern aversion to hell. He was educated into the first-century Jewish and Christian traditions, in both of which the God of love is equally the God of judgment. Surely, then, if he could talk with us, the evangelist would be unsympathetic with our contemporary queasiness about transcendent wrath and punishment. There is no indication from first-century Jewish or Christian texts that anybody back then perceived divine love and judgment as necessary antitheses.[74]

Allison's point is well made, but it is one thing to grant that divine love and judgment are not antithetical, and quite another to accept that vindictive

73. Davies and Allison, *Commentary on Matthew*, 3:715–16.
74. Allison, *Studies in Matthew*, 248–49.

and violent retribution is compatible with the caliber of divine love understood (even by Matthew) to be responsible for redemption. In other words, as Marshall argues, judgment need not necessarily imply violent retribution or retribution for its own sake.[75] Moreover, to accept that Matthew failed to perceive the theological-cum-moral problem of eschatological vengeance does not imply the absence of a problem, nor indeed that all of Matthew's (near) contemporaries failed to perceive it. As Allison himself demonstrates in a scintillating study of Luke 9:52–56, when Jesus rebuffs the offer by James and John to call down fire from heaven upon unreceptive Samaritans: there are Jewish and Christian traditions both prior to and contemporaneous with Matthew that recoil from notions of violent vengeance, admittedly by human beings, on the grounds of God's love and mercy.[76] François Bovon lends support to Allison's detection of the impulse against violence in Luke's writings,[77] and in later chapters I argue that the moral vision of both Mark and the Fourth Evangelist points in the direction of excluding eschatological vengeance.

Swartley and Reid seem to accept that the moral problem of eschatological vengeance in Matthew's Gospel is resolved by strictly demarcating between divine eschatological violence and nonviolent conduct explicitly expected of Jesus's disciples prior to the eschaton. On the one hand, they are correct: allowing that God is entitled to act violently when all other means have been exhausted does not imply that violent retribution on the part of human beings, even if understood to be acting on God's behalf, can be condoned. Indeed, Miroslav Volf and Scott Holland contend that, in certain circumstances, a nonviolent ethic necessitates anticipation of eschatological vengeance.[78]

On the other hand, those enamored of eschatological vengeance can just as easily support violent means to resolve conflict in the here and now. As Robert Wall points out in a study of "The Eschatologies of the Peace Movement,"[79] Christian hawks (who advocate "peacemaking" by means of military buildup) consider their position to be authorized by a Matthean-like eschatology, whereas Christian doves tend to appeal to an eschatology more similar to Luke's. "Isn't it true," he asks, "that the different theological warrants one finds in the current discussions about peacekeeping are being influenced by the different eschatologies one finds within the Bible?"[80] Wall endorses a position that accepts the canonical value of both Matthean and Lukan emphases, both as a challenge to exclusivist claims by hawks or doves to represent *the*

75. C. Marshall, *Beyond Retribution*, 175–97.
76. Allison, "Rejecting Violent Judgment," although he notes seeming contradictions to this peaceful orientation within Luke–Acts, such as Luke 19:27 and Acts 5:5, 10.
77. See Bovon, "The Child and the Beast." On Luke's ambiguity with respect to eschatological vengeance, see part 2.
78. Volf, *Exclusion and Embrace*, 275–306; Holland, "Gospel of Peace."
79. Wall, "Eschatologies of the Peace Movement."
80. Ibid., 9.

Christian position and as a reminder that any perspective on eschatology is necessarily partial and provisional. However one assesses Wall's view, my point is that attitudes and behaviors are shaped by what we hope for and expect; it is not a straightforward matter to separate morality from perceptions of divine reality. In other words, it is more difficult than either Swartley or Reid assumes to acknowledge the divine entitlement to violent retribution without arrogating the same prerogative to human beings, especially persons convinced that they are acting for God.

As indicated at the outset of this chapter, Matthew's prominent theme of eschatological vengeance poses serious problems for those who take their moral bearings from Jesus. The first is that it encourages a sub-Christian conception of God as one whose ultimate resort is overwhelming violence. A second problem is that to expect eschatological vengeance may foster vengeful attitudes and violent behaviors that are antithetical to the moral vision of Jesus. And insofar as Matthew foresees vengeance on the part of God, the question that arises is whether violence might be ontologically constitutive of reality. These difficulties are compounded both by Matthew's canonical status and by virtue of the reality that for much of the church's history, Matthew's Gospel has been its darling. In view of such seemingly intractable problems, how might one respond?

Shortly after the turn of the millennium, John Dominic Crossan responded to Dale Allison's portrait of Jesus as a "millenarian prophet,"[81] itself largely devoted to critiquing Crossan's own portrayal of Jesus as a "Mediterranean Jewish peasant."[82] Introducing "five necessary distinctions," which climax in the decisive interpretive choice between "violent or nonviolent apocalypse," Crossan wrote:

> We are now finally out of a terrible century, a century of worldwide killing fields, a century worse by execution if not by intention than any in our past. At such a moment, our very humanity demands that we reject definitively the lure of a violent ultimacy, a violent transcendence, or a violent God. If, on the other hand, we sincerely believe in a violent God, we must surely follow openly the advice of Mrs. Job: Curse God and die.[83]

Crossan's appeal—"Our very humanity demands that we reject definitively the lure of a violent ultimacy, a violent transcendence, or a violent God"—seems premised on some nexus between perception of divinity and

81. Allison, *Jesus of Nazareth*.
82. Crossan, *Historical Jesus*.
83. Crossan, "Eschatology, Apocalypticism," esp. 97–98. The other four distinctions are destructive or transformative apocalypse; material or social apocalypse; primary or secondary apocalypse; negative or positive apocalypse. For Crossan, the second option in each distinction comprises a moral imperative.

human conduct. Human behavior is affected by how we envisage God. What is demanded by "our very humanity," however, is open to multiple and even conflicting interpretations. In Jesus, various New Testament writers and later Christian thinkers perceived the measure of God. Nowhere is this expressed more clearly than in the prologue to the Fourth Gospel, where the divine *Logos* incarnate in Jesus is upheld as the exegete of God (John 1:1–18). Matthew's near-equivalent notion is *Immanu-el*, God present with humanity in the historical person of Jesus (Matt. 1:23). As Pregeant remarks, "As the one who is named 'God is with us' in [Matt.] 1:23, Jesus stands in God's stead. Since he speaks and acts for God, his words and deeds are God's own words and deeds: to obey his commands is to obey God, and to imitate his actions is to imitate God."[84] Whatever "divinity" we attribute to the "God with us" displayed in Jesus's mission and message should surely take priority over whatever residual knowledge of God remains to be disclosed eschatologically. In other words, within the Gospel according to Matthew, the memory of Jesus's nonviolent mission, which disciples are instructed to emulate, should be privileged over whatever lies beyond the capacity of any human being to know. Since "incarnation" (God present with us in Jesus) precedes the eschaton historically, so "incarnation" takes precedence over the eschaton epistemologically and ethically. As a result, for those who take their moral bearings from Jesus, this implies that with respect to the discrepancy in Matthew's Gospel between Jesus's nonviolent mission and his (apparent) expectation of eschatological vengeance, the former is determinative.

In this connection, Ulrich Luz offers instructive interpretive suggestions. Recognizing both the limitations and value of historical-critical approaches to biblical texts, his erudite work on Matthew's Gospel has focused on *Wirkungsgeschichte*, the continuing influence of biblical texts on later history. Since the historical influence of Matthew's Gospel is so mixed, Luz proposes two interlocking criteria for ascertaining a "true interpretation" of biblical texts: first, "correspondence with the essentials of the history of Jesus," which is not the same as correspondence with the Jesus of history; and second, love as the functional criterion for testing the effects or consequences of any particular interpretation.[85] In Luz's use of these two interlocking interpretive criteria, a double movement is discernible: he derives his interpretive criteria from the Gospel tradition, including (perhaps especially) Matthew's Gospel, but then evaluates that broader tradition, including Matthew's Gospel, in light of these criteria.[86] Indeed, for Luz, these two criteria coalesce, and his exposition of their interrelation is illuminating. It must be acknowledged, however, that *Wirkungsgeschichte* itself

84. Pregeant, *Knowing Truth, Doing Good*, 124.

85. Luz, *Matthew in History*, 75–97.

86. My own interpretive grappling with Matthew's violent eschatology is a variation on this double movement.

reveals that Matthew's "history of Jesus" has at various times and places had violent effects, justified by "love."

In an excursus on Matthew's conception of judgment, Luz's reflections on the continuing meaning of divine judgment in Matthew's Gospel lead him to explore two ways of apprehending this fundamental datum: "For Matthew it is Jesus and not an unknown who is the judge of the world."[87] One can take this to mean that whereas Jesus presently accompanies the church as *Immanu-el*, "God with us," he will ultimately confront all people as an unmerciful judge. One can also take comfort from this realization, however, since to know Jesus as *Immanu-el* precludes fearing him. While certain features of Matthew's Gospel encourage the first, more fearful reading, Luz opines that the Gospel as a whole supports the second, nonfearful reading: "The basic exegetical thesis lying behind this opinion is the conviction that in the Gospel of Matthew the *story of Jesus*, of the 'God with us,' takes precedence over, frames, and is decisive for the *proclamation of Jesus*, the Gospel of the kingdom, . . . of which the message of judgment is an essential part."[88]

In the quest to come to grips with the various problems associated with Matthew's violent eschatology, we can be grateful that we have four canonical Gospels rather than only one. If the early church had decided that differences between the Gospels required the acceptance of one alone as authoritative, that single Gospel might well have been Matthew's. Fortunately, Matthew's canonical counterparts mute the theme of eschatological vengeance to varying degrees. As a result, even at the exegetical level, there are scriptural resources for contesting Matthew's violent eschatology.

Although exegesis is important, the interpretive imperative is more important still, especially since Jewish and Christian Scripture contains more than one perspective on the moral validity and value of violence. In other words, interpretive choices can and indeed must be made. Exegetical studies indicate that within the Gospel tradition(s), eschatological violence is a Matthean emphasis, which can be plausibly explained as a response to specific sociohistorical circumstances. With the benefit of hindsight, especially in view of *Wirkungsgeschichte* and the reception history of Matthew's violent eschatology, it seems fair to say that one can hold tightly to Matthew's record of Jesus's mission and moral vision while sitting loosely to his anticipation of eschatological vengeance.

Matthew's depiction of eschatological reward and recompense should not simply be jettisoned, however. Even if the form of divine judgment foreseen by Matthew is morally problematic, his expectation that all human beings

---

87. Luz, *Matthew 21–28*, 292.

88. Ibid., emphasis original. Luz's "basic exegetical thesis" coheres with my contention that "incarnation" (the life story of *Immanu-el*) precedes the eschaton both epistemologically and ethically no less than historically. For a contrasting perspective, see Angel, "Inquiring into an *Inclusio*," 527–30.

are answerable to a higher authority is one means of investing human behavior and decision making with profound seriousness. "The coming judgment makes clear the true significance of human behavior," as Luz declares.[89] Or as Klaus Wengst writes in relation to Matthew's conception of final judgment:

> Anyone who thinks that they can act without responsibility, because there will be no consequences to their actions, is mistaken. There will be consequences which rebound upon the doer. This is guaranteed by the coming judge. Here is a hint as to why one must speak of judgment: it cannot be conceded that wicked deeds are without consequences for the doer and that it is accordingly irrelevant what is done.[90]

One might add that the notion of divine judgment safeguards against viewing historical winners as ultimate winners, which would authorize determining right by might. As Thorwald Lorenzen argues, in the absence of divine judgment, history is its own judge. Moreover, divine judgment in Christian perspective derives from Jesus's own vision of God and life, which implies that divine judgment is neither solely nor strictly retributive.[91] Indeed, Matthew 11:2–6 and other biblical passages lead me to conclude that although more restrictive ("to each their due") and retributive conceptions of justice and judgment are to be found in Jewish and Christian Scripture, divine judgment interpreted christologically is primarily restorative, even if it has a retributive dimension. Divine judgment condemns human pride, injustice, and violence, but within the context of God's all-embracing reconciling initiative.[92] Paradoxically, perhaps, divine judgment interpreted christologically also undermines the moral validity and value of violence, thereby raising yet another ethical caution against anticipating eschatological vengeance.

Since it is reasonable to affirm that not everything Matthew attributes to Jesus necessarily derives directly from Jesus, is one able to appeal to the historical Jesus to resolve the tension between Matthew's nonviolent ethic and violent eschatology? In *Jesus and the Transformation of Judaism*, John Riches argues that Jesus's emphasis on divine love, mercy, and forgiveness led him to moderate retributive and vengeful dimensions of Jewish eschatology—at least by comparison with his contemporaries. Jesus's "theism," in short, transformed traditional eschatological expectations.[93]

For understandable reasons, Hays equivocates on the role of the historical Jesus in New Testament ethics. He deems it unwise to make the (reconstructed)

89. Luz, *Matthew 21–28*, 288.

90. Wengst, "Aspects of the Last Judgment," 241; cf. Allison, *Resurrecting Jesus*, 96–99, who notes that however odious the traditional notion of hell may be, it nevertheless "presupposes a fundamental conviction that requires careful nurture": human responsibility and accountability.

91. Lorenzen, "Justice Anchored in Truth," esp. 297–98.

92. Further thoughts along these lines appear in Neville, "Justice and Divine Judgement."

93. Riches, *Transformation of Judaism*, esp. chap. 7, on "Jesus' Theism."

ethic of Jesus either the starting point for New Testament ethics or the criterion for evaluating any particular part of the New Testament, which he regards as "normative for the church's ethical reflection."[94] Even if only in an excursus, however, Hays considers it necessary to reflect on the relation between the historical figure of Jesus and New Testament ethics, and to give his own mini-reconstruction of Jesus's mission followed by "implications" of his reconstruction for Christian ethics.[95] While I recognize attendant difficulties, I nevertheless incline to the view that on certain points about which there is broad consensus, even among scholars who disagree about most other things, the (admittedly reconstructed) moral stance of Jesus as a historical figure should be juxtaposed alongside later developments, even within the New Testament, so as to allow for the possibility of critique. This should be done only with due care and caution, reflective of genuine humility in the face of texts that have nurtured the church for two millennia. If the voice of Jesus breaks through the strata of later interpretive traditions with sufficient clarity, however, it should be heeded. One such instance, I submit, is the moral stance of Jesus with respect to violence. Nonretaliation and love, even of perceived enemies, in imitation of the indiscriminate generosity of God—these are at the heart of Jesus's understanding of the appropriate human response to the reign of heaven. As a result, Matthew's depiction of Jesus's violent eschatology may be measured against Matthew's witness to Jesus's nonviolent mission and message.

Jesus undoubtedly expected eschatological judgment,[96] as did many of his Galilean and Judean contemporaries, and punishment may well have featured in his conception of judgment. Perhaps, like Matthew, he even anticipated "Gehenna."[97] Even so, the common story told by all four Gospel writers of how Jesus responded to violence and of what he taught his disciples with respect to violence is determinative. In other words, the story that Matthew tells contains within itself the wherewithal to deconstruct his own eschatological outlook. Thus part of the biblical interpreter's task is to desist from prejudging—and thereby preempting—the form that divine judgment might take. After all, when all has been said and done, *divine* judgment might turn out to display more of the Creator's inexhaustible creativity than anyone could have imagined.

94. Hays, *Moral Vision*, 160.

95. Ibid., chap. 7.

96. See Reiser, *Jesus and Judgment*, esp. 321–22, where Reiser, like Riches, states that Jesus's proclamation of judgment is distinctive by virtue of being unmotivated by any desire for revenge against perceived enemies.

97. See Allison, *Resurrecting Jesus*, 56–100.

2

Peaceful Power

Pleading Mark's Ethical Eschatology

It is widely acknowledged that the Gospel according to Mark reinterprets traditional conceptions of messiahship by presenting Jesus's suffering and service-oriented mission as God's way of reigning and of overcoming evil. This conception of divine reign is vividly expressed in Mark 8:22–10:52, within which Jesus's messianic mode serves as both pattern and norm for authentic discipleship. The same counterintuitive display of God at work in the world is also evident in Mark's account of Jesus's passion and death. It is also widely accepted that a significant part of Mark's purpose was to bolster hope by reassuring his audience that the crucified and risen One was soon to return as the Son of humanity to vanquish evil. If, however, the hope that Mark articulates is that when the Son of humanity comes, he will overpower evil forces in the same way—only definitively—as those forces had once overpowered him, this expectation militates against his express conviction that Jesus's nonviolent mission, voluntary suffering, and ignominious death disrupt evil. On this interpretation, Mark's peaceable Christology and other-oriented ethic are sabotaged by his eschatology.

Since Johannes Weiss rediscovered the significance of eschatology for comprehending the worldview of Jesus and early Christians,[1] New Testament

---

1. Weiss, *Jesus' Proclamation of the Kingdom*. Ever since Weiss first published this book in 1892, the relation between eschatology and ethics, both in historically descriptive and theologically constructive senses, has been a burning question in New Testament interpretation.

ethics has largely been conceived as conditioned by expectation of an imminent end-event. For Mark, the encroaching reign of God provides the rationale for Jesus's moral vision no less than for his call for change (1:14–15). But the general contour and specific content of Jesus's moral vision require that it be given critical status in relation to yet-to-be-realized aspects of the already-inaugurated reign of God. In Markan interpretation, in other words, ethics should impinge on eschatological expectation no less than eschatology impinges on ethics. Otherwise the reign of God is itself subject to Jesus's stricture in Mark 3:24–25 about any kingdom or house at odds with itself.

Vengeful eschatology seems to have been part of the convictional framework of some early Christians. In the New Testament, one thinks especially of the Gospel according to Matthew and the Revelation to John, about which John J. Collins asserts: "The expectation of vengeance is . . . pivotal in the book of Revelation."[2] But did all early Christians entertain a violently retributive eschatology? Though some consider that Mark's eschatology emulates and inculcates an ethic of empire,[3] my contention in this chapter is that Mark is an early Christian witness to an eschatological expectation more in keeping with the mission and message of his protagonist, whose instruction and conduct he held to be normative and exemplary.

Jesus, the crucified Nazarene (16:6), is presented by Mark in various ways: as herald-inaugurator of divine reign; as authoritative teacher whose words effect liberation, healing, discernment, and judgment; and as one who claims for himself the image of "one like a person" (see Dan. 7:13–14) as the most apposite—or perhaps least misleading—public designation of his identity.[4] These depictions coalesce to form a portrait of one who elicits faith, instills hope, and unveils the moral vision for a life of discipleship empowered by God's encroaching reign, even though Mark's narrative moves inexorably toward its denouement in the ignominious execution of Jesus on a Roman cross—and virtually ends there.[5] For Mark, crucifixion signifies not only Roman hegemony but also divine judgment and abandonment (15:34; cf. Gal. 3:13), yet he also interprets the humiliating death of Jesus as integral to divine action in, and on behalf of, the world. Paradoxically, God is present in

2. J. Collins, *Does the Bible Justify Violence?* 24. I am not convinced that the Apocalypse of John envisages literal eschatological vengeance, even if John's use of violent imagery is largely responsible for interpreting it along such lines. See chap. 7 below.

3. See Mack, *Myth of Innocence*; Liew, *Politics of Parousia*.

4. In support of the view that Dan. 7 is the interpretive backdrop for Mark's usage of the linguistically awkward phrase, "the son of the person" (ὁ υἱὸς τοῦ ἀνθρώπου), see Marcus, *Mark 1–8*, 528–32; Gathercole, "Son of Man."

5. In literary terms, Mark 15:40–16:8 is but an appendix to the much more detailed Passion Narrative in 14:1–15:39. Yet this epilogue is important since here Mark presents the resurrection of Jesus as God's reclamation of creation and reaffirmation of responsibility for the future of the created order, as I argue in Neville, "Creation Reclaimed."

Jesus's sense of godforsakenness and potently active in and through Jesus's voluntary powerlessness.[6]

This brings us to Mark's moral vision, which is both tradition-dependent, in that it is inexplicable apart from Jewish Scripture, and revisionary, insofar as traditional moral norms are critically revisioned—not simply revised—in light of Jesus's mission. No doubt Mark's reconfigured moral vision was molded by his scripturally resourced interpretation of the crucifixion of Jesus. No less than for Paul, and conceivably influenced by Paul,[7] the fulcrum of Mark's theology and ethics is Jesus as crucified Messiah. What he records of Jesus's teaching on self-renunciation and social reversal in Mark 8:31–10:45 coheres with his interpretation of Jesus's suffering and death.[8] But can one say the same of his understanding of the eschatological role of that humanlike One alluded to in Mark's three future-oriented references to the Son of humanity (8:38; 13:26; 14:62)?[9] In other words, did Mark envisage the Son of humanity's future realization of the reign of God to conform to the moral vision displayed in that selfsame Son of humanity's service-oriented mission, teaching on self-renunciation, and voluntary relinquishment of power in his passion? Or did Mark imagine that once God had vindicated the Son of humanity in his role as "suffering servant,"[10] it was acceptable that he execute the same kind of vengeance that had destroyed him?

Mark's Moral Vision

By comparison with the Gospels of Matthew and Luke, Mark's Gospel contains relatively little material that is explicitly ethical. As recent treatments of Mark's ethics have shown, however, it is not simply the teaching of Jesus that has moral significance. Equally important, if not more so, is the story world into which Mark invites readers and hearers so as to shape or reshape, challenge or reinforce attitudes and priorities. Moreover, as Allen Verhey points out, Mark's focus on the theme of discipleship patterned on the mission

6. I explore this paradox in Neville, "God's Presence and Power."

7. See Marcus, "Mark—Interpreter of Paul," esp. with respect to Paul and Mark's theological interpretation of the cross (*theologia crucis*).

8. See Rhoads, *Reading Mark*, chap. 3, "Losing Life for Others . . . : Mark's Standards of Judgment."

9. Mark 8:38; 13:26; and 14:62 are the most obvious allusions within Mark's narrative to the image of the humanlike One in Dan. 7:13–14.

10. Mark 9:12 suggests familiarity with a scriptural tradition associating the Son of humanity with suffering and shame, language reminiscent of the Servant figure in Deutero-Isaiah. A coalescing of the Son of humanity and Servant figures would help to make sense of Son of humanity texts that feature suffering (Mark 8:31; 9:31; 10:33–34, 45). See the Parables of Enoch (*1 Enoch* 37–71) for a parallel, but not identical, coalescing of these two scriptural figures.

of Jesus "makes the whole narrative a form of moral exhortation."[11] As a result, Mark's narrative as a whole, no less than any particular part within it, bristles with the potential to alter perspective, transform understanding, provoke character evaluation, and reorient assumptions about the nature of reality and standard patterns of human relationships, all of which are either profoundly moral in and of themselves or have moral implications. In this respect, the programmatic summary in Mark 1:14–15 is instructive. Jesus's proclamation of the good news *concerning God*, rather than from or about Caesar,[12] centered on the fulfillment of time as a result of the pressing (and pressuring) encroachment of divine reign, calls for radical reorientation that leads to the possibility of a life of faith and a faithful life.

While the whole of Mark's Gospel is morally meaningful, certain sections more clearly display his moral vision. One such section is Mark 8:27–10:45, which is bracketed by two stories of Jesus's restoring sight to blind men (8:22–26; 10:46–52). This central section concerns Jesus's efforts to alter his disciples' perception of and perspective on discipleship. It is carefully structured by means of three, three-part sequences: (1) Jesus predicts the Son of humanity's inevitable demise, (2) the disciples or representative disciples act in ways that reveal misunderstanding of Jesus's identity and mission, and (3) Jesus provides corrective instruction that reinforces the attitudes and conduct constitutive of authentic discipleship in the reign of God.

Within this central section, Jesus instructs would-be disciples that they must "renounce self" (8:34) and exercise a form of "social reversal" (9:35; 10:43–44). The language of voluntary social reversal in Mark 9:35 and 10:43–44 means much the same as the self-renunciation called for in 8:34. In an honor-shame culture, self-renunciation signified the voluntary relinquishment of status or rank, not the erasure of one's identity. It concerned how one perceived oneself in relation to others and therefore how one interacted with others. Each time Jesus corrects his disciples' misunderstanding, therefore, he addresses the basic issue of how interpersonal power is exercised within a network of social relationships. With ever-increasing clarity, Mark shows that an integral dimension of discipleship in the reign of God is the renunciation of honor, status, and rank rather than the culturally conditioned impulse to acquire the highest possible level of honor, status, and rank. And on what grounds? "For even the Son of humanity came not to be served [as though entitled by honor and status] but to serve [status-renunciation and social reversal], and to give his life as a ransom for many" (Mark 10:45).

11. Verhey, *Great Reversal*, 78.

12. The anti- or counterimperial dimension of much of the New Testament is now a commonplace. The crucial point is not that a Gospel, or Revelation, or a Pauline letter is anti-imperial, since what is anti-imperial so easily becomes imperialistic if the tables are turned. Mark's Gospel is not only anti-imperial but also counterimperialistic because in Jesus's mission the reign of God is displayed as qualitatively different from usual patterns of ruling.

Jesus's teaching reconceives and reorganizes social interrelations within the reign of God.

In view of later developments, it is significant that Jesus's instruction on self-renunciation and social reversal was directed toward those intent on enhancing their honor and status, not those without prospects of gaining honor and status. In this connection, Gerd Theissen's remarks regarding renunciation of status within the early Christian movement(s) are noteworthy:

> Thus in the Synoptic tradition humility is clearly "renunciation of status," *and this renunciation of status is bound up with a critical impetus against those who have a lofty status.* In the framework of this tradition humility is not a virtue of the lowly who fit into their lowly status by subordinating themselves to rule. On the contrary, humility is an imitation of the ruler of the world who voluntarily renounces his status. Humility is the virtue of the powerful.[13]

So, although Markan language about self-denial and servanthood has been used subsequently to maintain—rather than unsettle—status distinctions, this was not Mark's intent.

Theissen identifies both love of neighbor and renunciation of status as "the two basic values of the primitive Christian ethic,"[14] but Richard Hays declares that love is neither a prominent theme in Mark's Gospel nor features as a "distinctive mark of discipleship."[15] It is true that the vocabulary of love does not feature in Jesus's instructions to his disciples in 8:27–10:45. But in view of Jesus's remark to the perceptive scribe in 12:34, "You are not far from the reign of God," it would not be far-fetched to interpret Jesus's teaching on self-renunciation and voluntary social reversal as manifestations of loving one's neighbor as oneself. The dialogue between the scribe and Jesus in 12:28–34 reveals, at a minimum, the following three points: first, love of the one God together with love of neighbor as oneself comprises the heart of the "word of God"; second, love of God and neighbor surpasses sacrifices ordained by God; and third, comprehending these interrelated insights puts one near the reign of God, which suggests that to progress beyond understanding to living in accordance with these indivisible commandments is to enter God's reign and to participate in its world-altering impact (see 10:15, 23–27).[16]

Thus Mark records Jesus as interpreting love of the one God with all one's being and love of neighbor as oneself as both the pinnacle of Torah and of greater value than the divinely instituted sacrificial system: this surely places love at the center of Mark's moral vision. If one were in a position to ask

13. Theissen, *Primitive Christian Religion*, 75–76, emphasis added. Self-renunciation (renunciation of status) was not intended to maintain hierarchical distinctions.

14. Ibid., 63–80.

15. Hays, *Moral Vision*, 84.

16. See Marcus, "Entering into the Kingly Power."

Mark whether *self*-renunciation and *voluntary* social reversal express or enact love of neighbor *as oneself*, it is difficult to imagine him responding in the negative. As Udo Schnelle remarks, "Mark sees the double commandment [of love] as realized above all in mutual service (9:33–37; 10:35–45)."[17] In any case, whether or not love is the motivational basis for self-renunciation, itself patterned on Jesus's self-giving, both love of neighbor and voluntary social reversal fit harmoniously within a coherent moral vision.

Since Mark's moral vision is characterized by status renunciation and the reconceptualization of service as a paradoxical form of greatness, which in turn may be regarded as expressions of love for neighbor, the indispensable moral corollary of wholehearted love for the one God—this is not far from an ethic of peace. The vocabulary of peace is no more prominent in Mark's Gospel than that of love, but 9:50 echoes the Pauline emphasis upon practicing peace. On three separate occasions, Paul exhorts believers in the Greco-Roman world to live peaceably with others (1 Thess. 5:13; 2 Cor. 13:11; Rom. 12:18). In the two earlier letters, he focuses upon maintaining peaceful relations within the community of faith, but his exhortation is universalized in Romans 12:18. The verb εἰρηνεύειν (*eirēneuein*), to practice peace or to live peaceably, appears in these three Pauline references, in Mark 9:50, and nowhere else in the New Testament.

If this were the extent of the peace theme in Paul's Letters, its "echo" in Mark 9:50 might be historically interesting but hardly significant. Peace is central to Paul's theology, however, as evidenced by his characterization of God as "the God of peace" (ὁ θεὸς τῆς εἰρήνης, *ho theos tēs eirēnēs*). Both Ulrich Mauser and Willard Swartley emphasize the significance of the distinctive phrase "God of peace," which appears five times in four of the undisputed letters of Paul (1 Thess. 5:23; Phil. 4:9; 2 Cor. 13:11; Rom. 15:33; 16:20).[18] This same phrase recurs in the benediction of Hebrews 13:20, and "Lord of peace," used christologically, occurs in the benediction of 2 Thessalonians 3:16. Moreover, in 1 Corinthians 14:33, the theological rationale undergirding Paul's appeal for orderly and disciplined prophesying during worship is that God is a "God of peace," not disorder. In naming God "the God of peace," Paul was borrowing from his Jewish heritage, in which the nature and action of God could be expressed by combining the name of God with a predicate noun (e.g., "God of truth" in Isa. 65:16 KJV), but also innovating by aligning God's character and action with the concept of peace. Outside of the Pauline corpus and Hebrews 13:20, "God of peace" occurs in Jewish literature prior to or contemporaneous with Paul only in the *Testament of Dan* 5:2. Since Paul never refers to "the God of righteousness," which is remarkable in view of the significance he attaches to the righteousness of God (δικαιοσύνη θεοῦ,

---

17. Schnelle, *Theology of the New Testament*, 424.
18. See Mauser, *Gospel of Peace*, 105–6; Swartley, *Covenant of Peace*, 208–11.

dikaiosynē theou), and only once speaks of either "the God of hope" (Rom. 15:13) or "God of love" (2 Cor. 13:11, "God of love *and peace*"), the relative frequency with which he invokes "the God of peace" is theologically significant. As Mauser muses,

> In Paul's thought . . . "peace" is a reality and a power that deserves to be associated with God so closely that it can describe a fundamental aspect of the act and being of God. Paul knows of a wrath of God, and of judgments of God. But he never spoke of a "God of wrath" or of a "God of judgment." Peace is more deeply associated with God, more comprehensively descriptive, and more ultimately revelatory of God, than other words of human language that can and must be used as opposites to peace. . . . Paul is the servant of a God who loves, accomplishes, and preserves peace.[19]

A basic datum of Paul's biography is that not only his life but also his theology and moral vision were reconfigured as a result of his unexpected encounter with the risen Jesus. There is reason to think that Paul's reconstructed perception of the God of Hebrew Scripture as "the God of peace" was grounded in the peaceable and peacemaking mission of Jesus. Although Paul does not make much use of the language of "reconciliation" to interpret Jesus's saving significance (Rom. 5:1–11; 11:15; 2 Cor. 5:14–21), his more prominent use of "rectification" language (δικαιοσύνη, δικαιοῦν; *dikaiosynē, dikaioun*), traditionally expressed as "justification, justify," means much the same thing. As revealed in Jesus Messiah, the intrinsically right(eous) God acts in accordance with God's own nature or character by setting right—rectifying—all that is not rightly related to Godself.[20] Swartley is therefore correct to conclude, "The favored status of 'God of peace' for Paul is a key to his larger theology, for his central doctrinal emphases are much associated with peacemaking."[21] Indeed, given the conceptual and linguistic means by which Paul interpreted "Christ crucified" (1 Cor. 1:18–2:5), especially with reference to the relational notions of reconciliation and rectification, one might even hazard the suggestion that Paul's interpretive wrestling with the scandal of Jesus's crucifixion (see Gal. 2:15–3:29) formed the basis of his theology of peace.

In short, the "echo" of Paul's peace theme in Mark 9:50 resonates with a profound theology of peace, whether or not Mark was indebted to Paul. Furthermore, although the immediate context of the puzzling combination of

---

19. Mauser, *Gospel of Peace*, 106. Seen from this perspective, Paul's customary letter greeting, "Grace to you and peace . . . ," takes on added significance. See Rom. 1:7; 1 Cor. 1:3; 2 Cor. 1:2; Gal. 1:3; Phil. 1:2; 1 Thess. 1:1; Philem. 3; also Eph. 1:2; Col. 1:2; 2 Thess. 1:2; and with noticeable variation, 1 Tim. 1:2; 2 Tim. 1:2; Titus 1:4. See also Crossan, *God and Empire*, 146–47, who notes that most of Paul's undisputed letters also close with a salutation of peace.

20. On this central Pauline theme, see Keck, *Paul and His Letters*, 111–16; and Richard K. Moore, *Rectification ("Justification") in Paul*.

21. Swartley, *Covenant of Peace*, 210.

sayings in 9:49–50 seems to indicate that Mark contextualized these sayings solely on the basis of a series of verbal associations (fire, salt), the broader context is more revealing. The exhortation "Have salt among yourselves and practice peace among yourselves" is antithetical to the disciples' dispute over who among them was greatest (9:33–34), which provokes this particular segment of Jesus's corrective instruction. In place of self-aggrandizement, Jesus exhorts being peaceable or practicing peace, which requires self-renunciation or voluntary status reversal.

Disconcertingly, however, this passage containing Mark's sole reference to practicing peace also contains Mark's only references to the threat of hellfire (9:43, 45, 47–48). Even if 9:44, 46 are textually dubious, nevertheless 9:48 recalls the odious conclusion to the book of Isaiah, which suggests that life in God's new creation is enhanced by voyeuristic delight in the fate of the damned.[22] Although these hyperbolic Gehenna-sayings probably presuppose postmortem punishment, they are directed toward insiders rather than outsiders, and their primary purpose is to warn against conduct perilous to entering life or the reign of God. They may not challenge the traditional notion of hell, but neither do they confirm it. Since it is generally agreed that the sayings in Mark 9:42–50 are grouped together on the basis of catchwords and therefore impossible to situate in any meaningful life-setting within the mission of Jesus or even in that of Mark's audience, it is precarious to explicate Mark's conception of eschatological judgment on the basis of this passage alone.

Whatever one makes of Jesus's Gehenna-sayings in Mark 9:42–50, the peaceable note on which this passage ends is what stands out as characteristic of Mark's moral vision. Generally speaking, Mark's Gospel displays a peace-prone moral vision. Is one able to say the same about his eschatology, however, or do his references to Gehenna provide a better index to his end-time expectations?

Mark's Enigmatic Eschatology

Discussions of Mark's eschatology often focus on three future-oriented Son-of-humanity sayings (8:38; 13:26; 14:62).[23] In addition to texts that characterize Jesus's mission in terms of eschatological fulfillment, however, Mark has other future-oriented eschatological texts, such as 9:42–49 (on entering "life" or the reign of God versus Gehenna); 10:30 ("and in the coming age eternal life"); 12:18–27 (on resurrection life); and 14:25 (on drinking wine in the

22. It is widely accepted that Mark 9:48 alludes to Isa. 66:24, whose LXX wording is close to Mark's. For a sagacious discussion of the threat of hellfire in the Gospels, see Allison, "Problem of Gehenna," in *Resurrecting Jesus*, 56–110.

23. I refer to "future-oriented" rather than "apocalyptic" Son-of-humanity sayings so as not to cloud their meaning by evoking prejudicial associations.

future reign of God). Nevertheless, the placement of Mark's future-oriented Son-of-humanity sayings in significant contexts indicates that such texts are especially important.

Despite Mark's nonuse of the term *parousia*, the most common interpretation of 8:38; 13:26; and 14:62 is that these texts refer to the parousia, return, or second coming of Jesus. According to John Carroll, for example:

> Three times in Mark, Jesus taps Daniel's vision of the Son of humanity (Dan 7:13–14) to portray his own future coming in glory (8:38), or with clouds and great power and glory (13:26; 14:62). As in Daniel 7, Mark assigns the parousia both negative and positive functions. Negatively, the majestic presentation of the Son of humanity renders judgment against evil; positively, it vindicates the Son of humanity (and with him, the chosen people), and it is the occasion for the gathering or constitution in power of the elect community of God's faithful.[24]

Since some early Christians believed the parousia of Jesus to be imminent, it is reasonable to hold that Mark shared this belief. All too often, however, Mark's future-oriented Son-of-humanity sayings are interpreted in light of what is more clearly expressed in other texts, without careful attention to what Mark himself wrote or, perhaps more important, *did not write*. Whether or not Mark expected an imminent parousia is not the most important point, however. Far more significant than whether or not Mark anticipated an imminent parousia is the "character" of the returning Son of humanity. For it is not simply that interpreters have generally understood 8:38; 13:26; and 14:62 as references to the parousia but also that so many have conceptualized that return in ways contrary to the moral vision articulated, enacted, and embodied by the selfsame suffering yet authoritative Son of humanity. Commenting on Mark 8:38, for example, Craig Evans writes:

> God's reign on earth will be brought to completion in the drama of the coming of the "son of man," that heavenly humanlike figure described in Dan 7:13–14, accompanied by "holy angels." . . . As the suffering "son of man," Jesus will be dragged before Caiaphas and the Jewish council, and then before Pilate and his brutal soldiers; later, as the returning heavenly "son of man," Jesus will enter Jerusalem as a conquering warrior.[25]

Although Evans's viewpoint is not unanimously affirmed, it is representative. Any such perspective that envisages the returning Son of humanity in vengeful terms, however, exposes a serious christological problem. For, on this interpretation, either the inauguration of the reign of God by the suffering Son of humanity was ineffectual, so that the returning Son of humanity must revert

24. Carroll, "Parousia in the Synoptic Gospels and Acts," 11.
25. C. A. Evans, *Mark 8:27–16:20*, 27.

to retribution, or Mark's Christology suffers from something analogous to dissociative identity disorder. Too much of what is commonly asserted about Mark's eschatology is incompatible with the relatively clear—if humanly counterintuitive—description of how divine reign is exercised in the mission of Jesus, who, although potent to effect transformation, was voluntarily vulnerable in the face of coercive violence.

For different reasons, some readers interpret Mark's future-oriented Son-of-humanity sayings without reference to the parousia. For some, these sayings find their fulfillment in Mark's Passion Narrative or at least by the end of the Gospel.[26] For others, they refer to Jesus's exaltation to God's right hand, a heavenly vindication confirmed by some historical occurrence.[27] Among the latter group, the historical event most commonly nominated as confirming Jesus's vindication via exaltation is the destruction of Jerusalem and the temple in 70 CE, although some also point to ecclesial expansion.

Those who contend that Mark's future-oriented Son-of-humanity sayings relate primarily to the destruction of Jerusalem preserve Jesus from the charge of false prophecy by identifying an event within a generation of Jesus's crucifixion as fulfilling his solemn utterance in Mark 13:30 that "all these things" will have occurred within a generation. Certainly the destruction of Jerusalem proved Jesus's prophecy of the temple's demise to be correct. On this view, however, one must accept that Mark envisages the violence visited upon Jerusalem to be the work of the same God who authorized Jesus's nonviolent mission; the way of the coming Son of humanity is no less at odds with that of the suffering Son of humanity than on the parousia interpretation. One way or another, one must accept that although God's way in the historic mission of Jesus was nonviolent, either the vindication or the ultimate realization of his mission was or will be by means of divinely authorized violence.

The imagery of cosmic collapse associated with the second of Mark's future-oriented Son-of-humanity sayings (13:24–27) is especially important for those who argue that these sayings find their resolution in the destruction of Jerusalem. For example, N. T. Wright and Thomas Hatina argue that the language of 13:24–27 was not intended to be understood literally but rather metaphorically, to signify the sociopolitical ramifications of Jerusalem's destruction.[28] This thesis has been scrutinized by Edward Adams in *The Stars Will Fall from Heaven: Cosmic Catastrophe in the New Testament and Its World.*[29]

26. See, e.g., Lightfoot, *Gospel Message*; Mann, *Mark*; Myers, *Binding the Strong Man*; Bolt, *Cross from a Distance*.
27. So, e.g., France, *Gospel of Mark*; Wright, *Jesus and the Victory*, 339–68, 510–19; Dyer, *Prophecy on the Mount*; Hatina, *In Search of a Context*, 325–73. France has advocated this view since his early book *Jesus and the Old Testament*. Both France and Dyer accept that Mark 13 refers to the parousia, or "transcendent eschatology," but not before 13:31 (Dyer) or 13:32 (France).
28. Wright, *Jesus and the Victory*, 339–68, 510–19; Hatina, *In Search of a Context*, 325–73.
29. Adams, *Stars Will Fall.*

Against Wright, Hatina, and others, Adams argues—on the basis of a thorough investigation of biblical, postbiblical, and Greco-Roman sources—that in context the language of 13:24–25 (and other similar imagery within the New Testament) refers to anticipated cosmic catastrophe. He also defends the view that the Son-of-humanity saying in 13:26 (and its contextual parallels) is a reference to the parousia.

What Adams demonstrates is that a good case can be made for interpreting the imagery of cosmic collapse in Mark 13:24–25 as anticipating the actual disruption or dissolution of the natural order, but what he does not demonstrate is that a biblical writer could not have used the language and imagery of cosmic collapse metaphorically. With respect to making sense of the New Testament writers, Adams rightly emphasizes the way in which the language and imagery of cosmic collapse was employed and understood late in the Second Temple period, not simply the contextual presence of such language and imagery in the biblical sources themselves. While this is methodologically sound, one must be cautious about presuming that a New Testament author's appropriation of such biblical language and imagery must necessarily correspond with that of writers more nearly contemporaneous with the author. Appropriation precludes neither innovative interpretation nor indeed radical reinterpretation, as the reuse of biblical traditions reveals.

Peter's citation of Joel 2:28–32 in Acts 2:17–21 illustrates the point. As Adams notes, the second half of Joel, beginning at 2:28 (3:1 in the Hebrew Bible), comprises a collection of oracles in which the imagery of natural calamity is associated with the eschatological "day of the Lord."[30] Of the Jewish apocalyptic writings and related texts that Adams discusses, only *Testament of Moses* 10 seems to echo this prophetic passage, where the image of the moon as turning to blood accompanies the final coming of God to deliver Israel and to inflict retribution on its enemies.[31] In Peter's Pentecost speech, almost the whole of Joel 2:28–32 (virtually all of Joel 3 in the Hebrew Bible) is explicitly cited with reference to the Spirit-facilitated events of Pentecost; as Peter points out, these events follow from Jesus's wonder-working mission, crucifixion, resurrection, and exaltation (see Acts 2:14–36). In context, all that Luke cites from Joel 2:28–32, including the language and imagery of cosmic collapse, relates to the recent past, not to some foreseen future event. Luke even accentuates the eschatological force of Joel's text by prefacing his biblical citation with the phrase "In the last days." He need not have incorporated the substance of Joel 2:30–31, but since he did, such language and imagery reinforces the eschatological character and significance of Pentecost rather than foresees future cosmic collapse. Adams does not discuss Acts 2:16–21

---

30. Ibid., 46–48.

31. Ibid., 71–74. Adams (52, 98) also suggests that Joel 2:30–31 is the probable source for the idea of celestial disturbances as eschatological preliminaries.

but opines in a footnote that the cosmic phenomena of Acts 2:19–20 equate to the heavenly signs of Luke 21:25.[32] This is not the most natural way to read the citation of Joel 2:28–32 within the context of Peter's Pentecost sermon, however,[33] and what is possible for Luke is possible for Mark, especially in view of the creativity with which he evokes biblical motifs.

Whether or not Adams adequately defends the traditional view that Mark's future-oriented Son-of-humanity sayings relate to the parousia is best determined by discussing the passages themselves within their respective literary contexts. To anticipate, however, Adams has led me to accept that the parousia is in view in at least one of Mark's future-oriented Son-of-humanity sayings but not necessarily in all of them.

Mark 8:38–9:1 in Context

Mark's first future-oriented Son-of-humanity saying is situated at a decisive narrative juncture. It occurs near the beginning of the central section of the Gospel (8:27–10:45) in the wake of the first of three passion/resurrection forecasts that punctuate this section (8:30–32a; 9:30–31; 10:32–34). The first of these passion/resurrection forecasts occurs immediately following Peter's confession of Jesus as Messiah and does so with reference to the Son of humanity. Jesus does not repudiate Peter's insight that he is the Messiah, but in the exchange between Jesus and Peter that follows, Jesus qualifies his identity as Messiah by his vocation as the suffering Son of humanity, who will be vindicated by resurrection. Structurally speaking, therefore, Mark 8:38 is situated at a major turning point. Although 8:27–9:1 is often subdivided into three passages (8:27–30; 8:31–33; 8:34–9:1), to do so atomizes a coherent text segment.

As explained earlier, each of the three passion/resurrection forecasts initiates a threefold sequence in which the forecast is misconstrued by one or more of the disciples, thereby occasioning instruction by Jesus on the nature or ramifications of discipleship (see 8:30–9:1; 9:30–50; 10:32–45). In the first of these sequences, Jesus's passion/resurrection forecast is the first instance where he says that the Son of humanity must suffer. Jesus's two earlier references to the Son of humanity emphasize his authority (2:10, 28). Now, however, within the first of Mark's three, threefold sequences in his central section, one learns not only that the Son of humanity must suffer but also that beyond suffering and death he will experience resurrection and a "coming" in divine glory (8:31, 38). In short, the first suffering Son-of-humanity saying and the first future-oriented Son-of-humanity saying occur within the same threefold narrative sequence that opens Mark's central section. The pairing is decisive

32. Ibid., 177n219.
33. See Hatina, *In Search of a Context*, 361–62, and my discussion of this passage in chap. 5 below.

because both resurrection and coming in glory vindicate and validate the Son of humanity's willingness to suffer and submit to death. This is disclosed in what immediately follows.

Mark 8:38 relates closely not only to what precedes it but also to what follows. Although Mark 9:1 might once have been an independent saying, in its present context it reconfigures the Son-of-humanity saying in 8:38. As Morna Hooker observes, "Whoever was responsible for joining the sayings together presumably regarded the coming of the Son of man in glory and the coming of the Kingdom of God in power as closely related, if not identical."[34] Whether or not Mark was responsible for juxtaposing these sayings, it is reasonable, within his narrative and theological framework, to see them as mutually illuminating. Whatever its origin, then, Mark 9:1 uses different terms to reiterate the substance of the future-oriented Son-of-humanity saying in 8:38,[35] alongside Jesus's solemn assurance that some within his audience would witness the coming of divine reign. And in the transfiguration episode that follows, some do—at least proleptically. There is considerable debate about whether or not Jesus's assurance in Mark 9:1 is fulfilled in 9:2–8. For the following reasons, I think it is fulfilled, if only in an anticipatory way.

First, nothing else either recounted or alluded to in Mark's narrative more obviously fulfills the solemn assurance in 9:1 than the transfiguration. The crucifixion of Jesus is accompanied by signs of divine power and so should not be ignored in this connection, but it more naturally fulfills Jesus's prophecy about the suffering and death of the Son of humanity, not his coming in glory. Mark's account of the crucifixion, however, clearly envisages the hidden potency of God as active alongside or even through Jesus's experience of godforsakenness and powerlessness. So perhaps Mark did envisage that Jesus's promise in 9:1 was also partially realized at his crucifixion, but that does not preclude the transfiguration from being a partial or proleptic fulfillment of the same saying.

Second, Mark could not have made more obvious his perception that the transfiguration realized the promise of Mark 9:1 than by recounting that glory-filled event immediately after that promise. Moreover, as Joel Marcus points out, the opening phrase of Mark 9:2, "After six days . . . ," is rare, unusually precise, and scripturally redolent, alluding as it does to Moses's ascent of Mount Sinai to receive divine instruction (Exod. 24:16).[36] Jesus himself is transfigured, his clothing shimmering white. He is joined on the mountain by luminaries of Israel's past, Elijah and Moses, who had spoken for God.

34. Hooker, *Commentary on Mark*, 211.

35. The parallel version of this saying in Matt. 16:28 refers to the Son of humanity's coming in his reign or with his reign, thereby directly reiterating the future-oriented Son-of-humanity saying in 16:27.

36. Marcus, *Mark 8–16*, 631. In my view, the unusually explicit temporal connection between Mark 9:2 and 9:1 suggests a thematic relation.

A cloud (of divine presence) envelops Jesus, Elijah, and Moses, and from the cloud issues the divine voice, claiming Jesus as Son and commanding that the disciples should *listen to him*. Perhaps such details do not strongly evoke the reign of God as coming with power, but if Mark 9:1 reiterates 8:38, the transfiguration of Jesus naturally construes as a foreshadowing or proleptic fulfillment of the Son of humanity's *coming in the glory of his Father with holy messengers.*

Third, several key motifs bind Mark 8:27–9:13 together: Elijah, the Son of humanity, suffering, and resurrection. One might also mention Peter's personal prominence in these scenes, a new development since his confession of Jesus as Messiah,[37] and Jesus's commands to secrecy at the beginning and end of this section (8:30; 9:9). The figure of Elijah—and with him, John the Immerser (8:28; 9:13)—haunts this section. In addition to the sole reference to the glorious Son of humanity within this section (8:38), the suffering and/or rising Son of humanity is referred to on three occasions (8:31; 9:9, 12). Beyond this, the theme of resurrection from among the dead appears in Mark 9:9–10, and the suffering of "Elijah" as John the Immerser is alluded to in 9:13. In short, it is difficult to avoid the conclusion that Mark intended this narrative block to be read and comprehended as such.[38] If this is granted, that strengthens the case for interpreting the transfiguration as an anticipatory fulfillment of Jesus's promise in Mark 9:1.

All things considered, I accept the transfiguration in Mark 9:2–8 as an anticipatory fulfillment of the mutually illuminating sayings in 8:38–9:1. In Mark's understanding, the glorious coming of the Son of humanity or the powerful coming of divine reign remains a matter of hope, but hope grounded in and shaped by the vision of Jesus's transfiguration. There is also reason to think that the transfiguration anticipates the resurrection of Jesus.[39] Within Mark's narrative, therefore, the transfiguration foreshadows both the resurrection of Jesus and the glorious coming of the Son of humanity, each of which Mark affirms but neither of which he narrates.

What follows from this? With respect to eschatological expectation, one may affirm that Mark expects an imminent glorious coming of the Son of humanity, prefigured by the transfiguration. With respect to moral vision, however, it seems reasonable to look to the transfiguration to assist in interpreting the glorious Son-of-humanity saying in Mark 8:38. One must certainly attend to the details of 8:38, but if the transfiguration prefigures both the resurrection of Jesus and the glorious arrival of the Son of humanity, this implies that one's

37. See ibid., 612. Before Mark 8:27–29, Simon Peter is but the first-named among peers (1:16, 29, 36; 3:16; 5:37); following 8:27–29, he acts and speaks as an individual.

38. Lee, in *Transfiguration*, 10, regards Mark's transfiguration account as one of "two central panels at the mid-point of the Gospel (8:27–9:13)."

39. This is not to say that, for Mark, the transfiguration is a transposed postresurrection appearance account.

expectation of that arrival should cohere with the transfiguration. That this is not forced interpretation is confirmed by the eschatological dimensions of Mark's transfiguration account. As most commentators accept, the presence of "Elijah with Moses" alongside Jesus—not, as one might expect, Moses and Elijah—reflects Mark's understanding that Elijah was to initiate the eschatological consummation. This is confirmed in the conversation immediately following the mountaintop experience (9:11–13). Although acceptance of Elijah's role as eschatological precursor of the Messiah was not necessarily widespread in Second Temple Judaism, it nevertheless had scriptural warrant (Mal. 4:5–6) and was clearly prevalent enough for Mark, if not Jesus, to interpret its fulfillment in the activity of John the Immerser.[40] No details of the conversation between Elijah, Moses, and Jesus are given; what counts is the association of Jesus with these luminaries from Israel's past, whom some expected to play an eschatological role.[41]

While the eschatological role of Elijah is affirmed, however, the conversation after the transfiguration experience reveals that neither the role foreseen for Elijah nor Elijah's actual role in what is here inferred from the mission of John the Immerser features retribution.[42] The first part of Mark 9:12 is difficult to exegete, with some accepting that Jesus affirms Elijah's prior coming, and others contending that the first half of 9:12 should be understood as a question no less than the second half; in the latter case Jesus can be understood to be casting doubt either on Elijah's eschatological priority or on the particular role attributed to him—that of "restoring everything."[43] Since Jesus affirms that Elijah has already come, what he seems to dispute is Elijah's apparently anticipated role of restoring everything (cf. Acts 1:6; 3:20–21). The decisive point, however, is that what one learns of the eschatological Elijah's role is that he participates in the scripturally ordained suffering and shame of the Son of humanity. The one who fulfilled Elijah's eschatological role, John the Immerser, had done to him what others wanted, as written about him, no less than what Jesus indicates has been written about the Son of humanity must happen to him—that he must experience suffering and shameful rejection. In other words, as with the Son of humanity, the eschatological Elijah's role is fulfilled not by inflicting violence but by suffering it.

The climax of Mark's christologically focused transfiguration story is not a demonstration of divine power, at least not one recognizable as such, but the content of the command that issues from the cloud of divine presence: "This is my Son, the beloved; hear him!" (9:7). These words echo those of the

---

40. This is clear enough from Mark 9:13, but Matt. 17:13 makes things explicit.

41. See A. Collins, *Mark*, 423–24.

42. Nor, importantly, does retribution feature in Mark's description of John the Immerser's role as forerunner (1:1–15), although that is not to say that the theme of judgment is absent.

43. See the conflicting interpretations of A. Collins, *Mark*, 430–32; and Marcus, *Mark 8–16*, 642–51.

divine voice spoken to Jesus at his baptism in the Jordan by John (1:9–11). Now, however, they are addressed to the disciples, culminating with the curt command, "Hear him!" Not enough attention is paid to the role of this divine command in Mark's narrative, even though many recognize that it occurs near the beginning of Mark's central section concerned with the Way, used both geographically and metaphorically with respect to divine triumph and discipleship.

It is now widely appreciated that the "Way" motif plays a significant structural and thematic role within Mark's narrative, especially within his central section (8:22–10:52), which features Jesus's teaching regarding his own redeeming role and its rugged ramifications for disciples. "Influencing the whole section," Marcus writes, "is the Deutero-Isaian conception of God's 'way,' his triumphal progress up to Jerusalem in a saving act of holy war that will liberate and enlighten his elect people and demonstrate his gracious sovereignty over the world."[44] To be true to Mark, however, Marcus immediately qualifies the nature of this Deutero-Isaian influence by showing, with reference to his earlier work *The Way of the Lord* and to Rikki Watts's *Isaiah's New Exodus in Mark*,[45] that Mark's use of the "way of the Lord" motif involves "inversion," "adaptation," and "redefinition" of the holy war tradition. In retrieving this motif, Mark also renovates. Nothing about divine triumph taught by Jesus within this central section intimates that violence or vengeance plays a role. When the voice from the cloud (of divine presence) commands the disciples to pay attention to Jesus, therefore, that constitutes a divine validation of Jesus's interpretation of the "way of the Lord," a way that even in the quest for the reign of God entails suffering violence rather than inflicting it. The moral imperative for disciples of Jesus is clear: their way is the "way of the Lord" as interpreted and, even more important, enacted by Jesus.

Beyond this, however, is there not also an eschatological implication? If Jesus's teaching on the meaning of discipleship derives its coherence and legitimacy from the mission of the Son of humanity, who accepts suffering and death as the "way of the Lord," is it not perverse to read the future-oriented Son-of-humanity saying in Mark 8:38, whose fulfillment is prefigured in the transfiguration, as a warning of vindictive retribution against those ashamed of Jesus and his teaching?

Having considered the broader context of Mark 8:38–9:1, it is time to hone in on the future-oriented Son-of-humanity saying itself, especially the tit-for-tat warning centered on shame. Mark 8:38 sits within a carefully structured concentric text-segment beginning at 8:34 and ending with 9:1. The two rhetorical questions in 8:36–37 compose the center of the segment, with 8:35 and 8:38

---

44. Marcus, *Mark 8–16*, 591. The Deutero-Isaian "way of the Lord" motif is found in such texts as Isa. 35:8–10; 40:3 (cited in Mark 1:3); 43:16–21; 51:9–10; 52:1–12; 62:10–12.

45. Marcus, *Way of the Lord*; Watts, *Isaiah's New Exodus*.

paralleling each other both formally and thematically. Mark 8:34 functions as the "thesis statement" of the segment, while 9:1 concludes it.[46]

As a result, Mark 8:38 cannot be understood in isolation from the "thesis statement" of 8:34, where two dominant strains of Mark's ethic of discipleship are sounded for the first time. In 8:34, Jesus instructs the (previously absent) crowd along with his disciples that whoever is of a mind to follow him must practice self-renunciation in place of self-preservation and self-aggrandizement. A follower of Jesus must be prepared to "bear a cross," to accept suffering, humiliation, and loss of life if these turn out to be the cost of following Jesus and enacting his teaching. When, in 8:38, Jesus warns, "For if anyone should happen to be ashamed of me and *of my words* . . . ," he is surely referring to his teaching on self-renunciation as integral to discipleship.

This ethic of discipleship is developed further in Mark 9:33–36 and 10:42–45, where self-renunciation is more clearly defined in terms of "servanthood." In Mark's account of Jesus's teaching, however, "servanthood" is not simply self-abnegation but also greatness redefined; indeed, 10:42–45 indicates that "servanthood" modeled on the mission of none other than *the Son of humanity* is an alternative mode of exercising authority. If this interrelated set of instructions (8:34–9:1; 9:33–37; 10:42–45) on the meaning of discipleship derives its cogency and coherence from the mission of the Son of humanity, it is difficult to read 8:38 as a warning of vindictive retribution against those who are presently ashamed of Jesus and his teaching.

It is often recognized that in addition to Mark's version of this Son-of-humanity saying (8:38 and its contextually parallel versions in Matt. 16:27 and Luke 9:26), there is another version in which the language of renunciation rather than shame is used (see Matt. 10:32–33 // Luke 12:8–9). The language of renunciation might well have suited Mark by echoing the language of self-renunciation in the "thesis statement" of 8:34, "If anyone wishes to follow after me, let that person renounce self and take up their cross and follow me." Mark 8:38 uses the language of shame, however, not renunciation. This too is apposite, given that in an honor-shame culture, self-renunciation entails voluntary relinquishment of status or rank, or the deliberate bypassing of opportunities to enhance one's own honor at another's expense. Self-renunciation entails diminishment of status or rank in the sight of others, here because of one's voluntary association with Jesus. Thus self-renunciation is similar to embracing shame: diminishment of status or rank in the sight of others. The opposite of embracing shame is to be ashamed of another by maintaining one's own honor, status, or rank as a consequence of dissociating from one perceived to be shameful. According to Bruce Malina and Richard Rohrbaugh, "To be ashamed of a person is to dissociate oneself from that person, to not recognize that person's claims to honor, to distance oneself from that person's

---

46. For this analysis, see Lambrecht, "Q-Influence on Mark 8,34–9,1," esp. 289–90.

honor rating."[47] Interpreted from the perspective of "challenge and riposte" within an honor-shame social context, Jesus's warning in Mark 8:38 is principally a statement of eschatological reversal. Those now ashamed of Jesus and his words will find that God's eschatological agent will be ashamed of them. Or put differently, one who now finds Jesus and his words to be a source of social shame will ultimately discover that the reverse is true. Perceived this way, Mark 8:38 is, like 8:35, a saying of reversal. Seen in Gospel perspective, trying to preserve one's life or honor by distancing oneself from Jesus ultimately results in its loss.

The image of the coming Son of humanity as being ashamed of those who have been ashamed of Jesus is generally associated with eschatological judgment. There is good reason for this. One is reminded of envisaged judgment scenes in 1 Enoch, as in chapter 97, where the face of sinners will be darkened with shame when their lawless actions are recounted before God.[48] In 1 Enoch the setting of such sayings is clearly one of eschatological judgment, whereas in Mark 8:38 Jesus says only that one's being ashamed will rebound upon oneself, so to speak. The ramifications of this are not articulated, so perhaps Adela Yarbro Collins goes too far in inferring, "In the second part of the saying, the Son of Man's being ashamed of such people suggests that he will refuse to associate with them. Such rejection means that they will not be included when the Son of Man sends his angels to gather the elect (13:27)."[49] Mark leaves things indeterminate. Unlike Matthew 16:27, he does not record Jesus as saying that the glorious coming of the Son of humanity entails divine recompense for deeds or, to recall Ernst Käsemann's memorable phrase, "the eschatological *jus talionis*."[50] Although we are taught to read Matthew as interpreting Mark, we all too often interpret Mark in light of Matthew. Here that might be injudicious.

In Edward Adams's defense of a parousia reading of Mark 13:26, considerable attention is given to 8:38.[51] For Adams, Mark 8:38 is decisive for establishing a parousia reference within Mark's narrative itself, and he considers that 13:26 should be read in light of 8:38. Adams accepts that Mark 8:38 draws upon the imagery of Daniel 7:13 and indeed its wider context (7:9–14), but he is more impressed by how the imagery of Mark 8:38 varies from that of Daniel's vision. In Mark 8:38, he contends, the Son of humanity's arrival is for the purpose of judgment, unlike in Daniel. This crucial inference is based on the preceding

47. Malina and Rohrbaugh, *Social-Science Commentary*, 182.

48. See Nickelsburg and VanderKam, *1 Enoch*, 147–48. I have substituted the phrase "darkened with shame" for Nickelsburg's textual emendation "put to shame," to convey the sense of what one finds in the later Parables of Enoch such as *1 Enoch* 46–48; 62–63; 69:26–29; esp. 63:11, in which it is said of the mighty: "And after that their faces will be filled with darkness and shame in the presence of that son of man."

49. A. Collins, *Mark*, 411.

50. Käsemann, "Sentences of Holy Law," 77.

51. Adams, *Stars Will Fall*, 148–50.

context of Mark 8:38 and on an alleged association between "being ashamed" and eschatological judgment, particularly in the Septuagint (LXX). I accept this association, present also in *1 Enoch*, so long as judgment is not automatically taken to imply violent retribution or vengeance. Crucially, in *1 Enoch*, those put to shame in the context of eschatological judgment are those with status, rank, and honor because of their wealth and power. Interpreting Mark 8:34–9:1 within an honor-shame context adds nuance to what "being ashamed" implies. It is worth recalling that in 8:38, Jesus states that before the Son of humanity can be ashamed of anyone, someone must first be ashamed of him and his words. To infer that the Son of humanity's "being ashamed" implies judgment in the guise of violent retribution is to read too much into Mark 8:38. If Matthew 16:27 is based on a saying similar to or identical with Mark 8:38, as commonly supposed, Matthew evidently did not consider the nuance of eschatological recompense to be articulated clearly enough in his source.

Adams also points out other ways in which Mark 8:38 differs from Daniel's vision, including the details that the Son of humanity is to come in the glory of his Father (unparalleled in Daniel) and is to be accompanied by holy angels, not come into the presence of angels, as in Daniel. "In 8:38, therefore, Mark is quite evidently *not* trying to reproduce the entire picture of Daniel 7:9–14. The only concrete connection with the passage in Daniel is the image of a coming Son of man."[52] Beyond considerations relating to Mark's creative appropriation of the imagery of Daniel 7, Adams's most significant exegetical observation is that Mark 8:38 alludes not only to Daniel 7:13 but also to the eschatological imagery of Zechariah 14:5, "Then the LORD my God will come, and all the holy ones with him." For Adams, this coalescence of images drawn from Daniel 7:9–14 and Zechariah 14:5 reinforces an interpretation of Mark 8:38 as an anticipated coming of the Son of humanity from heaven to earth for the purpose of eschatological judgment.[53]

In view of the significance of Zechariah 9–14 for Mark elsewhere, especially beginning with Jesus's entry into Jerusalem, Adams's argument for reading Mark 8:38 as referring to the parousia is persuasive. Unless one holds that the sayings of Mark 8:38–9:1 are fulfilled without remainder within the confines of Mark's narrative, the conflation of imagery derived from both Daniel 7:13 and Zechariah 14:5 seems to require that one envisage the Son of humanity as coming from, rather than toward, heaven. Adding to the cogency of Adams's argument is that Jesus's affirmation in Mark 9:1 about the powerful coming of divine reign is thematically close to Zechariah 14:9, "And the LORD will become king over all the earth; on that day the LORD will be one and his name one."

Even if Mark 8:38–9:1 envisages the eschatological arrival or parousia of the Son of humanity, however, one should nevertheless read Mark with care.

52. Ibid., 149, emphasis original.
53. Ibid., 149–50.

By alluding to Zechariah 14:5 (and perhaps also 14:9), Mark does not necessarily affirm everything associated with the scriptural "day of the LORD." In
fact, the coming of the Lord with holy ones in Zechariah 14:5 is more closely
associated with divine rescue and restoration following a time of terror and
turmoil than with retribution. So even if the theme of eschatological judgment
is present in Mark 8:38–9:1, that is not the dominant note, nor is judgment
necessarily construed as divine destruction.

Mark 13:26 in Context

Mark 13 as a whole presupposes a traditional Jewish apocalyptic end-time
scenario. Before God's decisive intervention to vanquish evil and to right
wrongs, evil itself will intensify, with the result that suffering will increase.
Such suffering may be associated with human aggression and/or natural
calamities, persecution for faith, and familial strife. During such suffering,
discernment is needed to avoid being deceived by those offering false hopes.
Perceptiveness is also needed to ascertain the meaning and ramifications of
ambiguous (and ambiguously described) events. In such circumstances, people
of faith must cling to the hope that such an intensification of evil and the
suffering that comes with it signal imminent intervention by God on behalf
of the faithful.

There can be little doubt that Mark envisaged some such eschatological
scenario, which he expected would play itself out in the aftermath of Jesus's
death and resurrection. Indeed, in view of parallels between Jesus's "prophecy
on the mount" in Mark 13 and his own passion and death as described in Mark
14–15,[54] it is probably fair to say that Mark viewed Jesus's own suffering and
death as precipitating the end-time countdown. Jesus's forecast of the temple's
destruction sets the stage for the remainder of his teaching in this section,
and the historical reality that the temple was destroyed within a generation
of Jesus's own death leads many to conclude that what Jesus forewarns in
Mark 13 relates to the Jewish Revolt that provoked the Roman destruction of
the temple. Jesus's solemn assurance in 13:30 that "this generation" will not
have passed until all these things have eventuated encourages interpreters all
the more to relate Mark 13 to the temple's destruction in 70 CE.

Another factor plays an important role in Mark 13, as in other apocalyptic eschatological scenarios: ambiguity. While the sense of escalating chaos
and disorder is clearly expressed and even periodized to some extent, the
discourse as a whole is shrouded in perplexing ambiguity.[55] For example,

54. I have borrowed the description of Mark 13 as Jesus's "prophecy on the mount" from
Dyer, *Prophecy on the Mount.*
55. This feature of apocalyptic literature generally inclines one to opine that apocalyptic
language is not revelatory if it does not also mystify.

the imprecise expressions ταῦτα (*tauta*, these things) and ταῦτα πάντα (*tauta panta*, all these things) recur at key points in Mark 13. In Mark 13:4, four of Jesus's disciples demand of him the following clarification: "When will *these things* occur, and what sign will signal when *all these things* are about to be brought to completion?" Some of "these things" comprise the labor pains that begin the end-time countdown (13:8); some other of "these things" are a sure sign that something or someone is pressing near, even at the door (13:29), but to what "these things" point is not clearly identified. Do "all things" about which the disciples have been forewarned in Mark 13:23 echo "all these things" in their original question? What, moreover, does "all these things" in Mark 13:30 encompass? Adding to the ambiguity, the purposed end or appointed time is referred to more than once (13:7, 13, 33), but it is not entirely clear what is to end. Is it *the* End, the termination of history, or merely the end of humanity's history of resistance to divine reign? Or is the end referred to merely the end of the period of suffering and strife that must precede evil's cessation?

Despite the ambiguity, there does seem to be something of a temporal progression within this forecast of woe. Mark 13:8 speaks of beginnings of labor pains, a traditional image of eschatological tribulation, and 13:19–20 envisages tribulation such has never been experienced since the beginning of creation. Then is not the time to expect the Messiah (13:21–23) because after that period of tribulation, heavenly turmoil will trigger the eschatological countdown (13:24–25). "And then," Mark writes, "they will see the Son of humanity coming on clouds with much power and glory, and then he will send the angels, and he will collect his chosen ones from the four winds, from the ends of earth and heaven." Even where there is a glimmer of temporal clarity, however, Mark muddies the waters. His phrase "and then" at Mark 13:21 seems to refer to those days of unprecedented tribulation abbreviated by the Lord because of his chosen ones, but precisely the same phrase in 13:26, 27 seems to signal temporal succession: first cosmic catastrophe, *and then* the coming Son of humanity, *and then* the collecting together of the chosen ones.

Since Mark's temporal indications suggest that the cosmic collapse of 13:24–25 marks the beginning of salvation, much as the earthly upheaval of 13:7–8 marks the beginning of tribulation, I now focus on Mark 13:24–30:

> In those days after that affliction, however, the sun will be darkened and the moon will not give its light, and the stars will be falling from heaven and the heavenly powers will be shaken. And then they will see the Son of humanity coming in clouds with much power and glory. And then he will send the angels, and he will collect his chosen ones from the four winds, from the ends of earth and heaven. But from the fig tree you [pl.] must learn the figure: when its tender shoots have already sprouted and it produces leaves, you know that hot weather is near. So also you, when you happen to see these things occurring, you know

that it is near—upon the gates. Truly I say to you that this generation will not pass until all these things have occurred.[56]

This passage raises numerous questions, only some of which are addressed here. First, how do the signs of cosmic collapse relate to the earlier part of Jesus's prophecy? Second, what is the meaning of this symbolic language? Third, by whom will the coming of the Son of humanity be seen? Related to this, in what direction does the Son of humanity come—to earth or to heaven? Fourth, what is the significance of the role of the angels? And finally, what does the fig-tree analogy reveal to be near?

To begin with the first of these questions, the Greek conjunction ἀλλά (alla), with which Mark 13:24 begins, generally functions within Mark's narrative to show contrast. Together with the phrase "after that affliction," this contrastive conjunction serves to separate what comes after from what comes before. One might even translate the opening words of this passage as follows: "By contrast, in those days after that affliction. . . ." The heavenly signs of Mark 13:24–25 signal a new act in the end-time drama: they mark the beginning of salvation from tribulation, rather than the last of the labor pains.

Second, when Mark recounts Jesus's prophecy that the light of both sun and moon will fail and stars will fall from heaven, does he understand this in a literal or metaphorical way? Many interpreters view Mark's language here as symbolic but nevertheless referring to anticipated cosmic collapse in a literal sense.[57] Others, as has already been noticed, consider that Mark's language of cosmic calamity has nothing to do with the actual dissolution of the natural order but refers metaphorically to sociopolitical change, interpreted as divine judgment. For such authors, Mark 13:24–25 refers not to destabilization in the heavens but to an epochal sociopolitical reality: the destruction of Jerusalem. Since Jewish Scriptures alluded to by Mark associate such heavenly portents with divine judgment of sociopolitical powers, as in Isaiah 13 (Babylon) and 34 (Edom), Mark can be understood to have borrowed such symbolism to depict Jerusalem's destruction. Thus Mark 13:24–25 means not the literal end of the natural world, but the end of the way in which the sociopolitical world is ordered. Heavenly symbolism serves as theological commentary on a mundane, if momentous, event. Jerusalem will not only be destroyed but its destruction also composes divine judgment. On this view, moreover, Jerusalem's destruction is the earthly manifestation of the Son of humanity's exaltation and vindication.

---

56. This passage may well extend beyond 13:30, perhaps even to the end of the discourse, but the crucial concerns of this study coalesce in this passage relating to the coming Son of humanity.

57. Present-day cosmology also entertains the possibility of literal cosmic collapse, even if not imminent, so the idea that the natural world as we now know it has an end date is not simply a relic of an outmoded worldview. What differentiates the worldview of biblical writers from our own is that at least some of them envisaged cosmic catastrophe as a pressing prospect. Some today fear that, too, but for different reasons.

A metaphorical interpretation of Mark 13:24–25 is enticing. Mark clearly borrows from Scripture, so it seems reasonable to suppose that in a discourse beginning with reference to the destruction of the temple, Mark should borrow scriptural language associated with prophetic oracles of judgment to refer to Jerusalem's destruction. What cannot be sustained, however, is a sharp distinction between literal and metaphorical interpretations of Mark 13:24–25. No less than Edward Adams, Dale Allison and Brant Pitre demonstrate with reference to contextual literary data that the language of cosmic collapse could be and indeed was understood in a literal way within Mark's sociocultural context.[58] Yet that does not necessarily imply that such imagery is nonmetaphorical. The imagery of Mark 13:24–25 might legitimately be understood to refer to literal cosmic collapse *while also* signifying a corresponding historical calamity.[59]

The plethora of literary data discussed by Adams demonstrates that the imagery of cosmic collapse was understood realistically within Mark's sociocultural context, but I am not persuaded that Mark could not have used such imagery metaphorically to signal something other than the dissolution of the natural order. Even Adams makes this concession: "From Mk 13.24–27 alone, it is not possible to determine whether the convulsions occasion cosmic dissolution."[60] However, I do not think that Mark's appropriation of the imagery of cosmic collapse symbolizes the destruction of Jerusalem; rather, I am inclined to view such imagery in Mark 13:24–25 as preparing for, rather than paralleling, the arrival of the Son of humanity.

In a detailed investigation of the imagery of cosmic collapse in Mark 13:24–25, Joseph Verheyden demonstrates that Mark's utilization of scriptural passages is that of creative conflation rather than wooden dependence.[61] Through painstaking analysis of points of contact between Mark and his scriptural resources, Verheyden argues that Mark's creative reworking of scriptural traditions reveals him to have merged "day of the LORD" and divine theophany traditions, with the result that the retribution commonly associated with the "day of the LORD" fades from view. As he writes in his concluding paragraph,

> The transfer of certain motifs from one tradition to another begins already in the Old Testament, and the texts that are behind Mk 13,24–25 are the very illustration of this. . . . The eclipse and the shaking of the heavens can be used in quite distinct contexts. What turns them into "metaphors of judgement" is the explicit mention of God's judgement (as in Isa 13,6.9–10; 34,4–5.8; Joel

58. See Allison, "Jesus and the Victory"; Pitre, *Jesus, the Tribulation*, 330–48.
59. See Pitre, *Jesus, the Tribulation*, 336–37.
60. Adams, *Stars Will Fall*, 160; yet for Adams, when Mark 13:24–25 is read alongside 13:31, it refers to actual cosmic collapse.
61. Verheyden, "Describing the Parousia."

2,10–11; 4 [3 Eng.],15–16). When these motifs are taken out of that context, as in Mk 13,24–27, the connotation is lost.[62]

The creative conflation of "day of the LORD" and biblical theophany traditions need not necessarily imply that the theme of divine judgment commonly associated with the "day of the LORD" is erased. But if one attends to Mark's own description, his emphasis is the salvation associated with the arrival of the Son of humanity rather than judgment. This is decisive, no matter what other features of this enigmatic passage mean. Whatever judgment might be associated with the arrival of the Son of humanity, it occurs within the context of revelation and reclamation.

A third perplexing pair of questions relates specifically to the future-oriented Son-of-humanity saying in Mark 13:26. Who, one wonders, will see the Son of humanity coming in clouds with much power and glory? And what is the destination of his coming? Or put differently, to whom or what does the Son of humanity come?

The Greek text of Mark 13:26 does not explicitly identify those who will see the Son of humanity coming in clouds with much power and glory. According to Marcus, "Most scholars . . . take *opsontai* as an impersonal plural, equivalent to 'people will see' or 'the Son of Man will be seen.'"[63] In keeping with this interpretation, Adams avers, "Although the referent of 'they will see' is not made explicit, it does suggest an earthly vantage-point, and thus a descent to earth, not an ascent to heaven."[64] In context, however, the most obvious referent of "they will see" is the constellation of heavenly powers (Mark 13:25), whose shaking coincides with cosmic collapse. The only reason for not accepting these heavenly powers as those who will see the Son of humanity's coming in clouds is ideological, not grammatical. Most people today do not think of there being animate entities in the heavens or, if we do, we hardly imagine them to possess powers of perception. But Mark inhabited a different world with a different cosmology, and in his world the heavens were populated with animate powers.

In his exegetical notes, Marcus initially equivocates on who will see the coming Son of humanity in Mark 13:26. His first suggestion is that the false messiahs and prophets of 13:22 will see the Son of humanity. Later he accepts that the heavenly powers of 13:24–25 may be among those who see the coming Son of humanity, but the following observation makes his initial suggestion redundant:

This is the most grammatically natural way of taking the third person plural *opsontai* in 13:26, and in ancient contexts it is perfectly normal to think of

62. Ibid., 550.
63. Marcus, *Mark 8–16*, 904.
64. Adams, *Stars Will Fall*, 150.

heavenly bodies as animate and therefore capable of perception, thought, and emotion. . . . The contrast between the two instances of *dynamis* ("power") in 13:25 and 13:26 is consonant with this interpretation: the inimical *powers* of heaven will be shaken when they know their doom is near, as will immediately be confirmed when they see the Son of Man coming with a *power* greater than their own.[65]

By the time Marcus comes to comment on Mark 13:26–27, the heavenly powers comprise the implied subject of "they will see," at least "in the first instance."[66] Since the most grammatically natural way of interpreting 13:26 is to take the heavenly powers as those who will see the Son of humanity coming in clouds, and since this is comprehensible within the context of ancient cosmology, this is how this Son-of-humanity saying should be understood. At his coming in clouds with much power and glory, the Son of humanity will be seen by quaking heavenly powers.

Mark 13:26 clearly alludes to Daniel 7:13–14, in which a humanlike One comes with clouds to the Ancient of Days and is granted dominion and glory. While accepting this textual allusion, most interpreters consider that Mark envisages the Son of humanity as coming earthward from above rather than to God, as in Daniel. The principal reason for this is that most scholars presuppose that Mark 13:26 refers to the parousia of the Messiah. If those who will see the Son of humanity coming in clouds are heavenly powers, however, this supports a reading that envisages a coming of the Son of humanity toward God, as in Daniel 7:13, not toward earth. However, the Son of humanity's arrival would be perceivable by heavenly powers whatever the direction of his coming. Taking the referent of "they will see" as the heavenly powers of Mark 13:26 may be suggestive of exaltation rather than return, but it is not decisive.

Those who interpret Mark 13:26 as a reference to the Son of humanity's exaltation are rarely content to leave things at that. Exaltation to God is generally thought to correspond to some identifiable event, meaning some *perceptible* historical event. Most often, that event is the destruction of Jerusalem, as if the vindication-by-exaltation of the suffering Son of humanity must imply retribution on a grand and indiscriminate scale. But if the Son of humanity's coming to God is to be perceived by powers in the heavens, why must there be some corresponding historical event? If the reality of Jesus's resurrection can be affirmed without describing a postresurrection appearance, why is it not possible for Mark to affirm the reality of the Son of humanity's vindication-by-exaltation without describing a historical event that corresponds to it and thereby confirms it? And even if some perceptible event is deemed necessary, why should it not be the gathering of the elect rather than the destruction of Jerusalem, which is more likely associated with the intensification of affliction

---

65. Marcus, *Mark 8–16*, 903–4.
66. Ibid., 908.

(Mark 13:14–22)? If one allows that cosmic collapse prepares for, rather than parallels, the Son of humanity's arrival, it is difficult to associate his coming with the destruction of Jerusalem.[67]

Even if one remains convinced that the Son of humanity's arrival is to be seen in parallel with cosmic collapse, the description of which draws on biblical and postbiblical imagery generally associated with divine judgment, Mark associates such imagery with salvation rather than with tribulation. Within biblical tradition, salvation and judgment are not antithetical, so one should not suppose that judgment cannot belong to the posttribulation period. What can be said, however, is that in Mark's depiction of the period of salvation that begins with cosmic collapse, retributive judgment is muted, if not absent. This point is underappreciated, even though recognized by some. For example, according to George Beasley-Murray,

> It may fairly be said that so far as the interest of the eschatological discourse is concerned, the prime purpose of the theophanic parousia is for the deliverance of the people of God, but that cannot be imagined without the exercise of judgment. By accident or design, however, the discourse is silent on the latter aspect.[68]

And as Marcus observes,

> The Markan Jesus . . . seems to be drawing on well-known apocalyptic traditions about cosmic collapse but reconfiguring them in an original manner. The "punishment of the nations" theme, for example, is absent from our passage, and indeed from the whole eschatological discourse; the only mention of the nations is in 13:10, where they are to be an object of mission rather than condemnation.[69]

However Mark 13:26 is understood, whether as exaltation or as parousia, the Son of humanity's arrival is decoupled from retribution and vengeance. Mark's relatively peaceful end-time scenario is again brought into relief by comparison with the parallel version of this saying in Matthew 24:30, "And then *the sign of the Son of humanity will appear in heaven*, and then *all the tribes of the earth will lament*, and they will see the Son of humanity coming upon the clouds of heaven with power and much glory."[70] For Matthew, unlike Mark, the coming of the Son of humanity is cause for distress. As Walter Wink

67. See Adams, *Stars Will Fall*, 152–53, where he cites Wright as acknowledging that "there is *nothing* in the historical Jewish sources remotely approaching a parallel to the alleged application of the motif of the coming of the Son of man to the temple's destruction" (emphasis original with Adams). Cf. Wright, *Jesus and the Victory*, 519.

68. Beasley-Murray, *Jesus and the Last Days*, 430; his view that Mark 13:24–27 is influenced by divine theophany traditions no less than "day of the Lord" traditions is supported by Verheyden, "Describing the Parousia."

69. Marcus, *Mark 8–16*, 907.

70. Words in italics are unique to Matthew.

observes, "Whereas Mark's 'coming' of the son of the man was an occasion for rejoicing at deliverance from tribulation, Matthew has added 'then all the tribes of the earth will mourn' (24:30), shifting the focus to an adverse judgment that will overtake the enemies of the son of the man."[71] Divine judgment may also be intimated in Mark's version of this saying, but it is neither explicit nor emphasized, and the mode and manner of judgment is left up to the Son of humanity, whose character and manner of dealing with opposition, betrayal, and injustice are on display within Mark's narrative.

In Mark 13:27, the Son of humanity, having arrived (whether to or from God), sends out the angels and gathers his chosen ones from wherever they might be, thus provoking the fourth question raised by the passage. At first glance, Mark's description suggests that the Son of humanity's collecting of his chosen ones is independent of his sending angels. In all likelihood, however, angels gather his chosen ones for him. The gathering together of his chosen ones provides the rationale for sending out angels. In the vision from Daniel 7 alluded to in Mark 13:26, the Ancient of Days is attended by innumerable hosts (Dan. 7:10). The saying in Mark 13:27 probably envisages the Son of humanity as sending out these hosts to bring in his chosen ones. Having been exalted to God,[72] the Son of humanity is served by the heavenly hosts that serve God. And the particular service required of them is to gather together, from wherever they may be, the Son of humanity's chosen ones.

By contrast with the Gospels of Matthew and Luke, heavenly angels are mentioned relatively infrequently by Mark. The Lord's messenger appears at the beginning of the Gospel, but he is not a heavenly figure. In Mark 1:12–13, however, Jesus is served by angels during his time of testing. This brief note could well have eschatological overtones. Indeed, one is tempted to suggest that this reference prefigures the service that Jesus will ultimately receive as the exalted Son of humanity following divine vindication of his own suffering service. The next time angels are mentioned, in Mark 8:38, it is in relation to the first future-oriented Son-of-humanity saying examined above. Mark 12:25 declares that those raised from the dead do not marry, but are like angels in heaven. And Mark's two final references to heavenly angels occur in Mark 13:27, 32, which reveal little more than that Mark accepts angels as belonging to the company of heaven. The reference to angels in Mark 8:38 poses interpretive challenges but is probably best understood in light of 13:27. Mark 1:12 and 13:27 are the only two references to heavenly angels that provide insight into Mark's conception of their role. And in each case, their task is to serve either the needs of the tested Jesus or the command of the exalted Jesus. In Mark 13:27, it is noteworthy that the work of the angels

71. Wink, *Human Being*, 170.
72. Those who understand Mark 13:26 as referring to the parousia nevertheless accept that the Son of humanity's exaltation precedes his return.

is solely that of gathering the chosen ones. They play an eschatological role, but in comparison with Matthew's conception of the eschatological task of angels, especially as depicted in Matthew 13:36–43, 47–50, Mark's vision of the eschatological work of angels is remarkably positive and peaceful. This is in harmony with Mark's image of a Son of humanity whose determination to endure suffering rather than to inflict it is vindicated by resurrection and exaltation to the right hand of God.

In relation to this passage, there is a fifth and final question to consider: what does the figurative fig tree reveal to be near? In Mark 13:28–29, Jesus instructs his disciples to learn the parabolic lesson offered by the fig tree, whose budding leaves signal that hot weather is near. It is probably too neat to suggest that the sprouting of tender shoots and the subsequent production of leaves corresponds to the two-stage tribulation prophesied in 13:6–22, followed by imminent salvation, yet the imminence of eschatological deliverance from turmoil and trouble seems to be the fig tree's lesson. Nearness is emphasized in both the natural illustration and its eschatological analogy. What is unclear, since again Mark fails to be explicit, is what or who is near according to the eschatological analogy.

Much depends on the meaning of "these things" in Mark 13:29. The coincidence of "these things" in 13:29 with "all these things" in 13:30 echoes the occurrence of "these things" and "all these things" in the double question of the disciples that provokes Jesus's lengthy prophecy (13:4). This suggests that "these things" relate to the period of tribulation, while "all these things" include eschatological salvation as well as the tribulation that precedes it. On the basis of a clear allusion to Daniel 12:6–7 in Mark 13:4, Adams persuasively argues that the disciples' second question intimates the eschaton, by which he means the parousia, but he is reluctant to accept that "all these things" in 13:30 includes eschatological salvation. Instead, "all these things" in 13:30 relates to "these things" in 13:29 and is equivalent to "all things" prophesied by Jesus in 13:23. This enables Adams to dissociate the arrival of the Son of humanity from events prophesied by Jesus to occur within a generation.[73] On this point, however, Hatina is closer to the mark:

> While ταῦτα [*tauta*, these things] in v. 29 probably refers to events prior to v. 24 (especially since it is qualified presumably by the Son of Man's nearness), it seems more natural to read (or to hear) ταῦτα πάντα [*tauta panta*, all these things] in v. 30 as a reference to the entire prophetic discourse, much like a summary statement of all that has been prophesied up to this point.[74]

It is even possible that the reference to "all these things" in 13:30, understood eschatologically, explains the continuation of this discourse in 13:31 by recalling

73. See Adams, *Stars Will Fall*, 140–41, 164–65.
74. Hatina, *In Search of a Context*, 351.

the imagery of cosmic collapse: "Heaven and earth will fade away, but certainly not my words." In any case, what is near once "these things" are seen to occur is eschatological salvation associated with the arrival of the Son of humanity.

Probing Mark 13:26 in context has not produced complete clarity on whether this saying envisages the Son of humanity's exaltation or parousia. If 13:26 is to be read in light of 8:38, probably the parousia is in view, but that is not a necessary inference if heavenly powers are thought to witness the Son of humanity's coming. Strikingly clear, however, is the relatively peaceable nature of Mark's vision of eschatological salvation. Mark 13:24 marks the beginning of salvation from tribulation, and Mark's imagery of celestial collapse signals imminent salvation rather than divine judgment, unless one interprets such imagery to signify divine judgment of heavenly powers antagonistic to divine reign. There is much to be said for the view that Mark innovates by using the imagery of cosmic catastrophe in association with divine disclosure (theophany) rather than with divine destruction,[75] as argued by Beasley-Murray and Verheyden. Although the coming of the Son of humanity might well intimate judgment, the motif of retribution is absent. What receives emphasis is not retributive judgment but eschatological salvation in the form of collecting the elect.

Mark 14:62 in Context

The broader narrative context of Mark 14:62 is worth recalling before focusing on this saying itself. Since the prophecy on the Mount of Olives in Mark 13, Jesus has been anointed by an unnamed woman in preparation for his burial but also betrayed by Judas. Jesus has organized and shared a Passover meal with the Twelve, during which he presages his betrayal by one of his own in a forceful Son-of-humanity saying (14:21), alludes to his impending death by means of broken bread and shared wine, and looks forward to drinking wine in the reign of God. He has spent further time on the Mount of Olives, predicting his disciples' abandonment and agonizing over his impending death.

Jesus is then arrested and brought before an assembly comprising the high priest, chief priests, elders, and scribes, at which point evidence is sought to condemn him to death. This proves fruitless, so the high priest confronts Jesus with the question, "Are you the Messiah, the Son of the Blessed?" Jesus's reply in Mark 14:62 is sufficient for the entire assembly to concur that he deserves the death penalty because his response is considered blasphemous.[76]

75. To be clear, divine disclosure implies judgment no less than divine destruction, albeit a qualitatively different mode of judgment.

76. Remarkably, Jesus's earliest Son-of-humanity saying within Mark's Gospel occurs in the context of the charge of blasphemy (2:1–12) no less than in this final Son-of-humanity utterance. See Malbon, *Mark's Jesus*, 203.

In this section, Jesus's prescience is confirmed. His intimations of impending death are matched by the plot to put him to death and by the verdict of death pronounced by the Sanhedrin. His predictions of abandonment by his disciples and of Peter's denial are also proved true. Mark 14 begins with the anointing of Jesus bracketed by the plot to kill him (14:1–11) and ends with his hearing before the Sanhedrin bracketed by Peter's denials (14:53–72). As is often observed, the challenge to prophesy while being smitten and spat upon in 14:65 is briny with irony. The Sanhedrin itself has confirmed Jesus's various prophecies about his impending death, and his disciples have also confirmed his prescience, whether individually (Judas and Peter) or en masse. In the Gethsemane scene some also find the (partial) fulfillment of Jesus's warnings in 13:33–37 about remaining watchful. One reason why the confirmation of Jesus's prescience is so important is that it lends assurance to Jesus's future-oriented Son-of-humanity saying in 14:62, as Robert Gundry points out.[77]

The Greek in which Jesus's response to the high priest's question is conveyed in Mark 14:62 easily translates into English: "I am, and you will see the Son of humanity sitting at the right hand of the Power and coming with the clouds of heaven." Opinion is split on whether his opening words were simply "I am" or something closer to Matthew's "You have said so," but this textual question is not crucial. Much more critical are the source(s) and significance of Mark's intertextual allusions in this saying, which in turn feed into the question of what Mark understood to be the meaning of this saying.

As is generally agreed, Mark 14:62 alludes to two scriptural texts, Psalm 110:1 (109:1 LXX) and the text that stands behind Mark's two earlier future-oriented Son-of-humanity sayings, Daniel 7:13. In Mark's narrative, Jesus has already cited Psalm 110:1 within the context of posing an awkward question about the Davidic descent of the Messiah (12:35–37). Here, in response to a query about whether he himself is the Messiah, the Son of the Blessed, Jesus distinctly alludes to Psalm 110:1 but conflates this allusion with an equally clear allusion to Daniel 7:13. Indeed, despite the conflated (or perhaps competing) allusion to Psalm 110:1, the Son-of-humanity saying in Mark 14:62 more closely parallels Daniel 7:13 than any other such saying in the Gospel, as Morna Hooker recognized in her classic study, *The Son of Man in Mark*.[78]

Despite general agreement on the scriptural sources of the principal allusions in Mark 14:62, scholarly opinion is divided on what they signify in context. Some insist that Jesus's reply concerns his end-time return or parousia, others that this saying relates to divine vindication by exaltation to or enthronement at the right hand of God, others still that it has both exaltation and return in view. Perhaps the majority accepts that Mark 14:62 envisages exaltation

77. Gundry, *Mark*, 886.
78. Hooker, *Son of Man*, 163.

followed by end-time return, provided the emphasis falls upon the parousia rather than exaltation.

In support of the view that Mark 14:62 refers to the parousia, one might appeal to the way in which the imagery of this saying was understood by Christian writers from the postapostolic period. In *Ecclesiastical History* (2.23), Eusebius of Caesarea (ca. 260–339 CE) cites an account of the death of James, brother of Jesus, by Hegesippus, a Jewish-Christian writer from the second half of the second century. At one Passover festival during the early 60s, according to Hegesippus, Jewish scribes and Pharisees compelled James to stand atop the temple in Jerusalem and to explain the meaning of the enigmatic phrase "the door (or gate) of Jesus." James had earlier explained that this phrase signified that Jesus was "the Savior," but he now replied by using language and imagery reminiscent of Matthew 26:64 and Mark 14:62, "Why do you question me about the Son of humanity, since he is sitting in heaven to the right of the great power and is about to come on the clouds of heaven?" Infuriated by the effect of this response on those who had gathered, the scribes and Pharisees pushed James from the top of the temple and then stoned him before he was finally killed by a blow to the head.[79]

If Hegesippus is accurately recorded by Eusebius, Jesus's eschatological imagery in Matthew 26:64 and Mark 14:62 still had currency in the second half of the second century. Furthermore, this testimony of James clearly refers to the imminent return of Jesus following a session in heaven seated to the right of God. In this account the return of Jesus is not explicitly linked with judgment and the exercise of destructive power. As in Matthew 26:64 and Mark 14:62, the "great power" is a circumlocution for God. Nevertheless, in light of Hegesippus's remark that those who asked James to explain the meaning of the phrase "the door (or gate) of Jesus" believed neither in resurrection nor in one coming to reward people according to their deeds, Hegesippus (and Eusebius after him) probably understood the return of Jesus to entail judgment.

Both the substance and wording of Jesus's response to the high priest in Matthew 26:64 and Mark 14:62 are close, so it is unclear which version of this saying Hegesippus thought James had alluded to. Indeed, if Hegesippus was familiar with both Gospels, it is doubtful whether such a concern would have been meaningful to him. Given the preference for Matthew's Gospel over Mark's Gospel in the early centuries of the church, however, and the agreement between James's utterance and Matthew 26:64 regarding Jesus's anticipated arrival *on* (rather than with) the clouds of heaven, it is likely that Hegesippus was (more) familiar with Matthew's Gospel. This may well explain the clear reference to the return of Jesus in James's affirmation. Explicit references to the parousia

---

79. Eusebius, *Hist. eccl.* 2.23, trans. Lake (LCL), 1:168–79. Eusebius begins his account of the death of James by contending that Jewish leaders turned against him after their plot against Paul had been frustrated by the decision of Festus to send Paul to Rome. On Hegesippus's account of the death of James, relied upon by Eusebius, see Painter, "Who Was James?" 50–53.

of Jesus in Matthew 24:3, 27, 37, 39 (cf. 24:30–31, 44) might well have encouraged a reading of 26:64 as referring to the return of Jesus (cf. 24:30 and 26:64).[80]

Writing in the mid-second century CE, Justin Martyr seems also to have understood Daniel 7:13 and New Testament echoes of this text such as Matthew 26:64 and Mark 14:62 as predictions of a glorious "second coming" of Jesus from heaven. In his argument from biblical prophecy, which comprises the central section of his *First Apology* (30–53), Justin appeals to Daniel 7:13 (though he actually cites Jeremiah!) in support of the view that Jesus will come again from heaven. He then writes:

> For the prophets foretold two comings of Christ—one, which has already happened, as that of a dishonored and passible man, and the second, when as has been foretold he will come from heaven in glory with his angelic host, when he will raise the bodies of all . . . who have ever lived, and will clothe the worthy with incorruption, but send those of the wicked, eternally conscious, into eternal fire with the evil demons.[81]

According to Rudolf Bultmann, Justin was the earliest Christian writer to differentiate between *first* and *second* comings of Christ (*Dial.* 14.8; 40.4) and to refer explicitly to a "coming again" (118.2).[82] Nevertheless, in this respect, Justin simply made explicit what is implicit in most New Testament references to the parousia of Jesus (see Matt. 24:3, 27, 37, 39; 1 Cor. 15:23 [cf. 1:7–8]; 1 Thess. 2:19; 3:13; 4:15; 5:23; 2 Thess. 2:1, 8 [cf. 1:6–10]; James 5:7–8; 2 Pet. 3:3–4 [cf. 3:10–12]; 1 John 2:28). Writing some eighty years earlier than Justin, however, Mark did not use the Greek term *parousia*; even if he had, he would not necessarily have used it in the sense of a *second* advent or return (cf. 2 Pet. 1:16). For, strictly speaking, *parousia* denotes "coming," "arrival," or even "presence" rather than "return." So, although we have evidence from two second-century Christian writers that New Testament texts echoing Daniel 7:13 were understood to refer to the return or second coming of Christ, such evidence does not necessarily imply that Mark 14:62 refers to the parousia. Such an expectation was more likely to have been fostered by New Testament texts other than Mark's Gospel.[83]

---

80. See Davies and Allison, *Commentary on Matthew*, 3:531. On whether the imagery of Matt. 26:64 envisions the Son of humanity going to God (enthronement) or coming from God (parousia), Davies and Allison conclude: "But the decisive point, at least at the level of Matthew's understanding, is that everywhere else in our Gospel the coming of the Son of man refers to the *parousia*." For France, however, Matt. 26:64 cannot refer to the parousia but is a transparent reference to heavenly enthronement alone. See his *Gospel of Matthew*, 1024–28. According to Hegesippus (via Eusebius, *Hist. eccl.* 2.23), this is not how James understood things.

81. Justin, *1 Apol.* 52, trans. Hardy, in *Early Christian Fathers*, LCC 1:275.

82. Bultmann, *Theology of the New Testament*, 1:29. Bultmann's citations are to Justin's *Dialogue with Trypho*.

83. According to Stanton, an early form of the "two advents" schema found in Justin and in later Christian apologists is discernible in Matthew's Gospel as a means of countering Jewish

Mark 14:62 envisages the Son of humanity *both* sitting and coming—sitting to the right of God in a position of authority and coming with the clouds of heaven. For those who interpret this saying as referring both to exaltation and to the parousia, it is natural to understand these two positions as sequential: first sitting at God's right hand and then coming with the clouds of heaven. This viewpoint is well illustrated by Raymond Brown:

> While there is a complementarity in the two positions [sitting, coming], Mark means us to think of a sequence from one action to the other, for obviously one cannot sit and come at the same time. In Dan 7:13, after the beasts who represent the passing kingdoms of this earth have had their dominion taken away, there is depicted "coming with the clouds of heaven one like a son of man"; and to him is given the dominion, the honor, the kingdom, and an everlasting power. In Dan[iel] the "coming" of the figure is *to* the Ancient of Days who gives him these gifts, but the sequence to "sitting" in Mark demands that the coming be *from* the right (hand) of the Power to earth and human beings.[84]

For many, the order in which reference is made to the Son of humanity's sitting and coming in Mark 14:62 is critical. Despite dealing with the language of vision and despite the admitted divergence in meaning from the source text (Dan. 7:13), interpreters all too often insist that the order in which the Son of humanity's sitting and coming is mentioned must correspond to the order in which his heavenly session and his coming with the clouds of heaven occur. First he must sit, and then he must come. Not everyone who considers Mark 14:62 to refer primarily to the parousia sees things this way, however. Craig Evans, whose exegesis of Mark 14:62 emphasizes the return of the Son of humanity in judgment, envisages that the Son of humanity can both sit and return simultaneously because he is seated at God's right hand in the divine chariot-throne. The throne of the Ancient of Days in Daniel 7:9 has wheels of burning fire, likely alluding to the vision of the divine chariot-throne in Ezekiel 1.[85] According to Evans, "It would seem that Jesus has claimed that he will return as the figure depicted in Daniel's vision, seated at the right hand of God in the divine chariot-throne, and that he will return in judgment on his enemies."[86]

---

criticisms that the life and mission of Jesus failed to fulfill scriptural prophecies concerning the coming Messiah. See his *Gospel for a New People*, 185–91; idem, "Two Parousias of Christ."

84. R. Brown, *Death of the Messiah*, 497. Brown's sense is clear even if his final sentence is awkwardly phrased.

85. The description of the divine throne in Dan. 7:9 is likely dependent on Ezek. 1, and evidence for a form of Jewish mysticism focused on the divine chariot-throne extends back to the Hellenistic period of the Second Temple era. For the potential significance of this mystical tradition for interpreting Mark 14:62, see Schaberg, "Mark 14.62." Her argument focuses on the pre-Markan stage of tradition, but her analysis is applicable to Mark's Gospel itself.

86. C. A. Evans, *Mark 8:27–16:20*, 452.

If the mystical image of the divine chariot-throne had any influence on Mark 14:62, however, that would support an interpretation of this saying as envisaging exaltation rather than return, not exaltation followed by return. The image of the divine chariot-throne relates most closely to ascents to heaven, especially in Jewish literature roughly contemporaneous with Mark's Gospel.[87]

Even if the mystical imagery of the divine chariot-throne is considered irrelevant, Mark 14:62 need not be interpreted woodenly. Understood in a strictly literalistic way, the imagery of Mark 14:62 may seem problematic for an exaltation interpretation of this saying, but understood as complementary metaphors of vindication via enthronement, the two metaphors simply re-inforce each other. As Marcus observes, "Although the phrase 'sitting at the right hand' in [Mark] 14:62 is most directly an allusion to Ps. 110:1, it is also consonant with the picture in Dan. 7:13–14 of the humanlike figure being presented to the Ancient of Days and made his co-regent."[88] Also relevant is that Mark's allusions to both Psalm 110:1 and Daniel 7:13 are, as Christopher Bryan points out, "indirect and imprecise," the result of conflating citations from memory rather than from direct comparison of the relevant source texts.[89]

The view that Mark 14:62 envisages exaltation to God's right hand and/or enthronement has respectable precedent. According to Vincent Taylor,

> Not to speak of the fact that Dan. vii. 13 does not describe a descent, but a coming to the Ancient of Days . . . , the conjunction of Psa. cx. 1 and Dan. vii. 13 shows that a spectacular descent is not contemplated. What Jesus claims is that the glorious destiny which belongs to the Messiah, described in different ways by the Psalmist and the prophet, will be seen to be His. The emphasis lies on enthronement, and on enthronement as the symbol of triumph.[90]

In *The Son of Man in Mark*, Hooker devotes much of her discussion of Mark 14:62 to demonstrating that the Son of humanity's sitting and coming are "parallel expressions" for vindication via exaltation to God's right hand, although she equivocates on whether this is precisely Mark's perspective.[91] Over the course of a generation, France has in the same vein argued consistently that the Son of humanity saying in Mark 14:62 refers solely to vindication and exaltation, not the parousia. For example, in *Jesus and the Old Testament*, he writes:

> Until recently it was almost universally assumed that this was a prediction of the Parousia, but this interpretation is now frequently questioned. It is suggested

87. See Schaberg, "Mark 14.62," 77–79.
88. Marcus, *Way of the Lord*, 165. For Marcus, however, Mark 14:62 refers primarily to eschatological judgment at the parousia.
89. Bryan, *Preface to Mark*, 146–47.
90. Taylor, *According to St. Mark*, 569.
91. Hooker, *Son of Man*, 163–73; cf. idem, *Commentary on Mark*, 361–62.

instead that in Mark 14:62 Jesus is taking Daniel 7:13 in just the sense in which it was originally intended, that is, as describing his imminent vindication and exaltation to supreme authority. . . . The sitting at God's right hand and the coming with clouds are not, then, two events separated by an indefinite period of time, but two figures for the single idea of the vindication and exaltation of the Son of man. His "coming" is not a coming to earth, but, as in Daniel 7:13, a coming to God to receive power and glory.[92]

For France, this interpretation of Mark 14:62 is confirmed by two considerations. First, he maintains that it is reasonable to assume that Jesus alluded to Daniel 7:13 in its original sense unless clear evidence militates against this assumption.[93] Whether Mark enables one to assume this about Jesus is debatable, but even assuming that a New Testament allusion to Jewish Scripture replicates the sense or meaning of the text alluded to probably assumes too much. Mark's penchant for creative reinterpretation of Jewish Scripture, especially by composing passages from disparate textual fragments, is reason enough to be cautious about assuming that Mark simply reaffirms the sense or meaning of texts he cites or echoes. As Keith Dyer demonstrates, "composite quotations" or conflated allusions in Mark's Gospel imply a process of "dialectical interpretation" involving *both* reaffirmation *and* repudiation.[94] In the case of Mark 14:62, Dyer argues that Mark borrows from both Psalm 110:1 and Daniel 7:13–14 so as to reaffirm the exaltation and vindication of the Son of humanity (or as Dyer prefers, "the Human One"), along with the gathering of peoples that such vindication implies, but also to repudiate the themes of ruling from Zion and the violent judgment of the nations found in Psalm 110:2–6.[95] It is noteworthy, then, that after scrutinizing Mark 14:62 alongside four other composite citations, Dyer supports France's view that this final Son-of-humanity saying in Mark's Gospel refers not to the parousia but to exaltation and vindication.

France's second point in support of his interpretation of Mark 14:62 is that the verb ὄψεσθε (*opsesthe*, you [pl.] will see) implies that Jesus's immediate audience, those gathered to condemn him, would witness the fulfillment of his prophetic utterance. For France, confirmation of this implication is to be found in the temporal phrases preceding Matthew and Luke's contextual parallels to this saying (Matt. 26:64; Luke 22:69).[96] Matthew's version of this saying begins with the words "From now on you will see . . . ," and Luke's rather different parallel reads "But from now the Son of humanity will be sitting at the right hand of the power of God." For France, who accepts Matthew and

---

92. France, *Jesus and the Old Testament*, 141.
93. Ibid.
94. Dyer, "Conflicting Contexts."
95. Ibid., 205–6.
96. France, *Jesus and the Old Testament*, 141.

Luke's dependence on Mark, these two latter evangelists understood Mark 14:62 to mean that those to whom Jesus directed this saying would witness its fulfillment. Although the primary point of the saying is the vindication and exaltation of Jesus as the Son of humanity, France takes *opsesthe* to imply that the vindication and exaltation of the Son of humanity will be manifested historically within a time frame brief enough for those currently sitting in judgment on Jesus to witness it.

One need not adopt an exaltation interpretation of Mark 14:62 to agree that *opsesthe* implies imminent fulfillment. It is not unusual for those who advocate a parousia interpretation of this saying to acknowledge that Mark understood it to imply imminent fulfillment, not only in Jesus's day but also, and even more pressingly, in Mark's own time. Understood as a parousia prophecy, however, Mark 14:62 remains unfulfilled, whereas interpreted as a prophecy of exaltation and vindication, this saying can be affirmed as having been fulfilled in various ways. Following G. B. Caird,[97] France identifies the destruction of Jerusalem, understood in terms of divine judgment, as the most probable historical manifestation of the heavenly vindication of the Son of humanity.[98] This view is further nuanced in his commentary on Mark's Gospel, wherein both "the powerful growth of the NT church" and "the demise of Jerusalem and its temple as the focus of God's rule on earth" are suggested as fulfilling, in a publicly visible way, Jesus's prophecy in Mark 14:62. "We need not be more specific, since Mark is not," France writes, "but within this complex of events it would certainly be possible for Jesus's judges within their lifetime to see that the 'Messiah' they thought they had destroyed had in fact been vindicated and exalted to the place of supreme authority."[99]

How those gathered to condemn Jesus will see the Son of humanity sitting at the right hand of God and coming with the clouds of heaven is perhaps the most pressing problem for an exaltation interpretation of this saying. Divine vindication via exaltation and enthronement is not open to empirical observation, so advocates of this interpretation invariably propose some visible historical counterpart to the Son of humanity's heavenly vindication as the likely object of perception. Most often that corresponding historical occurrence is adjudged to be the destruction of Jerusalem, interpreted as divine judgment. The logic of this interpretive maneuver, based on scriptural precedent, is that divine vindication entails indiscriminate retributive judgment, but whether

---

97. Caird, *Jesus and the Jewish Nation*, 20–22. Caird's influence can also be traced through the work of N. T. Wright to Richard Hays. See Hays, "Why Do You Stand Looking?" 121. Responding to Wright, Hays confesses that "with regard to Mark 14:62, Wright has converted me." Like France, Hays cites the synoptic parallels to Mark 14:62 as confirmation that this saying of Jesus envisages enthronement rather than a return to earth from heaven.

98. France, *Jesus and the Old Testament*, 142.

99. France, *Gospel of Mark*, 613.

such logic coheres with Mark's christologically informed (and conformed) moral vision is difficult to demonstrate.

Raymond Brown's discussion of this problem reinforces how perplexing it is. He interprets the allusion to Daniel 7:13 in Mark 14:62 as a reference to the parousia, but he recognizes that Jesus's assertion that the entire Sanhedrin *will see* the Son of humanity both sitting and coming complicates matters. If the problem for an exaltation exegesis of this saying is how heavenly exaltation is to be perceived, the problem for a parousia perspective is how to "rescue" Jesus from false prophecy (according to the criterion enunciated in Deut. 18:22 and Jer. 28:9) since, despite the evident note of imminence in Jesus's saying, the parousia has yet to occur. Accordingly, Brown begins by suggesting that while Jesus's words were addressed to the Sanhedrin, Mark intended the Jewish leaders to play a representative role: "Whatever is predicted concerning them would for Mark's readers have some relation to Jews of their own time who continue to disbelieve and to mock Christian claims."[100] He also suggests that "Mark may also (but not principally) include in the 'you' his Christian readers, for whom this sight is triumphal verification."[101] Whatever plausibility might be granted to these suggestions, Brown's qualification to his second suggestion, "but not principally," deserves to be emphasized. Moreover, neither of his suggestions makes Mark 14:62 comprehensible. As Brown himself acknowledges,

> Something has to happen to be seen, even if the seeing means the ability to appreciate the significance of what happens. Perhaps the Sanhedrists could be said to "see" the Son of Man sitting at the right of the Power if the public proclamation that Jesus has been raised and been seen in glory forced their attention, as Acts 5:27–34 reports that it did. It is much harder to understand how they could be said to see the parousia.[102]

Here Brown concedes that an exaltation interpretation of this saying, or at least the exaltation aspect of this saying, is more compatible with the saying's main verb. Notably, he does not suggest the destruction of Jerusalem as the catalyst for appreciating the significance of Jesus's resurrection and exaltation. Rather, he appeals to Luke's report that the Jewish leadership was forced to pay attention to the social effects of early Christian convictions regarding Jesus's resurrection and exaltation. While I am wary of appealing to Acts to explain the meaning of Mark 14:62, Brown's suggested explanation of what he takes to be the exaltation dimension of this saying is at least as compelling

100. R. Brown, *Death of the Messiah*, 498.

101. Ibid., 498–99.

102. Ibid., 499. Acts 7:55–56 recounts that Stephen, *a believer*, sees the Son of humanity *standing* at God's right hand, but whether this is relevant for interpreting Mark 14:62 is difficult to determine.

as finding this saying's fulfillment in the destruction of Jerusalem, a suggestion that likely also derives from beyond the contours of Mark's narrative itself.

Recognizing that his two face-saving suggestions leave the meaning of Mark 14:62 unclear, Brown proffers three further observations: first, that the earliest Christians, no less than later believers, experienced difficulty in making sense of Jesus's teaching on what the future holds in store; second, that Jesus's response to the high priest's question does not imply self-exaltation but rather trust in God's vindication; and third, that Mark 14:62 is partially fulfilled in Mark's Passion Narrative, especially at Jesus's crucifixion.[103]

Each of Brown's additional observations is valuable from an interpretive perspective, but especially the latter two. His second suggestion resonates with the interpretive insight that Jesus's reply to the high priest parallels Jewish martyrological traditions in which those experiencing oppression express the hope that their oppressors will one day *see* God's vindication of those whom they have oppressed. Building upon the work of Rudolf Pesch, Marcus emphasizes how closely Mark 14:62 parallels *1 Enoch* 62:1–8, a text in which the Lord of Spirits (God) enthrones the Chosen One, also identified as that Son of humanity.[104] The passage begins with the Lord's commanding the powerful of the earth, "*Open your eyes* and lift up your horns, if you are able *to recognize* the Chosen One" (62:1). Following the Chosen One's enthronement, the text continues:

> And there will stand up on that day all the kings and the mighty and the exalted and those who possess the earth. And they will *see and recognize* that he sits on the throne of his glory; and righteousness is judged in his presence, and no lying word is spoken in his presence. . . . And one group of them will look at the other; and they will be terrified and will cast down their faces, and pain will seize them when *they see* that son of man sitting on the throne of glory. And the kings and the mighty and all who possess the earth will bless and glorify and exalt him who rules over all, *who was hidden*. For from the beginning *the son of man was hidden*, and the Most High preserved him in the presence of his might, and he revealed him to the chosen.[105]

Whether or not the Parables of Enoch predate Mark's Gospel, this passage witnesses to an interpretive tradition in which the Son of humanity is both enthroned by God and perceived as such by those presently in power. Mark 14:62 is a parallel expression of the eschatological hope envisioned in *1 Enoch* 62 and also in Revelation 11:12, where the two witnesses, revivified after having been slain, are called up to heaven, and their enemies *see* them

---

103. Ibid., 499–500. Brown prefaces his three additional observations with these words: "Although Marcan thought about the when and the how of the 'you will see' is not clear, these three observations may help."

104. See Marcus, *Way of the Lord*, 166–67.

105. Nickelsburg and VanderKam, *1 Enoch*, 79–80, emphasis added.

entering heaven in a cloud. As Marcus observes in his commentary, "This prophecy [of Mark 14:62] reflects a standard martyrological motif: the witness to the divine truth throws in his enemies' face that, although they are now persecuting and presuming to judge him, the tables will soon be turned and they will see God vindicate him and send them off to eternal punishment."[106] Nothing in Mark 14:62 intimates "eternal punishment," but Marcus is misread if one fails to reflect upon this perspicacious observation in relation to the prophecy of Mark 14:62 in context: "Once again the Markan theology of the cross transforms but does not obliterate a standard eschatological scenario."[107] While Mark 14:62 draws upon biblical and postbiblical motifs of Israel's kingship theology and ultimate messianic triumph, Mark's narrative progresses by featuring the humiliation and physical aggression suffered by Jesus. Mark's description of this is reminiscent of mistreatment experienced by the servant of the Lord in Isaiah 50:6, which implies that, even as Jesus endures humiliation and physical abuse, his vindication, prefigured in the scriptural image of the Suffering Servant of the Lord, is already in process of fulfillment. Marcus puts it this way:

> In the mockers' eyes, Jesus' claim to be the eschatological redeemer and rebuilder of the Temple is vitiated by his present state of helplessness and subjection to their will. For the evangelist and biblically literate readers, however, the echoes of the Suffering Servant passages in Isaiah 50–53 (silence before judges, spitting, slapping) may suggest that this absorption of abuse is actually effecting the defeat of the rulers of this world. Jesus, then, is not being vanquished but triumphing in his very humiliation.[108]

Vindication via exaltation is confidently affirmed, in other words, and that affirmation is paradoxically in process of realization in the very mistreatment endured by Jesus, seen as occurring according to the Scriptures.

In keeping with such an interpretive line, Brown's third and final observation is critical because, although he takes Mark 14:62 as first and foremost a reference to the parousia, he is able to interpret Jesus's saying with reference to dimensions from within Mark's narrative that are unrelated to the parousia:

> Is not the acclamation of Jesus as the Son of God the sign that the Lord has enthroned him on high (granted that there is a Davidic royal element in "the Son of God")? Is not the tearing of the veil of the sanctuary the sign of judgment on the Sanhedrists, since their holy place is no longer holy? The fact that Mark reports this as part of the centurion's *seeing* how Jesus died suggests that it is not impossible to interpret these actions as being seen. Such a glorification and parousiac judgment would be in the immediate future (the same day as Jesus'

106. Marcus, *Mark 8–16*, 1016.
107. Ibid., 1017.
108. Ibid., 1018.

prediction), but of course it would not nullify or substitute for the exaltation involved in the resurrection or the judgment involved in the final parousia. It would be the realization of all that *here and now* for the Sanhedrists.[109]

There is wisdom here. Although some have argued that each of Mark's future-oriented Son-of-humanity sayings is fulfilled within Mark's narrative, such a view takes things too far. Mark's accent undoubtedly falls on what is already fulfilled in the mission of Jesus rather than on what will be fulfilled in the (near) future, but eschatological anticipation is not entirely resolved intratextually. Hope for imminent fulfillment is not satisfied by what Mark recounts, even if it is fed by his narration of Jesus's mission as the beginning of the end.[110] In this connection, Wolfgang Schrage is probably correct: "Mark was well aware . . . that neither a theology of the cross (*theologia crucis*) nor a Christian life following in the footsteps of the crucified Jesus can be maintained without hope for an ultimate consummation."[111]

Even if a parousia perspective on this saying is maintained, Mark 14:62, like 8:38–9:1 and 13:26, is relatively peaceful. While this final future-oriented Son-of-humanity saying may intimate eschatological judgment, judgment is neither its focus nor its emphasis. In Mark 14:62 Jesus affirms his imminent vindication, not his vindictiveness.[112]

Pleading Mark's Ethical Eschatology

In their respective narrative contexts, each of Mark's three future-oriented Son-of-humanity sayings resists straightforward exegesis. This makes it difficult to know whether they share the same basic meaning or vary in meaning, depending on context and precise formulation. While I consider these three sayings to shed light on one another by virtue of their common allusion to Daniel 7:13–14, in each case additional intertextual connections preclude confidence that all three share precisely the same meaning. That Mark 8:38 alludes not only to Daniel 7:13–14 but also to Zechariah 14:5 suggests that the parousia is in view. That Mark 14:62 alludes not only to Daniel 7:13–14 but also to Psalm 110:1 suggests that *exaltation to God's right hand* is the primary point. The meaning of Mark 13:26 depends on how it is seen to relate to its immediate context as well as to 8:38–9:1 and 14:62. If the imagery of celestial collapse in Mark 13:24–25 is understood as preliminary to the Son of humanity's arrival rather than integral to it, there is little difficulty understanding 13:26 as referring to exaltation rather than the parousia. But if Mark 13:26 is

109. Brown, *Death of the Messiah*, 500.
110. See Marcus, *Mark 1–8*, 72.
111. Schrage, *Ethics of the New Testament*, 139.
112. See A. Collins, *Mark*, 705.

seen to evoke 8:38, that echo supports a parousia reading, which nevertheless presumes prior exaltation to God's right hand.

Although the debate on whether Mark's future-oriented Son-of-humanity sayings refer to the parousia or to exaltation is exegetically engaging, that is not the most crucial interpretive issue. Since the parousia presumes divine exaltation of the suffering Son of humanity who was raised from among the dead (Mark 8:31; 9:9–10, 31; 10:34; 14:25, 28; 16:6–7), both exaltation and parousia comprise the necessary convictional nexus between the resurrection of Jesus from among the dead and the general resurrection of the dead. For Mark, the reality of the resurrection of Jesus requires both his exaltation to God's right hand and his imminent return, which coincides with the arrival of divine reign in its fullness. Resurrection, exaltation, and return remain, for Mark, aspects of the one reality of divine reign impinging on the present and soon to be both realized and universally recognized as such. Put differently, the resurrection of Jesus from among the dead foreshadows the imminent resurrection of the dead, which is perhaps the single most significant eschatological manifestation of divine reign coming with power (Mark 8:38–9:1; 13:26–27).

The transfiguration of Jesus, coming as it does immediately after the first future-oriented Son-of-humanity saying in Mark's narrative, prefigures various facets of the one reality of divine reign soon to be realized—resurrection, exaltation to God's right hand, and the parousia. God's vindication of Jesus by resurrection and exaltation may also be foreshadowed by the preternatural signs at the crucifixion of Jesus (Mark 15:33–39), thereby within the confines of Mark's narrative confirming the prophetic authority of the Son of humanity, who embraced suffering as the means to divine reign. Transfiguration precedes suffering and crucifixion to authorize ("Hear him!") the scriptural path of suffering and shame embraced by this Son of humanity (Mark 8:31; 9:12, 31; 10:33–34, 38, 45; 14:21).

Insofar as the transfiguration *not only* provides divine authorization for the scriptural path of suffering and shame chosen by the Son of humanity *but also* prefigures divine vindication of that same Son of humanity by means of resurrection, exaltation, and the parousia, the transfiguration bespeaks peaceful eschatological power on the part of the coming Son of humanity. This is not only a theological-moral inference but is also borne out in the respective future-oriented Son-of-humanity sayings themselves. All too often read as inherently violent apocalyptic sayings, the apocalypse they envisage is a glorious display of peaceful power on the part of the Son of humanity, whose vision of divine Power (Mark 14:62) empowered self-renunciation for others. In Mark's theology, Christology, moral vision, and eschatology cohere.

In his account of *Christian Origins*, Christopher Rowland writes, "The Gospel of Mark is not an easy document to interpret as far as its eschatology is concerned."[113] Quite so! Rowland is reserved about endorsing an imminent eschatological expectation on Mark's part, suggesting instead: "It is more likely that the Gospel challenges Christians to maintain a way of non-violence and opt for a 'third way' between violence and political conformity, that of 'counter-cultural' politics."[114] Although I consider Mark's eschatology to express an expectation of imminent fulfillment, heightened by partial or anticipatory fulfillments within Mark's narrative itself, I nevertheless concur with Rowland's assessment of the moral bearing of Markan eschatology, especially in view of its relatively peaceable expression. This is especially significant if, as many consider, Mark is responding to a situation of crisis and conflict such as the Jewish Revolt of 66–73 CE.

In an earlier study of Mark's moral vision and eschatology,[115] I made four points in conclusion that seem as defensible now as then. First, the Gospel according to Mark deserves to be read on its own terms. In particular, Mark's eschatology should not be interpreted as if it intimates Matthew's more retributive eschatological outlook. However one sees the relation between these two Gospels, Mark's eschatological outlook is undeniably more peaceful.

Second, in light of Mark's christologically focused moral vision, it is reasonable to appeal to his portrayal of Jesus's nonviolent mission and message as a criterion for evaluating his eschatology. At the interpretive level, this is to say no more than my critical engagement with Matthew's violent eschatology; yet in Mark's case I consider that even at the level of exegesis, his moral vision ought to serve as a check on what one asserts about his eschatology. Although it is conceivable that Mark held incongruent convictions, such a view should not be presumed. Only if what Mark discloses about his eschatological expectations is clearly incompatible with his narrative account of the mission of Jesus should one concede that his eschatology conflicts with his moral vision. What stands out from detailed investigation of the future-oriented Son-of-humanity sayings in Mark 8:38; 13:26; and 14:62 is the absence of violent retribution. This is not to deny that judgment is intimated in this series of sayings. In view of the paradoxical way in which God is shown to work through Jesus's mission and the counterintuitive nature of much of Jesus's moral teaching, however, we should be open to the possibility that Mark's conception of divine judgment envisaged something more creative and restorative than strictly retributive forms of judgment, with which he was undoubtedly familiar. Judgment at the discretion of the Son of humanity, who chose to accept suffering over inflicting it, might well be different from vengeance.

Third, and following on from the previous point, present-day squeamishness about violent retribution does not validate interpretive violence. In other

113. Rowland, *Christian Origins*, 290.
114. Ibid.
115. Neville, "Moral Vision and Eschatology." The early part of this chapter is also adapted from this study.

words, my concerns about eschatological vengeance do not legitimize the coercion of nonretributive meaning from texts that anticipate divinely authorized retributive violence. Relative to other early Christian texts such as the Gospel according to Matthew and the Revelation to John, however, Mark's eschatological outlook is remarkably benign. Moreover, more than perhaps any other early Christian text apart from the Sermon on the Mount, Mark's Gospel is responsible for inculcating suspicion about the moral value and validity of violence.

Finally, no less than the disciples of Jesus within Mark's narrative, we find it difficult to imagine that violence and coercive power can ultimately be vanquished by anything other than greater violence and coercive power. Yet that is precisely the logic turned topsy-turvy by the paradoxically transforming power revealed in and by Mark's story of the crucified One.

Part 2

THE LUKAN LITERATURE

3

The Evangelist of Peace

If any of the canonical Gospel writers deserves the epithet "evangelist of peace," Luke is the one.[1] The peace theme recurs frequently throughout his two-part narrative, though it is struck more insistently and more meaningfully in his Gospel than in Acts. Moreover, the theme of peace resonates strongly with other distinctive features of Luke–Acts, such as Luke's particular concern for justice, his persistent attention to those at the margins of society, and his nuanced sociopolitical stance. This perhaps explains the focus on Luke's Gospel in *Jesus and the Non-Violent Revolution*, by André Trocmé; *The Politics of Jesus*, by John Howard Yoder; *My Enemy Is My Guest*, by Josephine Massyngbaerde Ford; and *Peace on Earth*, by Joseph Grassi—to name but a few books that feature the peace theme. In my view, however, the case for designating Luke *the* evangelist of peace has been prosecuted most

1. It is mystifying that the peace theme is so understated in the survey of Lukan research by Bovon, *Luke the Theologian*. "Peace" does not appear in the "Index of Subjects," although it makes an appearance (albeit not as a theme in its own right) in the "Bibliographic and Thematic Index on Luke–Acts, 1980–2005." By contrast, Bovon's article "Child and the Beast: Fighting Violence" highlights Luke's theme of enemy love as the means toward overcoming retaliatory violence. A text on New Testament ethics that seriously underplays the peace theme in Luke–Acts is Burridge's *Imitating Jesus*, which briefly discusses violence as an ethical issue in Luke's Gospel (269–70); but without his passing reference to Willard Swartley, one would not learn that peace is central to Luke's theological and moral vision. Much the same can be said of Pregeant's *Knowing Truth, Doing Good*.

persuasively by Willard Swartley, especially in his *Covenant of Peace: The Missing Peace in New Testament Theology and Ethics*.[2]

Swartley points out that the Greek term for peace, εἰρήνη (*eirēnē*), occurs fourteen times in Luke's Gospel, but with only one parallel occurrence in Mark 5:34 and one parallel occurrence in Matthew 10:34. The texts are Luke 1:79; 2:14, 29; 7:50; 8:48 (cf. Mark 5:34); 10:5–6 (3x); 11:21; 12:51 (cf. Matt. 10:34); 14:32; 19:38, 42; and 24:36.[3] This vastly more frequent usage of peace terminology clearly signals the theological and ethical significance that Luke attached to this theme. But it is not simply frequency of occurrence that counts. Equally important is Swartley's observation that the preponderance of Luke's distinctive peace references occur at structurally strategic junctures in his narrative:

> Three uses occur in Luke's infancy narratives (1:79; 2:14, 29) and thus set the mood of peace expectancy: the announced coming one will bring *eirēnē* as a new and unprecedented historical reality. A second structurally strategic cluster comes close to the beginning and end of Luke's special section (10:5–6; 19:38, 42). Jesus' teachings on discipleship that leads to the kingdom of God are framed by peace emphases. And conversely, when *eirēnē* is refused, judgment follows (10:10–12; 19:43–46). Jesus' *eirēnē* thus brings crisis, a point clearly expressed in 12:51. The third structurally crucial occurrence is 24:36 where peace is the resurrected Lord's self-identifying greeting to his disciples.[4]

While it is relatively easy to overlook this pattern of occurrences, it is critical from an interpretive perspective. Both the greater number of peace references and their narrative plotting contribute to comprehending how central peace is to Luke's understanding of Jesus's identity and the significance of his mission. As Swartley declares, "These uses together make it clear that for Luke peace (*eirēnē*) expresses the very heart of the gospel."[5]

Beyond Luke's explicit references to peace and their function in plotting his Gospel narrative, Swartley identifies other Lukan features that corroborate his peace emphasis. First, although it is perhaps surprising that this evangelist of peace records no blessing on peacemakers (cf. Matt. 5:9), Swartley shows how the content and arrangement of Jesus's teaching in Luke 6:27–36, the central section of Luke's parallel to Matthew's Sermon on the Mount, accentuate (peacemaking and peace-promoting) love of enemies.[6] There can be no argument against seeing moral instruction on love of enemies as cohering with an emphasis on peace and positive peacemaking.

2. See Swartley, *Covenant of Peace*, 121–76, building on several of his earlier works: "Politics and Peace"; *Israel's Scripture Traditions*; "War and Peace."

3. Swartley, *Covenant of Peace*, 122. Of these, the references to peace in Luke 11:21 and 14:32 lack the theological depth of the others.

4. Ibid., 129–30.

5. Ibid., 130.

6. Ibid., 130–31.

Second, building on the work of Yoder and Richard Cassidy, Swartley documents that Luke's sociopolitical stance is both critically countercultural, at least with respect to deep-seated Roman values, and congruent with a peaceful moral vision. Prominent dimensions of this moral vision include the following: concern for those ordinarily disregarded by those with power, rank, and status, meaning care for the poor, the infirm, and the disreputable; a critique of wealth and the wealthy; condemnation of injustice and oppression matched by a call for social relations to be based on humble service; and repudiation of violence.[7]

Third, an especially noteworthy feature of Swartley's analysis of Luke's Gospel is his attention to the prominence of the terminology of δίκαιος, δικαιοσύνη, δικαιοῦν (*dikaios, dikaiosynē, dikaioun*), which he translates as "justice" in the first instance.[8] Luke's use of this particular word family is more variegated in meaning than Swartley signals, in my view, but there is little doubt that this Gospel discloses the narrator's concern for genuine justice, which decisively complements his prominent peace theme. In Luke's presentation, Jesus is one who both proclaims and embodies *peace with justice*, construed as either peace-as-the-fruit-of-justice or justice-as-the-mode-of-peace. Indeed, Swartley shows how Luke's christological portrayal of Jesus is molded by peace and justice emphases to the extent that Jesus can fairly be described as "messiah of peace."[9]

When Luke turned his mind to narrating his second book (cf. Acts 1:1), did the materials at his disposal, whether oral or documentary, permit him to maintain his peace-with-justice focus? Swartley thinks so. He rightly contends that "Luke's purpose [in Acts] is to portray an alternative community with its own kingdom-Gospel-*eirēnē* agenda that is inherently neither pro- nor anti-Roman."[10] But it seems to me that in turning from the story of Jesus to the story of the movement he initiated, Luke's peace beacon dimmed. This is not simply because the term *eirēnē* occurs only half as frequently in Acts as in Luke's Gospel; even when it does occur, it often lacks the full-orbed dimensions it so often conveys in the Gospel. Acts 10:36 is a significant exception, with a Petrine speech summing up the mission of Jesus in its entirety as God's peace announcement. Swartley contends that the significance of the key phrase "preaching peace by Jesus Christ—he is Lord of all" is threefold: first, it reiterates the announcement of Isaiah 52:7–10 that God's good news

7. Ibid., 133–34. On Luke's nuanced sociopolitical stance, see also Theissen, *Gospel Writing and Church Politics*, 95–105.

8. Swartley, *Covenant of Peace*, 140–44.

9. Ibid., 145–48. On the relation between peace and justice in Luke–Acts, see also Swartley, "Relation of Justice/Righteousness to *Shalom/Eirēnē*," esp. 35–41.

10. Swartley, *Covenant of Peace*, 154. See also Mauser, *Gospel of Peace*, 83–103, esp. 85: "The concept of peace in the book of Acts is engaged in silent dialogue with the ideal of the Roman Peace (Pax Romana)."

of peace will reach the ends of the earth; second, the peace that is the object
of the good-news proclamation is a social reality, breaking down boundaries
between people groups; and third, this peace announcement is the direct result
of the mission of Jesus, which thereby reveals his universal lordship.[11] In short,
there is no doubt that the peace referred to in Acts 10:36 is both theologically
and socially profound. Elsewhere, however, the peace theme is muted in Acts,
both in the frequency with which it is sounded and in its meaning when it is
sounded.[12] One could argue that Luke intended the prominent peace-with-
justice emphasis of his Gospel to flow over into Acts, but if that were so, one
would expect more supportive textual data. It is hardly accidental that in Acts
10:36 the term *eirēnē* is so theologically and socially loaded; after all, as its
defining content it has the whole (and whole-making) mission of Jesus. When
the peace theme occurs in relation to the mission of the church, however, its
connotations are more mundane. This is telling, especially given Luke's evident concern to parallel as much as possible the church's mission with that of
Jesus. The evidence of Luke–Acts suggests that while the early Jesus movement
carried out its mission(s) in Jesus's name, it soon lost sight of Jesus's radical
commitment to peace and peacemaking at the heart of the good news.

Luke's Peace-Framing Texts

The early references to peace in Luke's Gospel cluster around the births of John
and Jesus. The first such occurrence is especially significant. It appears at the
conclusion of Zechariah's Spirit-inspired prophecy (known as the Benedictus)
following the unimaginable birth of his son and occurs within a rich tapestry
of interwoven themes—divine visitation, salvation, mercy, divine faithfulness
and compassion, revelation, and peace (1:67–79). Some of these same themes,
notably peace and salvation, likewise cluster together in old Simeon's paean of
praise (2:29–32) upon finally seeing the "Messiah of the Lord" (2:26). Thus the
responses of two devout, Spirit-led men to the births of both John and Jesus
cannot but associate these extraordinary births with peace. But it is not only
on earth that the peace note is sounded. In Luke 2:14, in response to the birth
of Jesus, an angelic host erupts into an exclamation of praise in couplet form:

> Glory be to God in the highest heavens,
>   and on earth peace among people (divinely) favored.[13]

11. Swartley, *Covenant of Peace*, 161–62.
12. Mauser and Swartley do as well as could be hoped for to show that Luke maintains an
emphasis on peace in Acts. Acts 10:36 notwithstanding, my sense is that Luke retains the peace
theme in Acts yet without as much emphasis on it.
13. The beauty and balance of this couplet are enhanced by the way in which the closing
word, εὐδοκίας (*eudokias*), aurally echoes the opening word, δόξα (*doxa*).

Thus, according to Luke, peace is integral to the theological meaning and significance of the births of both John and Jesus. Lest one regard the peace witnessed to in Luke's account of the births of John and Jesus as little more than rhetorical flourishes without theological, political, and social substance, Gary Yamasaki has demonstrated that Luke's initial references to peace are inextricably bound to divine salvation that results in material, political, and spiritual well-being.[14] Salvation, a theme widely acknowledged as central to Luke's concerns, cannot, for Luke, be understood except in relation to peace.

Not only surprising births display peace as integral to the dawning of a new period in salvation-history, however. With sublime narrative skill, the two theologically freighted peace references in Luke's birth narratives are echoed later in the Gospel at precisely the point when Jesus approaches Jerusalem to set in motion the denouement to the Gospel drama (19:28–44). These compositional resonances are decisive from an interpretive perspective, as will become clear in due course.

If original, the risen Jesus's peace greeting in Luke 24:36 is profoundly significant, from both narrative and theological perspectives. On internal grounds, Swartley adjudges this greeting of peace as original.[15] In this respect, he has the support of the majority of the Editorial Committee of the United Bible Societies' Greek Testament.[16] If original, however, it is difficult to comprehend how this peace greeting could have been omitted from certain manuscripts, most notably the so-called Western text (D), especially in light of John 20:19–23. Although I side with Swartley on this text-critical point, it is only fair to acknowledge that this judgment is influenced by theological and ethical commitments no less than by criteria such as internal thematic coherence and other points of contact between Luke's Gospel and the Fourth Gospel in their respective passion and resurrection accounts.

From a narrative perspective, it is delightful that the risen One's first words to the gathered assembly of disciples should echo words of peace proclaimed both from the heavens and within the temple in response to his birth. The whole of Luke's narrative account of Jesus and his saving mission is thereby enclosed by references to peace, indeed, peace that is synonymous with God's saving initiative. From a theological perspective, it is dumbfounding that one who was betrayed, scorned, shamed, vilified, and tortured to death should then make his presence felt among his own without so much as a hint of recrimination or retribution on his lips but rather with a greeting of peace. As

14. Yamasaki, "Shalom for Shepherds." His audience-oriented narrative approach (allegedly) precludes attending to echoes of his chosen text later in Luke's narrative, but in an audience-oriented study of Jesus's approach to Jerusalem in Luke 19:28–44, it should not preclude noting the echo of Luke 2:14 in 19:38b. Yamasaki's method is premised on an audience hearing a narrative once only, but can this be assumed in relation to Luke's Gospel?

15. Swartley, *Covenant of Peace*, 127n9.

16. See Metzger, *Textual Commentary*, 160.

Swartley observes, "God's mission of peace, and not the people's rejection of it, triumphs. . . . In view of Luke's preceding peace emphasis, the phrase must be considered more than a customary greeting in this context. The words signal the triumph of the incarnation's purpose according to Luke."[17] If resurrection implies divine validation and vindication of Jesus's peace-oriented mission of salvation, as it surely does, the risen Jesus's greeting of peace signals that the way of peace remains God's way. Violence against the way of God in the world is met not by divine retaliation but by a divine reaffirmation of the un-conquerable way of peace. The violence of Jesus's unjust death is addressed and indeed overcome by God's life-restoring *shalom* and *shalom*-restoring life.

Luke 9:51 begins Luke's central section, in which Jesus journeys toward Jerusalem and on the way teaches disciples his way with regard to discipleship, prayer, money, and the like. During this journey Jesus articulates some of his most memorable and distinctive parables: the compassionate Samaritan (10:25–37), the wealthy landowner (12:13–21), the fruitless fig tree (13:6–9), pride of place (14:7–14), the profligate son (15:11–32), the dubiously shrewd manager (16:1–8), the rich man and Lazarus (16:19–31), the persistent widow and unjust judge (18:1–8), and the self-satisfied Pharisee and the humble toll-collector (18:9–14). It is also during this journey that Jesus sends out seventy-two (or perhaps seventy) precursors (10:1–20); accepts the hospitality of Martha and her sister, Mary (10:38–42); on a couple of Sabbaths straightens a bent-double woman and heals a man with dropsy (13:10–17; 14:1–6); heals ten lepers, one of whom is a grateful Samaritan (17:11–19); and invites himself to the home of Zacchaeus (19:1–10). This central Lukan section is, in short, both distinctive and critical to Luke's compositional purpose and theological vision.

In *Covenant of Peace*, Swartley's observations on the clustering of peace texts near the beginning and end of Luke's distinctive central section are im-portant and illuminating. They largely reiterate comments made in his earlier 1983 study of politics and peace in Luke's Gospel. But these observations take on added significance in light of his 1994 book, *Israel's Scripture Traditions and the Synoptic Gospels*, in which he interprets Luke's central section as a recasting of Israel's exodus and conquest traditions, with Deuteronomy serving as literary model.[18] With respect to Deuteronomy's influence on Luke's central section, Swartley is dependent to some extent on the work of predecessors, especially C. F. Evans,[19] but his broader thesis is innovative and perspicacious.

Broadly speaking, Swartley demonstrates how all three Synoptic Gos-pels are shaped to varying degrees by four scriptural traditions relating to divine activity for human redemption: (1) exodus, (2) conquest, (3) tem-ple, and (4) kingship. With respect to Luke's distinctive central section, he

17. Swartley, *Covenant of Peace*, 127–28. By referring to incarnation, Swartley incorporates a concept alien to Luke, but as I suggest below, Luke works with a variation on this theme.
18. See Swartley, *Israel's Scripture Traditions*, 126–45.
19. C. F. Evans, "Central Section of Luke's Gospel"; idem, *Saint Luke*, 34–37.

acknowledges the influence of the exodus tradition but maintains that this block of material is shaped largely by the second tradition, which he designates "way-conquest." Since this tradition of Israel's occupation of the land of promise is troubling, especially when viewed from a peace perspective, it is somewhat startling to find Swartley contending that Luke's central section, bracketed by clusters of peace references, echoes Israel's conquest traditions. But by following his discussion, one learns that Luke's central section is a creative adaptation rather than simple adoption of the earlier story, with radical dissimilarities alongside evident similarities. In particular, the conquest motif is mostly subverted by Luke's depiction of Jesus as one who brings peace and justice and as one who overcomes enmity rather than enemies. According to Swartley, however, the conquest motif is retained and reiterated in relation to divine judgment against those who rebuff the good news of peace. Taking his cue from the parable in Luke 19:11–27, especially its chilling conclusion, Swartley writes:

> Even though Luke shows unambiguously that his followers are called to befriend and love the enemy, thus destroying the enmity, the category of "enemy" is not altogether eliminated. While the ethics for humans eschews it, the divine judgment includes it. . . . In keeping with the older story [Israel's conquest traditions], judgment falls upon those who hate the God of peace and love.[20]

Here Swartley reiterates a point made in relation to the opening part of Luke's central section: "A peace response becomes the criterion by which the people receive the kingdom of God or condemnation."[21] In these two comments, divine judgment is cast as condemnation grounded in the retention of enmity. Since this conception of divine judgment potentially undermines the good news of peace—that is, good news characterized as peace—there is benefit in looking again at the peace references that open and close Luke's central section.

Introducing these enclosing peace references in his earlier book, Swartley writes: "If one regards [Luke] 9:51–62 as introductory, then the first (10:1ff.) and last (19:28ff.) narratives in the section are laced with Luke's peace accent. The word occurs three times in 10:5–6, including the phrase, 'child of peace,' and three [sic] other times in 19:28–42. Each occurrence is strategic in Luke's literary design and theological intention."[22]

Swartley notes how the apparently innocuous peace references in Luke 10:5–6 serve to show that the mission of the Seventy-Two extends Jesus's own

20. Swartley, *Israel's Scripture Traditions*, 143. Here "his followers" must mean Jesus's followers, but only if, on Swartley's reading, the nobleman-king of Luke's parable is equated with Jesus.

21. Ibid., 135; cf. idem, *Covenant of Peace*, 125.

22. Swartley, *Israel's Scripture Traditions*, 135; cf. idem, *Covenant of Peace*, 125, where Swartley corrects his earlier reference to three occurrences of the term "peace" in Luke 19:28–42 to twice.

mission.[23] In *Covenant of Peace*, he interprets these initial peace references within the context of the beginning of Luke's central section to signify four key points: first, that peace is intrinsic to the Gospel; second, that the purpose of Jesus's mission is to search out children of peace; third, that "the peace gospel is God's way in Jesus and his followers to subdue evil"; and fourth, that the worldwide mission (symbolized by the Seventy-Two) is concerned to spread the gospel precisely as a gospel *of peace*.[24] In this interpretive summary, the third point, cited verbatim above, is crucial, for here Swartley acknowledges that Jesus's peace proclamation, as Luke presents it, is not simply well intentioned but is also the precise means by which God addresses anti-God forces. This is reinforced by the opening passage in Luke's central section, which Swartley designates as "introductory" but might better be termed "anticipatory" because of ways in which it prepares for the sending of the Seventy-Two.[25]

The phrasing of Luke 10:1 closely echoes that of 9:52 (lit., "and he sent . . . ahead of his face"), and in each case those sent by Jesus, whether messengers or the Seventy-Two in pairs, are precursors in the sense of preparing for his coming. Moreover, the paired themes of rejection and response to rejection are prominent in each passage, perhaps even dominant, provided one accepts Luke 10:13–16 as part of the larger passage beginning at 10:1. Thus Luke 10:1–16, within which one encounters a cluster of three references to peace, may be read as anticipated by 9:51–56. At a most basic level, one may at least affirm that after the experience of rejection in a Samaritan village, when Jesus next sends out emissaries to prepare for his own coming, he does so with a message of peace on their lips. And in view of Jesus's rejection of violent retaliation in Luke 9:54–55, it is hardly an idle question whether Jesus's warning of judgment in 10:12–15 should not be read as prophetic hyperbole to underscore the seriousness of rejecting his prophetic message, which also constitutes a rejection of God (10:16).

Such a reading gains support from Dale Allison's study of Luke 9:52–56 as an instance of critical repudiation of prophetic violence.[26] Allison demonstrates that Jesus's rebuke of James and John's request for permission to call down fire from heaven upon inhospitable Samaritans both recalls *and critiques* the story from 2 Kings 1 in which Elijah twice calls down fire from heaven as punishment. Moreover, the bulk of Allison's study shows that Luke 9:51–56 is of a piece with a Jewish-Christian theological trajectory that holds vengeance,

---

23. Swartley, *Israel's Scripture Traditions*, 135. Swartley accepts the textual reading of *seventy* in Luke 10:1, whereas I consider *seventy-two* more likely original, largely because the alteration from seventy-two to seventy rather than the reverse is more comprehensible (to me).

24. Swartley, *Covenant of Peace*, 125–26.

25. Perhaps as a result of utilizing earlier materials, Swartley's *Covenant of Peace* offers somewhat different assessments of Luke 9:51–56; cf. 125, where the whole of Luke 9:51–62 is "introductory," and 144, where Luke 10:1–16 is recognized as "a narrative follow-up" to 9:51–56.

26. Allison, "Rejecting Violent Judgment."

despite its scriptural sanction, as incompatible with divine mercy. He also draws attention to the way in which this passage coheres with other Lukan emphases, especially Jesus's teaching in Luke 6:20–49. As Allison observes, "Luke's Gospel . . . correlates human mercy with divine mercy."[27] The interpolator of the textual variant in Luke 9:56, "For the Son of humanity came not to destroy but rather to save people's lives," was a faithful interpreter (cf. 19:10).

Even apart from Allison's study, it is not much of a stretch to perceive Luke's peace note sounded at the outset of his central section. Jesus rejects the suggestion of violent retaliation; *more specifically*, he repudiates the suggestion of *divine vengeance* for failure to welcome him. Seen in light of this anticipatory passage, the instructed peace greeting in Luke 10:5 as the *first* utterance to escape the lips of the Seventy-Two takes on added significance. As if to emphasize that peace is integral to the good news—despite prior rejection and in full cognizance of vulnerability (10:3)—Jesus has his emissaries speak peace and let peace do its work, whether by remaining or returning (10:6).

Swartley's observations on the peace references at the beginning and end of Luke's central section are complemented by Paul Borgman's literary analysis of Luke–Acts.[28] In Borgman's treatment of dominant literary features relating to the oral-narrative dynamics of Luke's "big picture," within which individual details find their meaning and significance, he attends to "hearing clues" within certain sections of Luke–Acts that foreground the theme of peace. "Our exploration," he avers, "will bring to light meaning that is embedded in the drama and easily glossed over or even misunderstood and misappropriated."[29] Like most careful readers of Luke's Gospel, Borgman regards the central section beginning at Luke 9:51 as an especially significant feature of Luke's story of Jesus. In his view, Luke makes of this section, in which Jesus journeys toward Jerusalem, a metaphor for what he elsewhere terms the "way of salvation" (Acts 16:17) or "way of peace" (Luke 1:79). Luke also draws into this section much of the teaching of Jesus that he considers illuminating with respect to the means and manner of this "way."[30]

Borgman considers that Luke's entire central section, 9:51–19:44, is arranged concentrically around Jesus's response to the question "Lord, is salvation coming only to a few?" (13:23–30).[31] Borgman's concentric "echoes"

27. Ibid., 476. Tucked away in a footnote on the following page, however, Allison wonders "whether Luke–Acts is not here in tension with itself, for God does appear to sponsor violence in Luke 19:27 (cf. also Acts 5:5, 10)."

28. Borgman, *The Way according to Luke*.

29. Ibid., 1.

30. In Acts 9:2; 19:9, 23; 22:4; 24:14, 22, "the Way" represents the early Jesus movement. Within the New Testament, this designation is uniquely Lukan. Its association with the "way of the Lord" or "way of God" (Acts 18:25–26) or even the "way of salvation" (16:17) has stood the test of time, but during the course of the church's history, its association with the "way *of peace*" has been lost.

31. Borgman, *The Way according to Luke*, 77–78.

are overdrawn, in my view, but his contention that this central Lukan section is framed by passages that foreground the theme of peace (9:51–10:24; 18:35–19:44) is incontrovertible. Given the prominence of the peace theme in Luke's Gospel, there is nothing accidental about this particular motif cropping up at the beginning and end of Luke's most distinctive section relative to the general synoptic pattern of Jesus's mission and message. As Borgman writes,

> With departure in view, Jesus is shown preparing his followers for their responsibility in bearing the good news of peace. Here is the Way, the kingdom of God "come near to you." "Peace to this house" we hear as the heart of the first stage of the journey, the first principle [regarding the Way]. At journey's end, this theme focus is repeated, though now Jesus weeps over that which causes a desolate house—the failure of Jerusalem to recognize and implement "the things that make for peace."[32]

Borgman's discussion of the opening sequence in Luke's central section illuminates a tension that one detects in Luke's narrative, a tension between peace and vengeance. He rightly observes that the instruction given to the Seventy-Two by Jesus, "Peace to this house," is the antithesis of what James and John thought appropriate for unwelcoming Samaritan villagers.[33] But when it comes to Jesus's oracle of judgment on towns that are inhospitable toward his emissaries (10:10–15), Borgman slides over the incongruity between Jesus's own oracle of judgment *on that day* (10:12) and his rebuke of James and John for hankering after judgment *now*. He asks:

> But what is the end for those who consistently refuse welcome, the message of peace? The buried question spirals forward to its answer in the next sequence: do not be judgmental, because God judges. Local towns with perfectly ordinary Israelites . . . will receive an inevitable return for their ungracious refusal of God's own reign of peace among men and women. Two aspects of judgment are clear from what Luke has been saying: it will be delayed until it can be delayed no longer, and God will be the determiner of both the delay and the meting out of consequence.[34]

In fairness, Jesus's oracle of judgment in Luke 10:10–15 is not as explicit about the form of divine judgment that will inevitably be meted out as the fire from heaven suggested by James and John, but the reference to Sodom in 10:12 is suggestive of *fiery* judgment. Furthermore, while Luke 10:15 could

---

32. Ibid., 78–79. Borgman nowhere cites Swartley's work, even though this observation about Luke's central section being framed by clusters of peace texts had been made by Swartley as early as his 1983 "Politics and Peace" study.

33. Borgman, *The Way according to Luke*, 83.

34. Ibid., 84.

be taken as an image of reversal,[35] the parable of the rich man and Lazarus in Luke 16:19–31 indicates that Hades was, in popular imagination, a place of torment. It is therefore reasonable to hold that, in Luke's view, what differentiates Jesus's oracle of judgment from James and John's suggestion of divine vengeance is solely the timing. There is a day set for judgment (10:12, 14), which makes judgment *now* premature, but it is not entirely clear that the peace associated with the reign of God informs Luke's conception of eschatological judgment, even though, to reiterate Swartley's dictum based on Luke 10:18, "The peace gospel is God's way in Jesus and his followers to subdue evil."[36] If this is actually true, why should it not be ever true, especially if the agent of judgment is none other than the agent of salvation? In any case, even if the moral tension is not resolved thereby, to read Luke 10:1–16 in light of 9:51–56 opens up the possibility of mitigating the note of vengeance sounded in the later passage.

At the culmination of Luke's central section, he shares with his synoptic counterparts the story of Jesus's approach to Jerusalem on a donkey. Among the distinctive features of Luke's account, however, is his double reiteration of the peace theme. First, the company of disciples (rather than crowds generally) praise God in these words:

> Blessed be the one coming,
> *the king*, in the Lord's name;
> *in heaven peace and glory*
> in the highest heavens. (19:38)[37]

Then follows a uniquely Lukan passage before Luke's comparatively understated account of the scripturally authorized temple expulsion in which Jesus first responds to the Pharisaic demand that he reprove his disciples for their song of praise and subsequently utters an oracle of doom against Jerusalem. Weeping over the city, Jesus exclaims: "If only you had realized this day those things that lead to peace, but now they are concealed from your eyes" (19:42). Thus in brief compass, Luke's peace theme is forcefully reiterated at the very end of his central section. As Swartley states, "The structural function of these two *eirēnē* texts, closing off Luke's special section, underscores the prominence that Luke assigns to *eirēnē*."[38]

For Borgman, the closing frame of Jesus's journey to Jerusalem in Luke 18:31–19:44 not only echoes its beginning but also recapitulates Jesus's teaching

---

35. See Green, *Theology of Luke*, 90: "In a variety of ways the overarching theme of salvation-as-reversal is narrated repeatedly in the Third Gospel." For a full-scale analysis of this theme in Luke's Gospel, see York, *The Last Shall Be First*.

36. Swartley, *Covenant of Peace*, 126.

37. Distinctively Lukan phrases are in italics.

38. Swartley, *Covenant of Peace*, 127.

on what makes for peace along the way: "The journey began with the sending out of followers with the message of peace. The journey itself has focused . . . on the teaching of Jesus concerning peace. Now, at journey's end, Jesus breaks into tears at the sight of Jerusalem, with words intended for no particular audience—a cry from the heart: 'If you, even you, had only recognized on this day the things that make for peace.'"[39] Within this section designated by Borgman as the final frame of Jesus's journey to Jerusalem, however, two passages give one pause: Jesus's parable of the nobleman who would be king (19:11–27) and his lament over Jerusalem upon sighting the city (19:41–44).

Borgman offers a traditional eschatological interpretation of the parable of the nobleman who would be king, seemingly on the basis that the absent nobleman parallels the notice in Luke 9:51 that Jesus's time for departure was near.[40] Yet various difficulties haunt this well-worn interpretation.[41] The first is that Luke 19:11 suggests a noneschatological conception of the parable, as Luke configures it; Jesus tells the parable precisely to disabuse his audience of its misconception that, since he was near Jerusalem, the reign of God was about to appear.[42] One could conceivably contend that the parable counters the expectation that the return of Jesus should occur shortly after his departure, but the parable itself does not emphasize the duration of the nobleman-king's absence. More likely is that the parable in its Lukan setting warns against eschatological expectations focused on kingly rule as conventionally understood—in other words, expectations equating the reign of God with conventional, imperial modes of ruling. The parable mirrors what is constitutive of conventional kingdoms, which could well be what Jesus's audience has in mind if proximity to Jerusalem provokes expectations of the immediate arrival of the reign of God.

There is also the character of the returning nobleman-king. Virtually everything about him and his actions contravene the moral instruction of Jesus elsewhere in Luke's Gospel. First, he is preoccupied with wealth; the first thing recorded of him upon his return is that he assembles those slaves to whom he had entrusted money to ascertain how much had been made by trade. Luke's central section is replete with instruction on the challenge that wealth poses to authentic faith. Second, he instills fear because of his reputation for unjust

39. Borgman, *The Way according to Luke*, 86.

40. Ibid., 91.

41. My reassessment of this parable was provoked by two Australian scholars: Peter (Llewellyn né) Mendham, "In the Green Wood"; and Kitchen, "Parable of the Pounds."

42. Here I contest the interpretations of Luke Johnson and N. T. Wright, each of whom, in different ways, argues that this parable in its Lukan form and setting stresses the imminent arrival of God's reign: for Johnson, when Jesus enters Jerusalem and is acclaimed as king; and for Wright, when Jerusalem is judged by being destroyed. See Johnson, "Lukan Kingship Parable"; idem, *Gospel of Luke*, 288–95; Wright, *Jesus and the Victory*, 631–39. In this respect, I concur with Snodgrass, *Stories with Intent*, 538–39: "The intent of [Luke] 19:11 is to *refute* ideas that the kingdom would appear when Jesus got to Jerusalem."

gain; he is known as one who takes out what he does not put in and reaps what he does not sow, and Luke ensures that this detail is first uttered by the fearful slave and subsequently reiterated by the nobleman-king without hint of contradiction. And third, the way in which the nobleman-king deals with his enemies, ordering their slaughter, completely contradicts Jesus's teaching about love for enemies (Luke 6:27–36).

Of course, Luke 19:12–27 is a parable whose details should not be understood either literally or allegorically but analogically.[43] Even so, it is difficult to imagine Luke as conceiving of Jesus, whom he depicts as both the proclaimer and embodiment of peace, returning in the manner of the returning nobleman-king and thereby undermining three crucial dimensions of Jesus's moral teaching: the danger of wealth, concern for the underprivileged (justice), and love for enemies. This calls into question the traditional interpretation aligning the returning nobleman-king with the returning Jesus.

The parable of the nobleman-king is enclosed by references to Jerusalem, first Jesus's proximity to the city and then his continuing toward it (Luke 19:11, 28). The succeeding passage recounts Jesus's approach to Jerusalem (19:28–44).[44] In Luke 19:38, the praise of the disciples echoes two earlier passages, 13:35b and 2:14. For Borgman, the echo of the praise of the heavenly host (2:14) proclaims peace as well as glory *in heaven* rather than on earth.[45] In other words, the reminder of the promised peace on earth associated with the birth of the Savior is simultaneously an indication that such peace is yet far off. For Swartley, however, the disciples' praise in Luke 19:38 is better read as "earth's antiphonal response to heaven's declaration in 2:14."[46] Lukan composition balances the disciples' praise as Jesus approaches Jerusalem with the angels' praise at his birth.

The compositional significance of the peace references in Luke 2:14 and 19:38 is emphasized by Ulrich Mauser,[47] who shows that in form and content these exclamations of praise mirror each other. Like Borgman, however, he considers that the peace praise of the disciples falls short of the praise of the angelic host in recognition that the peaceable mission of Jesus is not wholly accepted. In view of Luke 19:42, there can be little doubt that rejection of the peaceable and peacemaking mission of Jesus casts a shadow over this part of the narrative. While the disciples' praise in Luke 19:38b does not refer to peace *on* earth, however, the key point is that it issues *from* earth as an echo of angelic praise from heaven. The disciples recognize *in Jesus* their messianic king and, in acclaiming him as such, their praise matches that of the angelic

43. See Snodgrass, *Stories with Intent*, 1–31, 540.
44. Three times in this pericope, Jesus draws ever nearer to the city of Jerusalem (Luke 19:29, 37, 41), but his entry into the temple in Luke 19:45 marks his entry into the city.
45. Borgman, *The Way according to Luke*, 93.
46. Swartley, *Covenant of Peace*, 127, 150.
47. Mauser, *Gospel of Peace*, 46–50.

host. For Luke, one must remember, it is Jesus's mission in its totality that comprises the good news of peace (2:14; cf. Acts 10:36).

The tearful oracle of woe against Jerusalem begins with Jesus's lament over the city's blindness *this day* to those things that lead to peace. This note of timing suggests that in Luke's view, the things that lead to peace reside in the one who has arrived at the city *as king* in the name of the Lord (19:38a). Jesus's forecast of Jerusalem's siege and sacking, in language relatively close to what occurred in 70 CE, interprets Jerusalem's destruction as punishment for failing to recognize God's visitation in Jesus's arrival to the city (19:44b). So although Swartley and Borgman draw attention to the way in which Luke's central section is framed by peace texts, these framing texts contain discordant notes suggestive of incongruence between the peace-accented teaching of Jesus and divine judgment that is anything but peaceable.

Jesus's Journey to God

Swartley and Borgman have set readers on the right path. Especially with regard to Luke's central section, however, their interpretive observations may be strengthened. Although Luke 9:51 marks the beginning of Jesus's journey to Jerusalem, the interpretive clue to the significance of this section is provided a little earlier, in the story of Jesus's transfiguration on the mountain (9:28–36).[48] While praying, Jesus's face changes in appearance, and his clothes become dazzlingly white. Moses and Elijah join him, and then we read this crucial statement: "They appeared in glory and discussed his exodus, which he was about to accomplish [or "fulfill"] in Jerusalem" (9:31). Those "appearing in glory" might well include Jesus, but the most significant part of this narrative comment is the topic of conversation between Moses, Elijah, and Jesus—his "exodus," which he was about to fulfill in Jerusalem.

There is considerable debate over the meaning of Jesus's "exodus" in Luke 9:31. For some, it is probably Jesus's death; for others, his resurrection; for others still, his ascension. Some consider that death, resurrection, and ascension together compose Jesus's "exodus." To translate "exodus" in Luke 9:31 as "departure," as is often done, is to overlook an important clue to the meaning of Luke's understanding of Jesus's journey to Jerusalem. The appearance of both the biblical personage, Moses, and the term "exodus" in the same passage must be more than coincidental. For François Bovon, "exodus" in Luke 9:31 is principally a "euphemism for death," while also, in Jesus's case, incorporating his resurrection and especially his ascension. "It is entirely possible that he also has in mind the fundamental experience of Israel, the exodus from Egypt."[49]

---

48. For an illuminating discussion of Luke's transfiguration account, see Lee, *Transfiguration*, 65–87.

49. Bovon, *Luke 1*, 376.

Surely the exodus allusion is more than simply possible. Indeed, according to David Moessner, the transfiguration episode is only part of the introduction in Luke 9:1–50 to the central journey narrative (9:51–19:44), in which "Luke sets forth a fourfold exodus typology of the prophetic calling of Jesus which conforms closely to that of Moses in Deuteronomy."[50] Whatever one makes of Moessner's proposal that Luke's Jesus recapitulates the portrayal of Moses in Deuteronomy, the key point (for my purposes) is that by analogy with the story of Moses, Jesus's exodus is more than simply his death, resurrection, ascension, or even all three together. The exodus from Egypt involved arduous journeying no less than departure from Egypt. Similarly, Jesus's "exodus" includes the journey *to* Jerusalem no less than departure in or from Jerusalem. In this respect, I agree with Moessner: "In the context of 9:51 where 'the days [pl.] of his taking up' in Jerusalem are 'becoming completely full' (i.e., 'had already arrived'), it is certain that the exodus that Jesus fulfills *in* Jerusalem is also one that he fulfills on his way *to* Jerusalem, that is, through a journey to that city. Hence his exodus is both a 'going out' to as well as a 'departure' from Jerusalem."[51]

Luke 9:31 indicates that Jesus's "exodus" will culminate (or be fulfilled) in Jerusalem, not that his entire "exodus" will transpire in Jerusalem.[52] The journey to Jerusalem in its entirety is, for Jesus, part of his own "exodus," whereas for his disciples and other followers, the journey to Jerusalem with Jesus is their novitiate into a new way of life. They learn this new way on the way, and in Luke's account the pathway they must tread is significantly longer and more burdened with things that must be learned and absorbed than in any other Gospel account.

As I see it, then, the reference to Jesus's "exodus" in the transfiguration episode prefigures the entirety of Jesus's journey to Jerusalem and beyond, which begins shortly thereafter at Luke 9:51, "And it happened that as the days of his 'taking up' were drawing near, he fixed his face to journey to Jerusalem." A meager fourteen verses interpose between the conclusion to the transfiguration story and the beginning of Jesus's journey to Jerusalem, but in these few verses Jesus's disciples are cast in a dim and desultory light. On the day following Jesus's transformation on the mountain, he castigates his disciples for their inability to release a boy from an unclean spirit (Luke 9:37–43a). He reminds his disciples pointedly that the Son of humanity is to be handed over

---

50. Moessner, *Lord of the Banquet*, 60.

51. Ibid., 66.

52. Swartley in *Israel's Scripture Traditions*, 76, also regards "fulfillment" terminology in Luke 9:31 as indicating "completion of action already begun." For Swartley, however, the beginning of what will be completed at Jerusalem is Jesus's Galilean ministry in its entirety. Swartley documents how exodus motifs shape Luke's Galilean section, but in narrative terms Luke 9:31 seems to look ahead to Jesus's own "exodus," as opposed to that which he has recapitulated in his Galilean mission. Swartley comes close to saying as much on 132.

into human hands (cf. Luke 9:22), but they fail to understand him and refrain from asking for clarification due to fear (9:43b–45). Instead, they enter into debate about which of them is the most prominent, whereupon Jesus instructs them on humility, with reference to a child (9:46–48).[53] Finally, Jesus corrects John for trying to hinder someone from expelling demons in Jesus's name (9:49–50). Ironically, those who could not drive out a demon from a child now try to prevent one who was succeeding "because he was not following *with us*" (9:49). Luke's phrasing here does not suggest that the person in question was not a follower of Jesus, only that he was not following along with those traveling with Jesus, which perhaps cast into stark relief their own incapacity to expel demons and thereby restore people to well-being.

Since Jesus's journey to Jerusalem culminates in his ascension,[54] his journey to Jerusalem is also his journey to God. When Jesus fixes his face for Jerusalem, it is a deliberate determination to act in accordance with what he understands to be a divine imperative,[55] a journey toward God that will include walking (and some riding), mixing with people, teaching, healing, challenging preconceptions, and provocation. At journey's end, he will experience betrayal, suffering, death, resurrection, and finally ascension into the presence of God. Jesus's journey begins with the mundane and ends in glory, prefigured in the transfiguration account.

The ascension is the culmination of Jesus's journey to God, not—as in the Fourth Gospel—his return to God, but a movement to God nonetheless.[56] And for Luke, Jesus's journey to God is what makes possible our turning to and movement toward God. We journey toward God in the wake of Jesus, who is, as the writer of the Letter to the Hebrews puts it, "the pioneer of our faith" (12:2). But journeying toward God in the *wake* of Jesus also implies being drawn into the *way* of Jesus itself—its direction, shape, and constraints.

The way of Jesus en route to God via Jerusalem is, in Luke's presentation, the way of peace (cf. 1:78b–79). To reiterate, the peace theme is prominent at both the beginning and end of the distinctively Lukan journey section, enclosing and thereby binding together all the teaching in this block of material—whether on discipleship, the mercy of God, money, or prayer. As Swartley discerns, "By

53. That Jesus instructs his disciples on humility with a child as object lesson is perhaps suggestive of the reason for their failure to expel a child's unclean spirit in Luke 9:38–42. Either lack of humility or disregard for the socially lowly is likely the problem.

54. See Parsons, *Departure of Jesus*, 91–93.

55. In relation to Jesus's life and mission, the impersonal δεῖ (*dei*), "it is necessary," appears in Luke's Gospel as often as in the other three Gospels combined. See esp. Luke 2:49; 4:43; 9:22; 13:33; 17:25; 19:5; 22:37; 24:7, 26, 44. In this way, Luke conveys his sense of Jesus's life and mission unfolding in accordance with God's plan and purpose.

56. See Senior, *Passion of Jesus*, 35–39. Senior also speaks of "Jesus' journey to God," but he overemphasizes the notion that Jesus's journey to God is a *return* to God. In Luke's account of Jesus's journey to God, there is an *intimation of homecoming*, but to speak of Jesus's journey to God as a return to God is to read Luke's Gospel through Johannine eyes.

introducing the peace motif prominently at the beginning and ending of his Journey Narrative (9:51–19:44), Luke wants his readers to see that Jesus' entire mission was one of bringing peace."[57] It is also toward the end of this journey to Jerusalem—indeed, at Jericho—that Luke provides his own distillation of the purpose of Jesus's mission and journey toward God: to seek out and to rescue the lost. At the conclusion of the uniquely Lukan encounter between wealthy Zacchaeus and Jesus, Luke records Jesus as saying: "Today salvation has happened to this house, insofar as even he is a son of Abraham. For the Son of humanity came to seek out and to save the lost" (19:9–10). Despite Jesus's provocation in the temple, perfunctorily recounted in Luke 19:45–46,[58] he endures with equanimity his betrayal; mocking by soldiers; various hearings before the Sanhedrin, Pilate, and Herod; and ultimately his execution by crucifixion. He even heals the ear of the high priest's slave after a disciple lashes out violently, prays for the forgiveness of his executioners, and offers reassurance to a co-crucified criminal who accepts the law of retribution for himself but defends Jesus's innocence. (These are distinctively Lukan features.)

In short, the journey to Jerusalem and thence to God via crucifixion, resurrection, and ascension is one characterized by peace on Jesus's part. Furthermore, resurrection and ascension to the right hand of God are divine stamps of approval on the mission of Jesus and the manner in which it is conducted. This is borne out in Acts 10:36, Peter's distillation of the meaning and significance of Jesus's mission. In a decisive episode that in Luke's view authorizes the mission to non-Jews, Peter characterizes Jesus's mission in its entirety as God's good news of peace to the people of Israel, a peaceable mission now to be extended to the nations. According to this text, it is not simply that Jesus's own teaching was irenic in content and tone but also that Jesus's mission in its entirety was a divine overture of peace.

We learn from Luke's distinctive conception of Jesus's mission that the journey of Jesus to Jerusalem and thence to God is a *way of peace* that disciples of Jesus are to emulate. More than that, however, we also learn that the way of Jesus turns out to be not only the way *to* God but also, decisively, the very way *of* God. The mission of Jesus is not only his peaceable seeking out and recovery of the lost but also God's intentional determination to wage peace in an unreceptive, violent, and often cruel world.

Acts 10:36, Luke's distillation of Jesus's mission in its entirety as God's announcement of peace, is prepared for and reinforced in the Gospel by a distinctively Lukan motif—*divine visitation*. If the Fourth Gospel is the Gospel of *incarnation* and Matthew's Gospel is the Gospel of *Immanu-el*, God's real

57. Swartley, *Covenant of Peace*, 149. This literary or narrative inference, which one might be tempted to attribute to a savvy reader, is reinforced by Acts 10:36 and Luke's evident emphasis on peace.

58. Luke places greater emphasis on Jesus's daily teaching within the temple precincts (19:47; 20:1; 21:37–38; 22:53).

presence with humanity,[59] Luke's variation on this theme is the *visitation of God in the prophetic persona and mission of Jesus.*[60] Of eleven occurrences of the verb ἐπισκέπτομαι (*episkeptomai*) within the New Testament, seven are in Luke–Acts. This is the verb twice used by the Son of humanity in Matthew's final judgment scenario to refer to visiting or not visiting him when he was sick and/or incarcerated (25:36, 43), but otherwise it occurs elsewhere in the New Testament only in Hebrews 2:6 and James 1:27. Of Luke's seven usages of this verb, only four convey the sense of *divine* visitation (Luke 1:68, 78; 7:16; Acts 15:14).[61] To these four theologically significant occurrences of this verb, one should also add Luke's use of the cognate noun, ἐπισκοπή (*episkopē*), in Luke 19:44. Within the New Testament, the only other comparable occurrence of this word family to signify divine visitation is in 1 Peter 2:12, which refers to the eschatological "Day of Visitation."

The precedent for this usage appears in the Septuagint, in which this vocabulary conveys the sense of God's visitation for the purpose of deliverance (LXX: Exod. 4:31; Ruth 1:6; Pss. 79:15 [80:14 Eng.]; 105:4 [106:4]).[62] It also has this theological sense in Jewish literature roughly contemporaneous with Luke's time of writing, for example, Wisdom 3:7; *Psalms of Solomon* 3:11; 10:4; 11:6; 15:12; *Testaments of Levi* (4:4), *Judah* (23:5), and *Asher* (7:3); and the Qumran text known as the *Damascus Document* (CD) 1.7–11, in which the Teacher of Righteousness is the focus of divine visitation. The Qumran parallel is decisive for Fitzmyer, whereas parallels in the *Testaments of the Twelve Patriarchs* stand out for Bovon.[63] Either way, Luke evidently tapped into Jewish tradition to convey something of his understanding of Jesus and his mission.

Acts 15:14 shows that for Luke divine visitation was not restricted to Jesus's mission and message. There Jesus's brother, James, sums up Simon Peter's appeal before the Jerusalem assembly by characterizing the conversion of the Roman Cornelius as divine visitation to retrieve from the nations a people representative of divine initiative (lit., "to take or receive from the nations a people for his name"). For Luke, this particular "visitation" is associated with the Holy Spirit (Acts 10:44–48; 15:8). So although divine visitation is not restricted to Jesus's own mission, it is clearly tethered to it, since in Acts the Holy Spirit is poured out by the ascended Jesus (2:32–33). While Acts 15:14

59. For a full-scale study of Matthew's "divine presence" theme, see Kupp, *Matthew's Emmanuel*.

60. See R. Brown, *Birth of the Messiah*, 390n38. Commenting on the visitation motif in Luke 1:68, 78, Brown remarks: "Here Luke moves close to the Emmanuel, 'God with us,' motif in Matthew's infancy narrative."

61. The usage in Acts 7:23 and 15:36 is parallel in meaning to that in Matt. 25:36, 43.

62. See Fitzmyer, *According to Luke (I–IX)*, 382–83; cf. Bock, *Luke 1:1–9:50*, 178–79, noting that Jer. 44:13 shows that divine visitation can be for judgment.

63. Fitzmyer, *According to Luke (I–IX)*, 383; Bovon, *Luke 1*, 69.

is of a piece with Luke's theologically loaded visitation motif, therefore, the motif itself is a Lukan means of explicating the meaning and significance of Jesus's divinely authorized mission in his Gospel, where it serves a narrative-theological role like the peace motif.

The passage that concludes Luke's journey to Jerusalem, Luke 19:41–44, reiterates not only Luke's peace theme (2:14; 19:38) but also the theme of divine visitation sounded at the beginning of the Gospel. In the Benedictus that concludes Luke's opening chapter, the Spirit-influenced prophecy of the priest Zechariah begins and ends with the theme of divine visitation for human salvation. "Blessed be the Lord God of Israel, because he has *visited* and has effected redemption for his people," is how Zechariah's prophecy begins (1:68). It ends poetically, affirming that through the compassionate mercies of our God, the dawn from on high will *visit* or break in on us to give light to those in darkness and to guide our feet into the way of peace (1:78–79). As at the end of Jesus's journey to Jerusalem, the themes of peace and divine visitation are here intertwined.

In Luke 7:16, those who witness the raising of the young man of Nain praise God by exclaiming, "A great prophet has been raised up among us." As a corollary of this, they infer that "God has *visited* his people." In other words, the presence in their midst of a great prophet signals divine visitation. Moreover, what induces this exclamation of praise and recognition is Jesus's restoration of a young man to life. In Zechariah's paean of praise, divine visitation is associated with redemption, revelation, and peace; here divine visitation is associated with restoration to life. At the culmination of Jesus's journey to Jerusalem, however, he forecasts that city's inevitable demise because of its failure to recognize the appointed time of "visitation." The Greek text of Luke 19:44 does not specify this "visitation" as divine, but in view of earlier occurrences of this word group, the inference is inevitable. As Moessner paraphrases, "Gazing down from the Mount of Olives upon the city of Israel's destiny, Jesus weeps for a nation that has failed to recognize its 'exodus visitation' of deliverance from God (*episkopēs*, 19.44; [LXX:] Exod. 3.16!; 13.19; cf. Gen. 50.24)."[64] In the prophetic persona of Jesus, people may encounter but may also overlook the divine presence that is offering healing salvation.

There is perhaps an echo of this theme of divine visitation in Luke 24:18, where the downcast Cleopas asks the risen but unrecognized Jesus whether he is the only *temporary resident* or *visitor* in Jerusalem not to know what has been happening there of late. The Greek term (παροικεῖς, *paroikeis*) is different, but its association with Jerusalem is tantalizing. Earlier, as Jesus approaches Jerusalem, he accuses the city of failing to perceive divine visitation in his person; now, as he joins others headed away from Jerusalem, he is asked, on the presumption that he is a visitor to the city, how it is that he is unfamiliar

---

64. Moessner, "How Luke Writes," 158.

with all that has happened—*to himself*! The irony is pungent. For, as Brendan
Byrne observes, "We know that he is the divine 'visitor' to Jerusalem who has
stood at the very center of what has been going on."[65]

In Lukan interpretation, it is relatively rare to find the theme of divine visitation in the prophetic persona and mission of Jesus given much prominence.
But Byrne has placed this motif at the center of his reading of Luke's Gospel:

> Luke sees the whole life and ministry of Jesus as a "*visitation*" on God's part to
> Israel and the world. From the start this raises the question: how will this guest,
> this visitor be *received*? The crucial point is that those who do receive him find
> that he brings them into a much wider sphere of hospitality: the "hospitality of
> God." The One who comes as visitor and guest in fact becomes *host* and offers a
> hospitality in which human beings and, potentially, the entire world, can become
> truly human, be at home, can *know* salvation in the depths of their hearts.[66]

Byrne's reading perspective is fruitful. In the divine visitation that is Jesus's
prophetic mission, Byrne detects a divine determination to effect reversal, not
only a reversal from guest to host but also a reversal of humanity's alienation
and dis-ease. Byrne might well have said that the mission of Jesus comprises
divine visitation *for*, no less than *to*, Israel and the world. Also helpful is his
association of divine visitation with the theme of salvation, a theme central
to Luke's conception of Jesus's mission. For Byrne, the Lukan passage that
best illustrates the double-sided theme of divine visitation/hospitality is the
story of Zacchaeus (Luke 19:1–10).[67] This story displays Luke's holistic understanding of the meaning of salvation, which can be experienced here and
now. Even the way in which Luke has Jesus sum up the purpose of his mission at the conclusion of this story can be read in terms of divine visitation/
hospitality: "For the Son of humanity came to seek [visit] and to save [offer
hospitality to] the lost" (Luke 19:10).

Expanding on the insight of Swartley (and Borgman) that the peace theme
encloses and thereby holds together the entirety of Luke's distinctive journey
section (9:51–19:44), the motif of divine visitation in the prophetic persona
and mission of Jesus extends this "enclosure of peace" back to the Benedictus
of Zechariah at the beginning of the Gospel. On Jesus's arrival at Jerusalem,
his twofold lament is that the city fails to recognize both that which leads to
peace and the divine visitation inherent in his mission (19:41–44). Zechariah's
prophecy of praise, itself enclosed by references to divine visitation, associates

65. Byrne, *Hospitality of God*, 187.
66. Ibid., 4; cf. Lee, *Transfiguration*, 65, who speaks of various features within Luke's account of the transfiguration as "symbolic of the divine visitation which is the centre of Luke's theology."
67. Byrne, *Hospitality of God*, 4–5. Probably not coincidentally, twice in his encounter with Zacchaeus Jesus uses the term "today," which at certain points in Luke's Gospel ties in with Luke's motif of divine visitation. See esp. Luke 2:11; 4:21; 5:26; 13:32–33; 19:5, 9. I am indebted to Swartley for alerting me to this connection in personal communication.

this visitation with the way of peace (1:67–79). As Luke 19:38 echoes 2:14, so 19:41–44 echoes 1:67–79, thereby comprising a double narrative interlacing that encloses the whole of Jesus's life prior to his entry into Jerusalem.[68] If one accepts Luke 24:18 as an echo of the divine visitation motif, Luke's narrative peace arc extends from before the birth of Jesus (1:78–79) to beyond his resurrection. This is already the case if the risen Jesus's greeting of peace in Luke 24:36 is original. Even if the peace greeting in Luke 24:36 is secondary, however, the divine visitation motif, inextricably associated by Luke with peace and restoration, brackets Luke's Gospel in much the same way as Matthew's *Immanu-el* motif brackets his Gospel. As variations on a shared theme (Jesus as the locus of divine presence) serving a common narrative function (*inclusio*), Luke's visitation motif and Matthew's *Immanu-el* motif function similarly.

Earlier I expressed the view that Jesus's "exodus"—his journey to Jerusalem and thence to God via crucifixion, resurrection, and ascension—was not only his own peaceable way to God but also God's own way of peace. Dorothy Lee characterizes the Lukan Jesus's "exodus" as "his path through life and death which is the path of God's visitation."[69] Luke's narrative interlacing of divine visitation with peace makes it possible to affirm both perspectives as integral to Lukan theology: divine visitation implies and is constitutive of peace; peace is the shape and signature of divine visitation. As with Matthew's *Immanu-el* motif, Luke's motif of divine visitation *in Jesus* provides insight into the character of God and God's way in the world. As such, the theme of divine visitation in the prophetic persona and mission of Jesus serves a critical function with respect to aspects of Luke's two-part narrative that militate against this theme.

Jerusalem's Judgment

Luke may be the New Testament's evangelist of peace, but discordant notes jangle against his peace emphasis. For example, the visitation motif in Luke 19:41–44 is reminiscent not only of Zechariah's prophecy of praise, in which divine visitation is associated with the way of peace, but also the theme of Jerusalem's judgment. Judgment per se is not incompatible with a peace focus, but strictly retributive, purely retaliatory, or vindictively violent expressions of judgment hardly cohere with a peace-oriented theological and moral vision. What, then, is one to make of Jesus's prophecies of retributive judgment against Jerusalem and his apparent anticipation of eschatological vengeance? The next two chapters focus on Lukan eschatology in both his Gospel and Acts; meanwhile, what may be learned about the relation between peace and

68. For further resonances between Jesus's lament for Jerusalem and Zechariah's Benedictus, see Tannehill, *Narrative Unity of Luke–Acts*, 1:159–60.

69. Lee, *Transfiguration*, 73.

judgment from an examination of Luke's understanding of the foretold destruction of Jerusalem?

It is widely (though not universally) accepted that Luke's composition of both his Gospel and Acts occurred after the destruction of Jerusalem and the temple in 70 CE. At no point does Luke refer to Jerusalem's destruction as an event that has already occurred, perhaps because his two-part narrative breaks off with Paul in Rome before the beginning of the First Jewish Revolt (in 66 CE). But many see in what Luke recounts of Jesus's pronouncements regarding Jerusalem's destruction (Luke 13:35; 19:43–44; 21:5–6, 20–24; 23:28–31) some familiarity with this historical event, which he used to give greater specificity to Jesus's predictions.[70]

It is not simply that Luke gives greater specificity to Jesus's pronouncements of judgment against Jerusalem. As Bradley Chance points out in *Jerusalem, the Temple, and the New Age in Luke–Acts*, "There is no question that Luke wished to emphasize the destruction of Jerusalem and the temple."[71] More important, Chance argues that Luke understood the destruction of Jerusalem and the temple to be the direct result of Israel's rejection of Jesus, the church, and the church's universal mission.[72] Examination of Luke 13:34–35; 19:41–44; 21:5–6, 20–24; and 23:28–31 bears out Chance's observations, especially with respect to the emphasis that Luke placed on Jerusalem's destruction and the "rationale" for destruction in its rejection of Jesus.

Jesus's lament over Jerusalem in Luke 13:34–35 is almost identical to its parallel in Matthew 23:37–39, but Luke contextualizes this lament in his central journey section within a block of text that is largely unique to himself (L or special tradition). Luke 13 begins with a uniquely Lukan passage that warns of destruction in the absence of a change of mind and direction (13:1–9) and is followed by the uniquely Lukan story of Jesus's release of a daughter of Abraham from an oppressive spirit (13:10–17). Then follow his version of Jesus's parables of the mustard seed and leaven (13:18–21), the first of which he shares with both Matthew and Mark, the second with Matthew alone. Next, in response to a question about whether salvation is coming only to a few, comes Jesus's warning, shared with Matthew, on exclusion from the eschatological reign of God (Luke 13:22–30), after which some Pharisees warn Jesus of Herod's intent to kill him (13:31). In response, Jesus reasserts the purpose of his mission but also reaffirms his commitment to journey toward Jerusalem, his reason being that it is unthinkable that a prophet should perish outside Jerusalem.

Then follows his first lament over Jerusalem, in which he utters these words: "Behold, your house is forsaken to you" (Luke 13:35). The word *house* is here

70. See, e.g., Fitzmyer, *According to Luke (I–IX)*, 54.
71. Chance, *Jerusalem, the Temple*, 115.
72. Ibid., 116–27.

often interpreted to signify the temple, but it might also mean the house of Israel as a whole. Either way, this "house" is inextricably associated with Jerusalem and left to its own devices as a result of spurning Jesus's prophetic care and protection. As Peter Walker observes, "In the light of the preceding verses with their emphasis on Jerusalem (vv. 33–34) this 'house' clearly includes the Temple."[73] Luke's composition here also associates the city's rejecting care with its killing of prophets. Thus there is an implicit connection between the perishing in Jerusalem of the prophet Jesus and the (divine) forsaking of Jerusalem's "house," however that is understood.

Jesus's lament at journey's end (Luke 19:41–44) is uniquely Lukan and emphatic in both its prediction of destruction for Jerusalem and the reason for that destruction. Luke 19:43–44a predicts both a suffocating siege of the city and its utter leveling, with the inevitable loss of (human) life that destruction of such magnitude necessarily implies: "and your children within you." The reason then provided is that Jerusalem's destruction is the direct consequence of failing to appreciate the time of (divine) visitation (19:44b). "This is the payment for Jerusalem's rejection," as Darrell Bock states bluntly.[74] Bock accurately conveys Luke's meaning, but in view of the term ὅτι (hoti) at the beginning of Luke 19:43, one wonders whether the final clause of 19:44 is not Lukan redaction of a traditional oracle of judgment.[75] This prophecy reads somewhat differently if one takes the ὅτι of Luke 19:43 in a causal sense, as follows: "But now that [comprehension of things that make for peace] is concealed from your eyes so that [or "insofar as"] days are coming upon you . . ." (19:42b–43a). This reading accepts Jerusalem's destruction as a consequence of failing to appreciate the things that lead to peace and makes redundant Luke's explicit rationale for destruction in 19:44b. For Luke, however, indiscriminate destruction of Jerusalem is clearly payback for its rejection of Jesus.

In an intriguing study, Brent Kinman explores Luke's depiction of Jesus's entry into Jerusalem against the backdrop of Hellenistic celebratory welcomes or παρουσίαι (parousiai).[76] After discussing the Greco-Roman matrix within which arrivals of dignitaries to cities would be understood, Kinman documents how Jesus's royalty is emphasized by Luke but also how understated Luke's description of his welcome to Jerusalem is. The gist of Kinman's argument is that Jesus deserved and expected a celebratory welcome to Jerusalem but

73. Walker, *Jesus and the Holy City*, 61.
74. Bock, *Luke 9:51–24:53*, 1561.
75. Ἀνθ' ὧν (anth hōn, lit. "in return for which") in Luke 19:44b seems almost to "trump" the ὅτι (hoti, because) of 19:43a. Elsewhere in Luke–Acts, this expression signifies divine punishment (see Luke 1:20 and esp. Acts 12:23). "The expression occurs frequently in the LXX," according to Fitzmyer. "See Jer 5:14, 19; 7:13; 16:11, especially with retributive force." See Fitzmyer, *According to Luke (X–XXIV)*, 958.
76. Kinman, "Parousia, Jesus' 'A-Triumphal' Entry," 279–94.

received nothing of the kind. For this reason, he pronounced his oracle of
doom against the city (Luke 19:43–44).

The evidence adduced by Kinman to show that Luke presents Jesus's arrival
to Jerusalem as a shameful affront to Jesus on the part of its leading citizens
is compelling. Jesus does not enter Jerusalem in triumph. Less compelling,
however, is Kinman's inference that this explains his prophecy of Jerusalem's
destruction. First, Jesus's pronouncement of judgment against Jerusalem is
not presented as an outburst of vindictive retribution; rather, upon seeing
Jerusalem, Jesus weeps over (perhaps even *upon*) it (19:41). Distress rather
than honor-insulted fury on Jesus's part is what Luke conveys. Second, Luke
13:35a indicates that Jerusalem's judgment was, in Luke's view, already sealed
well before Jesus's arrival to the city. And third, as Kinman himself points out,
at the beginning of Jesus's journey to Jerusalem, he experienced a similar
rebuff but explicitly refused to call down vengeance on the offending village.
If anything can be described as Jesus's response to Jerusalem's failure to welcome him in a manner befitting his royal status, it is his "occupation" of the
temple (19:45–48). Even if Kinman were correct on this point, however, that
would only exacerbate the already-existing tension between Jesus's peaceable
mission, as Luke presents it, and Luke's linkage of Jerusalem's destruction
to its rejection of Jesus.

By comparison with Mark 13, Chance shows that Luke 21 at various points
emphasizes the destruction of both Jerusalem and the temple (21:5–6, 20, 24).[77]
This Lukan emphasis shows up yet again in the distinctively Lukan account of
Jesus's warning to mourning women while being led to his crucifixion. Here
the prophetic oracle is more allusive than previous prophetic pronouncements,
but most interpreters see in this prophecy a reference to Jerusalem's misery
and despair during the Roman siege of Jerusalem. Various interpretations
have been offered of the proverbial question in Luke 23:31, "For if to the green
wood they do such things, to the dry what will happen?" Something along these
lines seems to be the gist of it: if this can be done to a green, living tree (Jesus
himself), what is likely to happen after it has been killed? The implied answer
is that the fate of the green tree will be meted out on those responsible for killing the green tree, perhaps even that the dead-dry wood of the once-green tree
will kindle the retribution. One need not press for anything too precise, but
some such interpretation comports with the view expressed in Luke 19:41–44.[78]

In short, among the canonical Gospel writers, Luke most explicitly relates
Jerusalem's demise by Roman violence to divine vengeance for Jewish rejection
of Jesus and his mission. The parable of the vineyard, shared among all three
Synoptic Gospels, hints at divine retaliation against the Jewish leadership but

77. Chance, *Jerusalem, the Temple*, 72–73. Luke 21 receives more attention in chap. 4 below.
78. For another plausible interpretation, see Walker, *Jesus and the Holy City*, 76–79. Walker's
paraphrase of Luke 23:31 reads: "If the Romans treat in such a way one whom they admit to be
innocent, what will they do to the guilty?"

without explicitly connecting this with the destruction of Jerusalem (Matt. 21:41; Mark 12:9; Luke 20:16). Matthew 22:7 may also hint at divine retaliation against Jerusalem. The invective in Matthew 23:29–36 (cf. Luke 11:47–51) more obviously associates the destruction of Jerusalem with divine vengeance, especially in view of the oracle against Jerusalem that immediately follows (Matt. 23:37–39 // Luke 13:34–35). But no text more clearly attributes the destruction of Jerusalem to divine retaliation for rejecting the mission of Jesus than Luke 19:41–44.[79] Here and in Luke 21:20–24, Luke's view is barely distinguishable from that of his Jewish contemporary Josephus, who also attributes Jerusalem's devastation at the hands of the Romans to divine punishment.[80]

Once accept that Jerusalem's destruction at Roman hands was divine judgment for the city's rejection of Jesus's peaceable mission and the mode of expected eschatological judgment is almost inevitably retributive. It is one thing to acknowledge that Jesus intuited Jerusalem's demise and to affirm that its destruction proved his prophetic insight to be correct, or even that Jerusalem's destruction was an inevitable consequence of failing to follow in Jesus's peace path. But it is another matter altogether to equate the destruction of Jerusalem with divine vengeance on its inhabitants for rejecting Jesus and his way. This would seem to have been Luke's understanding, however, even though it grates against so much else that contributes to designating him as the evangelist of peace. How does the perception that Jesus's mission in its entirety was divine visitation for the purpose of announcing peace and salvation to Israel cohere with the conviction that the divine response to Israel's rejection of that overture of peace and restoration is vindictive retribution in the form of destruction and slaughter?

This question can be answered with the care it deserves only after Luke's vision of eschatological judgment is explored more fully in the next two chapters. But some preliminary observations may be made. First, Jesus is a prophetic figure for Luke, and divine judgment for covenant unfaithfulness was a prophetic mantra. In this connection, prophetic insight in biblical tradition is usually expressed in symbolic and indeterminate terms.[81] In other words, biblical prophecy is visionary and intuitive, not empirical-in-advance. Moreover, prophecies of divine judgment could, as Jonah learned, be conditional. Christopher Marshall notes how a number of Lukan pronouncements of

---

79. Compare Travis, *Christ and the Judgement*, 217–18. For Travis, Luke 19:41–44, read in tandem with 13:34–35, indicates that divine judgment of Jerusalem takes the form of divine abandonment into the hands of enemies, not the direct infliction of divine vengeance via Roman destruction.

80. Josephus, *Jewish War* 6.93–110. To avoid confusion, Josephus does not attribute Jerusalem's demise to divine retribution for Jewish animosity against Jesus or James, as some patristic authors claimed. On the misuse of Josephus by early Christian writers, see Mason, *Josephus and the New Testament*, 7–24; chap. 6 of Mason's book compares Josephus and Luke–Acts.

81. See Meyer, *Aims of Jesus*, 246–47. Myer helpfully discriminates between prophetic knowledge and "empirical-knowledge-by-anticipation."

divine judgment on Jerusalem allude to Hosea 9–10, then comments: "Yet just as Hosea's threats are followed by the counternote of mercy, . . . so Jesus's warnings of judgment are not necessarily the last word on the matter but are meant to provoke Israel to repentance."[82]

Second, Luke was a person of his time. It was evidently commonplace within contemporary Palestinian and Diaspora Judaism, as well as in early Jewish and non-Jewish Christianity, to conceive of God as both just judge and dispenser of mercy, even though, strictly speaking, these conceptions mix like oil and water. Moreover, the theme of divine retribution is well attested in Jewish Scripture, especially among the prophets. If there is a tension in Luke's writings between peace with justice on one hand, and divine retribution on the other, that tension fits Jewish and Christian literature of the period and can claim scriptural precedent.

At one level, belief in divine judgment is fully compatible with a *shalom*-oriented moral vision. One might even affirm that divine judgment is the necessary theological basis for a moral commitment to peace. But this depends on the content and character of divine judgment. Divine judgment that is solely retributive or vengeful hardly undergirds peace as primary because ultimately the divine will is maintained by divine violence. Luke's understanding of Jerusalem's destruction as divine retribution for rejecting Jesus leans too far in the direction of retaliatory vengeance, especially in view of his peace emphasis, *an emphasis encompassing not only human morality but also divine initiative.* Both in Luke's Gospel and in Acts 10:36, divine visitation in the life, mission, and teaching of Jesus is characterized as an overture of peace to humanity, and Jesus's own journey to God is characterized as the way of peace. In the context of that theological and moral vision, which Luke himself constructs, a view of divine judgment that is solely retributive jars and jangles. Perhaps it comes down to a question of emphasis, that is, which side of Luke's theological and moral vision one subsumes under the other. In view of his conception of Jesus's mission as a divine overture of peace, I am inclined to relativize his view of divine judgment as retributive and vindictive. But may that inclination be maintained and defended in light of Luke's view of eschatological judgment?

Third and finally, Walker's reflections on the Lukan pronouncements against Jerusalem, most notably the last in Luke 23:27–31, underscore an "integral connection" between Jesus's own death and Jerusalem's dire destiny. What Walker means is that, for Luke, Jesus's innocent death is not simply the cause of Jerusalem's subsequent destruction, understood as divine judgment, but also its precursor. From this Walker infers a number of points, the most helpful of which is his observation that "Luke's Jesus is not just one who judges

---

82. C. Marshall, *Beyond Retribution*, 165. Marshall detects the following Lukan allusions to Hosea: Luke 13:6–9 / Hos. 9:10, 13, 16; Luke 19:41–44 / Hos. 9:7; 10:2, 4; Luke 21:22 / Hos. 9:7; Luke 23:28–31 / Hos. 10:8.

Jerusalem; he also suffers that judgement himself and identifies with the city in its [sic] death. His words are not distantly critical, but are backed up by costly identification."[83] This rings true and thereby creates an interstice in which to perceive in Jesus's death the possible impossibility of divine forgiveness where retribution is deserved. After all, Luke's crucifixion account follows hard upon the enigmatic saying of Jesus in Luke 23:31, "For if to the green wood they do such things, to the dry what will happen?" Although textually uncertain, Jesus's next words, spoken from the cross, are "Father, forgive them, because they do not know what they are doing" (Luke 23:34). And one crucified alongside Jesus who recognizes that he deserves retribution is promised a place in paradise (23:39–43).

Conclusion

To set the scene for a discussion of moral vision and eschatology in Luke–Acts, this chapter has marshaled the evidence for recognizing Luke as the evangelist of peace. This conclusion rests on the relative prominence of the peace theme in Luke–Acts as a whole, the clustering of theologically loaded references to peace at significant junctures in Luke's Gospel, and the summary in Acts 10:36 of Jesus's mission in its entirety as God's peace-announcement. It is also supported by strong resonances between peace and other prominent Lukan themes, especially justice and concern for those at the margins of society.

Not every other Lukan theme sits comfortably with Luke's peace emphasis, however. Especially discordant is the Lukan motif of divine retribution, which sits cheek by jowl with the theme of peace at both beginning and end of Luke's central section concerned with Jesus's peaceable journey toward God. Particularly perturbing are prophetic pronouncements of divine vengeance against Jerusalem, most of which are unique to Luke. How is this thematic tension best addressed? Not everyone perceives the tension, but the discrepancy between peace and divine vengeance is pronounced if Luke conceived of Jesus's mission in its entirety as a divine overture of peace but expected eschatological vengeance modeled on the destruction of Jerusalem rather than eschatological salvation modeled on Jesus's mission of peace.

Is Swartley correct that despite Luke's construction of Jesus's mission in its entirety as God's peace-announcement to humanity, God nevertheless retains the prerogative to indulge in vengeance toward enemies not won over by the overture of peace in Jesus? Luke's understanding of Jerusalem's destruction as divine retribution suggests that he may be correct, as do aspects of Luke's eschatology. Luke's eschatology is not a single current, however, as the following two chapters reveal.

---

83. Walker, *Jesus and the Holy City*, 77–78. It is unclear whether Walker's intention was to refer to Jerusalem's or Jesus's death, but his basic point is nevertheless clear.

4

"As in the Days of Noah and Lot"

Retributive Eschatology in Luke's Gospel

In the previous chapter, Luke was shown to be the evangelist of peace. The peace theme is not only dominant in his Gospel, but the way in which this theme is plotted within his narrative also signals that peace is integral to Luke's understanding of the mission and message of Jesus. It is not only that Luke endorses peace as an appropriate stance for disciples of Jesus, nor even that he regards Jesus's own journey through life and death and beyond to be inherently peaceable, but also that this "way of Jesus" reveals the way of God to be peaceable. Among the writers of the first three Gospels, Luke's eschatological outlook is perhaps the least impending, except in relation to the demise of Jerusalem. Although Luke dissociates the destruction of Jerusalem from the coming of the Son of humanity, both his association of Jerusalem's destruction with divine judgment and his anticipation of similarly devastating displays of divine judgment at the eschaton stand in considerable tension with the peaceable ethos that Luke correlates with the reign of God proclaimed and embodied by Jesus. This chapter examines future-oriented eschatological passages in Luke's Gospel with a view to weighing retributive eschatology against Luke's theology of peace.

Luke's Eschatological Schema

"Everything began with history and eschatology." So begins François Bovon's survey of scholarship on *Luke the Theologian*, in which the opening chapter is devoted to "The Plan of God, Salvation History, and Eschatology."[1] Bovon's opening sentence makes sense only when one appreciates that his survey begins in 1950 with the work of such scholars as Philipp Vielhauer, Ernst Käsemann, and especially Hans Conzelmann, who placed an alleged revisionist eschatology at the forefront of Luke's theological concerns. For more than a quarter-century, eschatology retained a prominent place in Lukan studies, although in 1983 Bovon could report that "the flood of publications on eschatology in Luke has subsided."[2] Even so, since 1975 a number of major works on Lukan eschatology have been published, as Bovon documents.[3]

Before turning to two influential interpretations of Lukan eschatology, it is worth trying to make sense of Luke's eschatological outlook on the basis of his two-part work itself. His eschatological outlook has a discernible schematic structure. First, Luke's history of Christian origins is premised on the conviction that the events he recounts are themselves instances of eschatological fulfillment. This is evident from Luke's elegant preface, in which he refers to events that have been fulfilled among us, literally, "the having-been-fulfilled-among-us events" (Luke 1:1). Various texts convey Luke's conviction that the decisive eschatological event is precisely the life and mission of Jesus, in fulfillment of scriptural promises (1:54–55, 68–74; 2:30–32; 3:4–6; and esp. 4:21; 7:19–23; 10:23–24). This perspective is reinforced by other texts that point to the presence of God's reign in aspects of the mission of Jesus (10:9, 11; 11:20; 17:20–21). In Acts 3:11–26, Luke records Peter as saying that Jesus's suffering and death were the means by which scriptural prophecy that the Messiah must suffer was fulfilled by God. For Luke, therefore, realized eschatology—that which has already been fulfilled in accordance with God's eschatological plan and purpose—is decisive.

The second aspect of Luke's eschatological schema is fulfillment of prophecy and promise within the time frame of his salvation-historical narrative. Such eschatological fulfillment is organically related to the first feature of Lukan eschatology insofar as it occurs either within the matrix of the story of Jesus or in immediate sequence to it. For example, the birth of John, narrated in Luke 1:57–80, occurs in fulfillment of the angel's words to Zechariah in 1:8–20 (see esp. 1:20, "my words, which will be fulfilled at their appointed time"). Similarly, the prophetic words of Simeon to Jesus's mother, Mary, in Luke 2:34–35, are at least partially fulfilled by the conclusion of Luke's Gospel. Likewise, Jesus's own prophetic words about a time when the bridegroom

---

1. Bovon, *Luke the Theologian*, 11.

2. Ibid., 474. Between 1950 and 1975, Bovon detects a shift in interest from eschatological to ecclesial concerns, with a further shift in the quarter-century between 1980 and 2005 from ecclesiology to ethics. In a sense, this present chapter reexamines an aspect of Luke's eschatology from the perspective of a key theologico-ethical theme—peace, which hardly features in Bovon's survey of scholarship.

3. Ibid., 520–24.

would be taken away from the disciples (5:35) is fulfilled within the Gospel narrative. But perhaps most important for this "second-stage realized eschatology" is the fulfillment at Pentecost (Acts 2) of Jesus's promised gift of the Holy Spirit (Luke 24:49; Acts 1:5), which according to Luke is also eschatological fulfillment of scriptural promises (Acts 2:14–21). Thus, for Luke, the preparatory mission of John, the grace-filled mission of Jesus, and the gift-endowing "baptism" of the Holy Spirit comprise the decisive eschatological moment in his salvation-historical schema. What precedes this decisive moment is here fulfilled and what follows this moment is thereby determined, meaning that all later events find their true orientation here. In Luke's salvation-historical schema, future-oriented eschatological expectation takes its bearings from realized eschatology.

The third aspect of Lukan eschatology is prophetic utterance on the part of Jesus that is not recounted as being fulfilled within Luke's two-part narrative but is likely presupposed as having already occurred. The decisive event in this category is the destruction of Jerusalem and the temple, which is predicted by Jesus in Luke 13:35; 19:41–44; 21:6, 20–24; and (probably) 23:28–31, but never actually recounted. Yet the manner in which Jerusalem's demise is predicted suggests that Luke's familiarity with certain aspects of the historical siege and destruction of Jerusalem influenced his recording of Jesus's prediction.[4] What is especially noteworthy is that the destruction of Jerusalem is considered by Luke to be "days of vengeance" (Luke 21:22), perhaps even divine retribution on "this generation" for violence committed against God's prophets since the creation of the world (11:49–51). In 19:44, Jesus apparently infers that Jerusalem's impending demise is as a result of failing to recognize "the season of your visitation [by God]." Thus the temple's destruction in 70 CE instantiates divine judgment as historical event within Luke's salvation-historical schema.

If the destruction of Jerusalem is characterized as "days of vengeance," the coming of the Son of humanity is characterized as a "day of deliverance" (Luke 21:28, 34–35). There are those who identify the destruction of Jerusalem with the coming of the Son of humanity, a position that finds some support in Luke 17:22–37, which equates the "revealing" of the Son of humanity with calamity. But if the promised return of Jesus (Acts 1:11) is what Luke understands by the "coming" or "revealing" of the Son of humanity,[5] this seems to be something still future for Luke, not past, as Jerusalem's demise probably is. It seems that

4. I accept that Jesus's predictions of Jerusalem's destruction are not so-called "prophecies after the event," but that is not to say that Luke's recounting of such predictions was not influenced by knowledge of the events themselves, even if the specific language used could well have been gleaned from Jewish Scripture. See Dodd, "Fall of Jerusalem."

5. If, for Luke, the return of Jesus and the coming of the Son of humanity are one and the same, Luke is rather sure about the manner of his return, to be like his departure (ascension), but noncommittal about the timing.

the destruction of Jerusalem falls between ascension and anticipated return, perhaps the third major event following the ascension of Jesus, the first and second being (1) the gifting of the Holy Spirit at Pentecost and subsequently to non-Jews (Acts 11) and (2) the mission in Jerusalem, then to wider Judea, Samaria, and beyond to Asia Minor, Macedonia, Achaia, and ultimately to Rome.[6] Luke recounts these earlier two and seems to presuppose the third (Jerusalem's destruction), all of which (and much else besides!) occur between ascension and return, the fourth aspect of Luke's eschatological schema.

Associated with the returning Son of humanity is some form of recompense (see Luke 9:26–27; 12:8–9). Is this event the same as "that Day," or "the judgment" (10:12–15; 11:30–32; 21:34), or the resurrection of all people? And what is the relation between the returning Son of humanity and the drawing near of divine reign (21:31–32), which has already drawn near enough to be present in the mission of Jesus (10:9, 11; 11:20; 17:20–21)? Acts 3:21 suggests that the ascension, which Luke here describes as Jesus's being received into heaven, lasts until the "restoration of all things," which in Acts is associated with the return of the ascended Jesus.

Beyond the arrival of the Son of humanity, as a fifth eschatological feature, Luke seems to envisage an age to come, with two "destinations" for persons: one is characterized as "reward in heaven" (Luke 6:23, 35; cf. 14:14), "eternal life" (10:25; 18:18, 30), habitation in "eternal dwellings" (16:9), or sitting at table in the kingdom of Jesus (22:29–30); the other is characterized as being cast into Gehenna (12:5; 16:19–31) or sharing the fate of the faithless (12:46). But Jesus's promise to the penitent bandit, "Today you shall be with me in paradise" (23:43), seems either to dispense with an age to come or to suggest that one may somehow experience it at the point of death. This dimension beyond (or perhaps before) the return of Jesus is the most hazy and amorphous aspect of Luke's eschatological schema.[7]

Conzelmann and Carroll on Luke's Eschatology

Since the 1950s, discussion of Luke's eschatology has tended to orient itself to the work of Hans Conzelmann, whether by acceptance of his basic thesis, by readjustment, or by outright repudiation. In 1952 he published *"Zur Lukasanalyse,"*[8] which presaged his publication of *Die Mitte der Zeit*

---

6. Acts 2:33 suggests that the ascension, "being lifted by God's right hand," results in Jesus's receiving the promised Holy Spirit, then pouring out the Spirit on his followers. This is despite the fact that Luke construes Jesus's mission as already being conducted by the power of the Spirit.

7. Some consider that "individual eschatology," the destiny of individuals at the point of death, is a crucial feature of Luke's eschatology. The texts on which this judgment rests are Luke 12:16–21; 16:9, 19–31; 23:39–43; Acts 7:55–60. Except incidentally, this dimension of Luke's eschatology is not my concern here.

8. Conzelmann, *"Zur Lukasanalyse."*

(The Middle of Time) two years later.[9] Conzelmann's central thesis is that Luke, writing toward the end of the first century CE, dealt with the cognitive dissonance caused by the delay of the return of Jesus, the parousia, by differentiating between salvation-historical eras with a view to dampening imminent eschatological expectation. No one disputes Conzelmann's exegetical industry, but it should be acknowledged that his basic thesis derives from his *Doctorvater*, Rudolf Bultmann, and had already been articulated in broad terms by other scholars within the Bultmann school, such as Vielhauer and Käsemann. Indeed, as Udo Schnelle points out, the basic features of Conzelmann's hypothesis had already been proposed a quarter-century earlier by Heinrich von Baer in his study of the role of the Holy Spirit in Luke's writings.[10] Perhaps working from the assumption that a redactor's changes to source materials reveal the redactor's mind better than what is retained unaltered, Conzelmann rightly discerned a certain dampening of eschatological fervor on Luke's part. But he overstated the degree to which Luke sought to reinterpret sayings of Jesus that apparently anticipated imminent fulfillment.

More than half a century later and after countless studies, one can say that many regard Luke's eschatological outlook to be more nuanced than Conzelmann allowed. A more balanced assessment of Luke's eschatological perspective is to be found in John Carroll's doctoral dissertation, *Response to the End of History: Eschatology and Situation in Luke–Acts.*[11] By careful analysis of texts that have featured in debates on Luke's eschatology, Carroll presents a cogent case for acknowledging that Luke did indeed seek to show that Jesus had not taught his disciples to expect his return prior to the time in which Luke was writing. Luke also sought to show that some of what Jesus had prophesied had already taken place in the mission endeavors recounted in Acts, thereby accenting the trustworthiness of Jesus's prophetic words. Moreover, according to Carroll, Luke's intent in showing that the return of Jesus should not have been expected before his own time of writing was nevertheless to reinforce imminent eschatological expectation among those for whom he wrote. For Luke, in other words, imminent eschatological expectation had not been appropriate prior to when he wrote, but it was the only appropriate stance after he wrote because only constant expectation of the imminent return of Jesus would ensure the proper attitude toward mission and an appropriately watchful moral ethos.[12]

9. Conzelmann, *Die Mitte der Zeit* (1954), ET as *The Theology of St. Luke*. These publications were followed by his commentary on Acts, *Die Apostelgeschichte* (1963).

10. Schnelle, *History and Theology*, 255n356. Baer's study was *Der Heilige Geist in den Lukasschriften* (1926).

11. Carroll, *Response to the End*.

12. A distillation of Carroll's perspective on Lukan eschatology may be found in Carroll et al., *Return of Jesus*, 26–45.

Carroll's analysis does more justice to Luke's eschatological outlook than Conzelmann's, but there is a sense in which Conzelmann's view of Lukan eschatology might have served Luke's audience better. For Conzelmann, Luke's redactional alterations to his sources, especially in his Gospel, effectively postponed the parousia to the indefinite future by making significant salvation-historical space for the mission of the church. On this view, Luke's adjustment away from imminent eschatology permitted early Christians to get on with business associated with the church's mission without being undermined by doubt resulting from Jesus's failure to return. Indeed, although this was probably not Luke's perspective, one might surmise that it is the basic stance encouraged by the retention of Luke's two-part history of Christian origins in the Christian canon.

In Carroll's more nuanced analysis, Luke effectively updated the more imminent Markan eschatological outlook by showing, via compositional arrangement as well as by redactional alteration, that the recent past since the prophetic mission of Jesus had been anticipated by Jesus. In other words, the prophetic words of Jesus indicate that he himself had expected a "holding back" of his return for a season to allow time for the church's mission to the nations. Luke also renovated the Markan eschatological perspective by indicating that in view of the (wholly expected) postponement of Jesus's return, his audience could—and should—expect that return at any time. Imminent eschatological expectation had not been appropriate before the completion of events written about by Luke, especially relating to the various missions of Philip, Peter and John, Stephen, and Paul. But now, after the events recounted in Luke's "second book" (cf. Acts 1:1), the only appropriate stance was readiness for Jesus's imminent return. With the benefit of hindsight, one can say that even if Luke did resolve (or alleviate) the so-called *Parousieproblematik*, on Carroll's reading he could not have done so for long.

However that may be, there is a further and more perplexing problem located at the heart of Luke's eschatology: the discrepancy between his peaceable Christology and moral ethos on one hand, and retributive aspects of his eschatology on the other. Most investigations of Luke's eschatology are concerned with whether or not his eschatological outlook is imminent, but whether or not it is inescapably retributive is more theologically pressing. Carroll identifies four interwoven variables in Luke's eschatological perspective: (1) timing, which has most exercised exegetes and interpreters; (2) content, meaning what Luke expected to occur at the eschaton; (3) "the significance of the eschaton, and of eschatology in general, in Luke's total perspective"; and (4) the situation that provoked Luke's eschatological outlook.[13] Though Carroll focuses on variables 1 and 4, timing and situation, my concern is with variable 2, the content or nature of Luke's eschatological expectation.

13. Carroll, *Response to the End*, 29–30.

In particular, given Luke's Jesus-inspired peace-shaped ethos, did he envisage that although divine visitation in Jesus was peaceable, this peaceableness would be exhausted by and by?

One best wrestles with this question by examining specific passages in Luke's two-part narrative, carefully attending to what is and—sometimes more important—what is not affirmed, and also entering into critical albeit respectful conversation with such texts. The remainder of this chapter explores three key future-oriented eschatological texts in Luke's Gospel, and the next chapter focuses on Acts.

In the Gospel according to Luke are three significant teaching blocks relating to future-oriented eschatology associated with the coming of the Son of humanity: Luke 12:35–48; 17:20–37; and 21:5–36. While the last of these is contextually parallel to the eschatological discourse of Jesus in Matthew 24–25 and Mark 13, both of Luke's earlier passages also have conceptual and verbal parallels with the one eschatological discourse of Matthew and Mark, albeit with little, if any, overlap with Luke 21.[14] For whatever reason, Luke decided against concentrating Jesus's eschatological instruction in one major block. He was not averse to repetition of material, presumably for emphasis, so perhaps his three future-oriented eschatological texts disclose a prominent concern with this theme. Especially noteworthy is that the earlier two of these three texts occur within Luke's central section, one in the first half and the second in the second half. In other words, these texts, which on the face of things feature foreseen eschatological vengeance, occur within the larger block of material bracketed by texts that feature Luke's peace emphasis (as well as warnings of judgment). To these texts we now turn, focusing on the nature or character of the event that comprises the eschatological horizon rather than its imminence or apparent postponement.

Expect the Unexpected (Luke 12:35–48)

Luke 12:35–48 sits within a larger section, 12:1–13:9, in which eschatological themes and motifs recur relatively frequently.[15] But the various parabolic sayings in 12:35–48 pertain particularly to Luke's prominent motif of vigilant readiness for the arrival of the Son of humanity. The passage begins by sounding the note of vigilance and continues by emphasizing the benefits experienced by servants who are ever ready to welcome home their master from a wedding feast. Indeed, these benefits are hyperbolically compared to the delight such servants would experience when their master rewards them by serving them at table—an implausible sociocultural scenario (see 17:7–10). Yet this implausible reversal of sociocultural status is of a piece with other aspects of

14. See Bock, *Luke 9:51–24:53*, 1420–21.
15. See Carroll, *Response to the End*, 53.

Luke's depiction of Jesus's mission and message. "In a wide variety of ways the overarching theme of salvation-as-reversal is narrated repeatedly in the Third Gospel," as Joel Green observes.[16] In Luke 12:37–38 this theme finds expression in an eschatological context. The returning master, according to Luke, is unpredictable and hence quite likely to turn the tables on those who both wait for him and wait on him.

Luke 12:37–38 stands out by virtue of its chiastic structure. It begins and ends with "macarisms" or blessings: "Blessed [are] those slaves. . . . Blessed are those [slaves]." And sandwiched between these two asseverations of blessing is the wildly implausible scenario of a master serving his slaves, introduced by the solemn declaration: "Truly I say to you. . . ." The following statement is contextually inapposite, introducing the motif of a break-in. This suggests that it is an isolated saying juxtaposed by Luke alongside the earlier analogy to reinforce the theme of unexpected arrival. In this respect, it does no harm, apart from detracting from the exquisitely crafted countercultural dominical saying preceding it. Seen from the perspective of this astonishing utterance, the warning about the Son of humanity's arrival in Luke 12:40 might well counsel readiness with respect to *outcome* no less than with respect to *timing*. Indeed, the astounding saying of Jesus in Luke 12:37b envisages the home-coming master (or Son of humanity) comporting himself in precisely the way Jesus himself characterizes his demeanor among his friends at his final meal with them. There, after posing the question about who has greater status, one who sits at table or one who serves, Jesus observes, "I myself am in among you as one serving" (Luke 22:27c). In Jesus's parabolic warning, the returning master turns the tables on those waiting for him in precisely the way Jesus characterizes his mission as one of service. On this reading, the coming Son of humanity might well surprise by his conduct as well as by his timing. In any case, here we catch a glimpse of moral congruence between the mission of Jesus and the conduct of the coming Son of humanity. As Robert Tannehill remarks in relation to this passage, "That the Lord who returns in glory still takes the role of servant for his people suggests that this is now an indelible part of his character."[17]

Careful readers will notice, however, that Luke presents this surprising scenario as contingent on the servants' watchfulness; only if the returning master is gladdened by his servants' alertness will he turn the sociocultural tables. But it is profoundly important that in this passage primacy is given to the positive consequences of eschatologically oriented vigilance. All too often readers skip over the promised blessing associated with the call for readiness in their rush to learn what is in store for those who are unprepared. In this larger passage, primacy belongs to Luke 12:35–40, which in tone and content

16. Green, *Theology of Luke*, 90.
17. Tannehill, *Luke*, 211.

is wholly positive. Only in response to Peter's question about whether his call is addressed solely to his disciples or to everyone does Jesus reinforce this call for readiness with a warning about the consequences of abusing power.

Jesus's response to Peter's query is puzzling because he apparently carries on with further parabolic teaching without addressing the question. The imaginary setting of a master's household remains the same, but now the focus shifts from readiness to responsible leadership. A macarism matching that of Luke 12:37 is found in 12:43, except that the latter slave is blessed if his master returns to find him going about his business, not alertly keeping watch. If, however, as a result of the master's delay, the slave mistreats those under his management and overindulges his appetites, he will receive, unexpectedly and without warning, vengeful retribution of a kind that snuffs out life and consigns the victim to the fate of the faithless.

It would seem, both on the basis of the distinction broached by Peter's question ("To us or to all?") and on the shift in focus from readiness to responsibility, that Jesus's grim warning is directed at those in leadership within the Christian community. It is not for all but for "us," meaning those who exercise leadership on behalf of the Lord. Jesus's question in Luke 12:42 implies as much: who is trustworthy and wise enough to place in a position of authority over other servants in order to look after them? Faithful service in that capacity will be rewarded, but unfaithful—that is, abusive and indulgent—leadership will inevitably be cut short.

This warning of punishment for irresponsible leadership is carried over into Luke 12:47–48, albeit with consideration for levels of culpability. Luke clearly envisages such teaching as having paraenetic value. Although the overriding concern within Luke 12:35–48 is uncertainty regarding the timing of the Son of humanity's arrival, as Carroll observes, "the governing motif is a paraenetic one. The burden of this pericope is its summons to a particular manner of living."[18] In other words, Luke recorded this block of eschatological instruction with a view to making a practical impact: to maintain an attitude of alertness and to encourage faithful and responsible behavior. Put positively, "concern with ethos and a living eschatological hope go hand in hand."[19] Put negatively, "with delay comes a lure toward complacent living correlated with uneschatological faith."[20] Succinctly stated, Luke's concern was to correct lukewarm faith and discipleship resulting from fading eschatological expectation.

More than this, however, if the shift in focus from readiness to responsibility at Luke 12:41 is correctly discerned, Luke was concerned to emphasize the seriousness of responsibility for leadership within the community of faith. The warnings of retribution in Luke 12:45–48b are principally directed at

18. Carroll, *Response to the End*, 55.
19. Ibid., 56.
20. Ibid., 59.

leaders within the community of faith, not all and sundry. But the primary point of Luke 12:35–48 is the overwhelmingly positive and surprising prospect of eschatological reversal: the master's serving servants, just as Jesus himself later characterizes his presence among his disciples at their last meal together. Luke 12:35–40 both comes first and is instruction for all. While the break-in motif at 12:39 is somewhat jarring, what Luke records of Jesus's eschatological instruction before Peter's query is wholly positive and entirely consistent with what else Luke recounts about Jesus's mission.

For those with leadership responsibility within the community of faith, however, additional responsibility brings inevitable retribution in its wake if such responsibility is abused or exploited. At one level, such a warning of scaled punishment for degrees of failure to exercise leadership with due care coheres with Luke's moral concern for the poor, powerless, and dispossessed. But it also needs to be said that for those leaders secure in the knowledge that they are in the right, the image of how power greater than their own can be used against faithless, irresponsible, or abusive behavior all too easily justifies their own retributive measures against inferiors. Thus, while Jesus's teaching in Luke 12:35–48 is primarily positive, even warning against abuse of positions of relative power, its image of a severely punitive master who deals in dicing no less than drubbing casts a somber moral shadow. After all, even though one who is complacent, unfaithful, irresponsible, or abusive may be encouraged or cowed to change in view of potentially imminent judgment in the form of retribution, the anticipated mode of judgment, no less than its inevitability or potential immediacy, also impacts on ethos. Anticipation of the strictly retributive mode of punishment envisaged in Luke 12:46 can scarcely be counted upon to inculcate the peaceful ethos Luke correlates with the reign of God present and pervasive in the mission of Jesus. And if this is so in parabolic mode, what is one to make of comparisons between the future arrival of the Son of humanity and the wholesale destruction associated with the stories of Noah and Lot?

At various points, Carroll contends that Luke 12:35–48 is significant because it "establishes a baseline" for eschatological expectation. Indeed, in concluding his discussion of this section, he writes: "This passage establishes a base from which eschatological hope may not—with respect to its content—waver. The precise date and hour of the arrival of the Son of man, the culminating eschatological image in Luke–Acts, are and must remain unknown."[21] But Carroll's qualifying statement regarding "the precise date and hour of the arrival of the Son of man" suggests that he means the *timing* of eschatological hope and not its *content*. If there can be no wavering from the *content* of

21. Ibid., 60. For similar statements, see 30 and 55. On the other hand, Carroll characterizes Luke 21:5–36 as "Luke's programmatic statement on eschatology" (103–4); cf. idem, "Parousia in the Synoptic Gospels and Acts," 35: "Luke 12:35–48 joins the motifs of the Lord's delayed return and his arrival at an unexpected hour. This pattern marks the extensive eschatological discourses in 17:22–18:8 and 21:5–36 as well."

eschatological hope depicted in Luke 12:35–48, the expected arrival of the Son of humanity is one of profoundly mixed blessings, and its anticipation likewise results in mixed moral blessings here and now.

Life Interrupted (Luke 17:20–37)

Luke 17:20–37 looks to be a discrete block of teaching, with little intrinsic connection to what comes before or after it.[22] Nevertheless, Luke 17:11 reminds readers that the larger context of this instruction is Jesus's journey to Jerusalem (and thence to God). Also noteworthy is that although this passage contains verbal and conceptual parallels with both Matthew and Mark, most such parallels are to the so-called Synoptic Apocalypse, of which Luke 21 is the contextual parallel. In some sense, therefore, Luke 17:20–37 is a "doublet" of Luke 21, which suggests that one should be read in light of the other.

Luke 17:20 has Pharisees asking Jesus about the timing of the arrival of God's reign, but in 17:22–37 Jesus instructs his disciples regarding the day(s) of the Son of humanity.[23] For Luke, the coming reign of God and the day(s) of the Son of humanity are clearly related[24] but not necessarily identical. Indeed, according to Luke 17:21b, the reign of God is a present reality, whereas the day(s) of the Son of humanity seems to be on the horizon.

Some hold that Jesus's saying in Luke 17:21b indicates that the reign of God is an inner, spiritual reality. More likely, Jesus's saying relates the reign of God to his own mission: God's reign need not be looked for here and there because it is already present and active in the mission of Jesus. If this be granted, the reign of God is to be understood in terms of the character of Jesus's own mission and message, an important dimension of which is peace with justice or justice leading to peace. In responding to the Pharisees' question about the timing of the arrival of divine reign by identifying that reign with his own mission, Jesus gives priority to what can be ascertained about divine sovereignty from the shape and content of his own character and mission. According to Udo Schnelle, "Luke expresses a basic principle of his eschatology in Luke 17:20–21,"[25] and this is what I understand that basic principle to be: the nature or character of divine reign is discernible in Jesus.

22. Carroll, *Response to the End*, 71–76, considers that this eschatological teaching block extends to Luke 18:8. Despite the eschatologically oriented conclusion of the parable comprising 18:1–8, however, the parable itself serves a different purpose from 17:20–37 (see 18:1). Even if Carroll is correct, his structural observations pertain more to the interpretation of Luke 18:1–8 than 17:20–37.

23. In this passage, Luke refers to "one of the days of the Son of humanity" (17:22), his "day" (17:24, 30), and "the days of the Son of humanity" (17:26). If there is any difference in meaning between these phrases, it is difficult to show what it is. I take the singular "day" to be primary and the other two phrases as contextual variations.

24. See Carroll, *Response to the End*, 73.

25. Schnelle, *Theology of the New Testament*, 517.

But might things ultimately be different? Will the returning Son of humanity display the selfsame reign of God or one with a different tenor? Luke 17:22–37 suggests the latter.

Although Luke interrelates the reign of God and the revealing of the Son of humanity by juxtaposing these sayings of Jesus in Luke 17:20–37, he clearly differentiates between them with respect to timing. Regarding the reign of God, it will not be said, "Look here" or "Look there," because it is a present reality. As for the day(s) of the Son of humanity, however, even if it is said, "Look there" or "Look here," Jesus advises not to take notice because it is not yet a present reality and will be unmistakable to all when that time comes, indeed, as unmistakable as lightning that lights up the entire (night?) sky (17:24). So although the reign of God is already present in the mission of Jesus, the day(s) of the Son of humanity lies in the future beyond the end of the mission of Jesus, which is characterized by his suffering and rejection by "this generation" (17:25). Nevertheless, if there is any cogency to my earlier inference that, for Luke, future eschatology takes its bearings from realized eschatology, its litmus test is the relation between divine reign impinging on the present in the mission of Jesus and the coming day(s) of the Son of humanity. From Luke's depiction of the reign of God, what one can be confident about with respect to what lies ahead is contingent upon the already-present reign of God in the mission of Jesus, which, as Willard Swartley shows, is inextricably related to the proclamation of good news, salvation, and peace: "All three terms, proclaim good news, salvation, and peace, are linked in various texts with 'kingdom of God,' so that Luke's view of 'gospelizing the kingdom of God' . . . is bringing to people *salvation and peace*."[26] At an interpretive level, therefore, Luke's own depiction of the character of divine reign in the mission of Jesus relativizes the retribution apparently associated with the day(s) of the Son of humanity in Luke 17:27, 29.

At this point in Jesus's mission, then, his eschatological instruction seems to envisage the revelation of the Son of humanity occurring not before the conclusion of his own mission but at any point thereafter. Not coming to grips with delay but with unexpectedness and catastrophe seems to be the burden of Jesus's instruction in these sayings. In seemingly ordinary times, as people are engaged in day-to-day activities, the day(s) of the Son of humanity will dawn suddenly, with catastrophic consequences. This, at least, seems to be the primary point of the analogies of Noah and Lot. All seemed normal, with each day like the one before, until Noah in his day entered the ark and Lot in his day left Sodom, at which point wholesale devastation ensued, by flood or by fire. "In accordance with such (events) will the day of the Son of humanity be revealed," Luke has Jesus say (17:30). "The Son of Man's day will follow

---

26. Swartley, *Israel's Scripture Traditions*, 81, emphasis original. "Gospelizing the reign of God" appears in Luke 4:43; 8:1; 16:16; Acts 8:12.

this same pattern," Darrell Bock paraphrases.[27] But in these analogies, does Jesus emphasize the unexpectedness, the calamitous consequences, or both?

The careful analysis of Luke 17:26–30 by Robert Tannehill demonstrates that the primary effect of the two similes relating the past days of Noah and Lot to the future day(s) of the Son of humanity is to emphasize the unanticipated interruption of the normal rhythm of daily life.[28] The explicit focus of these parallel sayings is not the wickedness of Noah and Lot's contemporaries but rather the mundane routine of daily life being interrupted. Nevertheless the exact repetition of the note of total destruction in Luke 17:27, 29,[29] especially following the reference to the rejection of the Son of humanity in 17:25, indicates that divine retribution analogous to that displayed against the kinds of wickedness associated with the biblical stories of Noah and Lot is in view (cf. 2 Pet. 2:5–7).

Tannehill seeks to mitigate the note of destruction in Luke 17:26–30: "Note that nothing definite is said about the kind of destruction which might come. This remains hidden behind the similes. Thus the indirectness of its language gives the text some freedom from the apocalyptic conceptions which were associated with it in early Christianity."[30] Although nothing definite is said about the specific form of destruction associated with the day(s) of the Son of humanity, that is not especially consoling if the coming destruction is near-indiscriminate divine retribution. Even the warning of Luke 17:31–32 intimates devastation no less than sudden urgency. Preservation from destruction might just be possible provided one does not falter at the decisive moment. One who hesitates, like Lot's wife, is lost! But that warning, together with the possibility of self-preservation it apparently holds out, is seemingly negated by Luke 17:33, which cautions that to attempt to preserve one's life is a recipe for losing it.

In this passage, therefore, Jesus forewarns his disciples that they should not anticipate the day (or days) of the Son of humanity until after the conclusion of his mission. Beyond that point, however, that day might be any day.[31] But Jesus's sayings about the disclosure of the day of the Son of humanity also associate that day with calamity and devastation. Despite the peace orientation of his mission and hence of the reign of God present in his mission, Jesus apparently envisages the day of the Son of humanity as a time of vengeance. But various sayings within this eschatological complex unsettle such a neat

27. Bock, *Luke 9:51–24:53*, 1434.

28. Tannehill, *Sword of His Mouth*, 118–22.

29. Carroll, *Response to the End*, 90, points out that in both of these verses, the word πάντας (*pantas*, all) occurs in an "emphatic final position"; cf. idem, "Parousia in the Synoptic Gospels and Acts," 36, claiming catastrophic disaster to be the burden of Luke 17:22–37.

30. Tannehill, *Sword of His Mouth*, 121; cf. idem, *Luke*, 261: "The nature of the interruption is not specified. It is hidden behind the biblical images. But it is destructive for those whose life is wrapped up in the activities of heedless people."

31. This particular point reiterates the burden of Jesus's sayings in Luke 12:35–40, but not the following clarifications (12:41–48)!

conclusion. The maxim of reversal in Luke 17:33 is one such saying, as are the apparently intrusive passion prediction in 17:25 and the inscrutable concluding aphorism, "Wherever the body, there also will eagles be gathered" (17:37b).

In light of Luke 17:22, 25, it is tempting to interpret Jesus's enigmatic saying in 17:37b about birds of prey gathering around a body as alluding to his own crucified body, surrounded by Roman soldiers.[32] In Luke 17:22 Jesus forewarns his disciples that a time is coming when they will long to see one of the days of the Son of humanity, but will be frustrated in their longing. The time between Jesus's arrest and crucifixion might well be such a time, but Luke 17:23 seems to discount this interpretive option. Luke 17:25, however, clearly refers to Jesus's own suffering and rejection by this generation as needing to occur before the conspicuous day(s) of the Son of humanity. As a result, the ominous saying about eagles gathering around a body might conceivably be (or at least might once have been) a forecast of Jesus's death at the hands of the Romans.

In context, however, it is difficult to sustain such an interpretation of this saying. Steven Bridge surveys some twenty interpretations of this saying (under seven categories),[33] none of which coincides with that considered above. Bock follows Howard Marshall in viewing this saying as emphasizing the finality of divine judgment intimated in the preceding images of division. For Bock,

> Judgment will be visible, universal, and permanent. Once separation occurs, there is no turning back. Vultures gather to feed off the dead bodies. . . . This point that once judgment is rendered it is final seems the most likely sense. . . . All will see the judgment's horrific finality. . . . The graphic and emotive image of vultures is a warning that the return will be a grim affair. The return of the Son of Man saves some but permanently condemns others. The return will be what was longed for in 17:22, but when it comes it will mean ultimate judgment for those who are not prepared. This is classic day-of-the-Lord warning to the unprepared.[34]

Since the theme of judgment implicitly pervades much of this eschatological passage, Bock and others are probably correct to interpret the culminating saying as foreboding judgment. But Bock extrapolates no less than he exegetes. Where is anything said about vultures feeding off dead bodies? And if the finality or permanence of judgment is intimated, that seems to be emphasized by Bock more than by Luke. Matthew's version of the birds-of-prey saying follows hard upon his parallel to the lightning saying (Matt. 24:26–28). By contrast,

32. The term for birds of prey used here by Luke probably refers to eagles. See Bridge, "*Where the Eagles Are Gathered*," chap. 3. Fitzmyer accepts a possible allusion in Luke 17:37b to the eagle emblem carried by Roman soldiers; see his *According to Luke (X–XXIV)*, 1173.

33. Bridge, "*Where the Eagles Are Gathered*," 3–20; cf. Bock, *Luke 9:51–24:53*, 1439–40.

34. Bock, *Luke 9:51–24:53*, 1440; cf. I. H. Marshall, *Gospel of Luke*, 669.

Luke seems to have separated these (originally contiguous?) sayings to enclose the bulk of this eschatological passage. While the latter saying is perhaps more ominous, it probably parallels the lightning saying in meaning, especially if it envisages birds of prey circling in flight, thereby comprising parallel images set in the sky. No less than when lightning illuminates the entire sky, the day of the Son of humanity will be as *unmistakable* as the presence (and perhaps even the location) of a body from gathering birds of prey.

By contrast with Bock (and the interpretive tendency he represents), Bridge's study of the enigmatic eagles saying in Luke 17:37b emphasizes deliverance rather than destruction. For Bridge, the eagles saying is to be interpreted metaphorically, with the eagles understood as the righteous and the body as the resurrected and exalted Lord. Rather than focusing on the fate of those who will be destroyed, "Luke presents Jesus's saying as a word of comfort to the elect, assuring them of their deliverance from the inevitable destruction of the final days."[35] In support of this thesis, Bridge discusses the eagles saying both within the literary context of Luke 17:11–18:14 and in light of eschatological emphases in Luke 21. By examining ornithological references from antiquity, Bridge shows that Luke probably envisaged the gathering of eagles rather than vultures. He also argues that Luke was influenced by a Jewish deliverance tradition that features eagle imagery.

There is much to commend in Bridge's study. His investigations into ancient ornithology are instructive, and his literary and redactional analyses of eschatological texts are both insightful and informative. His interpretation of the eagles saying also finds strong support among patristic commentators, which Bridge helpfully catalogs in an appendix.[36] Especially appealing is that an emphasis on eschatological deliverance resonates with Luke's peace theme. The alleged influence of Jewish deliverance traditions that employ eagle imagery in analogous ways is, however, suggestive rather than compelling. Moreover, although Bridge's deliverance-focused interpretation of Luke 17:37 resonates with the rescue of Noah and Lot from calamity, it is doubtful whether such an interpretation resonates with the tenor of 17:26–30 as a whole, in which total destruction is the dominant note. Indeed, even in Bridge's view, Luke 17:37 is a text of deliverance only because it is addressed to "survivors" rather than "victims" of eschatological destruction. In other words, Bridge's deliverance-focused reading of Luke 17:37 presupposes eschatological vengeance, even if addressed to those who will (apparently) escape it. As a result, as appealing as Bridge's deliverance-focused interpretation of Luke 17:37 is, it fails to address the prospect of eschatological vengeance on the day of the Son of humanity.

35. Bridge, *"Where the Eagles Are Gathered,"* 20.
36. Ibid., 151–55. Among recent commentators, Bridge's interpretation of the eagles saying in Luke 17:37 is supported by John Nolland and François Bovon.

Even if the eagles saying also intimates judgment, as seems likely, consideration should nevertheless be given to Luke's coupling of its "framing twin," the lightning saying, with the passion prediction of Luke 17:25. Bock observes that this passion prediction is one of six in Luke's Gospel and the only one set within the context of future-oriented eschatological instruction.[37] If the lightning saying in Luke 17:23–24 is qualified by the reference to Jesus's suffering and rejection in 17:25, perhaps the eagles saying in 17:37 harks back not only to the lightning saying but also to the passion prediction. In other words, inasmuch as Jesus cannot look ahead to the day(s) of the Son of humanity without presaging his inevitable suffering, perhaps the eagles saying resonates with the Son of humanity's suffering no less than it anticipates the unmistakable future disclosure of the selfsame Son of humanity. The "body" of Luke 17:37 may not signify the dead body of Jesus, as suggested earlier, but it may recall the suffering, rejection, and death experienced by the Son of humanity before his conspicuous future "day." If so, this perplexing climactic saying functions to tether the future revelation of the Son of humanity (17:24, 30) to the historical mission of the suffering Son of humanity (17:25), in whom divine reign was embodied and enacted peaceably.

Both the passion prediction in Luke 17:25 and the maxim of reversal in 17:33 look conspicuously out of place. Not only so, but both also echo the decisive passage in Luke 9:18–27, in which Peter identifies Jesus as God's Messiah, and Jesus responds by commanding silence, by predicting his suffering, rejection, death, and resurrection, and also by teaching on discipleship. Luke 17:25 echoes 9:22, the first of Jesus's various passion predictions in Luke's narrative (cf. 9:44; 12:50; 13:33; 17:25; 18:31–33). Reinforcing the intertextual links between Luke 17:20–37 and 9:18–27 is 17:33, a "doublet" of 9:24, which itself is a close contextual parallel of Matthew 16:25 and Mark 8:35.[38] To explain why Luke reiterates this maxim of reversal within this particular context has proved challenging to interpreters. Perhaps, as John York argues, "The aphorism of v. 33 presents the bi-polar reversal, again in the context of two opposing attitudes that were introduced in vv. 31–32. Verse 33a represents the fate of Lot's wife, who tried to hold on to the past and turned back, thus losing her life (Gen. 19.26). Verse 33b represents the positive result of not returning for one's possessions at the coming of the Son of man (v. 31)."[39]

To my mind, however, the maxim of reversal in Luke 17:33 unsettles rather than illustrates. Within an eschatological context, it reiterates the counterintuitive rule of discipleship that unsettles any assurances about life and its

37. Bock, *Luke 9:51–24:53*, 1430–31. Four of Luke's passion predictions are explicit (9:22, 44; 17:25; 18:32–33), and two are implicit (12:50; 13:32–33).

38. Matthew 16:25 itself echoes 10:39, whereas Luke's "doublet" in 17:33 echoes the saying in its contextually parallel threefold form (Matt. 16:25; Mark 8:35; Luke 9:24). There is also a Johannine version of this saying in John 12:25.

39. York, *The Last Shall Be First*, 84–85.

security. In any case, the key point about both this saying and the passion prediction in Luke 17:25 is the reminiscence that they jointly effect between the future-oriented instruction of this passage and 9:18–27, in which both passion prediction and maxim of reversal occur together for the first time at a crucial juncture in Luke's narrative.

Reading Luke 17:20–37 in reminiscence of 9:18–27 raises some interesting interpretive possibilities. First, and most important, the earlier passage makes plain that in Luke's perspective the Son of humanity is none other than Jesus himself. Second, it makes crystal clear that Jesus's identity as "the Messiah of [or "from"] God" (9:20) entails suffering, rejection by religious authorities, premature death, and resurrection (by God) (9:22). Third, one who follows this Messiah of God must participate in the quality of life displayed by the Messiah, which involves self-renunciation and a willingness to relinquish life. The way of the Messiah of God is the way of God in the world. Finally, Luke 9:26, which closely parallels Mark 8:38, indicates that if one is ashamed of Jesus and his words, the Son of humanity will be ashamed of that person when he comes in glory.[40] As argued earlier in connection with Mark's ethical eschatology, to be shamed in the glorious presence of the Son of humanity undoubtedly bespeaks judgment but not necessarily destruction.

In view of the various intertextual links between Luke 17:20–37 and 9:18–27, one is entitled to ask whether the later passage may be read in light of the former. The clear thematic connections between the two passages are suggestive. As a result, I am inclined to interpret the saying in Luke 17:33 as something of a reality check. In view of Jesus's mission, which makes divine reign present, what matters most is to lose one's life after the pattern of God's Messiah (cf. 17:25), for so to lose one's life is to be ready for the day(s) of the Son of humanity—at any time. While the day of the Son of humanity is associated with wholesale devastation, borrowing from traditional imagery, this underscores the inevitability rather than the mode of judgment. Judgment in the day(s) of the Son of humanity is inevitable, impossible to anticipate, and total, but it is nevertheless the judgment of the selfsame Jesus whose peaceable mission made present and active God's sovereign reign. In view of the precise manner in which the mission of Jesus fulfilled scriptural promises, strictly vindictive retribution on the part of the Son of humanity would hardly qualify as coming in glory.

In this connection, it is worth reflecting on Jesus's words regarding his mission in Luke 12:49–53, which follow hard upon his first block of future-oriented eschatological teaching. Speaking of his historic mission, Jesus spits out these words:

40. The coming of the Son of humanity in glory in Luke 9:26 is also echoed in the motif of the day(s) or revealing of the Son of humanity in 17:22, 24, 26, 30—yet one more intertextual connection between these passages.

I came to cast fire upon the earth, and how I wish it were already alight. I have a drowning by which to be drowned,[41] and how distressed I am until that occurs. Do you suppose that I arrived to establish peace on earth? Not so, I tell you, but rather division!

As one reads on, however, it becomes clear that here Jesus refers to the inevitable *impact* of his mission rather than the reason, the purpose, or even the means of his mission. His mission provokes judgment, lethal retaliation, and familial divisions, but these are neither its intent nor means. Here is prophetic hyperbole relating to his current mission, which, if apposite to Jesus's historic mission, might also be apposite to the eschatological day of the Son of humanity.

This is not an interpretation that will find support in most exegetical treatments of Luke 17:20–37. Nevertheless, various factors nudge me in this direction. First, Luke's juxtaposition of sayings about the eschatological day of the Son of humanity with a *preceding* saying about the presence of divine reign in his historical mission provokes the question of the relation between realized and future eschatology. Second, strong intertextual resonances between this passage and Luke 9:18–27 lead me to read the later passage in light of the former. Third, the problematic saying in Luke 17:33 suggests that one should not read the passage within which it jarringly sits at face value. Fourth, like Luke 12:35–48, so also 17:20–37 falls within Jesus's journey to Jerusalem, which is bracketed by the theme of peace. As Carroll writes, "Our interpretation of the meaning and literary function of 17:20–18:8 must be guided by its placement in the Gospel narrative. This passage is the second of three large blocks of eschatological teachings located within the travel narrative."[42] And fifth, Luke is the evangelist of peace because he discerned within the mission and message of the Messiah of God the peaceable reign of God. It may be that he lost sight of the peaceable way of God when writing about the anticipated day(s) of the Son of humanity, but if so, he also provided readers with resources for challenging an easy association between the eschatological disclosure of the Son of humanity and vindictive vengeance.

The Day of Deliverance (Luke 21:5–36)

By contrast with Matthew and Mark, who depict Jesus as delivering his final discourse in the hearing of disciples alone while seated on the Mount of Olives,

41. In Luke 12:50a, Jesus uses the language of baptism or immersion, but since this can hardly mean anything other than his death, the image of drowning seems apposite.

42. Carroll, *Response to the End*, 74. While I concur with Carroll on the interpretive significance of the narrative placement of Luke 17:20–37, my interpretive judgments differ largely because my focus differs. In this citation, Carroll holds Luke 17:20–18:8 to be a unified block of eschatological teaching, and he also considers the parable of the nobleman-king in Luke 19:11–27 to pertain to Luke's future-oriented eschatology.

it is within the very temple itself that Luke presents Jesus both prophesying the temple's demise and clarifying (to some degree!) the relation between Jerusalem's destruction and the future arrival of the Son of humanity, seemingly in the hearing of an audience much larger than his disciples (see 20:45; 21:5, 7, 37–38). In Conzelmann's words,

> Luke abandons the symbolism of Mark's setting, according to which Jesus speaks from the Mount of Olives "over against" the Temple, and transfers the speech to the Temple, before an audience which has been listening to Jesus each day. This is in keeping with Luke's scheme, according to which there are before the Last Supper only two places in which Jesus is found: in the Temple by day, and on the Mount of Olives by night (xxi, 37f.).[43]

For Luke, therefore, the clearest description of Jerusalem's inevitable fate issues from within the very temple itself and is apparently overheard by "all the people" (20:45). This adds to the dramatic impact of Jesus's third block of eschatological instruction in Luke's Gospel. But what does Jesus's teaching in Luke 21 contribute to a consideration of retributive eschatology in relation to peaceful ethos in this Gospel? As the third and culminating block of eschatological instruction, it is clearly significant for that reason alone.[44] One expects to find previously articulated eschatological themes and emphases reinforced or clarified. This turns out to be the case—in at least four respects.

First, Luke's eschatological timeline is clarified considerably,[45] while still preserving indeterminacy regarding the timing of the Son of humanity's arrival. Political upheaval and international conflict are inevitable but not signs of an imminent end (21:9–10a). On the immediate horizon, persecution will undoubtedly come to those loyal to Jesus (21:12–18). This is the time for witness (21:13), a time about which Luke writes in Acts but that presumably extends until at least the shaking of heavenly powers (21:25–26). Jerusalem's demise (21:20–24) falls within this time of witness but is never recounted by Luke (perhaps because that event postdates Paul's sojourn in Rome). These "days of vengeance" (21:22a, 23b) mark the beginning of the "times of the Gentiles" (21:24), which must also precede the Son of humanity's arrival.

Beyond this, however, things are hazy, although some clarity is achieved by reading Luke 21:10–11 as a preview of the general sequence of events expected to occur in the near future. According to Carroll, by the addition of uniquely Lukan references to heavenly portents in 21:11, "Luke employs vv. 9–11 to

---

43. Conzelmann, *Theology of St. Luke*, 125.

44. Carroll, *Response to the End*, 103–4: "Luke presents his eschatological perspective with greatest clarity and elaboration in the eschatological discourse of Luke 21:5–36, which amounts to a programmatic statement on the subject of last things in relation to history."

45. Compare ibid., 107–14, speaking of "eschatological phase clarification in Luke 21:5–36."

provide an overview of the entire eschatological scenario."[46] On my reading, however, Luke 21:10–11 (without 21:9) is a parenthetical eschatological
preview: first come international conflicts, then natural disasters, and finally
heavenly portents. The first two sociopolitical and natural phenomena overlap
with the time of witness and the times of the Gentiles. Jerusalem's destruction is an instance of war and disorder, but not a sign of the end (21:9). Only
signs in the heavens, the result of disruption to heavenly powers, signal that
the Son of humanity's arrival is imminent (21:25–28).

Much depends on reading Luke 21:10–11 as an "eschatological preview."
Later in the discourse, dread-inducing signs in the heavens are not sharply dif-
ferentiated from the prophecy of Jerusalem's siege and trampling (21:25–26).
Such heavenly signs are introduced by the imprecise phrase "and there will
be," without any explicit temporal demarcation from the prior description of
Jerusalem's "days of vengeance" (21:22). This encourages some scholars, such
as Allan McNicol and Tom Wright, to interpret the heavenly signs as scriptural
metaphors for Jerusalem's destruction.[47] This is not far-fetched, especially
in view of Josephus's description of various heavenly signs accompanying
Jerusalem's siege and destruction.[48]

If Luke 21:10–11 comprises a parenthetical preview of what must precede
the Son of humanity's arrival, however, the heavenly signs of 21:25–26 likely
follow, rather than parallel, Jerusalem's destruction. Various considerations
combine to confirm that Luke 21:10–11 functions to preview the eschatological sequence of events in the remainder of the discourse, events before the
Son of humanity's arrival: first, only Luke has Jesus refer to heavenly signs
at this early stage in the discourse (cf. Matt. 24:7–8; Mark 13:8); second,
Luke's uniquely intrusive introduction to Jesus's words at the beginning of
21:10, including its phrasing, suggests that what follows serves as a summary; third, the double use of the enclitic particle τε (*te*) along with καί (*kai*)
in 21:11 couples together (1) great earthquakes with famines and plagues
and (2) terrors with great signs from the heavens; finally, the continuation
of the discourse in 21:12, "Before all these things, however . . . ," reads like
a backtracking resumption. The opening section of Jesus's response to the
question posed in Luke 21:7 concludes with the words, "for these things
must occur first, but the end is by no means imminent" (21:9). Following

46. Ibid., 112.

47. See McNicol, *Jesus' Directions for the Future*, 125–42. For the bulk of Luke 21, McNicol
considers Luke to have reworked Matt. 24 rather than Mark 13. For Wright, not only heavenly
signs but also the coming of the Son of humanity signify Jerusalem's destruction. His views
are expressed in various publications, as in the first two volumes of his theology of the New
Testament, *Christian Origins and the Question of God*, and in *Surprised by Hope*. For a suc-
cinct statement, see Wright, *Luke for Everyone*, 249–60. To date, Wright seems to afford Luke
a privileged role for interpreting the synoptic tradition and indeed Jesus himself.

48. See Josephus, *Jewish War* 6.286–315. For Josephus, however, such signs apparently accompanied the Roman destruction of Jerusalem rather than symbolized it.

immediately thereafter, the words in Luke 21:10–11 interrupt the flow of the discourse thus far to form a new beginning: "*At that time* he *was saying* to them, 'People groups will rise against people groups and kingdoms against kingdoms; not only will there be great earthquakes but also, from place to place, famines and plagues, not only terrors but also great signs from heaven.'"

Instead of identifying only the "beginning of end-time labor pains" (Matt. 24:8; Mark 13:8) at this early point in Jesus's final discourse, in Luke's reconfigured presentation, Jesus previews the full sweep of events preceding the coming of the Son of humanity. Read as an eschatological *preview*, the summary statement in Luke 21:10–11 enables one to differentiate between the destruction of Jerusalem and heavenly signs later in the discourse.

Second, beyond clarifying the eschatological timeline, Luke reiterates and reinforces his emphatic note of judgment against Jerusalem. Although he incorporates Jerusalem's destruction into his overarching eschatological timetable, he makes plain that this event does not signal the end; rather, the trampling of Jerusalem initiates an indefinite period of the Gentiles. Luke's main point regarding Jerusalem is that the city's demise comprises "days of vengeance" in fulfillment of Scripture (21:22), a view in keeping with the idea expressed earlier that Jerusalem's destruction is divine judgment for Israel's rejection of Jesus.

In Conzelmann's view, Luke dissociates Jerusalem's destruction from eschatological hope,[49] whereas for Carroll, Luke distinguishes but does not separate Jerusalem's desolation from the Son of humanity's arrival: "Luke's task, in clarifying the relation of Jerusalem's demise to the parousia, was to correct a mistaken identification of the two, yet without severing their connection."[50] Once again, Carroll's reading is perhaps truer to Luke than Conzelmann's, but from the perspective of hindsight, Conzelmann's interpretation might have served Luke (and his readers!) better. Moreover, especially with regard to content rather than timing, retaining a connection or relation between Jerusalem's "days of vengeance" and the arrival of the Son of humanity is ethically ambivalent because the destruction of Jerusalem can then be seen as paradigmatic of eschatological judgment, as Joseph Fitzmyer illustrates:

> The Lucan discourse looks back at the catastrophe in Jerusalem (A.D. 70) in a microcosmic view; it sees the crisis that the earthly coming of Jesus brought into the lives of his own generation, but sees it now as a harbinger of the crisis which Jesus and his message, and above all his coming as the Son of Man, will bring to "all who dwell upon the entire face of the earth" (21:35). Both of the events are examples for Luke of God's judgment, even if their temporal connection is

49. Conzelmann, *Theology of St. Luke*, 133.
50. Carroll, *Response to the End*, 112.

no longer that which Mark stressed. As Jerusalem met its fate, so will all who dwell upon the face of the earth.[51]

This interpretive correlation between the "days of vengeance" for Jerusalem and what is expected in conjunction with the arrival of the Son of humanity is much more troubling than the vexed question of the temporal relation between these events. For this reason, no less than with respect to clarification of Luke's eschatological timeline, much depends on how Luke 21:10–11 is understood. If this passage is read as an eschatological preview, it compensates in advance, so to speak, for the absence in Luke 21:25 of any explicit demarcation between the description of Jerusalem's destruction and anticipated heavenly signs, thereby putting distance between them—both chronologically and, in view of 21:28, theologically.

Third, Luke again couples the concepts of the Son of humanity's arrival and the nearness of the reign of God. In Luke 21:27–28 Jesus tethers the future arrival of the Son of humanity to heavenly signs (21:25–26); in 21:31 he reiterates the point, only this time referring to the nearness of God's reign. This brings these concepts into even closer relation than earlier, in Luke 17:20–37. Here they are more or less synonymous,[52] whereas earlier they were simply juxtaposed, without obvious correlation. This strengthens the case for the interpretive judgment that, with respect to Luke's theology, future-oriented eschatology should be understood in relation to realized eschatology. In Jesus's mission, the character of divine reign has already been disclosed, and it is precisely that reign already encountered in Jesus's past mission that is anticipated as arriving in its fullness at the Son of humanity's future coming. The reign of God already attested to in the mission and message of Jesus draws near yet again when the Son of humanity comes with power and glory.

Fourth, as earlier, eschatological anticipation serves paraenetic ends. Luke 21:34–36 echoes the by-now-familiar exhortations to remain alert so as not to be caught unawares and to desist from moral torpor. As Carroll observes,

> Eschatological phase clarification is not for Luke an end in itself. This "revisionist history" is not a theoretical project, but rather serves a governing pastoral motive. In a fashion anticipated by the paraenetic tenor of Luke 12:35–48 and 17:20–18:8, Luke 21 approaches the problem of eschatology with an eye to the ethos of the Lukan community. Luke's interest in eschatological phase clarification corrects a faulty reading of the eschatological timetable that has rendered imminent future hope suspect in his own situation.[53]

51. Fitzmyer, *According to Luke (X–XXIV)*, 1329. So too Bock, *Luke 9:51–24:53*, 1675: "It would seem that Luke sees in Jerusalem's collapse a preview, but with less intensity, of what the end will be like."
52. See Tannehill, *Luke*, 307–8.
53. Carroll, *Response to the End*, 115.

While one can agree that eschatological clarification on Luke's part served a pastoral motive, indeed, that Luke addressed "the problem of eschatology with an eye to the ethos of the Lukan community," it must also be acknowledged that Luke bequeathed to his audience, both intended and unintended, another pastoral problem relating to eschatology and ethos. Although Luke was not alone in this respect, it is morally disconcerting that this evangelist of peace looked forward to eschatological vengeance meted out on the day of the Son of humanity. That seems to be accurate in relation to the eschatological instruction of Luke 12 and 17, but is it true to Luke 21?

Although in most ways Luke 21 either reinforces or clarifies previously articulated eschatological themes and emphases, in one important respect eschatological expectation in Luke 21 differs from expectations sounded earlier: the absence of vindictive retribution *explicitly* associated with the arrival of the Son of humanity. The Son of humanity is expected to come with power and glory (21:27), but not with exterminating sword or punishing staff (cf. 12:45–48a); the coming of the Son of humanity is a time of deliverance (21:28), not wholesale destruction (cf. 17:27, 29). Commenting on the coming of the Son of humanity in Luke 21:27–28, Fitzmyer writes:

> He will bring deliverance to Christian disciples who will have to learn to "shape up" and hold their heads high in joyful expectation. For the judgment passed on Jerusalem merely presages a judgment of greater dimension and import. As Jerusalem was faced with a crisis when Jesus appeared to teach there, so will the world be faced when he comes as the Son of Man. In contrast to the judgment to be passed on the world, Christian disciples will then realize that their deliverance is near.[54]

The theme of judgment is certainly sounded in Luke 21:34–36, but not in such a way that judgment must be seen solely in terms of retributive vengeance. Luke 21:25–36 undoubtedly affirms judgment before the Son of humanity but characterizes his coming with power and glory as effecting "your redemption."[55] Lest the Son of humanity's arrival be considered a "time of deliverance" solely for his own, as Fitzmyer infers, it should be recalled that the audience of Jesus's temple discourse in Luke 21 is not restricted to his disciples, even though some of the discourse applies only to them (21:12–19).[56] Much mayhem is

54. Fitzmyer, *According to Luke (X–XXIV)*, 1349.
55. Even Bock, who emphasizes the theme of retributive judgment in Luke 21, recognizes that Luke 21:28, 36 are essentially nonretributive. Luke 21:28, like Mark 13:27, focuses on redemption, and Luke 21:36 is likely a positive image of "standing with approval in deliverance." See Bock, *Luke 9:51–24:53*, 1687, 1694–95.
56. Compare Carroll, *Response to the End*, 113, referring to the arrival of the Son of humanity, "bringing with him redemption of the faithful." Carroll and Fitzmyer's restrictive interpretation of Luke 21:28 might be true to Luke, but it is nevertheless an elaboration of the text that reads, "because your redemption nears."

forecast in Luke 21, but only that relating to Jerusalem's demise is explicitly associated with divine judgment. One can appreciate why Lukan interpreters fasten on Jerusalem's "days of vengeance" as the template and precursor for eschatological judgment, but it deserves to be recognized that this interpretive inference is precisely that, without explicit textual grounding, and that whatever premonitions of judgment are signaled from Luke 21:25 onward do not construe divine judgment as either inherently vengeful or exclusively retributive.

Reviewing Luke's Retributive Eschatology

From what Luke records of Jesus's eschatological teaching, what may be said about the content of his future-oriented eschatology? The primary point, which cannot be emphasized too strongly, is that Luke's eschatological horizon is inextricably associated with the Son of humanity, whether the unexpected arrival of the Son of humanity (12:40), the inevitable and unmistakable day of the revelation of the Son of humanity (17:22–24, 26, 30), or the arrival of the Son of humanity with power and glory (21:27, 36). For Luke, however, this is the selfsame Son of humanity known in Jesus. Only if the future-coming Son of humanity is someone other than Jesus or a fundamentally changed Jesus can the judgment associated with his arrival be solely retributive. It may be that with respect to Jesus's (self-designated) role as Son of humanity, Luke's Christology suffers from some form of dissociative identity disorder, but careful examination of the relevant texts indicates that the problem may be more one of diagnosis than of genuine disorder. In Luke's climactic block of eschatological teaching, anticipation of the arrival of the Son of humanity is bereft of the note of eschatological vengeance; and in the two earlier blocks of eschatological instruction, the theme of retributive judgment, while present, is relativized by other textual details.

Furthermore, both of the two earlier blocks of eschatological instruction occur within Luke's central section, in which all of Jesus's instruction (on whatever theme) is enclosed within bracketing peace texts, which thereby relativize intimations of eschatological vengeance. On its own, this interpretive observation might be easily dismissed, but it coheres with Luke's broader concern with peace as the fruit of justice.[57] More important, it also coheres with what might be described as Luke's Christology of peace, according to

57. Lest I be misunderstood, I here reiterate that biblical justice is broader than strictly retributive (or distributive) justice. See Swartley, "Relation of Justice/Righteousness to *Shalom/Eirēnē*," esp. 30: "Compassion and mercy are inherent to justice in the biblical understanding." See also Neville, "Justice and Divine Judgement," in which I argue that certain scriptural construals of justice transcend and transfigure conceptions featuring strict reward, recompense, or retribution. "Theologically and ethically," I conclude, "biblical conceptions of justice move beyond notions of strict distribution and retribution towards ideals of restoration and transformation."

which the entirety of Jesus's mission and message comprises not only divine visitation but also a divine announcement of peace. Warnings of future retribution uttered by one whose mission as a whole is characterized as a divine announcement of peace and sounded within a narrative context framed by peace texts—such warnings are fundamentally different in kind from the same (or similar) warnings unrelated in any discernible way to a Christology of peace and a peaceable ethos and ethic.

Wholly consistent with a Christology of peace and a peaceable ethos and ethic is the literary datum that Jesus's warnings of eschatological violence are themselves enclosed within eschatological expectations that are nonretributive. Read together, Luke 12:35–40 and 21:25–36 envisage an eschatological scenario much more in keeping with the tenor of the historic mission and message of Jesus. Earlier I noted Carroll's view both that Luke 12:35–48 "establishes a base from which eschatological hope may not—with respect to its content—waiver" and that Luke 21:5–36 is "Luke's programmatic statement on eschatology." I here concur, provided that Luke 12:35–40 is regarded as the base with respect to the content of eschatological hope, and 21:25–36 is considered eschatologically programmatic. Read this way, Luke's retributive expressions of eschatological judgment are enclosed within—and hence relativized by—nonretributive, indeed, surprisingly benign expressions of eschatological judgment. Moreover, insofar as Luke 21 is regarded as the "programmatic doublet" of Jesus's eschatological teaching in Luke 17:22–37, the hope of redemption at the coming of the Son of humanity (21:27–28) draws the venom and vehemence from the (implied) retribution conveyed by comparing the day(s) of the Son of humanity with the devastation that befell those who lived in the days of Noah and Lot.

Notwithstanding all that has been said to mitigate the adverse theological and moral ramifications of Luke's texts of eschatological terror, his conception of the destruction of Jerusalem as retribution for rejecting the divine overture of peace in Jesus's mission remains perplexing. This is especially problematic because although Luke dissociates Jerusalem's destruction from the arrival of the Son of humanity in power and glory, nevertheless it marks an important phase in Luke's salvation-historical scheme—the beginning of the times of the nations (or Gentiles). If the God whose announcement of peace was conveyed through the peaceable mission of Jesus is nevertheless responsible for the retribution meted out on Jerusalem for rejecting that peace announcement, this theological interpretation of Jerusalem's destruction undermines Luke's peace emphasis and suggests that ultimately the day(s) of the Son of humanity might well be as violent. Perhaps, after all, Luke–Acts is, as Garry Trompf contends, but another "narrative of retributive justice."[58]

---

58. See Trompf, *Early Christian Historiography*, chap. 2: "The first Christian historian: Luke and his two books." Trompf's argument is discussed toward the end of the next chapter.

Having examined the major blocks of future-oriented eschatological instruction in Luke's Gospel, it is time to turn to pertinent passages in the Acts of the Apostles. Do the notes of retributive eschatology in Luke's Gospel resound through Acts? If the peace theme is somewhat muted in Acts, at least by comparison with the Gospel, is this reflected in eschatological texts? These questions are answered in rather surprising ways in the following chapter.

5

"In the Same Way"

Restoration Eschatology in Acts

choing earlier evaluations, Richard Pervo declares: "Eschatology, long a burning issue in the study of the Gospel [of Luke], is not a prominent topic in Acts."[1] In the International Critical Commentary on Acts, however, C. K. Barrett gives eschatology pride of place in his overview of the theology of Acts.[2] Eschatology is undoubtedly a less prominent topic in Acts than in Luke's Gospel, but that does not imply that eschatological convictions are either unimportant or on the retreat to oblivion. The theme of eschatological fulfillment is prominent early in Acts, most notably in three crucial passages within the first three chapters of the book, and eschatological motifs surface at various points later in Acts. Responding to evaluations like that of Pervo (above), John Carroll shows how certain events narrated in Acts effectively fulfill Jesus's prophetic words in Luke 21:12–19, thereby identifying the period covered by Acts with the designated time of witness and persecution in Luke's eschatological schema.[3] For Carroll, the correlation between Acts and a particular section of Luke 21 by means of clear verbal echoes makes imminent eschatological expectation otiose in Acts; events within Acts fall within a particular period of salvation-history prophesied by Jesus. Be that

1. Pervo, *Acts*, 25.
2. Barrett, *Acts of the Apostles*, 2:lxxxii–iii.
3. Carroll, *Response to the End*, 117–19.

as it may, it is nevertheless striking that both eschatological fulfillment and eschatological expectation in Acts are more in keeping with the evangelist of peace than certain passages within Luke's Gospel.

The opening chapters of Acts naturally set the stage for the rest of Luke's narrative, although some restrict this stage-setting function to the first two chapters, which recount the ascension and the first Christian Pentecost. In the opening chapter of Acts, Jesus presents himself to his disciples over a forty-day period, promises that they will be baptized with the Holy Spirit so as to be empowered for mission, and ascends into heaven, after which Peter instigates the replacement of the twelfth apostle. In chapter 2, the promised empowering by the Spirit occurs at Pentecost, and Peter delivers a speech that interprets the event and encourages a positive response. This is followed by a brief, idealized summary of early Christian solidarity. At the beginning of chapter 3, a lame man is healed through Peter and John, no doubt as a further demonstration of apostolic Spirit empowerment but perhaps also as an intimation that the eschatological era has dawned. As in chapter 2, the event is followed by another interpretive speech by Peter. During these first three chapters, the apostolic witness is unhindered,[4] but chapter 4 opens with official intimidation against the apostolic proclamation focused on the resurrection of Jesus from the dead. However one views the first three chapters of Acts in relation to the remaining narrative, it is within these opening chapters that Luke's most explicit eschatological teaching in Acts occurs.

Ascension and Promised Return (Acts 1:1–11)

It is difficult to determine where the opening passage of Acts ends—whether at verse 5, 8, 11, or 14. On the one hand, Acts 1:12–14 serves well to conclude Luke's introduction, since it recounts the original apostles (apart from the betrayer) ensconced in *Jerusalem* (cf. 1:4) and devoted to communal *prayer* with some women and members of Jesus's family (mother and brothers). On the other hand, Acts 1:12–14 also serves as a transitional passage that sets the stage for the replacement of Judas by Matthias. Acts 1:1–11 therefore comprises the substance of Luke's introduction to Acts, which also recapitulates significant information from Luke's Gospel.[5] If 1:11 is taken as the end of Luke's introduction to Acts, the theme of Jesus's ascension is sounded early and recounted at the end.[6] This is programmatic for the remainder of the

4. This is also the note on which the book of Acts ends, perhaps to evoke promising beginnings in Jerusalem that inevitably provoke resistance.

5. See Barrett, *Acts of the Apostles*, 1:59–90. Barrett designates the whole of Acts 1:1–14 "introduction and recapitulation."

6. The ascension is also echoed in Acts 1:22 as the culmination of Jesus's public mission, which was initiated when John baptized him.

narrative. As Marion Soards points out, "That Jesus is raised and ascended into heaven is presupposed by elements in several subsequent speeches, for example, Stephen's speech (7:56); Paul's speech at Pisidian Antioch (13:33–37); Paul's Areopagus address (17:31); Paul's speech to the Jerusalem Jews (22:6–8); Paul's speech before Agrippa (26:13–15)."[7]

Various other eschatological motifs appear throughout this introductory section: the reign of God (Acts 1:3), the imminent coming of the Spirit (1:5, 8), the "restoration" of Israel (1:6), the divinely set timetable for events (1:7; cf. Mark 13:32 and Matt. 24:36, which are without a contextual parallel in Luke's Gospel), "cloud conveyance" (Acts 1:9), angelic clarification (1:10–11), and exaltation followed by return (1:11). In such a strikingly eschatological text, it is noteworthy that while the "end of the earth" is mentioned (1:8), it is not referred to in a cataclysmic sense but solely in terms of the farthest reaches of the world as the goal of mission, which for Luke means Spirit-empowered witness to Jesus (1:8; cf. 1:21–22). Nor does anything else in Acts suggest a cataclysmic end to earth, even though the theme of divine judgment is occasionally sounded (see 3:23; 10:42; 17:30–31; 24:25).

Jesus's commission to bear witness to himself, which in Acts 1:21 Peter equates with being a witness to the resurrection of the Lord Jesus, has the "end of the earth" in view, but for its salvation rather than its destruction. It is perhaps not accidental that the phrase "until the end of the earth" is immediately followed by Luke's description of Jesus's ascension as his apostles look on. "And having said these things," Luke writes, "as they were watching, he was taken up and a cloud removed him from their vision" (Acts 1:9). Furthermore, while Jesus is still in transit, so to speak, the apostles' stupefied staring upward is interrupted by two angelic figures, who reassure them that "this Jesus who was taken up (and away) from you into heaven will return in the same way that you observed him journeying into heaven" (1:11).

The two men clothed in white at Jesus's ascension are reminiscent of the two men in gleaming clothes whom women encounter at the open and empty tomb in Luke 24:4. As in Acts 1:10–11, the two men come alongside the women at the tomb, pose an incriminating query but also bring some clarity and reassurance to the situation. The two scenes are parallels, as Robert Tannehill points out, providing yet one further connection between the end of Luke's Gospel and the beginning of Acts.[8] Whether or not the two men in both scenes are the same is unimportant but have the same apocalyptic roles: to interpret the situation and to turn confusion or stupefaction into comprehension and purposeful behavior.

The two men in white at Jesus's ascension recall not only the two men at Jesus's empty tomb but also the two men who appear in glory at Jesus's

7. Soards, *Speeches in Acts*, 25.
8. Tannehill, *Narrative Unity of Luke–Acts*, 2:19–20.

transformation, Moses and Elijah (see Luke 9:28–36).[9] Having gone up a mountain to pray, Jesus's face changes as he prays, and here it is *his* clothes that become dazzlingly white. The appearance of Moses and Elijah "in glory" is probably to be understood in much the same way as Jesus's own transformation; after all, in Luke 9:32b, the waking disciples see *Jesus's* glory as well as the two men with him. The motif of a cloud, which J. A. Fitzmyer describes as an "apocalyptic stage prop,"[10] also links Luke's accounts of the transfiguration and ascension of Jesus, although the function of the cloud varies.

One more decisive detail binds ascension and transfiguration together for Luke. On the mountain of transformation, Moses and Elijah speak with Jesus about his "exodus," which, Luke informs us, he was about to fulfill in Jerusalem (Luke 9:31). I concur with those who interpret Jesus's exodus as at least including his ascension, especially in view of Luke 9:51, which reads: "And it happened that as the days of his 'taking up' [in all likelihood, his ascension] were drawing near, he fixed his face to journey to Jerusalem." In the words of H. J. Cadbury,

> That the ascension was no mere insertion or afterthought of Luke is probably attested by the use of that word in Luke ix. 51. In this editorial introduction to a major section of his Gospel the writer points to the climax to which he is leading in a word which could conceivably mean death or resurrection but which more naturally is understood of the ascension as concluding or including the three items.[11]

As argued earlier, however, I also consider that the exodus motif intimates a more extended movement within the Lukan narrative than the culmination represented by death, resurrection, or ascension—or all three together. Jesus's journey to Jerusalem—with all that it entailed, including the mundane no less than the extraordinary—was part of his "exodus." As a journey that culminated in ascension, however, Jesus's exodus was a journey to God that makes possible our turning to and movement toward God. Moreover, Jesus's journey to God turns out to be the way of peace, not only Jesus's own way of peace that disciples should emulate but also God's own announcement of peace and peaceable way in the world, as demonstrated in Jesus's mission as divine visitation.

What bearing, if any, does this have on Luke's introduction to Acts, especially with respect to the ascension and promised return of Jesus? If the ascension

9. See Parsons, *Departure of Jesus*, 172–73; Lee, *Transfiguration*, 71–74. The phrase "and behold two men" appears in Luke 9:30 and 24:4, as well as in Acts 1:10. Some suggest that the two men are Moses and Elijah on each occasion, but in Luke 24:4 and Acts 1:10 their function is more significant than their identity.

10. Fitzmyer, *Acts of the Apostles*, 208–11.

11. Cadbury, "Acts and Eschatology," 306.

of Jesus is the culmination of his peace path to God and, as such, the flip side of God's overture of peace in Jesus's mission, what implications might that have for Jesus's promised return? The transfixed apostles are reassured that the *very same* Jesus who was taken up and away from them will return *in the same way* as he was observed departing (Acts 1:11). Exegetically, what this implies is that the same person who ascended will return and that the manner of his return will be that of his departure. "Conditions are to be similar," according to Cadbury, "actual transit, visible to spectators, and probably accompanied with angels and a cloud. Possibly in the tradition, not only the place but the manner of the expected return supplied features for the manner of his going."[12]

In this connection, although the angelic reproof in Acts 1:11 interprets the ascension as something of a prolepsis of Jesus's return,[13] the actual description of Jesus's ascent in 1:9 is reminiscent of the Son of humanity's eschatological arrival in Luke 21:27.[14] Only Luke 21:27 refers to "power and pluriform glory" to characterize the Son of humanity's arrival, but the shared motif of a cloud accompanying both the Son of humanity's future arrival and the ascent of Jesus in Acts 1:9 suggests that in recounting the ascension, Luke envisaged it as Jesus's return in reverse.[15] This tightly tethers both ascension and return in Lukan theology, whether return is seen in light of ascension (as narrated) or ascension is recounted in light of anticipated return (as suggested by the narrative progression of Luke's two-part work). According to Acts 1:9–11, ascension prefigures return, and return mirrors ascension.[16]

Carroll points out that the "correlation" between ascension and return in Acts 1:9–11 probably addresses doubt about the likelihood of Jesus's return: "Affirmation of Jesus's present status as exalted Lord (and Christ, 2:36) serves to reinforce expectation of his parousia. In view of the delayed parousia which will enable the worldwide mission of the church (1:6–8), eschatologically oriented faith has evidently been shaken. Luke undergirds hope in Jesus's return by employing the ascension as a pledge."[17]

---

12. Ibid., 309. David Peterson warns against interpreting the promised similarity between ascension and return too restrictively, however, since Jesus's second coming promises to be more public than his ascension; see his *Acts of the Apostles*, 115–16. I agree that parallels between ascension and return should not be interpreted too restrictively, but for different reasons.

13. Compare Parsons, *Departure of Jesus*, 197, where "Jesus' ascension is an earnest of Jesus' parousia."

14. See Soards, *Speeches in Acts*, 25–26.

15. Barrett in *Acts of the Apostles*, 1:64, 84, suggests that Luke's imagery in narrating Jesus's ascension is drawn from his conception of the parousia.

16. I understand those who emphasize the ascension in Luke's eschatology, but not at the expense of parousia expectation. For Luke, the ascension is both presupposition and pattern of the parousia. Compare Flender, *St. Luke*, 91–106; Franklin, "Ascension and the Eschatology of Luke–Acts"; idem, *Christ the Lord*, 9–47. I concur with Franklin that the ascension "determines the manner" of the parousia, but to characterize the ascension in Luke's thinking as the "complete eschatological event" isolates and thereby overstates its significance.

17. Carroll, *Response to the End*, 126.

In view of Luke's dominant peace theme, however, more may be said than that Jesus himself will surely return in the manner of his departure. To say that this *same* Jesus will return also implies that his character and disposition will be unchanged upon his return. In other words, the "correlation" between ascension and return extends into the ethical domain. Ascension to the right hand of God is not for the purpose of "character reprogramming"; after all, Jesus's peaceable orientation reflects the divine plan and purpose for his mission: to announce peace to God's people (Acts 10:36). Furthermore, if ascension is the culmination of Jesus's peace path to God, must one not also infer that Jesus's return will be peaceable? This goes beyond what Luke likely intended to imply in Acts 1:11, but it rings true to Luke's depiction of Jesus's mission as both a divine overture of peace and a peace-oriented journey toward God.

What Luke signals about ascension and return in his introduction to Acts is decisive for anything further that might be said in Acts about Jesus's return, his "office" at the right hand of God, and his just judgment (or God's judgment through him).[18] The returning Jesus is the very same Jesus through whom God announced peace to the children of Israel and whose own mission was a peace path toward God. The ascended Jesus at God's right hand is none other than he whose exodus occurred peaceably (on his part) and made for peace. What the ascended Jesus dispenses is what he receives, the promised Holy Spirit (Acts 2:33; cf. 10:38), who extends the divine announcement of peace to all nations. And since Jesus, crucified and raised, is the divinely designated judge of the living and the dead (10:39–42; 17:30–31), just judgment no longer implies simple payback or retribution (cf. Luke 23:41) but must measure up to justice that restores peace peaceably. In this respect Acts 3:20–21, which also implicitly correlates ascension and return,[19] reinforces Luke's peaceable eschatology in Acts with reference to restoration. Before turning to that puzzling passage from Peter's second missional speech, however, there are important issues to be considered in the opening portion of his Pentecost speech, which sheds further light on the type of eschatology found in Acts.

Joel's Prophecy Fulfilled (Acts 2:14–21)

On the day of Pentecost, when assembled believers are filled with the Holy Spirit and are understood by Diaspora Jews in their own native languages,[20]

18. As he is wont to do, Bock somehow detects the theme of judgment in Acts 1:11. See Bock, *Acts*, 42, 70. Future judgment is undoubtedly a Lukan theme in Acts, but it is absent from the reassurance of Jesus's return in the manner of his taking up.

19. See Soards, *Speeches in Acts*, 26.

20. Whether Luke intended this to be understood as a miracle of speech (speaking in unlearned foreign languages) or hearing (perhaps but not necessarily in response to ecstatic utterance) is interesting but ultimately irresolvable.

Peter proffers to a skeptical audience an explanation of this corporate experience by appealing to an eschatological passage from the book of Joel. This passage, however, seems to say more than is necessary to explain the experience of the Spirit's outpouring at Pentecost. Acts 2:17–18 speaks of divine determination to pour out the Spirit indiscriminately, but 2:19–20 catalogs divinely orchestrated cosmic phenomena that will serve as a prelude to the "day of the Lord." For Carroll, "The Joel citation (Joel 3:1–5 LXX [2:28–32 Eng.]) has both programmatic and prophetic functions in the Acts narrative. . . . Scriptural prophecy . . . serves not only to interpret the event just narrated (Acts 2:1–13), but also to point the reader forward to the worldwide mission that will unfold in the 'last days' preceding the 'day of the Lord.'"[21] In other words, whereas the first half of the Joel citation in Acts 2:17–18 interprets the Pentecost experience as fulfillment of prophecy, the whole of the citation retains its prophetic force for the narrative to follow.

In support of Carroll's reading of the Joel citation within its context in Acts 2, Soards observes:

> The quotation from Joel is a freely cited version of the Septuagint tailored to fit the act of Christian proclamation at Pentecost. (A) The reference to "visions" (ὁράσεις) in the lines from Joel (2:17) finds complements in the reports of visions (ὅραμα) in later speeches (11:5; 22:17–18) as well as in the event of the narrative (9:10; 10:3, 11, 17, 19; 16:9–10; 18:9). (B) The mention in v. 19 of τέρατα, "portents/ wonders" (in Joel), and σημεῖα, "signs" (not in Joel but added here by Luke), is echoed subsequently in speeches in 2:22; 7:36; 4:30 (though there σημεῖα καὶ τέρατα, "signs and wonders") and in the narrative in 2:43; 5:12; 6:8; 14:3; 15:12.[22]

For both Carroll and Soards, then, the whole of the Joel citation within Acts 2 looks forward to future fulfillment, for the most part but not entirely within the time frame of the subsequent narrative of Acts; yet the first half of the citation also interprets the Pentecost experience as fulfillment of the prophetic promise in Joel that God intends to pour out a portion of the divine Spirit upon all to facilitate prophecy by all.

Carroll considers that the second half of the citation from Joel in Acts 2:17–21 functions like the eschatological discourse in Luke 21:5–36, even if less precisely, by previewing what must occur before the end. This situates the church between the fulfillment of prophecy at Pentecost (along with events recounted within Acts) and the yet-to-be-fulfilled prophecy reiterated from Joel in Acts 2:19–20. Correlating the cosmic signs of Acts 2:19–20 to those of Luke 21:25–26, Carroll comments, "Only the supramundane events prophesied also by Jesus (Luke 21:25–27) are still outstanding as the 'eschatological remainder.'"[23]

21. Carroll, *Response to the End*, 128–29.
22. Soards, *Speeches in Acts*, 32–33.
23. Carroll, *Response to the End*, 132–33.

While I am in basic sympathy with Carroll's interpretation of Lukan eschatology, including his view that Luke held even the "eschatological remainder" to be imminent for his audience, I remain unconvinced that the "wonders and signs" of Acts 2:19–20 belong to that "eschatological remainder," even though Carroll finds support among a significant number of Lukan scholars. As F. F. Bruce observes in relation to Acts 2:19–20, "The wonders and signs to be revealed in the world of nature may have more relevance in their immediate setting than is sometimes realized."[24] I agree, even though eminent Lukan scholars see things differently.

For Ernst Haenchen, Luke naturally searched the LXX for a text that foretold ecstatic utterance, which in Haenchen's view is the startling phenomenon underlying Luke's account of the linguistic miracle recounted in Acts 2:4–13, whether interpreted as a miracle of speech or a miracle of hearing. Luke allegedly fixed upon the prophecy of Joel 3:1–5 (LXX [2:28–32 Eng.]) so as to interpret the Pentecost phenomenon as the fulfillment of the divine promise to pour out a portion of the Spirit on sons and daughters, young men and old, menservants and maidservants, even though "Luke could not directly link the cosmic omens of the last days with the context of the sermon; for him there lay between the coming of the Spirit and those heavenly signs . . . a lengthy interval."[25] Commenting on Acts 2:17–21, he avers: "In Lucan theology the last days do not begin as soon as the Spirit has been outpoured! . . . The cosmic events describe the terrible end which threatens, when only he who calls upon the name of the Lord (= Jesus!) shall be saved."[26] Unlike Carroll, Haenchen holds to the Conzelmann thesis that Luke had abandoned, or at least modified, imminent expectation, but Haenchen's view of the Joel citation within the context of Acts 2 matches Carroll's closely.

In Barrett's view, the Joel citation in Acts 2:17–21 offers insight into Lukan eschatology: "God has begun, but not completed, the work of fulfilment; Christians are living in the last days, but the last day has not yet come."[27] In other words, the prophecy of Joel is only partially realized by Pentecost, even if at this point in the narrative the stress is on fulfillment. On Acts 2:19, Barrett comments that "he [Luke] wished to add to heavenly portents signs, miracles, worked by the apostles which provided further proof that the age to come was now dawning. . . . Signs are being done on earth in these last days; but (except so far as they may be included in the wind and fire of the day) portents in heaven have not yet appeared."[28] Again Barrett places the emphasis on fulfillment even as he asserts that prophesied heavenly portents have yet to occur. But his assertion is qualified by his parenthetical remark, "except

24. Bruce, *Book of the Acts*, 61.
25. Haenchen, *Acts of the Apostles*, 186.
26. Ibid., 179.
27. Barrett, *Acts of the Apostles*, 1:135.
28. Ibid., 1:137.

so far as they may be included in the wind and fire of the day," which opens the door to interpreting the Pentecost experience as fulfilling the whole of the Joel citation, even if not woodenly by checking off each of Joel's cosmic omens. This is reinforced by Barrett's further observation that although Luke freely adopts Joel's heavenly portents, his main concern is to incorporate the statement regarding the promise of salvation with which his citation from Joel concludes (Acts 2:21; Joel 3:5a LXX [2:32a Eng.]).[29]

Fitzmyer's interpretation of Luke's citation of Joel goes further in the direction of Barrett's parenthetical possibility. While he acknowledges that the prophecy of Joel included "apocalyptic warning," he nevertheless writes:

> Luke uses these words of Joel about cosmic disturbances to characterize the noise heard and the fire seen at the coming of the Spirit on the first Christian Pentecost. . . . They are not to be understood as extraordinary natural features that will precede the end of time. They may have had that connotation in Joel, but Luke uses the description as a way of explaining what has accompanied the outpouring of the Spirit.[30]

Here Fitzmyer contests much scholarly opinion on Luke's citation from Joel, but he asserts his case rather than arguing for it, unless one accepts as argumentation two points that inform his interpretation. The first is his contention that "Peter's introductory comment tells of the fulfillment of Joel's words. . . . Peter sees it as the inauguration of the 'last days'; for the time has come when the Christian message is about to move out from Jerusalem to 'the end of the earth' (1:8)."[31] Informing Fitzmyer's initial point is his study of Qumran parallels to the way in which Luke introduces his citation from Joel, and also his acceptance that Luke altered the wording of Joel 3:1 (2:28 Eng.) in the LXX from "after this" to "in the last days."

That Luke himself altered the Greek version of Joel 3:1 in this way is contested by both Haenchen and Pervo, who contend that this was a later scribal amendment.[32] On this intractable text-critical point, I side with those who see Luke himself as responsible for modifying the opening phrase of Joel 3:1 in the Hebrew Bible (whether in Hebrew or Greek), including Carroll and Bruce Metzger.[33] Certainty is unattainable, however, and I readily concede that to envisage Luke as modifying the opening phrase of Joel 3:1 in the Hebrew Bible ties in with my support for Fitzmyer's interpretation of Acts 2:16–21.

---

29. Ibid. Barrett notes that Luke could have omitted the cosmic signs of Acts 2:18–19 if he had wanted to. But this cuts against Luke's general conservatism with respect to the LXX.

30. Fitzmyer, *Acts of the Apostles*, 253.

31. Ibid., 252.

32. See Haenchen, *Acts of the Apostles*, 179; Pervo, *Acts*, 76–79.

33. See Carroll, *Response to the End*, 135–37; Metzger, *Textual Commentary*, 256. Metzger's discussion of Acts 2:17–21 explains why text-critical determinations on this passage cannot be doctrinaire.

The second consideration informing Fitzmyer's interpretation of Acts 2:16–21 is the critical observation he makes in his introductory discussion of Luke's use of the Old Testament in Acts. There he observes that Lukan citations of Scripture not only serve his promise-fulfillment motif but also emphasize the role of the Spirit in the salvation-historical period of the church. "This use of the OT is seen in the second speech of Peter on the first Christian Pentecost (2:14–36)," he writes, "in which the prophet Joel is quoted *and the burden of the quotation is to emphasize the outpouring of the Spirit.*"[34] In other words, on the issue of fulfillment of scriptural prophecy, the principal role or function of the citation from Joel relativizes specific details within it.

Fitzmyer's reading of Acts 2:16–21 may not be unimpeachable, but he nevertheless gives due consideration to the way in which the citation from Joel is introduced. This is not always the case with commentators, who perhaps find Acts 2:16 all too transparent. In context, Peter denies that the enigmatic events of that Pentecost morning are due to inebriation and offers another explanation: "Rather, this is what was spoken through the prophet Joel" (Acts 2:16).[35] In other words, what the gathered crowd finds astounding and perplexing such that some put it all down to intoxication is explained by Peter on the basis of Joel's prophecy. Darrell Bock concurs, pointing out that the formulaic "this is" expression of Acts 2:16 "serves to identify and connect two things,"[36] although he then proceeds to interpret the wonders and signs of Acts 2:19–20 as yet to occur. In my view, however, the whole of Peter's citation of Joel in Acts 2:17–21 is to be read in light of *this is* in 2:16.

There are further interpretive considerations in favor of Fitzmyer's interpretation. First, the Pentecostal noise *from the heavens* and *firelike* tongues of Acts 2:2–4 provide partial parallels to the *heavenly wonders* and *fiery sign on earth* of Acts 2:19. Second, the earthly signs of blood, fire, and cloud of smoke are reminiscent of the exodus from Egypt under Moses and can therefore be conceived as signs of deliverance as much as signs of impending doom and gloom.[37] And insofar as the earthly signs of Acts 2:19 are reminiscent of Passover and exodus, it is noteworthy that the major cosmic display of darkening the sun has already occurred, in Luke's narrative, some fifty days earlier, at Jesus's crucifixion in the wake of Passover (see Luke 22:7; 23:44–45). While all three Synoptics refer to the darkness at noon associated with Jesus's crucifixion,

---

34. Fitzmyer, *Acts of the Apostles*, 92.

35. Compare Culy and Parsons, *Acts: A Handbook*, 30, who translate Acts 2:16 as follows: "Instead, this is (exactly) what was said through the prophet Joel."

36. Bock, *Acts*, 111–12.

37. Even the original context within Joel's prophecy is concerned with deliverance for Israelites, albeit restricted to Mount Zion and Jerusalem. See Pervo, *Acts*, 79: "The original context, which spoke of deliverance for returning Israelites, restricts itself to Jerusalem, and proceeds to denounce gentiles, is not helpful [for Luke's purpose]. The citation therefore omits the last part of v. 5 [Joel 3:5 LXX = 2:32 Eng.]."

only Luke mentions the *failing of the sun* (23:45a), which makes the parallel to Acts 2:20a that much stronger. This leaves only the reddening of the moon unaccounted for, but it would not be a great stretch to subsume the sign of the moon under the sign of the sun (as in Joel 2:10b and 3:15a [4:15a LXX]!). Finally, as Fitzmyer notes, in the LXX version of Joel's prophecy cited by Luke, the "day of the Lord" was already described somewhat differently from the Hebrew original in one key respect: as "great and glorious/resplendent" rather than "great and awesome/terrifying."[38] Perhaps this helps to explain why Luke saw no need to excise the natural wonders of Acts 2:19–20 but chose instead to make minor modifications for effect.

To avoid misunderstanding, I do not deny the presence of *any* future orientation in the citation from Joel in Acts 2:17–21. The burden of this citation within its present context, and hence the burden of my argument, however, is that the prophecy of Joel is realized with the outpouring of the Spirit at Pentecost. Perhaps the wonders and signs of Acts 2:19–20 are fulfilled in anticipatory fashion, but even so that anticipatory fulfillment establishes the parameters for future consummation. As in the case of Luke 17:20–37, future-oriented eschatology is tethered to and conditioned by realized eschatology.

Taking all these considerations into account, Pentecost no less than the parousia may be seen as at least a partial realization of the "day of the Lord," especially in view of Peter's statement later in the same speech that the risen and ascended Jesus, now also "Lord," dispenses as well as receives the Spirit (Acts 2:32–33, 36). I do not suggest that Pentecost *rather than* the parousia realizes the epiphanic "day of the Lord." But since Luke immediately has Peter stipulate that he is referring to "Jesus the Nazarene, a man accredited by God by means of works of power, *wonders, and signs* done by God through him" (Acts 2:22),[39] it is not too far-fetched to interpret the Pentecost experience as fulfilling, at least in anticipatory fashion, Joel's prophecy. And if that be granted, then Pentecost as well as ascension paves the way for conceptualizing the awaited parousia of the crucified, risen, ascended, and Spirit-gifting Jesus.

According to Pervo, "The theological ground of the speech [in Acts 2] is the theme of promise and fulfillment."[40] Nevertheless, his discussion of the Joel citation in Acts 2:17–21 indicates that he concurs with those who find only its

---

38. Fitzmyer, *Acts of the Apostles*, 253. For Pervo, *Acts*, 80, this altered adjective might well resonate with Lukan readers' view of the anticipated parousia as epiphany.

39. In this connection, Luke (in Acts 2:19) adds the word *signs* to the Greek text of Joel 3:3 (2:30 Eng.). Pervo, *Acts*, 77, notes that the atypical order, "wonders and signs," in Acts 2:22 matches the expanded citation from Joel in Acts 2:19. So too does the first reference to "wonders and signs" done by the apostles in 2:43, which leads Tannehill to infer that in both cases, the phrase signals fulfillment of the amended citation from Joel, even though he shares the view of those who see the wonders and signs of Acts 2:19–20 as belonging to an "eschatological remainder." See Tannehill, *Narrative Unity of Luke–Acts*, 2:29–32.

40. Pervo, *Acts*, 74.

first half (2:17b–18) fulfilled by the Pentecost experience, albeit with further "limited fulfillment in the subsequent narrative."[41] As for the second half,

> The general purpose of vv. 19–20 is to give a clear frame for Christian existence (cf. 1:6–8), which takes place between (and is determined by) Pentecost and parousia. In that epoch believers will be sustained by the gift of the Spirit. The details are more vague, not least because Luke has inserted "signs" to make v. 19b a distinct clause that refers to the time of Jesus and the life of the church. . . . In any event, the reader of Acts is invited to admire "signs on earth" but is not encouraged to investigate cosmological phenomena.[42]

Pervo's final statement above may be true to Luke elsewhere, but it is difficult to sustain on the basis of the Joel citation in Acts 2. Yet his opening observation is thought provoking. What is the character of Christian existence that takes place between—and is determined by—*both* Pentecost and parousia? A reading of Acts 2:19–20 that envisages a violent and retributive parousia, as so often in the church's history, is unlikely to inculcate Christian existence that is in tune with Pentecost, that is, with the Spirit gifted by one whose journey to God was characterized by peace. In Luke's salvation-historical schema, Pentecost precedes the parousia and prefigures it in the sense of manifesting in yet one more mode the divine response to the human predicament. In response to the violence of crucifixion, God liberated Jesus from death and raised him (Acts 2:23–24), God lifted him up, and God conferred upon him the Holy Spirit for the express purpose of being poured out to empower human witness to the crucified, risen, and ascended One. What is revealed in the resurrection, in the ascension, or in the bestowal of the Spirit to make anyone think that the one returning in the manner of his ascension will act contrary to his demeanor on his journey to God?

Eschatological Refreshment and Restoration (Acts 3:19–21)

In a speech following the restoration of a lame man to full working order, Peter reiterates the point made in his previous speech that although Judeans were responsible for the death of Jesus, albeit in ignorance, he and his fellow apostles are witnesses to God's raising of Jesus from death.[43] The note of scriptural fulfillment is also reiterated, as is the call for radical change:

> Change, therefore, and turn for the purpose of expunging your sins, so that anticipated times of refreshment may come from the face of the Lord and he

---

41. Ibid., 79.
42. Ibid., 79–80.
43. Regarding resemblances between the speeches of Peter in Acts 2 and 3, see Zehnle, *Peter's Pentecost Discourse*, 19–26. Despite their common features, Zehnle holds the literary qualities of the speech of Acts 3 in low esteem.

may send your preappointed Messiah Jesus, whom heaven must retain until the times of the restoration of all things, about which God spoke through the mouth of his holy prophets from antiquity. (Acts 3:19–21)

This single sentence is complex in construction, idiosyncratic in formulation, obscure in detail, but nevertheless relatively transparent in meaning. The blotting out or erasure of sins is peculiar, but not the typically Lukan notion of radical change as preliminary to dealing with—by forgiving—sins. The two phrases, "anticipated times of refreshment" and "the times of the restoration of all things," are utterly atypical, and their relation to each other is contested. Other terms and phrases are also unusual or used unusually. The implicit Christology of Acts 3:20 has been much discussed, especially in relation to 2:36, with scholars such as J. A. T. Robinson suggesting that this verse retains a vestige of a primitive christological formulation that envisaged Jesus as destined by his resurrection to *become* Messiah and eschatological judge *only at his return*.[44] Fitzmyer designates Acts 3:20–21 an "apocalyptic digression," presumably because of the peculiarity of the eschatological language and the curiousness of its function within the speech as a whole.[45] Especially striking, however, is that eschatological expectation intended to engender transformation should be so unambiguously and indiscriminately hopeful and nonretributive.[46] In line with Acts 1:11, Peter's expressed hope is that the risen and ascended One will return, resent by God, and that his return will be associated with refreshment and restoration, not retributive violence. The following composite scriptural citation in 3:22–23 introduces a warning of retribution, but that is not Luke's emphasis.

It is generally accepted that Acts 3:20–21 reinforces the Lukan schema that the period of the church falls between ascension and parousia. In other words, this passage both presupposes Acts 1:9–11 and builds upon it. The ascended One dispenses the Spirit (2:33) and thereby continues to effect change in the world, but his locus is with God "in heaven" until his return. But are "anticipated times of refreshment" a function of his present exalted status or, like "the times of restoration," associated with his return?[47] At one level, not

44. See Robinson, "Most Primitive Christology."
45. Fitzmyer, *Acts of the Apostles*, 282–83.
46. See Tannehill, *Narrative Unity of Luke–Acts*, 2:55–56.
47. Not everyone accepts that "the times of the restoration of all things" in Acts 3:21 are associated with the return of the ascended Jesus, largely because of the plural form of "times," which does not match Luke's usage elsewhere for the eschaton (likewise with "seasons"). See, e.g., Bayer, "Christ-Centered Eschatology," esp. 245–48; Gaventa, *Acts*, 88. Luke's linguistic and conceptual expression in Acts 3 diverges significantly from his usage elsewhere, however, and I have yet to be convinced that the "day" of the Son of humanity means anything different from the "days" of the Son of humanity in Luke 17:22–37. Similar imprecision regarding the eschatological "day" or "days" is to be found in *1 Enoch* 96:8, to which I was alerted by Bridge, *"Where the Eagles Are Gathered,"* 102–3. To my mind, therefore, "the times of the restoration

much is contingent upon the answer to this question. But if *both* refreshment and restoration relate to the parousia or, as Haenchen opines, the times of the restoration of all things will be experienced as seasons of refreshment,[48] this further supports my contention that, in Acts, the way of Jesus from God at his return is the way of Jesus throughout his "exodus" or journey to God. The most obvious meaning of 1:11 is that the manner of Jesus's return will be like that of his ascent, in short, by means of or along with a cloud. But if the return of Jesus implies seasons of refreshment no less than the times of restoration, that also implies that the parousia is in moral harmony with the ascension as the culmination of Jesus's peace path to God.

So, is the return (or resending) of Jesus associated with the anticipated "times of refreshment" as well as "the times of the restoration of all things," or only the latter? Barrett probably makes the most forceful case for viewing "times of refreshment" as occurring before the parousia. In his view, to associate the anticipated "times of refreshment" with the parousia "does not do justice to the plural καιροί [*kairoi*, times or seasons] (a number of specific points of time) or to the meaning of ἀνάψυξις [*anapsyxis*, refreshment], which suggests temporary relief rather than finality."[49] Beyond these lexical points, Barrett also appeals to Lukan theology:

> Luke does not see the period that must intervene (δεῖ [*dei*], v. 21) between the resurrection and the parousia as one of unrelieved gloom. There are repeated conversions, as one after another is won to the new faith; there are moments of collective inspiration, such as 2.1–4; 4.31. These are brought about as men [and women] are penitent and turn to God, receiving the forgiveness of their sins and the gift of the Holy Spirit. It is characteristic of Luke that he does not abandon the notion of a futurist collective eschatology but believes this to be anticipated in a series of individual realizations. Miracles provide further examples of such moments of refreshment.[50]

Perhaps Barrett reads Luke too woodenly here. Pervo's syntactical analysis of the single sentence that comprises Acts 3:19–21 is illuminating and leads to a different conclusion. He observes that the second promise linked to the twofold summons to repentance includes both "times of refreshment" and the sending of the Messiah.[51] In other words, not only may the term for time, *kairos*, connote an appointed or anticipated occasion, but here the plural *kairoi*, or seasons, of refreshment are also specifically associated with the return (or resending) of Messiah Jesus. Pervo accepts that if Acts 3:20 is read

---

of all things" in Acts 3:21 most naturally relate to the return of the ascended Jesus. The question is whether the same applies to "the seasons of refreshment" in Acts 3:20.

48. Haenchen, *Acts of the Apostles*, 208.
49. Barrett, *Acts of the Apostles*, 1:205.
50. Ibid.
51. Pervo, *Acts*, 107.

in light of 2:38, Peter's earlier call for radical change and baptism, "the 'periods of refreshment' would be the present eschatological blessings enjoyed by the baptized, followed—at some unspecified point—by the parousia." Yet on the basis of "rhetorical doubling," he accepts as "probably preferable" an interpretation of "periods of refreshment" and "times of restoration" that sees them as synonymous.[52]

On this interpretive point, Fitzmyer is adamant: "*Chronoi apokatastaseōs pantōn* must be another way of saying *kairoi anapsyxeōs* (3:20); they are related and mutually explain each other. *Kairoi* would indicate the beginning of the period, and *chronoi* the duration of it."[53] While Fitzmyer's final assertion pushes things too far, the two phrases do seem to be mutually illuminating. Carroll concurs, only in his view both phrases relate not to the parousia per se but to the present period of the church's mission. This, at least, is his position in *Response to the End of History*.[54] In *The Return of Jesus in Early Christianity*, however, his perspective on Acts 3:19–21 seems to have shifted in the opposite direction. With reference to Peter's summons to repentance, Carroll glosses: "He [Peter] then announces as the goal and benefit of repentance the experience of 'times of refreshing'—namely, the sending (again) of the Messiah Jesus (v. 20). Although he resides in heaven for the present, he will return when the time of the 'restoring of all things,' as declared by God through the prophets, has arrived."[55] Here "times of refreshment" and "times of restoration of all things" are seemingly associated with the parousia, although Carroll cites his earlier discussion without suggesting any change of interpretation and also draws attention to the interpretation offered by Luke Johnson in his commentary on Acts. Johnson's discussion does not help us to understand Carroll, however, because despite emphasizing interpretive difficulties associated with Acts 3:19–21, Johnson adopts a position close to Barrett's, claiming that "seasons of refreshment" are available during the time of the church whereas "the times of the restoration of all things" relate to the Messiah's return.[56]

On balance, while I accept that it is impossible to be certain about the precise meaning of Acts 3:19–21, I incline to the view that the two phrases under consideration are parallel in meaning,[57] that both pertain to the return of the ascended Jesus, and therefore that they are mutually illuminating. While the two phrases are parallel, however, they are not synonymous because the

52. Ibid., 108.
53. Fitzmyer, *Acts of the Apostles*, 288.
54. Carroll, *Response to the End*, 142–48.
55. Carroll et al., *Return of Jesus*, 44.
56. Johnson, *Acts of the Apostles*, 69, 74.
57. Compare Conzelmann, *Acts of the Apostles*, 29. See also Pervo, *Acts*, 108: "Both the verbal form of 'restoration' and the nouns 'times and seasons' appear in 1:6–7, indicating that the statements are parallel."

phrase most obviously associated with the parousia refers to the "restoration of all things."[58] In the entire New Testament, the noun ἀποκατάστασις (*apokatastasis*, restoration) occurs here only, but its cognate verb, ἀποκαθίστημι (*apokathistēmi*, to restore), occurs eight times, twice in Luke–Acts. In Luke 6:10 it is used of the restoration to wholeness of a man's withered hand, and in Acts 1:6 it appears on the lips of Jesus's apostles when they ask whether now, in the aftermath of Jesus's resurrection, sovereignty is to be restored to Israel. Luke's contemporary Josephus uses the noun ἀποκατάστασις (*apokatastasis*) with reference to Jewish *restoration* following the Babylonian exile, as Fitzmyer notes.[59] Luke's meaning in Acts 3:21 is illuminated by these associations, but in all probability is also informed by both prophetic and apocalyptic writings that anticipate cosmic restoration, such as Malachi 3:24 (Heb.; 3:23 LXX; 4:6 Eng.); Isaiah 62:1–5; 65:17; 66:22; 1 *Enoch* 45:4–5; 96:3; 2 Esdras (or 4 *Ezra*) 7:75, 91–95; and perhaps the *Assumption of Moses* 10:10.[60] Haenchen characterizes this eschatological image as "'restitution,' the realisation of all prophetic promises, which is at the same time a restoration of the original order of creation."[61] And Barrett conveys Luke's meaning precisely and concisely: "Jesus as the coming Messiah will restore God's perverted world."[62]

It would be naive to interpret "the times of restoration of all things" sentimentally, as if divine reconstruction could occur without wholesale deconstruction. Nor need one follow Origen and Gregory of Nyssa without demur to appreciate that this passage envisages an altogether different and much healthier conception of end-time judgment than that which the church has generally projected.[63] This anticipated hope of restoration—however self-reconstructing and life-altering it may be—is in keeping with Luke's peace emphasis. As such, it is a significant scriptural resource for contesting eschatological vengeance.

In view of the wholly restorative eschatological expectation in Acts 3:19–21, however, what is one to make of Peter's scriptural threat in 3:23 that those (Jews) who do not attend to the prophet like Moses—Jesus—face exclusion from God's people? Here, cheek by jowl with the hope of restoration is a threat of divine retribution. As Bock points out, the principal verb of Acts 3:23 appears only here in the New Testament and certainly sounds severe.[64] Taken literally, it denotes destruction, but in context the phrase "will be destroyed

---

58. Yet cf. the illuminating discussion of the phrase "times of refreshment" by Bauckham, "Restoration of Israel in Luke–Acts," esp. 477–82. He holds that "times of revival" expresses Luke's meaning better, in which case the two phrases of Acts 3:20–21 are that much closer in meaning.

59. Fitzmyer, *Acts of the Apostles*, 288–89.

60. See ibid., 289.

61. Haenchen, *Acts of the Apostles*, 208.

62. Barrett, *Acts of the Apostles*, 1:206.

63. See Fitzmyer, *Acts of the Apostles*, 289, for other notable scholars who followed Origen in building on Luke's conception of "the times of restoration of all things."

64. Bock, *Acts*, 179.

from among the people" might well mean to be cut off from God's people. Moreover, however final these words may seem, and despite their occurrence in an eschatological context, they more likely refer to Jews whose nonacceptance of Jesus precludes their incorporation into the (new) people of God constituted by faith in Jesus.

In narrative terms, it can hardly be coincidental that this threat of judgment constructed on the basis of Deuteronomy 18:19[65] comes shortly before a narrative juncture in which, for the first time in Acts, the Jewish leadership reacts with hostility to the proclamation of Peter (and John). Reflecting on whether this warning refers to historical or eschatological judgment, Tannehill remarks that "the harsh warning in 3:23 may anticipate the imminent turn for the worse in the relation between the apostles and the temple authorities. . . . Such anticipation of rejection in a speech before its actual appearance occurs elsewhere in Luke–Acts (see Luke 4:23–30; Acts 13:40–47)."[66] In other words, quite apart from the historical reality that Peter's threat of divine judgment expresses his (and Luke's) conviction that there is salvation in no one other than Jesus (see Acts 4:12), this warning seems to be an integral part of the theme of Jewish rejection of Jesus, which permeates Acts. This theme, however, is not to the exclusion of Jewish *acceptance* of Jesus, which is the dominant note in Acts 2–3 and also persists throughout Acts. It also merits mentioning that the biblical warning of judgment is not the note on which Peter's sermon in Acts 3 ends. Rather, as Richard Bauckham emphasizes, "although the possibility of rejecting the Messiah is clearly stated in Peter's sermon as a warning (3:22–23), it is on the positive note of blessing and restoration for Israel that the sermon ends."[67] Perhaps most important, the warning of divine judgment couched in scriptural terms within Acts 3:23 takes on a different complexion when read in light of later texts of eschatological judgment.

Eschatological Judgment (Acts 10:42; 17:30–31)

Beyond Acts 3, the return of the now-ascended Messiah recedes from view, but the warning of judgment sounded by Peter in Acts 3:23 is echoed by fleeting references to eschatological judgment in Acts 10:42; 17:30–31; 24:25. Of these three references, the most important are Acts 10:42 and 17:30–31. The reference to "coming judgment" in Paul's witness before the governor Felix and his wife, Drusilla (Acts 24:25), is best interpreted in light of the two earlier passages. Carroll passes over these texts in which the motif of future

---

65. Scholars convinced that Luke is working from the LXX consider that Luke conflates Deut. 18:19 with Lev. 23:29, but Bauckham insists that Luke conflates Deut. 18:19 with Num. 15:31. See Bauckham, "Restoration of Israel in Luke–Acts," 480.

66. Tannehill, *Narrative Unity of Luke–Acts*, 2:57.

67. Bauckham, "Restoration of Israel in Luke–Acts," 481.

judgment occurs because they are silent about "the timing or nature of end-time judgment."[68] With respect to timing, Carroll may well be correct, but with respect to the *nature* of eschatological judgment, some crucial points, often overlooked, need to be noticed.

The speech of Peter in Acts 10:34–43 is a high point in Acts, even if the Spirit found what Peter was saying interruptible. It prepares for the influx of non-Jewish people into Jewish Christianity (or perhaps Christian Judaism), one of Luke's principal themes in Acts. It is within this speech that Peter characterizes the mission of Jesus in its entirety as a divine announcement of peace to the people of Israel. After summarizing Jesus's mission following his baptism by John as Spirit-empowered and restorative due to God's presence with him (10:38), Peter proceeds to recount Jesus's crucifixion at the hands of Jews, his resurrection by divine agency, and his appearances to chosen witnesses, among whom Peter counts himself. Then he makes this statement: "And he [Jesus] commanded us to proclaim to the people, indeed, declare emphatically that he himself is the one appointed by God as judge of the living and the dead" (10:42).

To comprehend the significance of Jesus's divine appointment as judge over all humanity, both the living and the dead, the following points from this speech of Peter's are salient: first, the divine appointer is none other than the divine announcer of peace; second, the one divinely appointed as judge is the same one whose mission and message composed the divine announcement of peace to Israel; third, the one divinely appointed as judge is the same one whose Spirit-empowered mission entailed doing good and bringing release to those oppressed by evil; fourth, the divine restoration of Jesus from the clutch of death mirrors—and hence approves—Jesus's own restorative mission; and fifth, it is precisely the one divinely restored to life from death, restored after the manner of his own restorative life and mission, who is divinely appointed as judge of both the living and the dead.

It is also noteworthy that those commissioned to witness are said, in this instance, to have been commanded to witness to Jesus's appointment as judge, not, as so often elsewhere in Acts, to his resurrection. This further suggests that Jesus's divine appointment as judge is of a piece, so to speak, with his resurrection by divine agency. Since resurrection from the dead is in some sense analogous to—and thereby vindicates—Jesus's own restorative mission, this authorizes an interpretation of divinely authorized judgment by Jesus as ultimately concerned with restoration rather than retribution alone. Divine judgment deserves to be interpreted in terms of characteristically divine initiatives, and in this passage such initiatives are identified as overtures of peace, anointing with the Spirit for restorative action, and resurrection. These divine initiatives are more determinative for understanding the nature

68. Carroll, *Response to the End*, 122n14.

of divine judgment enacted by the "Lord of all" (10:36) than forms of judgment to which we are accustomed.

In Acts 17:22–31, Paul addresses the Athenians at the Areopagus. In this speech, Luke recounts Paul's affirming the Lord of heaven and earth as the Creator of the world and all that is in it, as the source of all human life, and consequently as the judge of all humanity or the inhabited world. Five crucial points about divine judgment are made in Acts 17:31. First, divine judgment occurs in God's good time. Second, such judgment is God's *own* judgment. Third, divine judgment will occur in accordance with righteousness, that is, justly. Fourth, even though this judgment is God's own judgment, it will be made effectual and effective through a divine delegate. And fifth, as the concluding phrase of Acts 17:31 makes clear, the divine delegate has already been appointed by virtue of his resurrection from the dead. Cadbury was correct to say that "the resurrection of Jesus is a credential of the coming judgment by Jesus,"[69] but *resurrection as credential of judgment* also signals that just divine judgment will conform to the mode and manner of life of the Righteous/Just One vindicated and validated by resurrection. Here divine judgment is christologically constrained. It is meted out by the risen Messiah in accordance with the righteousness or justice that characterized his earthly life. Moreover, if resurrection from the dead is as much the universal pledge of this judgment as the validation of the kind of life that was, in this instance, cut short by death, resurrection may also provide the best and clearest indication of the mode or form of divine judgment.[70] Hence a key question: What might judgment shaped by—and therefore shaped like—resurrection be like? At the very least, judgment that is analogous to resurrection must be closer to restoration and transformation than to retribution and deformation.

The Restoration of Israel (Acts 1:6; 28:20)

Situated near both the beginning and end of Acts are words that raise the question of the role of Israel in Luke's eschatology. In the eschatologically charged opening to Acts, assembled apostles put this question to the risen Jesus: "Lord, are you now restoring divine reign to Israel?" (1:6; cf. 1:3). Jesus's reply makes clear that the matter of timing is a divine prerogative and therefore not for people to know, but there is nothing in his response to suggest that the hope for restoration of divine reign to Israel is either inappropriate or forlorn. Toward the end of Acts, Paul is newly arrived in Rome, calls

69. Cadbury, "Acts and Eschatology," 310.

70. With respect to Lukan eschatology in Acts, Bruce is able to discuss the theme of "judgment and resurrection" without once considering whether the resurrection of Jesus as pledge of his future role as judge might bear on the mode, form, or nature of eschatological judgment. See his "Eschatology in Acts," 56–59.

together the Jewish leadership there, and informs these leaders that his reason for wanting to speak with them is that he is chained "because of the hope of Israel" (28:20). At an appointed time, large numbers of fellow Jews listen to him argue his case about the reign of God and Jesus. Some are even convinced, according to Luke, but Paul provokes contention among his listeners by citing Isaiah regarding Israel's lack of perception and by advising that the "salvation of God" has been sent to the nations (28:23–28). Since Paul's theme in Acts 28:23 (and also 28:31) echoes Jesus's instruction on divine reign in 1:3, these passages not only enclose the narrative of Acts as a whole but also reveal how significant Israel is to Luke's eschatology.[71]

Luke's attitude toward Israel, the Jews, and Jewish Law or tradition is a turbulent topic.[72] The evidence one must evaluate is mixed and open to conflicting interpretations. Of particular interest for this study is what has been made of Luke's alleged animosity toward Judaism and what that supposedly reveals about his eschatology, especially eschatological judgment.

In *Early Christian Historiography: Narratives of Retributive Justice*, Garry Trompf opens his chapter on Luke's contribution to Christian historiography by drawing attention to the curious coincidence within the New Testament of a plethora of injunctions toward other-oriented compassion alongside warnings of eschatological vengeance. "What happens in earliest Christian thinking," he asserts, "is that retributive vengeance on evildoers tends to be projected into future, divinely-charged eschatological events."[73] For all the social change inspired by the moral vision of Jesus and his earliest followers, "the staying power of traditionalist, normative logics of retribution was immense."[74] Trompf seeks to sustain this thesis in Luke's case by situating Luke–Acts within the context of contemporaneous Greco-Roman and Jewish writers. He shows that among nonbiblical writers of the period, a chief concern was to extol virtuous conduct and to demonstrate that unvirtuous behaviors brought in their wake inevitable negative ramifications. Among Roman writers such as Tacitus, Plutarch, and Cicero, diverse explanations were proposed about how blameworthy deeds are requited. As for Jewish authors of the period, especially Josephus, the notion of divine recompense, even after death, becomes a leitmotif.

Turning to Luke, whose two-part work Trompf accepts as the earliest exemplar of Christian historiography, though it combines *bios* with *historia*—"it is significant" for Trompf "that a hallmark of [Luke's] opus is a concern with retribution, or more specifically, with showing reflections of divine requitals in events, and with directing his readers to key issues of reciprocity and

71. While Carroll considers it reasonable to bypass texts of eschatological judgment in Acts, the final passage addressed in his study is the ending of Acts. See his *Response to the End*, 155–64.

72. For a range of perspectives, see Tyson, *Luke–Acts and the Jewish People*.

73. Trompf, *Early Christian Historiography*, 48.

74. Ibid., 50.

judgement."[75] When Luke's work is perceived within its sociocultural milieu, Trompf argues, retribution is an essential strand, perhaps even a dominant thread, within its narrative fabric.

Important for Trompf's case is what he describes as "a clear tendency in Luke toward 'anti-Judaism,'" which, although intimated at various points throughout Luke's two-part narrative, culminates in Paul's (apparent) repudiation of fellow Jews in Rome in favor of non-Jews, who will assuredly listen. According to Trompf, "It is on Paul's arrival in Rome that Luke chooses to accentuate God's judgement against the disbelieving Jews in favour of the receptive Gentiles. That is significant, for it was the Romans who destroyed the holy city of the Jews."[76] Luke's interpretation of Jerusalem's destruction as "days of vengeance" (Luke 21:20–24) is suggestive of a retributive mind-set, but Trompf's assertion regarding Paul's reception by Roman Jews and Paul's response is overstated.

At various points earlier in Acts (13:14, 42–49; 18:5–11; cf. 19:8–10), Paul turns his attention to non-Jews in response to Jewish hostility. Nevertheless, *the pattern of speaking first to Jews wherever Paul goes continues.* Even in Rome, Paul's first point of business is to meet with local Jewish leaders to advise them that he is chained "because of Israel's hope" (28:20). Later a large Jewish audience hears him out for an entire day as he seeks to persuade them about Jesus based on Torah and the Prophets. Although some remain unpersuaded, *some are convinced by Paul*, according to Acts 28:24. If anything, Paul's reception by fellow Jews is more positive in Rome than earlier in Pisidian Antioch (Acts 13) and Corinth (Acts 18:1–11), although even *after* determining to go to the Gentiles in Acts 18:6, Paul's first recorded converts comprise the household of Crispus, a synagogue leader (18:8). In other words, on earlier occasions Paul's "turning to Gentiles" does not entail an in-principle "turning away from Jews." Although cognizant of this prior pattern, Trompf ignores its relevance for interpreting the ending of Acts. Moreover, his alleged accentuation of divine judgment against Jews in Rome can only refer to Paul's implicit denunciation in Acts 28:26–27, citing Isaiah 6:9–10, followed up with the warning that the "salvation of God" has been sent to others more likely to listen.[77] Perhaps Paul's provocative language reflects Luke's awareness that although the early Christian movement grew out of Jewish soil, its appeal was ultimately stronger to non-Jews. But that is a far cry from "anti-Judaism."[78]

75. Ibid., 64.
76. Ibid., 66.
77. Toward the end of his chapter, Trompf glosses Acts 28:25b–28 as follows: "The decision of God that the 'pagans' are to be proselytized and that there is to be a rupture between synagogue and Church is strikingly affirmed as if it is from Rome outwards that this rupture will have its greatest effect in the future (verse 28)." See ibid., 87. This is scant justification for Trompf's inference regarding divine retribution.
78. See also Johnson, "New Testament's Anti-Jewish Slander," who shows that rhetorical rage between different Jewish groups was common during the period in which Luke wrote.

There is no compelling reason why Paul's final words in Acts should be interpreted differently from earlier occasions on which he announced that the focus of his mission was shifting to non-Jews.[79] Largely on the basis of the climactic position of Paul's final announcement, however, others see things differently. For Pervo, "This third example of the formula comes at the very end of the book and 'carries special narrative weight.'"[80] "Narrative weight" need not signify variation from an established pattern, however. In narrative patterns, why must the climactic instance contradict the pattern rather than confirm it? Certain details within this culminating passage encourage this more positive reading. First and foremost is the detail that some of Paul's Jewish audience accepted what he had to say. Internal to the narration of this episode itself, therefore, is evidence that Jews no less than non-Jews will indeed hear, understand, and turn, despite Paul's provocative scriptural citation. Second, although Luke's depiction of Paul's mission in Ephesus is less clearly parallel to the end of Acts than his descriptions of Paul's response to Jewish opposition in Pisidian Antioch and Corinth, in certain respects it foreshadows the end of Acts better than the earlier, more exact parallel occurrences. For example, in Ephesus, as in Rome, Paul's theme is the reign of God (Acts 19:8; 28:23, 31), and the duration of Paul's stay in both Ephesus and Rome is two years (19:10; 28:30). In Ephesus, Paul abandons the synagogue for the more conducive space provided by a certain Tyrannus, but Luke goes out of his way in Acts 19:10 to indicate that the Asians who heard the word of the Lord from Paul *included Jews*. In light of this, it is hardly far-fetched to envisage Jews as being among those welcomed by Paul during his two years in Rome. Indeed, given the focus on Roman Jews from the time of Paul's arrival in Rome (28:16), one wonders whether Luke's concluding comments in 28:30–31 also pertain primarily to Jews in Rome. Finally, as on earlier occasions, Paul's final words are directed to a particular Jewish community, not to Jews per se. On the basis of this final point in particular, Richard Bauckham argues that Luke envisages "a relatively open future" for Israel.[81]

Returning to Trompf, he recognizes that Jesus's mission, as Luke presents it, has a markedly prophetic dimension, but in view of Luke's more exalted Christology he contends that "the Evangelist's manifest interest in matters of retribution cannot be contained solely within the framework of prophetic judgment."[82] Trompf elaborates upon this by attending to Luke's conception

79. See Barrett, *Acts of the Apostles*, 2:xcvii. Also Witherington, *Acts of the Apostles*, 800–806.

80. Pervo, *Acts*, 681. The phrase "carries special narrative weight" is borrowed by Pervo from Joseph Tyson; cf. Carroll, *Response to the End*, 158–59, who thinks the length of Paul's scriptural citation in Acts 28:26–27 also sets this culminating episode apart from earlier comparable occasions.

81. Bauckham, "Restoration of Israel in Luke–Acts," 484–87.

82. Trompf, *Early Christian Historiography*, 68.

of the proclamation of God's reign, which in Trompf's view includes two aspects: cosmic judgment and a universal challenge.[83] A conception of cosmic judgment permitted Luke to envisage what many contemporaneous writers could not—ultimate resolution—even if this also made more precarious any effort on his part to discern divine retribution within historical events. According to Trompf,

> Luke reports that the preaching of the Christians includes the proclamation of the second return (the *parousia*) of Christ as final "judge of the quick and the dead" (as Peter in Acts 10:42b), or as the man appointed to "judge the world in righteousness" on a day fixed by God (as Paul at 17:31), at a resurrection to distinguish the just from the unjust (Paul at 24:15; cf. also 23:6b). Now the formulation of judging "the living and the dead" . . . foreshadows the one part of Christian credal statements distinctly concerned with retribution (as both punishment and reward).[84]

In view of Luke's acknowledgment of the crucified, raised, and ascended Christ's prerogative to judge ultimately, Trompf makes a point of drawing attention to Luke's careful emphasis on divine favor preceding and outweighing divine retribution. "In both volumes," Trompf avers, "Luke's educative strategy in terms of a prospective divine cosmic event is positive before any warnings are enunciated."[85] As a result, the Lukan ambience is decidedly sunnier than that of his Matthean counterpart, even if eschatological vengeance is not absent from Luke's worldview.

As for the second dimension of Trompf's understanding of the proclamation of divine reign, its universal implications, Trompf hones in on Luke's central section, asserting that in comparative terms it emphasizes three themes: "security [via wealth], discipleship, and the retributive consequences of rejecting or accepting the divine intention."[86] With respect to both security and discipleship, Trompf emphasizes how Jesus's teaching on the reign of God subverts existing cultural mores, but in relation to warnings of retribution, Luke apparently remained fixed to his religiocultural moorings. He innovates as a historian, according to Trompf, by subjecting all human experience to eschatological appraisal,[87] but not so far as the logic of retribution itself is concerned. Trompf seems to assume that Lukan asseverations of divine judgment within history are effectively coessential with final judgment. As he opines, with respect to Luke's dual perspectives concerning divine retribution, "God's final Judgement at the end of this order of existence evidently does not leave

83. Ibid., 69–78.
84. Ibid., 69.
85. Ibid., 70.
86. Ibid., 73. Trompf goes so far as to say that the last of these is given most space by Luke.
87. Ibid., 75.

the historian with nothing to say about divine judgements during this order; *all judgements are necessarily consistent.*[88] But nothing Trompf appeals to in the remainder of his discussion bears this out. Indeed, the few instances he cites of Luke's interest in ultimate judgment indicate reticence on Luke's part regarding knowledge of precisely how things will pan out. God's mercy or patience or predisposition toward those generally held to be of no account precludes cocksureness about God's final arbitration.

As for instances of divine judgment within historical processes, for example, the deaths of Judas and Herod Agrippa, Trompf observes that no retributive measure is actually narrated in Luke's Gospel but is rather reserved for Acts. Indeed, Trompf goes so far as to suggest that this might be a decisive reason for Acts: "What Jesus had warned about was coming true, and those who rejected him had to face the consequences."[89] In Acts, however, members of the early Jewish-Christian community such as Ananias and Sapphira, Stephen, and James (son of Zebedee) also die prematurely, and the deaths of Ananias and Sapphira are as close to being described as the result of divine judgment as is Herod Agrippa's.

Perhaps Trompf rightly sees in the deaths of Ananias and Sapphira instances of divine retribution for deceit, and there is coherence to his discussion of how Luke disentangles the premature and violent deaths of John the Baptist, Jesus, James, and Paul from the logic of retributive justice.[90] If, on the other hand, he is correct to characterize Luke as a "historian of retributive logic" and to see, as an important reason for Acts, the narration of episodes interpreted as divine retribution within history, one would expect the retributive strand in Luke's eschatology to be not only retained but also reinforced—even ratcheted up—in Acts. This is not the case, however. In Acts, Luke does not reinforce but rather rarefies the strain of eschatological vengeance present in his Gospel.

Like Bruce (and others), Trompf finds it acceptable to discuss divine judgment in Acts without reflecting on the difference it makes to see *in Jesus* God's peace announcement to Israel (Acts 10:36) or the divinely authorized judge (10:42; 17:31). Surely Luke's Christology should bear on what one thinks about—or how one wrestles with—divine judgment, whether in relation to historical events or in ultimate terms. Trompf also infers too much from the ending of Acts, which in view of parallel passages earlier in Acts is significantly more ambiguous than Trompf allows. As a result, despite Trompf's case for regarding Luke as a "historian of retributive logic," such a characterization

88. Ibid., emphasis added.
89. Ibid., 77.
90. Ibid., 78–89, under the heading "The Issue of Satisfactory Conclusions to Luke and Acts." Luke knew of Paul's death (see Acts 20:22–24, 36–38; 21:11–14), according to Trompf, but drew down the curtain on his story where he did to avoid recounting his death. "That Luke should round things off in this way has everything to do with his sense as a historian of retributive logic" (83).

accounts for less than the whole of Luke's narrative of Christian origins and, indeed, less than the best of Luke's theology and moral vision.

Restoration Eschatology in Acts

In turning from Luke's Gospel to Acts, it must be acknowledged that eschatological vengeance remains a part of Luke's conceptual schema. Despite his Christology of peace and peaceable moral ethos, retributive eschatological judgment is apparently indispensable. In relation to Luke's Gospel, I have sought to show that even in texts within which eschatological vengeance is foreseen, it is neither so primary nor so prominent that Luke's conception of divine judgment must be seen as strictly or solely retributive. Luke's eschatology in Acts takes us further in this direction.

Within the three eschatological texts in the first three chapters of Acts, the note of retribution is well-nigh absent. What emerges from attending to these passages is an association between the return of Jesus and restoration rather than retribution. From the perspective of these passages, early Christian hope was peaceable and restorative. Moreover, later texts in Acts that foresee eschatological judgment do not undo the restorative tenor of the earlier texts. In chapter 3, I expressed the view that in turning from the story of Jesus to the story of the movement(s) he initiated, Luke's peace beacon dimmed. In general terms, that view remains defensible, but not, surprisingly, in relation to Luke's eschatology. Overall, the eschatology of Acts is devoid of retributive dimensions that jar with Luke's peaceable Christology and moral ethos. This, some might argue, is simply because eschatology is muted in Acts. On the other hand, one might as easily argue that if retribution rather than restoration were the dominant note of Luke's eschatology, that would pierce through in texts that presume rather than develop his eschatological convictions. To be clear, I do not contend that the note of retribution is absent from texts of eschatological judgment in Acts, only that this is not the dominant refrain. In light of Luke's theology in its totality, judgment at the hands of *this* divinely authorized judge can hardly be strictly retributive, even if the restoration of all things (Acts 3:20–21) has a retributive dimension.

Luke–Acts: Eschatological *Shalom* or Vengeance?

Luke is the evangelist of peace and in Jesus perceived divine visitation for the purpose of proclaiming peace to Israel.[91] In general terms, Luke's eschatology coheres with his peaceable theology and moral vision. Texts of eschatological

91. Compare Swartley, *Covenant of Peace*, 129. He notes that most of the distinctive peace texts in Luke's Gospel "serve the purpose of showing that Jesus in his proclamation of the

terror are relatively rare in the Lukan literature, and even those that sound the note of retribution, such as Luke 12:46 and 17:26–30, do not overshadow the predominantly peaceful tenor of Luke's vision for the future. In view of Luke's emphasis on fulfillment of divine or divinely authorized promises, however, such texts do raise the question of the moral status of promises allegedly originating with Jesus regarding future retribution. Nevertheless, the contexts within which these retributive texts occur provide resources for reading these texts in line with Luke's peace-oriented Christology and moral vision.

In the case of Luke 12:46, the image of the vengeful returning master is primarily a warning for those in leadership within the Christian community. This troubling image is also relativized by the culturally strange but christologically coherent image associated with the Son of humanity's coming in Luke 12:35–40. As Luke's earliest depiction of what to expect at the Son of humanity's future arrival, this expectation should be given interpretive priority, especially if such anticipation is congruent with what is associated with the Son of humanity's expected arrival with power and much glory in Luke 21:25–36.

Although some interpreters associate the Son of humanity's coming in Luke 21 with Jerusalem's destruction, it seems more reasonable to dissociate these events in Luke's broader eschatological schema. If this be granted, nothing in Luke 21:25–36 explicitly associates the Son of humanity's arrival with retribution or vengeance. Rather, the keynote of Jesus's eschatological instruction in Luke 21 is *deliverance*. No doubt Luke held together the notions of divine deliverance and divine judgment, but Luke 21:25–36 provides no grounds for equating divine judgment with vengeance or retribution.

In Luke's Gospel, then, the first and last words on the Son of humanity's future coming are words of hope rather than words of despair. These first and last words cohere with Luke's peaceable theology and therefore provide the hermeneutical horizons for interpreting dissonant texts. In the case of Luke 17:26–30, which focuses on the future "day" of the Son of humanity, reading this text in light of 12:35–40 and 21:25–36 is further encouraged both by the context of this passage (immediately following 17:20–21) and by resonances between this passage and Luke 9:18–27, which articulates both the counterintuitive manner of the Messiah's mission and the equally counterintuitive (but coherent) requirements for discipleship. Read together, Luke 9:18–27 provokes the question whether the coming Son of humanity can be construed differently from the Son of humanity who fulfilled his mission nonviolently.

In short, in relation to eschatological vengeance, which lowers from time to time in Luke–Acts, Luke's standing as the evangelist of peace serves to relativize such texts, especially in view of two features of his theological vision: first, his characterization of Jesus's mission in its totality as a divine

---

kingdom of God announces and incarnates the Gospel of peace (*eirēnē*)." This assessment is reinforced by Acts 10:36.

overture of peace; and second, his prioritizing of realized eschatology in the mission of Jesus. Since Luke accentuates what God has already done in Jesus, his description of Jesus's mission and message establishes the standard for evaluating expectations associated with Jesus in the future.

Lurking in the shadows, however, and threatening to stymie eschatological expectation that envisages divine judgment as more restorative than retributive, more peaceable than vengeful, is Luke's evident conviction that the destruction of Jerusalem was divine retaliation for Jewish rejection of Jesus and his mission. So long as the most plausible way to interpret Luke's laments against Jerusalem is to see them as prophecies of divine judgment for spurning God's overture of peace in Jesus, the possibility remains that Jerusalem's destruction provides the template for Luke's conception of eschatological judgment. Once that possibility is embraced, however, Luke's status (and stature) as the evangelist of peace is strained. More than the relatively rare texts of eschatological terror, Luke's texts relating to Jerusalem's destruction as divine punishment jeopardize his standing as the evangelist of peace. This anomaly remains irresolvable to me. I would like to be satisfied with Mikeal Parsons's thesis that Luke's depiction of Jerusalem and the temple is ambivalent,[92] but too much is at stake in this ambivalence and too few seem alert to all that is at stake.

Someone who seems open-eyed to much of what is at stake in the Lukan laments for Jerusalem is Bruce Fisk. In a careful and detailed discussion titled "*See My Tears*: A Lament for Jerusalem (Luke 13:31–35; 19:41–44),"[93] Fisk makes a cogent case for interpreting Jesus's forebodings of judgment against Jerusalem as similar in kind to Jeremiah's provisional prophecies of judgment, which later were followed by promises of restoration. Although primarily concerned with the question of whether or not Luke holds out any hope for Jerusalem beyond its destruction, Fisk makes three points that bear on whether Luke's conception of Jerusalem's destruction as divine vengeance undermines his peaceable theology and moral ethos. First, he follows Dale Allison in interpreting the conclusion to Luke 13:31–35, "I tell you, you will not see me until you say, 'Blessed is the one who comes in the name of the Lord,'" as a contingent prophecy,[94] thereby opening up the prospect of hope beyond devastation, especially if the two laments of Luke 13:31–35 and 19:41–44 are permitted to shed light on each other. Second, he observes that the lament against Jerusalem in Luke 19:41–44 is restricted to the immediate future, again leaving open the possibility of restoration beyond devastation. And third, he draws attention to the frequent offers of forgiveness within Luke–Acts after Jesus's prophecy of woe upon Jerusalem. For Fisk, these considerations do not resolve matters completely but rather open up possibilities for contemplation. As he writes,

92. See Parsons, "Place of Jerusalem." See also idem, *Luke: Storyteller*, 84–95.
93. Fisk, "*See My Tears*."
94. Allison, "Matt. 23:39 = Luke 13:35b as a Conditional Prophecy."

These points do not prove that Luke anticipated the salvation of "all Israel," nor do they reveal how far Jesus could see beyond the devastation of Jerusalem. On the other hand, if we let Jesus' two laments interpret each other, and if we play both refrains in the key of Jeremiah, we may decide that Luke's tale of Jerusalem should not be reduced to one of refusal and utter abandonment.[95]

Fisk's study opens the door to the possibility that Jesus's forebodings of destruction for Jerusalem might not be God's final word for Jerusalem, but he does not challenge Luke's evident perception that Jerusalem's destruction was an instance of divine judgment. While I presently accept that Luke understood Jerusalem's destruction to comprise divine judgment, two concerns lead me to place a question mark against such an understanding: first, the tenuousness and indeed temerity of attributing any historical event to divine will or action; and second, the fissure such a perception implies within Luke's theology and moral vision. Surprisingly, neither of these concerns seems to trouble Richard Hays.

Discussing Luke–Acts in *The Moral Vision of the New Testament*, Hays structures his treatment of Luke's moral vision by beginning with Luke's Christology and relating that theme to Luke's vision for the church, then turning to Luke's depiction of the Spirit-empowered community, and subsequently considering how eschatology frames his ethical perspective.[96] In Hays's view, Luke's eschatology is not too different from Matthew's. Although there are some "distinctive accents" to Luke's eschatology, most notably in relation to the church's continuing role in history under the influence of the "eschatological Spirit," Luke shares Matthew's penchant for encouraging appropriate moral behavior by warning of eschatological judgment.[97] In general terms, this may be correct, but the prospect of eschatological judgment plays a more restricted role in Luke–Acts than in Matthew's Gospel, except perhaps in relation to individual eschatology. Not only is the threat of eschatological judgment muted, but Luke's peace emphasis also throws the relatively rare warnings of eschatological vengeance into even starker relief than in Matthew's Gospel.

Responding to Fitzmyer's observation that Luke refocuses things to make room for the period of the church in salvation-history, Hays remarks, "This making room for the church in history is one of Luke's most important contributions to New Testament theology and ethics."[98] For Hays, moreover, "The outpouring of the Spirit prefigures the end, and thus the community that lives and acts in the power of the Spirit is an eschatological community, bringing God's future into being in communal life and thus witnessing to the world about the power of the resurrection."[99] But if, within this eschatological community, Jerusalem's

95. Fisk, "*See My Tears*," 175.
96. Hays, *Moral Vision*, 112–37.
97. Ibid., 129.
98. Ibid., 131.
99. Ibid.

destruction is interpreted as divine judgment, and the deaths of individuals such as Ananias and Sapphira no less than Herod Agrippa are seen as divine punishment,[100] does not such a mind-set prefigure strict eschatological retribution? "Where the Spirit is at work in the church," according to Hays, "nothing is static: old barriers and conventions fall as the Spirit gathers and shapes a new people."[101] How new is the logic of strict retribution, however, especially in view of Luke's conviction that the Spirit who empowers the church is the same Spirit who empowered Jesus's own mission of peace and was conveyed to the church by the risen and exalted Jesus (Acts 2:32–33) to enable witness to Jesus? Hays rightly reads the general movement of Luke's presentation of the church under the guidance of the "Spirit of Jesus" (16:7), but, except in relation to Jesus's own mission, Luke himself seems not to have grasped all the implications of the Spirit's witness to Jesus as God's peace announcement. He did, however, provide the necessary resources for subsequent witnesses to divine visitation in Jesus to take things further along the peace path he etched.

Hays concludes his discussion of Luke's eschatology by recognizing both the prominence and various social ramifications of "eschatological reversal."[102] Few disagree that eschatological reversal is a prominent theme for Luke, but few ponder publicly whether, in light of the mission of Jesus, the logic of strict retribution has also been reversed. For example, according to Carroll, "Luke's God is the God of surprising reversals; history in the hands of such a God is laced with irony. And the deepest irony of all is the heavenly reign of the one who was rejected by the nation and crucified. He has been vindicated by God and installed in the seat of power, where he waits 'from now on' ([Luke] 22:69) while his enemies on earth are vanquished (20:42–43)."[103] Here Carroll attests to Luke's understanding of divine reversal but also intimates that beyond reversal lies *reversion* to eschatological vengeance. Although there are texts in Luke–Acts that would seem to authorize such an interpretation, there is much more in Luke's Gospel and Acts to encourage a deconstructive reading of Luke's relatively few texts of eschatological terror. Nothing is more redundant than vengeance following the recognition of divine visitation in Jesus's peace proclamation. If, as Hays affirms, "the overturning of the expected is a motion that lies in the deep structure of Luke's construal of the good news,"[104] I venture to hope, on the basis of Luke's own Christology and moral vision, that God's "overturning of the expected" applies ultimately to expectations of eschatological vengeance.

---

100. While the death of this Herod is clearly narrated as an instance of divine punishment, it is perhaps noteworthy that the deaths of Ananias and Sapphira are not explicitly interpreted as divine judgment, even though this seems to be the inevitable inference.

101. Hays, *Moral Vision*, 131–32.

102. Ibid., 132–33.

103. Carroll, "Parousia in the Synoptic Gospels and Acts," 40.

104. Hays, *Moral Vision*, 132–33.

Part 3

JOHANNINE TRAJECTORIES

6

Nonviolent Apocalypse

The Peace Witness of the Fourth Gospel

Turning from the first three Gospels to the Fourth Gospel, we encounter something both recognizably familiar and strangely different. One meets the selfsame protagonist as in the Synoptic Gospels, but the interpretive element in the Johannine narration of Jesus's mission and message is dramatically heightened. This is especially so in relation to eschatological aspects of Jesus's teaching. The future-oriented dimension of this teaching is muted, and one instead finds an emphasis on present fulfillment in the life of believers. Long considered as incompatible elements within Johannine theology, the presence within the Fourth Gospel of both realized and future-oriented eschatology is here considered to reflect the dialectical cast of the Fourth Evangelist's creative mind.[1] Dialectical dexterity and fertile freshness also help to account for the radical renovation achieved by reconfiguring apocalyptic motifs in line with the *shalom*-shaped mission of Jesus the Messiah.

The Fourth Gospel as Reconfigured Apocalypse

One of the many ways in which the Fourth Gospel differs from the other three biblical Gospels is the absence of specific exorcisms on Jesus's part. In the

---

1. See Barrett, *New Testament Essays*, chap. 4, "The Dialectical Theology of St John" (49–69); cf. Kysar, *John, the Maverick Gospel*, 118–26, where Johannine eschatology is described as *dialectical*. Within the Fourth Gospel, this more accurately describes the relation between realized and future-oriented eschatology than the term "complementary," as in O'Donnell, "Complementary Eschatologies."

Synoptic Gospels, Jesus's exorcisms signal the encroaching reign of God into territory under the sway of demonic forces. "If by the finger [or "Spirit"] of God I drive out demons," Jesus is remembered as saying, "then the reign of God has undoubtedly come upon you" (Matt. 12:28; Luke 11:20). As such, within the first three Gospels, exorcisms comprise a significant aspect of the fulfillment of eschatological hope. Jesus, vanguard of God's reign, scatters demonic forces in anticipation of their ultimate demise. In the Fourth Gospel, however, there are no confrontations between Jesus and demons, no displays of demonic agitation in Jesus's presence, no cries of anguish as demonic forces are driven from their human habitations.

In John 12:31, however, the following words are uttered by Jesus in response to a heavenly voice: "Now is judgment of this world; now the ruler of this world will be cast out." The context of this saying is crucial. It occurs in the aftermath of the final sign of Jesus's public mission, the raising of Lazarus, and shortly before the impending Passover festival, following Jesus's entrance into Jerusalem while mounted in kingly fashion on a donkey's colt. In response to a request by some "Greeks" who want to see him, Jesus responds that the time, or "hour," for the Son of humanity's glorification has arrived (12:23). The remainder of the exchange between Jesus and his interlocutors, who are never precisely identified, shows clearly that Jesus's death by crucifixion is in view (12:20–36a). For this evangelist, Jesus's death by crucifixion is his exaltation and glorification, but also the occasion of the world's judgment and expulsion of the world's tyrannical ruler. In short, despite the absence of specific exorcisms within the Fourth Gospel, the culmination of Jesus's mission is characterized as an exorcism.

This characterization of Jesus's death as "exorcism" bespeaks an apocalyptic orientation and mind-set.[2] Rather than seeing the divine confrontation with evil forces in individual exorcisms, however, the evangelist reconstructs this apocalyptic confrontation as occurring at Jesus's death, which in the Fourth Gospel is the culmination and completion of Jesus's mission in the world. Crucially, the expulsion of this world's ruler coincides with the messianic Son of humanity's attraction of all people to himself. In response to the heavenly affirmation that the Father's name has already been glorified and will be glorified again, which some interpret as thunder and others as the voice of a heavenly messenger, Jesus himself says: "Not for my sake did this voice occur but rather for yours. Now is judgment of this world; now the ruler of this world will be cast out. And when I am lifted from the earth, I will draw all to myself" (John 12:30–32). The evangelist's gloss on this startling claim is that Jesus said this to indicate what kind of death he was about to experience (12:33).

2. Although I came to this conclusion by different means, it finds support in the study by Kovacs, "Jesus' Death as Cosmic Battle."

From the perspective of narrative progression, Jesus's death by crucifixion remains in the immediate future, but when writing, the Fourth Evangelist could look back on years, likely decades, since Jesus's crucifixion. The tyranny of the world's ruler still seemed entrenched, and but a minority of people seemed drawn to acknowledge Jesus as God's Messiah. Nonetheless this evangelist affirms that Jesus's death was the apocalyptic event that rearranged reality. Writing from the perspective of hindsight, he was in a position to affirm that divine judgment of the world, the expulsion of the world's evil ruler, and the attraction of all humanity to Jesus would occur at the last day (cf. John 12:48). Instead, however, he affirms, seemingly against all evidence, that all this had *already occurred* in "the hour," the "now" of Jesus's death. The apocalyptic event has already transpired; the eschatological effects of Jesus's death have been realized.

Especially noteworthy is the Fourth Evangelist's depiction of the *manner* of Jesus's apocalyptic exorcism. The world's tyrannical ruler is dethroned and banished not by heavenly hosts, nor by military messianic might, nor even by calamitous cosmic conflagration, but by "loving to the end" (John 13:1). According to the Fourth Gospel, eschatology and violence are interrelated in the story of Jesus, but violence is not the eschatological agent's means against evil. Rather, it is the willingness of Jesus to endure suffering and death as integral to his mission in the world that scuttles evil. Indeed, it is precisely in and by that "loving to the end" that evil is undone. For this reason, Jesus's dying utterance is "It is accomplished" (John 19:30).

In 1991 two major works on the Fourth Gospel appeared: *Understanding the Fourth Gospel*, by John Ashton; and *The Quest for the Messiah*, by John Painter.[3] Independently of each other, these authors emphasize the importance of interpreting the Fourth Gospel within the matrix of late Second Temple Jewish apocalypticism. Introducing the revised edition of *Understanding the Fourth Gospel*, Ashton comments that the close affinity between the Fourth Gospel and apocalyptic writings to which he had drawn attention in the first edition had been all but ignored by others, Christopher Rowland being the only exception of whom he was aware.[4] But in a concluding section added to chapter 2 of the revised edition of *The Quest for the Messiah*, Painter comments, with reference to Ashton's work: "It is a feature of *Quest* that it argues that Jn owes more to apocalyptic motifs,

3. Ashton, *Understanding the Fourth Gospel*; Painter, *Quest for the Messiah*. Both books have been republished in substantially revised editions, Painter's in 1993 and Ashton's in 2007. Unless otherwise indicated, references to these works are to their second editions.

4. Ashton, *Understanding the Fourth Gospel*, 6–7. Ashton seems also to have overlooked Kovacs's study of John 12:20–36, "Jesus' Death as Cosmic Battle." C. H. Dodd referred to the Fourth Gospel as a "realized apocalypse" on the basis that the various "signs" recounted in the Gospel, especially the cross and resurrection, together comprise the promised vision of heaven opened in John 1:51. See his *Interpretation of the Fourth Gospel*, 294.

indeed to an apocalyptic *Weltanschauung*, than is normally recognized."[5]
With Ashton and Painter, I also recognize apocalyptic resonances within
the Fourth Gospel, although such resonances are radical renovations rather
than routine reiterations.

Part 2 of the revised edition of Ashton's book begins with a chapter titled
"Intimations of Apocalyptic." Accepting Rudolf Bultmann's insight that the
key concept of the Fourth Gospel is *revelation*, Ashton makes the context of
the Jewish apocalyptic tradition decisive for his analysis of this distinctive
Gospel. On the basis of four literary motifs—mystery at long last revealed,
revelation in stages, revelation via riddling discourse, and "correspondence"
between heaven and earth—Ashton avers that "the Fourth Gospel is profoundly indebted to apocalyptic in all sorts of ways."[6] This evangelist's
indebtedness to apocalyptic is not wooden or passively receptive, however.
Reflection on the mission and message of Jesus was facilitated by recourse
to apocalyptic motifs, but in the process such motifs were also recast under
the impress of both the story of Jesus and the subsequent experience of
Johannine believers such that Ashton can state: "Thus the fourth evangelist
conceives his own work as an apocalypse—in reverse, upside down, inside
out."[7]

Against the current trend to regard the canonical Gospels as generically
biographical, Ashton aligns himself with those who perceive the Gospels as
analogous to apocalypses:

> Reflecting on the gospel genre and comparing it with the apocalyptic patterns
> studied in the previous chapter ["Intimations of Apocalyptic"], one can hardly
> fail to be struck by the formal resemblances. Of its very nature the Christian
> gospel falls into two stages, the first inchoate and opaque, the second clear
> and unconfined. In the Gospels the two ages of apocalyptic, where the crucial
> distinction is between the hidden mystery and the revealed truth, coalesce
> with the two stages, which focus rather upon the difference between an initial
> revelation of an essentially puzzling character and one in which the puzzle is
> finally resolved.[8]

Painter sees no reason to deny the influence of Greco-Roman biographical
writings on the Gospels, yet he also highlights the influence of Jewish literary
traditions on the development of the Gospels, traditions such as the *Testaments (of the Twelve Patriarchs* et al.) and Jewish apocalyptic.[9] Irrespective

5. Painter, *Quest for the Messiah*, 134. There is no reference to Painter in the revised edition of Ashton's *Understanding the Fourth Gospel*, but his collection of essays, *Studying John*,
betrays familiarity with Painter's book.
6. Ashton, *Understanding the Fourth Gospel*, 310.
7. Ibid., 328–29.
8. Ibid., 334–35.
9. Painter, *Quest for the Messiah*, 131–35.

of the relative influence on the Gospels of the Hellenistic biographical genre, especially since Gospel and apocalypse need not be mutually exclusive genres,[10] what Ashton and Painter agree upon (apocalyptic) is more important than the point on which they disagree: whether or not the Gospels are biographical. By examining a number of Johannine features and themes relating to the "apocalyptic imagination," to borrow the apt phrase used by John J. Collins as the title for his illuminating study of Jewish apocalyptic,[11] it can be shown that the Fourth Evangelist did indeed write an apocalypse of sorts, but one reconfigured in light of the historic mission of Jesus.

Dualism: Imagery, Worldview, and Morality

Three signal themes are sounded in the opening lines of the prologue to the Fourth Gospel: the source and identity of the *Logos* (Word); the creation by the Logos of all that is; and the imagery of light versus darkness (John 1:1–5). As Painter has shown, the dualistic imagery of the Fourth Gospel, like that of certain Qumran texts, reflects a dualistic worldview, albeit modified by the Jewish doctrine of God's creation of all things.[12] All things derive from God, yet—inexplicably—the agent of creation encounters opposition precisely among those whose life derives from him:

> The light shines in the darkness, and the darkness has never vanquished it. . . .
> The true light, which enlightens everyone, was coming into the world. He was in the world, and the world came into existence through him, yet the world did not know him. He came to his own home, but his own people did not receive him. (John 1:5, 9–11)

The imagery of light dispelling darkness, albeit not entirely, and being resisted by the darkness, albeit not entirely successfully, rings true only within a conceptual framework in which the people of the world ought to recognize and welcome its Creator but do not. If they were to do so, the imagery of light as piercing darkness and thereby dispelling some (but not all) of it would be incongruent.

This modified cosmological dualism also entails a moral dualism. Ashton contends that "what looks like and has often been interpreted as a cosmological

---

10. The most obviously apocalyptic writing in the New Testament, the Revelation to John, is mixed with respect to genre, combining vision, letter, and prophecy. The Fourth Gospel mixes biography with apocalyptic vision.

11. J. Collins, *Apocalyptic Imagination*.

12. Painter, *Quest for the Messiah*, 8, 35–52. See also idem, "Monotheism and Dualism." Painter is not alone in drawing attention to the significance of Johannine dualism, which features in most discussions of Johannine thought. See, e.g., Bultmann, *Theology of the New Testament*, vol. 2, part 3, chap. 2; Ashton, *Understanding the Fourth Gospel*, chap. 10; Kysar, *John*, chap. 2.

dualism close to Gnosticism is really a moral dualism: the good (in this case those who accept the revelation of Jesus) versus the wicked (those who reject that revelation—'the Jews')."[13] Closer to the truth, it seems to me, is Painter's notion of a dualistic worldview derived from Zoroastrianism yet modified by Jewish belief in the creation of all things by the one God who is good. In certain respects, this worldview bears the impress of cosmological dualism, even if it balks at accepting a divine principle in ontological opposition to God the Creator, and it entails (but cannot be reduced to) moral dualism. Such relative cosmological dualism is reflected not so much in the imagery of "above and below" and "of/not of this world" (John 8:23) as in the notion that despite the world's creation by God, it has another, antagonistic "ruler" (12:31; 14:30; 16:11). As is evident from John 12:31, the mission of Jesus is not simply to enlighten those blinded by darkness but also to expel the source of darkness and thus the darkness itself. The train of thought developed in John 12:20–36 implies that the hour of the Son of humanity's glorification (12:23) has three interlocking ramifications: (1) glorifying the Father's name (12:27–28); (2) judgment of the world by means of the expulsion of its ruler (12:31); and (3) drawing all people to himself (12:32). The passage concludes by shifting from language focused on the Son of humanity to the imagery of opposition between light and darkness:

> Jesus said to them, "For a little while yet the light will be among you. Walk while you have the light, so that darkness may not vanquish you; one who walks in the darkness knows not where s/he is going. While you have the light, believe in the light, so that you may become children of light." (John 12:35–36a)

The starkly oppositional and indeed conflictual imagery of this passage, wherein darkness is an antagonistic and threatening reality both to the light and to those invited to become children of light, is one aspect of the dualistic worldview shared between the Fourth Gospel and Jewish apocalyptic texts.[14] To affirm a shared apocalyptic conceptual framework, however, should not be taken to imply no difference in theological outlook between the Fourth Gospel and Jewish apocalyptic. A shared dualistic or apocalyptic worldview there may be, but this evangelist's familiarity with and interpretation of the story of Jesus leads to innovative reconceptualization. As Painter observes,

> Jn has modified the apocalyptic vision in that Jesus, as the emissary from above, has entered this world/age as the revelation of the age to come in this age. But he is more than this; he is already, in his coming and going, the decisive intervention of God in this world. This does not, however, exhaust or completely fulfil

---

13. Ashton, *Understanding the Fourth Gospel*, 390.

14. The opposition of darkness to light also features in 1 John 1:5–2:11, where it expresses deep theological and moral convictions.

the purpose of God for this world. Because of this Jn's eschatological views are complex and the perspective of future fulfillment remains important.[15]

Incarnation as Stage One of Eschatological Fulfillment

The prologue, either written or adapted by the Fourth Evangelist to serve as the interpretive lens for understanding his Gospel, presents numerous exegetical and interpretive conundrums. These include the appropriate contextual matrix for understanding key themes such as Logos and light, whether an independent source was used, and if such a source was used, the extent both of the source and of the evangelist's modifications to it.[16] These are important matters, but here only two features of the prologue are addressed: (1) the eschatological orientation of the prologue and (2) the theological and ethical significance of the prologue's characterization of the Logos-become-flesh as the definitive disclosure of the will and way of God.[17]

The eschatological orientation of John 1:1–18 is set out in Painter's essay "Theology, Eschatology and the Prologue of John."[18] Here Painter plumbs the eschatological depths of the prologue, which he regards as a late addition to the Gospel, by showing how it functions as a worldview or metaphysical framework for the story of Jesus that follows. Crucial in this connection is Painter's appeal to the parallels between the prologue to the Fourth Gospel and ancient cosmologies:

> In the ancient world (Egypt and Mesopotamia) cosmologies were used by priestly schools to ground the image of the city state (the *status quo*) in the divine ideal. The cosmology of Genesis 1 also functions in this way, grounding the Law (Sabbath) in the pattern of creation. But the cosmologies of the Hellenistic age have a teleological/eschatological orientation. Thus when John made use of a cosmology in the Prologue, he was using a popular and persuasive means of communication and one which was intended to provide a *Weltanschauung*.[19]

15. Painter, *Quest for the Messiah*, 52. These sentences conclude a section of text added to the revised edition, in which Painter clarifies his understanding of the relation between Johannine dualism and apocalyptic.

16. Among those who emphasize the Jewish Wisdom tradition for understanding the prologue are Ashton, *Studying John*, chap. 1, "The Transformation of Wisdom"; and Painter, *Quest for the Messiah*, 137–62. Wisdom parallels to the Logos in the prologue are displayed in Dodd, *Interpretation of the Fourth Gospel*, 274–75; and in Tobin, "Logos," 353–54. Since his *Quest for the Messiah*, Painter has developed his distinctive approach to the prologue in a series of studies, the earliest of which is discussed below. See Painter, "Point of John's Christology"; idem, "Earth Made Whole"; idem, "Rereading Genesis in the Prologue of John?"; idem, "Creation, Incarnation, and Resurrection in John."

17. To avoid misunderstanding, by using the term *definitive* in relation to divine disclosure in the incarnate Logos, I mean decisive and determinative but not exhaustive.

18. Painter, "Theology, Eschatology and the Prologue."

19. Ibid., 28. Rather than equate the prologue to the Fourth Gospel with a cosmology, I am more inclined to say that the prologue bespeaks an *implied* cosmology.

Painter's reference to the cosmology of Genesis 1 foreshadows his discussion later in this essay (and in various other studies) of the crucial intertextual links that bind the Johannine prologue to the creation account in Genesis 1:1–2:3. Such links not only reflect this evangelist's commitment to a profoundly Jewish understanding of God as Creator but also signal a certain reconceptualization of God as a result of tension between the Christian group represented by the evangelist and contemporary Judaism(s). This reconceptualization of Jewish convictions about God as Creator and revealer (especially through Torah) is brought about by means of three "intra-textual transforming strategies," as Painter calls them: (1) replacing the Jewish conception of Wisdom with Logos, (2) setting the stage for making sense of the dualistic imagery contained in the Gospel narrative, and (3) reinterpreting eschatology.[20] Each of these strategies, but especially the last, warrants attention.

In Jewish tradition, *Word*, *Wisdom*, and *Torah* could be more or less synonymous as expressions of the divine will and creativity. In the prologue to the Fourth Gospel, however, the Logos of God active at and responsible for creation is identified not with Torah but with Jesus Messiah. A determinative dimension of Jewish tradition is thereby challenged by the evangelist's conviction that the definitive self-disclosure of God (Word/Wisdom, Light, Life, Grace, Truth) occurred in and through the Word who became flesh rather than in and through the Jewish Law (see John 1:17).[21]

By establishing within the prologue an antithesis between "light" and "darkness," the evangelist prepares readers for the dualistic imagery that pervades the Fourth Gospel and reflects an apocalyptic worldview. Like Ashton, Painter affirms that "the antithetical language of John manifests an underlying dualistic *Weltanschauung* characteristic of apocalyptic writings."[22] But since the dualism of Jewish apocalyptic literature and, by extension, the Fourth Gospel, is relativized by attributing the origin of all things to divine utterance or handiwork, this dualistic worldview necessarily implies a hoped-for eschatological resolution. After all, neither thoroughgoing dualism nor unresolved relative dualism offers any basis for hope in the ultimate triumph of God the Creator. Hence the evangelist's third "transforming strategy": eschatological reinterpretation as a response to relative (but nevertheless real) dualism.

Despite the world's origins in God's creative utterance, darkness no less than light has its divinely approved place in the created order. Used as an image for evil or opposition to the divine will, however, darkness is an anomaly in God's grace-filled world. No faith stance can with integrity ignore the pain of the world caused by disease and destruction, whether natural or the result of

20. Ibid., 31–41.
21. I say "rather than" instead of "as" because this seems to be the gist of John 1:17, but there is no contrastive conjunction in this verse. Even the "tenting" of the Logos-become-flesh in John 1:14 echoes the "tent of divine presence" in Exod. 40.
22. Painter, "Theology, Eschatology and the Prologue," 33.

human violence. For this reason the evangelist affirms the persistent shining of the light of the Logos into the darkness and the incapacity of the darkness to vanquish that light (John 1:5). Having affirmed this, however, the evangelist goes further, and his going further is what Painter means by his reinterpreting of eschatology: "Here the evangelist has creatively reinterpreted the eschatology of early Christianity which can now be defined in terms of the specific historical confrontation of the darkness by the light as distinct from the eternal shining of the light of the eternal creative λόγος [logos]."[23]

Painter discusses the "specific historical confrontation of the darkness by the light" in connection with five themes, which he identifies as stages in the evangelist's eschatological response to relative (but nevertheless real) dualism. These five stages are (1) the incarnation; (2) the ministry of signs as the most luminous instances of light's breaking into the darkness, which thereby provokes resistance no less than faith; (3) death/exaltation as the "end" of incarnation; (4) being born of God and continuing judgment through the Spirit; and (5) future judgment. Here brief remarks on the first, third, fourth, and fifth themes must suffice.

According to Painter, "If eschatology is the evangelist's response to the dualism, then the event of the incarnation is the first stage of the response."[24] In his brief remarks on the incarnation as the initial stage of the Fourth Evangelist's response to a dualistic apocalyptic ideology, Painter is concerned to prevent the conclusion that the incarnation was sufficient in and of itself to dispel the darkness. In this, he is correct. But more may be said—and will be shortly—than that the incarnation is but the first stage of a response to the problem exposed by dualism.

With respect to the theme of death and exaltation (or death *as* exaltation), Painter helpfully explicates death on a cross as the inevitable concomitant of incarnation. He points out not only that the logic of incarnation entails death, as for all flesh, but also that this particular stage in response to the darkness of the world does not militate against but rather conforms to God's love and goodness displayed in the incarnation. As Painter puts it,

> In the world dominated by the darkness the λόγος made flesh is on his way to death, the lot of all flesh. The "became flesh" signifies the assumption of a life directed inexorably towards death, and the willingness of Jesus to die is understood as a manifestation of his limitless love, 13.1. Because he is the λόγος made flesh, his self-giving is a manifestation of the love of God. Thus, if the λόγος is the symbol of God in relation to the world, the symbol of the incarnate λόγος is the cross. The light of the incarnate λόγος penetrates the heart of darkness (3.19–21; 8.12; 9.5, 39–41) in a way that shows that the goodness of God can only overcome the darkness by taking it into himself and absorbing it. Thus

23. Ibid., 34.
24. Ibid.

the light of the incarnate λόγος is manifest not only in his coming but also in his return to the Father by way of the cross.[25]

Painter comments that this theme of death/exaltation is also expressed by means of the coming and going of the Light of the world (3:19–21; 8:12; 9:5–6, 39–41; 12:35–36) and the descent and ascent of the Son of humanity (3:13–15; 6:62), which in turn connect with the Johannine theme of judgment of the world—another apocalyptic theme explored later in this chapter.

In relation to the theme of being born of God and continuing judgment, Painter observes how the role of the Paraclete in the Fourth Gospel is not only to continue to make possible being born by God, begun in the incarnation of the divine Logos, but also to continue judging the world, as begun by the Light's coming into the world. Finally, in relation to future judgment, Painter observes that this theme is absent from the prologue to the Gospel. Nevertheless, the various stages of the evangelist's response to the problem signaled by his dualistic worldview, however crucial, have yet to resolve the problem. "The fact that the dualism has not been resolved even by the exaltation of Jesus and the coming of the Spirit implies a future resolution. Here we should note Jesus' language about 'coming again' (14:1–4) which should not be dissolved into the coming of the Spirit."[26] In other words, while the prologue does not refer to future eschatological judgment, the empirical reality that the evangelist wrote in the context of continuing darkness necessarily implies that he anticipated eschatological judgment. References to the "last day" (6:39–40, 44, 54; 11:24; 12:48) are therefore not alien but integral to the evangelist's dialectical eschatology.

From a strictly logical perspective, one wonders whether Painter is correct to assert that "future resolution" is *implied* by the fact that neither the exaltation of the Son of humanity nor the presence of the Spirit has resolved the dualism inherent within the Gospel. But since future-oriented eschatology finds a place within the narrative, Painter is probably correct to see "future resolution" as a necessary implication of the evangelist's dualistic vision of reality. "The future eschatological judgement, though not mentioned in the Prologue, sits quite comfortably in relation to it and is demanded to resolve the problem of the prevailing darkness."[27]

Responding to Painter's remarks on the incarnation, I indicated that more could be said than that the incarnation was, for this evangelist, the first stage of his response to the problem posed by the pervasiveness of darkness in a world created by a good, gracious, and generous God. While anticipation of future eschatological judgment might well be necessitated by the persistence of darkness, despite the coming of the Light, nevertheless the emphasis on present (or

25. Ibid., 37–38.
26. Ibid., 40.
27. Ibid., 42.

realized) eschatology in the Fourth Gospel implies the decisiveness of the revelation associated with the incarnation of the Logos. Both the preeminence of the Logos and the indivisible connectedness between the Logos and God, as between sole son and father, permeate the prologue. Insofar as the prologue is the interpretive prism for the Gospel, the condescension of the divine Logos in becoming human and tenting among people in the manner described within the Gospel *discloses in a definitive way* both the will of God and the way of God in the world.

The revelation of God in the incarnation may not exhaust the mystery of God. There is nevertheless an unavoidable implication of the affirmation that the only-begotten One, whose closeness to God is the closeness of sharing in God's divinity, exegeted God for us when his closeness to humanity consisted in his complete sharing of our humanity (John 1:18). The inescapable implication is that this particular human life is *the* touchstone for true, if not exhaustive, knowledge of God and God's way in the world. For the evangelist, therefore, the incarnation of the divine Logos comprises an interpretive criterion, both theologically and ethically. The glory, grace, and truth of Jesus Christ reflect the glory, grace, and truth of divine reality, both within Godself and in relation to the world. There may be more to the inner life of God than is revealed by God's interpretive agent, but God cannot be different from or incompatible with God's self-disclosure via the Logos that shares God's nature. And since the Logos shares in divine existence before all else existed and continues to share the closest intimacy with God, the self-disclosure of God in the incarnate Logos is true through and through, not susceptible of change. In short, God is as Jesus is, and God's way of working in the world is precisely that of Jesus.

This has profound implications for Christian theology and ethics. While it might be correct to affirm, with Painter, that the incarnation is but the first stage toward resolving the conundrum of evil in God's good world, that first stage is determinative for all successive stages. No subsequent stage should be out of kilter with this first, determinative stage. Painter is compelling in his apposite remarks about the cross's being a symbol of the incarnate Logos in the same way as the Logos is the defining symbol of God in relation to the created order. Understood as parallel expressions of divine self-giving love for the world, incarnation and cross belong together. There is theological integrity and moral coherence between them. The same may be said in relation to the distinctively Johannine conception of the role of the Spirit. So, too, there should be theological integrity and moral coherence between incarnation and eschatological judgment, whether present or future.

Incarnation, Creation, and Peace

According to the prologue to the Fourth Gospel, the Logos who tented with us as a person is the selfsame Logos through whom all things came into existence.

It is a commonplace of Johannine interpretation that John 1:1–18 both recalls and interprets passages from the Torah, most notably the creation account in Genesis 1:1–2:3. The first two words of the prologue undoubtedly echo the word with which the Hebrew Bible begins and the opening words of the Septuagint. In this primordial creation story, God orders the world into existence through uttering the divine will. For the evangelist, the Logos is the personified speech of God by which all things were uttered into existence. In Johannine perspective, each time that God speaks in Genesis 1, that is the divine Logos enacting God's will. Whereas human speech is somehow detached from the speaker, the speech of God is no less divine than God and for that reason is no less efficacious than God to make effective the divine will. For the evangelist, it is the divine Logos instrumental in the world's generation who became flesh and dwelt among people so as to communicate yet again the divine will.

In Genesis 1:3, the very first divine utterance results in light. In John 1:4, the agent of life, the Logos through whom all life was generated, is characterized as the source of life and hence the light of humanity. As in the creation account, once light is present, the darkness is unable to engulf the light (Gen. 1:3–5; John 1:4–5). Light rather than darkness becomes determinative (cf. Gen. 1:2). Although darkness is regulated by light rather than altogether removed by ever-present light, nevertheless light, as the consequence of God's first utterance, is given a certain primacy over darkness. In addition to being the result of God's initial creative utterance, light is also first to be pronounced good (Gen. 1:4), and on each successive day of creation, the light of morning disperses the darkness brought on by evening. So it is, according to the evangelist, with the Logos, who as the source of life is therefore the light of humanity: this light illumes in darkness and thereby illuminates what is concealed by darkness (John 1:5).

Like speech that communicates, light reveals. For the evangelist, the true Light—true because it is the source of life—enlightens every human life by coming into the world (John 1:9). This enlightenment relates to the perception of divine glory. The coming of the Light into the world, coterminous with the Logos becoming flesh, is what makes possible the perception of divine glory, both the glory of the Only-begotten from the Father, full of grace and truth, and the glory of the Father, disclosed by the only begotten God, who is the Father's intimate. In the Logos-become-flesh, divine glory glows bright in the world, meaning both that God's own being is exegeted in and for the world and that humanity is thereby enlightened about the way to become children—no less than creatures—of God.

The numerous connections between the prologue to the Fourth Gospel and the creation account in Genesis 1 indicate that the evangelist was concerned to interpret the life story of Jesus in relation to the creation story with which Jewish Scripture begins. The same God responsible for verbalizing the world into being speaks yet again in Jesus. Since it is the same God already known in

Jewish Scripture as the Creator of the cosmos and since the manner of divine disclosure is the same as that by which the cosmos was created, one may infer that the evangelist's witness to Jesus incorporates what the creation story in Genesis 1 discloses about the Creator.

There is much to say about the Creator on the basis of the creation account in Genesis 1. One crucial feature of this creation story is the orderly and peaceable manner in which creation occurs. "A peaceable character pervades the Priestly cosmogony," observes William Brown. "All hints of conflict and opposition are effectively banished from this account."[28] Creation occurs as a consequence of God's good pleasure. God brings into being by speaking, expressing the divine will. Even what is apparently inadequate and threatening—darkness and deep waters—is not obliterated but ordered within a rhythm of life that makes room for darkness and deep waters. A jarring note is sounded in 1:28 (echoing 1:26), following the creation and blessing of humankind, where God instructs humanity to *subdue* the earth and to *exercise dominion* over all other life-forms. But the creative work of God itself is unhurried, carefully and indeed caringly ordered, and peaceable.

This is all the more noticeable if one compares the creation story in Genesis 1 with certain other ancient Near Eastern cosmogonies, in which the creation of the cosmos is associated with divine violence in some form or other. There is reason to think that the creation story in Genesis 1 was formulated in response to the Babylonian creation story, the *Enuma Elish*, with which Israelites no doubt came into contact as a result of the sixth-century exile in Babylon.[29] Intrinsic to the *Enuma Elish* is that the cosmos and all that compose it emerge from violent conflict among the gods. The cosmos is formed from the corpse of the primordial mother god, Tiamat, brutally slaughtered by Marduk, god of Babylon. Moreover, human beings are formed from the blood of another murdered god. The story is both brutal and bloody.[30] The worldview it reflects is that reality is inherently violent. If, as seems likely, the creation story in Genesis 1 is a counternarrative to the *Enuma Elish*, the absence of creation via violence in Genesis 1 stands out all the more than on first inspection. The orderliness, serenity, care, and peaceableness of the Hebrew creation story intimate a profoundly different worldview, one in which *shalom* (harmonious wholeness) rather than chaotic violence is constitutive of the created order.[31]

---

28. W. Brown, *Ethos of the Cosmos*, 46.

29. Even if the form of the creation story in Gen. 1 is preexilic, as some argue, that does not imply the absence of familiarity with the *Enuma Elish*. For a relatively recent discussion of the influence of the *Enuma Elish* on Gen. 1 and other so-called priestly portions of the Pentateuch, see Sparks, "*Enūma Elish* and Priestly Mimesis."

30. For the text of the *Enuma Elish*, see Pritchard, *Ancient Near Eastern Texts*, 60–72.

31. Here I echo Wink, *Engaging the Powers*, 13–17. Wink, in turn, borrows from Ricoeur, *Symbolism of Evil*, 175–210.

The depths of the prologue to the Fourth Gospel are unplumbable, but several observations may be made in relation to the theme of peace. The opening lines of the prologue clearly recall the cosmogony of Genesis 1, in which God beckons forth creation in an orderly and peaceable way, solely by the efficaciousness of divine speech. Even the chaotic forces that might be thought of as the "raw materials" of creation are ordered into a rhythmic life cycle rather than simply deposed and disposed. "God is comfortable with 'chaos,' incorporating it constructively."[32] While there is a premonition of destructive violence associated with the creation of the human species (Gen. 1:28), this is counterbalanced by the divine decree that follows, in which flora rather than fauna is stipulated to sustain life.[33] Insofar as John 1:1–18 both recalls Genesis 1 and functions as a metaphysical framework for the Gospel story of Jesus, it presupposes an "ontology of peace" rather than a metaphysic of violence.[34]

While the prologue to the Fourth Gospel recalls Genesis 1, it also interprets the Israelite creation story for a new day. Perhaps most pertinent in this connection is the note of conflict struck within the prologue by the imagery of light and darkness. Whereas in the creation story darkness is ordered into a larger rhythmic whole, in the prologue darkness remains at odds with the Light. Much more than in the creation story, conflict features in the Johannine prologue. Crucially, however, the note of conflict arises from the lack of receptivity to the Light. The evangelist appreciates the inevitability of human antagonism to the Light, absurd as that is in view of human dependence on the Light for enlightenment (1:9), but nowhere is such conflict expressed as purposed by the Light. For the Fourth Evangelist, all life derives from the Logos, whose own life is light for humanity and whose coming into the world incorporates creatures into God's family as children. One may say, then, that the reason for the Light's coming into the world is to reclaim God's world for God, to restore to God what was created to relate to God. This provokes inevitable conflict, but any such conflict provoked by the coming of the Light is, according to the prologue, the result of human resistance to the very source of life. So although the prologue does not simply reiterate the creation story in Genesis 1, its reinterpretation in light of the mission of Jesus reaffirms the *shalom*-oriented divine creativity displayed in Genesis 1. In Genesis 1, divine creativity expresses itself in creation as a whole; in John 1:1–18, divine creativity expresses itself by entering into creation to make it whole.[35]

32. W. Brown, *Ethos of the Cosmos*, 42.

33. For a countercolonial reading of Gen. 1:28 within the broader context of Gen. 1–11, see Brett, *Decolonizing God*, 32–43.

34. The phrase "ontology of peace" derives from Milbank, *Theology and Social Theory*, part 4, "Theology and Difference."

35. On the Fourth Evangelist's interpretation of the mission of Jesus as in some sense completing creation, see Painter, "Earth Made Whole"; J. Brown, "Creation's Renewal."

The prologue's concluding lines signal that the "ontology of peace" both presupposed by it and intimated within it has far-reaching ramifications. For the evangelist, the divine Logos-become-flesh makes possible true perception of divine glory. The unsurpassable generosity of divine grace is nowhere more evident than in God's self-expression in human form: Jesus Christ, the only-begotten God, whose self-disclosure makes it possible for us to speak of God as "Father." Much can be—and has been—made of this evangelist's doctrine of incarnation. In the prologue to the Fourth Gospel, however, "incarnation" expresses the conviction that in Jesus, God speaks again and indeed speaks in terms—*human terms*—that unveil divine mystery *to the extent* that people may know God to be no less than and no different from him who interprets God as grace and truth. Anything else that might be inferred from the incarnation of the divine Logos must cohere with that fundamental theological insight. Incarnation exegetes God: divine utterance reaches humanity in and through a person, Jesus Messiah, making possible true, though not exhaustive, knowledge of God. As the evangelist puts it, paradoxically, the one most intimate with the Father as only-begotten God has explicated divine mystery (1:18). Thus, as Jesus is, God is. There is no doubt more to God than what may be inferred from the life story of Jesus, but God, according to this evangelist, is neither less than nor incongruent with the grace and truth expressed in Jesus.

As with the Gospels according to Matthew and Luke, albeit in a definitive way, the Fourth Gospel binds—but without restricting—divine being, presence, character, and action to the life story of Jesus. For Matthew, Jesus is *Immanu-el*, "God with us." For Luke, Jesus is "divine visitation," seeking out to save. And for this evangelist, Jesus is divine Logos-become-flesh, God's self-expression in person, so that the world might know God as grace and truth—and peace, as at the beginning when God spoke peaceably, and all that is came to be. Bultmann characterized the Johannine depiction of Jesus as "disturber of the world's peace,"[36] but this disturber of the world's peace is none other than the agent of creation through whom the world was brought into being peaceably and in whom the Creator reaches out with restoring intent.

The Peace Theme in the Fourth Gospel

If the prologue to the Fourth Gospel links incarnation to *shalom*-oriented creation, as I consider, is there anything else in the narrative to reinforce this interpretive association? The first point to appreciate is that Jesus's mission is peaceful in the Fourth Gospel no less than in the other biblical Gospels. Although one must acknowledge Jesus's verbal vehemence in John 8 no less than in Matthew 23, this likely reflects the (similar) life-settings of these two

---

36. Bultmann, *Theology of the New Testament*, 2:32.

Gospels, in which local Jewish-Christian communities of faith were sorting out their tense relationship with non-Christian Judaism(s). But even if Jesus himself engaged in the rhetoric of rage, such a phenomenon is explicable in sociocultural terms far removed from inexpiable violence.[37] Jesus's mission was nonviolent, whichever biblical Gospel one consults.

Although the vocabulary of peace is not as extensive in the Fourth Gospel as in Luke's Gospel, it nevertheless clusters in such a way as to function similarly. Having accepted as authentic Jesus's peace greeting in Luke 24:36, I find it remarkable that this same peace greeting recurs repeatedly in the Fourth Evangelist's postresurrection appearance accounts (John 20:19, 21, 26). John 20, which perhaps concluded an earlier edition of this Gospel, comprises two main sections, rounded off with a statement of purpose in 20:30–31. The first section centers on Mary of Magdala, the first person to witness the open tomb and also the first person to encounter the risen Jesus. Similar to the pattern of Luke's postresurrection narrative, Jesus first appears to a nonprominent follower and later that same day appears to the disciples en masse, which begins the second main section in John 20. In this second section, Jesus greets his disciples three times with the words "Peace to you," twice on the first occasion and once again later, when Thomas is present and utters the confession, "My Lord and my God!" (20:28; cf. 1:1, 18). This culminating confession in the second half of the Gospel recalls the confession of Martha toward the end of the first half of the narrative, when she acknowledges Jesus to be "the Messiah, the Son of God, and the One coming into the world" (11:27; cf. 1:9). In the latter appearance, therefore, the peace theme occurs in the context of the climactic christological confession of the Gospel.

In the earlier appearance to the gathered disciples (20:19–23), there is a remarkable set of associations with the reiterated peace greeting. First, Jesus's peace greeting addresses the fear of the gathered disciples. Indeed, on both occasions the evangelist makes a point of stating that Jesus's appearance occurs despite closed doors. In 20:19, the reason for the closed doors is identified: fear of "the Jews." Thus on each occasion the one who suffered crucifixion mollifies the fear engendered among his associates by his crucifixion. As in the farewell discourse(s), the peace of the Messiah is the antidote to fear (see 14:27; cf. 16:32–33).

Second, the peace greeting in 20:21 follows closely upon the first (20:19) and may therefore be read as both emphatic and preparatory. John 20:21–23 reads as follows:

37. I appreciate that rhetorical vehemence, if not violence, is a significant dimension of ethical interpretation in relation to the Gospels and Acts, but this topic has been discussed extensively. It is related—but not restricted—to the question of "anti-Judaism" in the Gospels and Acts. See my section in chap. 1 on "The Construction of Violence in Matthew's Gospel" and the literature cited there. Later in this chapter, I return to this theme in conversation with Adele Reinhartz.

> Then again he said to them, "Peace to you. As the Father has sent me, so also I am sending you." And after saying this he breathed out and said to them, "Receive the Holy Spirit. If you release the sins of any, they are released; if you retain those of any, they remain."

This reiterated peace greeting emphasizes the peace conveyed by the risen Jesus. He whose crucifixion completed his exegesis of divine glory (see John 19:28–30) stands again among his friends with peace on his lips, not vengeance. As the source of life was willing to lay down his life for others, so now the life of God in the resurrected Jesus speaks peace, not retaliation. This signals the way of God in the world. Even the power to triumph over death is expressed in peaceful terms, not in the manner of the power that conspired against Jesus.

Jesus's second, emphatic peace greeting also draws his associates into his own mission.[38] Following hard upon his second peace greeting, Jesus commissions his disciples to carry on his own mission. As he was sent by the Father, he now sends his disciples. The second peace greeting, however, encourages one to consider whether it is more than simply a sending as Jesus was sent. It seems reasonable to suppose that if Jesus sends his own as he was sent by the Father, so also the manner and purpose of the disciples' sending should conform to the first sending. Put differently, Jesus sends his disciples in the spirit of his own sending.

The spirit of Jesus's own sending by the Father is confirmed and reinforced by the Spirit conferred upon the disciples when Jesus breathes out and instructs his disciples to receive the Spirit. Like Jesus, the Spirit is also one sent from the Father (14:26; cf. 15:26; 16:7), even if by means of the risen Jesus's expiration. Thus, in this postresurrection encounter between Jesus and his disciples, the peace theme is closely associated with divine agency in the world through incarnate Logos and Holy Spirit. The sending of Jesus by the Father, as intimated by the prologue, is precisely a mission of peace, and the sending of the Spirit is for the purpose of extending that selfsame mission in the world through the disciples.

In view of the clear resonances between the prologue to the Fourth Gospel and Genesis 1, it should not go unnoticed that the expiration of Jesus that confers the Holy Spirit in John 20:22 alludes to the vivifying divine breath of Genesis 2:7. There, at the beginning of the second creation account (Gen. 2), God forms an earthling from the earth and animates it by breathing life into

---

38. The Johannine association of peace and mission provides the focus for Swartley's discussion of the Fourth Gospel in his *Covenant of Peace*, chap. 11. Swartley's exposition of the peace and mission connection in John 20:19–23—in which the themes of peace, sharing Jesus's mission, reception of the Holy Spirit, and forgiveness are juxtaposed—identifies dynamic peacemaking resources. His treatment of the story of Jesus and the Samaritan woman in John 4 as a peacemaking text creatively reinforces the point that the biblical story of Jesus, in whatever manifestation, is primarily a peaceable one that elicits a peacemaking response in all spheres of life.

its nostrils.[39] In John 20:22, the expiration of Jesus confers upon the disciples the Spirit, who animates and sustains their mission in the manner of Jesus's mission, their sending after the pattern of Jesus's sending.

"Peace to you" is thus the risen Jesus's reaffirmation of the peaceable Creator's work in and for the world. The significance of the apostolic witness that the risen Jesus reaffirmed peace rather than breathing threats of vengeance cannot be asserted too assertively or restated too redundantly. Resurrection validates peace rather than violence. "Peace to you" is also the risen Jesus's antidote to fear, often the root of violence. "Peace to you" displays the character and tenor of the mission commissioned by the risen Jesus. "Peace to you" is sealed by the gift of the Spirit, breathed upon the disciples in a manner reminiscent of the divine breath of life in Genesis 2. The agent of life, now restored from death to life, breathes out the Spirit of life upon his disciples. In short, within this astounding postresurrection scene, life means peace and peace means life.

The prologue, by virtue of its resonances with the creation story of Genesis 1, may be read as a *shalom*-oriented text. Along with the prologue, the thrice-recurring peace greeting in John 20, with its various life-affirming associations, serves to enclose the whole of the mission of the Logos-become-flesh. Jesus's later self-disclosure at Lake Tiberius is important for various reasons, including the validation of the Fourth Gospel's witness to Jesus, but the epilogue of John 21 adds nothing to Jesus's mission that contravenes the evangelist's peace-framing texts.

Even apart from the prologue, however, the evangelist's peace references serve an enclosing function, bracketing as they do the Johannine account of Jesus's arrest, hearings before the high priest and Pilate, denial by Peter, flogging, crucifixion, and burial (John 18–19)—in short, *all the violence perpetrated against Jesus*. Twice in the farewell discourse(s) of John 13:34–16:33,[40] the peace theme occurs in passages of profound significance. Toward the end of what may once have served as the conclusion to an early version of the farewell discourse, Jesus offers these comforting words:

> I have spoken these things to you while remaining with you, but the Paraclete—the Holy Spirit, whom the Father will send in my name—will teach you everything and will remind you about everything I have said to you. Peace I leave you, my peace I give to you; I give to you not as the world gives. Do not let your heart

39. While markedly different from the creation story in Gen. 1, the creation account in Gen. 2 is no less peaceful. While a form of "surgery under anesthetic" is required to make a suitable partner for the original human, nevertheless the molding of humanity from the life-sustaining earth and the animating breath of God compose a peaceable image of human origins.

40. I distinguish between the farewell discourse(s) and the farewell scene, which extends from John 13:1 to 17:26. The recurrence of material in John 15–16 that seems a reprise of material in John 14 is commonly explained by different versions or editions.

be troubled, neither be afraid. You heard that I said to you, "I am departing and coming to you." If you loved me, you would rejoice that I should happen to journey to the Father, because the Father is greater than I. And now I have told you before things happen, so that when they occur you may believe. Not much longer will I speak with you all, because the world's ruler is coming, yet he has nothing over me. Rather, this is so that the world may know that I love the Father, and just as the Father commands me, so I do. Arise, let us depart from here. (John 14:25–31)

One of the important themes of the farewell discourse(s) is the imminent departure of Jesus, first sounded within this section at John 13:33, and the consternation this causes for the disciples. This theme is reiterated in John 14:25–31. At times within the farewell discourse(s), Jesus's talk of departure sounds as though it might refer solely to his death, followed by his return to his disciples after his resurrection; in other instances, it seems more naturally to refer to his departure or ascension to the Father, followed by a return at an indeterminate time. Further complicating things is Jesus's assurance of the Father's sending another Paraclete, whose presence will in some sense compensate for Jesus's absence by replicating, in certain respects, Jesus's historic presence.

There are those who hold that the sending of the Paraclete replaces without remainder the promised return of Jesus, but to collapse the promised return of Jesus into the sending of the Spirit takes things too far. Although Jesus's departure is the precondition for the sending of the Spirit, and though the role of the Spirit closely replicates that of Jesus and thereby compensates for his absence, nevertheless the Spirit's presence is focused on disclosing the meaning and significance of Jesus's mission. The Spirit aids in interpreting what was accomplished by the Logos-become-flesh, but the Spirit neither reunites believers with Jesus (John 14:2–3; 17:24) nor brings to a final resolution Jesus's mission in the world (see 1:9–11; 3:17). So long as the world created by the divine Logos remains unredeemed and all people have not been drawn to believe that Jesus is the Messiah and Son of God, the mission of the Logos-become-flesh remains incomplete, however complete Jesus's work may have been in principle.

John 14:25–26 is important for comprehending the evangelist's peculiarly christocentric pneumatology. It is hardly accidental that this particular understanding of the Holy Spirit should be developed within the farewell discourse(s), for a significant dimension of Johannine pneumatology is the conviction that the Spirit compensates for the absence of Jesus. An important feature of this text within its immediate context, however, is that the promise of the Spirit sent by the Father in Jesus's name immediately precedes Jesus's parting gift of peace. The Spirit's role is here described as teaching the disciples everything and reminding them of everything Jesus has said to them. It is probably not too far-fetched to interpret the second clause as epexegetical, that is, clarifying what is meant by "teaching everything." Or perhaps both clauses are qualified by the concluding phrase, "that which I have said to you." In other words, the Spirit's role is to teach the disciples everything by interpreting for them what Jesus has said and by persistently reminding them, drawing them back, to everything he has said.

In any case, the decisive point is that the Spirit's role is focused on the precedent of Jesus's own teaching. And the words of Jesus that immediately follow his assurance of the Spirit's presence and role concern *peace*, his own peace, bestowed upon the disciples in a way that is different from the way in which the world confers peace. Since the world opposed to God conceives of peace as achieved through coercion and violence, John 14:27 indicates that the peace bequeathed to the disciples, Jesus's own peace, is gained and hence passed on peaceably, not coercively or violently. This is reinforced by the exact repetition in John 14:27b of 14:1, "Do not let your heart be troubled," followed by the rider, "Do not be afraid." As in John 20:19–29, the peace of Jesus is the antidote to fear.

Thus the role of the Spirit within the community of faith is tethered to Jesus's parting gift of his own qualitatively different peace to his disciples. As a consequence, whatever teaching or reminding emanating from the Spirit should cohere with Jesus's own peace. In the farewell discourse(s), Jesus gives his disciples a new commandment of love: they are to love one another as Jesus has expressed his love for them (John 13:34; cf. 15:9–17). He also promises that the Father will give the disciples another Paraclete to be ever with them (14:16).[41] The next time he speaks of the Paraclete (14:26–27), Jesus gives his own qualitatively different peace to the disciples. In preparation for his departure, Jesus addresses his disciples' apprehension by giving them his new commandment of love, patterned on his own love and his own qualitatively different peace. He also promises that on his departure, they will be given another Paraclete. These three gifts—the command to love, Jesus's own peace, and the promised Paraclete—form the bedrock of the Johannine community of faith during Jesus's absence.[42] As a theological-ethical vision of life, christologically grounded love, peace, and the Spirit cohere together harmoniously.

Seen in this light, it should come as no surprise that the farewell discourse(s) ends as follows: "I have spoken these things to you so that in me you may have peace. In the world you will experience distress, but take courage: I have conquered the world" (John 16:33).[43] In short, the purpose of Jesus's farewell discourse(s) in its entirety is to instill in his disciples the peace that comes from belonging to him by believing in him. This makes the peace theme much

41. In John 15:26 and 16:7, Jesus promises to send the Paraclete (from the Father).
42. On the primacy of Jesus's love command within the "Johannine mode of peacemaking," cf. Swartley, *Covenant of Peace*, 296–300.
43. While the prayer of Jesus in John 17 may be regarded as part of the farewell discourse(s), it is parenthetical in a narrative sense insofar as it is not directed toward the disciples.

more important within this section of the Fourth Gospel than its two explicit occurrences would suggest. Not only does Jesus grant his disciples his own qualitatively different peace, but his teaching throughout this entire block of material is also motivated by a concern to instill his peace in his disciples.

In John 16:33, Jesus's reassurance is premised on his conquering of the world within which his disciples will experience distress. The peace promised by Jesus presumes conflict, but does it also signal that peace derives from divine or divinely authorized violence? In Johannine perspective, the "conquering" of John 16:33 must be read in light of 12:31–32, which reveals the manner in which the world's conquering occurs. So although the peace theme presupposes conflict by addressing its reality and inevitability, the peace promised by Jesus and premised on his "conquering" of the world neither promises divine violence nor is premised on it.

The theme of peace—as defined by Jesus—is therefore critical to the second half of the Fourth Gospel: it is the subtext for the farewell discourse(s) as well as Jesus's parting gift to his disciples; it is exemplified in Jesus's willingness to endure his pathway to death nonviolently (see esp. John 18:10–11, 22, 36; 19:1–2, 17–18, 26–27); and the thrice-recurring peace greeting on the part of the risen Jesus confirms this peace emphasis. In view of the unmerited violence meted out to Jesus during his time of suffering, it is profoundly significant that this section of the Fourth Gospel, in which human injustice and violence feature, should be bracketed by texts in which peace expresses the way of God in the world.[44]

In my estimation, the critical role of the peace theme in the second half of the Fourth Gospel resonates with the *shalom*-evoking prologue to the Gospel narrative. Taken together, these texts signal that the creative Logos responsible for the peaceable coming into existence of all that is encounters humanity in a peaceable yet challenging way through taking on our humanity and conducting a peaceful mission in a hostile environment. Indeed, when one considers possible alternatives to incarnation as a means of communicating the divine will and way, incarnation as displayed in the Jesus story is undoubtedly peaceful. Incarnation, no less than creation, bespeaks peace as primary and determinative.

The Son of Humanity and Judgment

Both the level of debate and lack of consensus about the meaning and significance of the Son-of-humanity epithet in the Fourth Gospel give pause about

44. D. Moody Smith and Craig Koester, in their respective theologies of the Fourth Gospel, note the pattern of the evangelist's peace references but find little to say about their theological-ethical function within the narrative. See Smith, *Theology of John*, 150–51; and Koester, *Word of Life*, 134, 158.

addressing it here. Nevertheless, the association of apocalyptic motifs with this expression more generally and its linkage with the theme of judgment in both the synoptic and Johannine traditions combine to make its consideration unavoidable. As in other respects, the Fourth Evangelist's use of the Son-of-humanity expression is both like and unlike its occurrences in the Synoptic Gospels. Whether or not he was familiar with its usage in the Synoptic Gospels, his own use of the Son-of-humanity idiom reflects his creative adaptation of traditional motifs to express a distinctive understanding of Jesus's identity and significance.

One's idea of the conceptual matrix within which the Fourth Evangelist made use of the Son-of-humanity expression inevitably affects one's interpretation. For this reason, here I provide a sketch of my understanding of conceptual resources with which this evangelist was probably familiar. First, I side with those who foreground Jewish Scripture and tradition as decisive for understanding the Son-of-humanity concept in the first century CE. Second, although no Johannine Son-of-humanity saying has an exact synoptic parallel, certain affinities suggest an acquaintance with thematic features associated with the Son of humanity in the synoptic tradition. Third, while various scriptural texts might well be alluded to by one or more Johannine Son-of-humanity references, the image of "one like a person" in Daniel 7 seems to be the basis for the development of a tradition upon which the Fourth Gospel relies. Fourth, within Jewish tradition roughly contemporaneous with the Fourth Gospel, the Parables of Enoch (1 Enoch 37–71) demonstrate how the Son of humanity could be conceived as a transcendent messianic figure with the authority to judge. Allusions to Daniel 7 in chapter 13 of the apocalypse known as 4 Ezra (or 2 Esdras) add weight to the view that a Jewish myth of a messianic "Son of humanity" had developed and was both known to and exploited by the Gospel writers, if not Jesus himself. Both this interpretive matrix and specific features associated with the Son of humanity within the Fourth Gospel lead to the conclusion that, for this evangelist, the Son of humanity is a heavenly messianic figure with the authority to judge, as in the Parables of Enoch.[45] This Son-of-humanity myth was used to interpret the story of Jesus, but it was also reinterpreted in light of the evangelist's understanding of Jesus.

The Son-of-humanity epithet occurs thirteen times in the Fourth Gospel, all but once in the first half of the narrative concerned with Jesus's public mission (1:51; 3:13, 14; 5:27; 6:27, 53, 62; 8:28; 9:35; 12:23, 34 [twice]; 13:31). Indeed, the final occurrence, in John 13:31, is at the beginning of the farewell discourse(s) and largely reiterates the substance of 12:23. As in the Synoptic Gospels, this expression is used almost exclusively by Jesus in the Fourth

45. On the Son-of-humanity myth in first-century Judaism, see esp. J. Collins, *Scepter and the Star*, chap. 8. See also A. Collins and J. Collins, *King and Messiah*, chaps. 4, 7, and 8. Also illuminating is Boyarin, "How Enoch Can Teach Us about Jesus." For a helpful discussion by a Johannine scholar, see Ashton, *Understanding the Fourth Gospel*, chap. 5.

Gospel. The two exceptions in John 12:34, at which point a crowd inquires of Jesus concerning the identity of the Son of humanity, is (apparently) in response to Jesus's assertion to Andrew and Philip that the time has arrived for the Son of humanity to be glorified (12:23).[46] John 5:27 is also exceptional by virtue of its being the sole instance in the Gospels that the expression "Son of humanity" occurs without any definite article. Though this linguistically awkward idiom generally contains two articles, literally, "*the* son of *the* person," in John 5:27 it lacks both articles.

A survey of the Johannine Son-of-humanity sayings reveals associations with several distinctive motifs. John 1:51, which serves as the culmination and probable refinement of a series of earlier christological affirmations (including Lamb of God, Son of God, Messiah, and King of Israel), has Jesus say to his earliest followers, "Truly, truly, I say to you [pl.], you will see heaven opened and the angels of God ascending and descending upon the Son of humanity." This enigmatic saying, whose meaning likely relates to the vision of Jacob at Bethel in Genesis 28,[47] features the apocalyptic motif of heavenly ascent and descent, which elsewhere pertains to Jesus, albeit in reverse. If this were the only Son-of-humanity saying to feature this motif, one might be inclined to focus on the Son of humanity as the *means* of heavenly ascent and descent, like the stairway in Jacob's vision. But the very next reference to the Son of humanity in John 3:13 has Jesus informing Nicodemus, "No one has ascended into heaven except the one who descended from heaven, the Son of humanity." John 6:62 reinforces the association between this epithet and the motif of heavenly descent/ascent.

The third Son-of-humanity saying in John 3:14–15, which is juxtaposed to the second such saying in the previous verse, refers to the necessity that the

46. The double question of the crowd in John 12:34 presupposes that although it misheard the heavenly voice as thunder (12:28–29), it nevertheless overheard Jesus's statement to Philip and Andrew in 12:23, correctly understood Jesus's statement about being lifted up in 12:32 as a reference to his impending death, and associated the Son of humanity with the promised Messiah. Why it must ask about the identity of the Son of humanity when it has already associated the Son-of-humanity saying in 12:23 with Jesus's statement about his own lifting up in 12:32 is puzzling.

47. This long-standing interpretive association is understandable in view of the probable allusion to Gen. 28:12 in the phrase "angels of God ascending and descending" (John 1:51), which reverses the Johannine sequence of descent from heaven to earth followed by ascent from earth to heaven (3:13; 6:33, 38, 41–42, 50–51, 58, 62; 16:28; 20:17). Not everyone accepts an association between John 1:51 and Jacob's vision in Gen. 28. See, e.g., Painter, *Quest for the Messiah*, 323–28. In context, however, the probable allusion to Gen. 28:12 in John 1:51 is illuminating. In Gen. 28, the *departing* Jacob is assured both of divine *presence* with him and his *return* to the land of promise. Departing and promised return in Gen. 28 is paralleled in the Fourth Gospel by one who has descended from heaven and will ascend to heaven. In context, the vision of heaven opened and "angels of God ascending and descending" on (or perhaps toward) the Son of humanity bespeaks divine presence and accompaniment, made explicit in John 8:29 (cf. 3:2; 16:32). John 1:51 envisages Jesus as assuring his disciples that they will come to see him as a heavenly figure who mediates divine presence and accompaniment.

Son of humanity be "raised up," as Moses elevated the snake in the desert (see Num. 21:4–9), so that all who believe in him may experience eternal life. Two later sayings also refer to the elevation or exaltation of the Son of humanity (8:28; 12:34). Closely associated with such sayings are those in which Jesus speaks of the glorification of the Son of humanity (12:23; 13:31). The raising of the Son of humanity by means of crucifixion is precisely the selfsame Son of humanity's glorification, through which God is also glorified.

The juxtaposition of the motifs of heavenly ascent and exaltation in John 3:13–14 leads many to conclude that the Son of humanity's elevation (on the cross) is also (the means of) his ascent to heaven. To relate these motifs is understandable, but equating them makes a questionable interpretive inference. Although conceptually related,[48] these motifs do not function interchangeably within the Fourth Gospel, as do the motifs of exaltation and glorification. Moreover, within the narrative itself, the evangelist distinguishes between Jesus's death, understood as his exaltation and glorification, and his heavenly ascent (20:17). John 20:17 is not a Son-of-humanity saying, but the use of the same heavenly ascent motif as used in John 1:51; 3:13; and 6:62, but elsewhere avoided in direct relation to Jesus's crucifixion, suggests that exaltation via the cross and heavenly ascent are not synonymous.[49]

The atypical saying in John 5:27 associates the Son of humanity with divinely granted authority to judge. Indeed, his status as Son of humanity seems to be the rationale for his authority to judge. Remarkably, in John 5:24–30 the evangelist brings together his three "Son" titles into some form of coalescence. "Son of God," "Son," and "Son of humanity" occur in quick succession within John 5:25–27 and in such a way as to identify each title with the one person: Jesus (as 5:24 and 5:30 make clear).

The Son-of-humanity sayings in John 6:27, 53 echo 3:14–15 by associating the Son of humanity with life in its full sense, and the saying in 9:35 echoes the theme of faith in the Son of humanity, also sounded in 3:14–15. For the evangelist, one may trust in the Son of humanity and thereby gain eternal life. In certain respects, these Son-of-humanity sayings in John 6 and 9 are also reminiscent of other earlier associations. In John 6:62, following the disturbing bread-of-life discourse, Jesus asks his disgruntled disciples, "What, therefore, if you should happen to see the Son of humanity ascending to where he was previously?" This saying presumes the Son of humanity's descent, but within the bread-of-life discourse, what descends from heaven is the bread of God or bread from heaven (6:33, 41, 50, 51, 58). Since the food that lasts and brings eternal life is granted by the Son of humanity and can even be said to comprise

---

48. See Nicholson, *Death as Departure*; Loader, *Christology of the Fourth Gospel*, 82–85, 93–135.

49. The case for differentiating between—but not dissociating!—the motifs of exaltation and heavenly ascent is strengthened if Martinus de Boer is correct to identify the theme of Jesus's departure with his resurrection rather than with his death. See his "Jesus' Departure to the Father."

the Son of humanity's own flesh and blood (6:27, 53), within the bread-of-life discourse the descent dimension of the descent/ascent motif is taken over by the bread of God that descends from heaven, while the ascent aspect remains with the Son of humanity (6:62).

As for John 9:35, which occurs near the end of the story of the man born blind, the theme of belief in the Son of humanity is connected by Jesus with that of judgment (9:39), a theme already directly related to the Son of humanity in John 5:27. Introducing a discussion of the Son-of-humanity sayings in the Fourth Gospel, Walter Wink asserts that "John's 'Son of Man' sayings show no trace of the apocalyptic motifs associated with that title in the Synoptics."[50] Such an assertion can be correct only if "apocalyptic motifs" are thought to relate solely to end-time resolution. Indeed, what Wink means to say becomes clearer upon reading these words: "'The son of the man' in FG [the Fourth Gospel] is not the apocalyptic figure we find in the Synoptics who will come on the clouds of heaven at the end of time."[51] But this is significantly different from claiming that apocalyptic motifs associated with synoptic Son-of-humanity sayings are absent from the Fourth Gospel. As Wink himself documents in his larger work on the Son-of-humanity tradition, the motif of the judging Son of humanity is present in the Synoptic Gospels, especially in Matthew's Gospel.[52] There he recognizes that the judging Son of humanity features also in the Fourth Gospel, only within a "non-apocalyptic framework."[53] Perhaps what Wink means by this is that the Fourth Evangelist reconstructs the image of the judging Son of humanity, but that is different from demonstrating that the Fourth Gospel is nonapocalyptic. In my view, the Fourth Gospel is no less apocalyptic in character or conception than any other of the biblical Gospels, indeed, no less apocalyptic than the Apocalypse of John. But this evangelist reinterprets the apocalyptic tradition no less than borrowing from it, and this is seen nowhere more clearly than in his dialectical renovation of the notion of judgment.

To return to a crucial passage wherein the evangelist's apocalyptic orientation reveals itself, John 12:31 affirms that the world's judgment occurs in and by the crucifixion of Jesus.[54] Lest the absence of any observed difference to the world after the crucifixion of Jesus should lead to the inference that nothing has really changed, in John 16:7–11 Jesus identifies the three-part role

50. Wink, "'Son of the Man' in the Gospel of John," 117.

51. Ibid., 120.

52. Wink, *Human Being*, chap. 11.

53. Ibid., 177.

54. That the "now" of John 12:31 refers to the "hour of glorification" (12:23) at Jesus's crucifixion is shown not only by the juxtaposition of Jesus's contiguous sayings about judgment and being elevated in 12:31–32 but also by Jesus's references to the world's ruler in 14:30 and 16:11, the first of which signals his imminent arrival from a precrucifixion perspective and the second of which affirms his accomplished judgment from a postcrucifixion perspective (enabled by the Paraclete).

of the promised Paraclete as being to confound the world about sin, justice (or righteousness), and judgment.[55] With respect to judgment, the Paraclete's role is to convict the world that its ruler has *already been judged* (16:11), in other words, to reiterate and to reinforce Jesus's own judgment regarding his crucifixion and its effects (12:31). In Johannine perspective, the crucifixion of Jesus is not something for which God must retaliate in order to overcome evil but rather the precise means by which that overcoming is accomplished.[56] Such a counterintuitive, dialectical perspective is intrinsic to this evangelist's theological-moral vision.

If the world in antagonism to God is judged by Jesus's crucifixion, what does this imply about judgment of individual human beings? John 12:44–50, which serves as a coda to the first half of the Gospel, reiterates central features of the Johannine conception of judgment.[57] Here the reader is reminded that Jesus is the Light of the world, reiterating John 1:4–5, 9; 3:11–21; 8:12; 9:4–5, 35–39. Outside of the prologue, the arrival in the world of the Light of the world paradoxically provokes the judgment of those in the world (3:19–21; 9:39), even though the express purpose of the coming of the Light is to res-cue the world rather than to judge it (12:47). This helps to make sense of the seemingly contradictory statements in John 3:17 and 9:39.[58] Judgment is a secondary function of the arrival of the Light, an expression of the reality that, despite its rescuing intention, the Light's arrival provokes disbelief and rejection no less than belief and acceptance. "Offering Life—Confronting with Truth" is how Craig Koester encapsulates the dynamic of divine judgment in the Fourth Gospel.[59] Rejection of divine disclosure in Jesus entails judgment. That judgment is but the outworking of disbelief, however, the consequence of the disbeliever's self-segregation from the source of life. One might say that Jesus repudiates the role of judge (12:47a) but respects the Father's authority to judge eschatologically on the basis of a person's response to his message

55. In John 7:24, which occurs within the context of a Sabbath dispute, Jesus endorses judg-ment in accordance with justice. "Do not judge according to appearance [or 'on face value'],"
he says, "but rather judge in accordance with just judgment." In John 5:30, Jesus claims that he judges justly.

56. The saying of John 8:50 is interesting in this connection. Responding to the suggestion that he is a Samaritan and has a demon (8:48), Jesus replies, in part: "I do not seek my own glory; there is one seeking it and judging." Since the "hour" of Jesus's glorification coincides with his crucifixion, John 8:50 may be interpreted to signify divine judgment by means of Je-sus's crucifixion.

57. With the exception of John 16:8, 11, explicit reference to divine judgment is restricted to the first half of the Fourth Gospel (chaps. 1–12).

58. John 9:39 expresses the peculiarly Johannine notion of judgment as division between people depending upon their response to Jesus. It also seems to reflect the Johannine situation of synagogue conflict. See Painter, *Quest for the Messiah*, chap. 8. On the basis of the association of the themes of light and judgment with the Son of humanity in John 9, Painter identifies the Son of humanity with the Light of the world.

59. Koester, *Word of Life*, 33–36.

(12:48–49). While repudiating the role of judge, Jesus's message, sourced in God, cannot but be the standard of eschatological judgment.[60]

John 12:44–50 points readers back to two crucial passages, 3:11–21 and 5:19–30, in which the distinctively Johannine conception of judgment is elaborated. The earlier passage, in which the theme of judgment is first sounded, makes the following three points. First and foremost, the divine purpose in sending the Son was not to judge the world but to rescue it (3:17).[61] As the first saying about divine judgment in the Gospel, this point deserves to be given primacy in one's understanding of the Johannine view of judgment. Consistent with the Johannine perception of God as love first and foremost (see 1 John 4:7–21),[62] this evangelist affirms that divine communication with the world is for the wholly positive purpose of salvation or granting eternal life. Judgment there may be, but judgment neither expresses the heart of God nor offers insight into God's determination to reach out to the world.

Second, John 3:18 indicates that one who believes in Jesus as God's only Son escapes judgment, whereas one who does not so believe is judged already. For this evangelist, judgment may not explain why God's only Son was sent into the world, but it is nevertheless a by-product of God's sending the Son. In this connection, it is helpful to recall the insight of both Bultmann and C. H. Dodd that κρίσις (krisis, judgment) and κρίνειν (krinein, to judge) have a two-fold sense: division and judgment.[63] Seen in this light, whether one responds in faith or unbelief to the sending of the Son is itself one's judgment in the self-discriminating sense of responding to the divine initiative either positively (reception) or negatively (rejection). How one judges Jesus rebounds as one's self-discrimination, so to speak, and one's self-discrimination occurs in the moment of one's judgment for or against Jesus. The paradox that one's judgment for or against Jesus is simultaneously one's own judgment (self-discrimination) is matched by the paradox that eschatological judgment occurs now.

Third, as if cognizant that John 3:17–18 runs counter to existing conceptions of divine judgment, the evangelist explains the dynamic of his notion of judgment in John 3:19: "This is judgment, that the light has come into

---

60. Coming where it does, at the conclusion to the first half of the Gospel, it is tempting to interpret John 12:48b in such a way as to relate the message (logos) that Jesus speaks with the divine communication (Logos) he incarnates. On such a reading, the Jesus story in its totality serves as the basis for eschatological judgment.

61. There are those who consider that the contrast between salvation and judgment implies that judgment here means condemnation. See, e.g., Travis, Christ and the Judgement, 263. This is supported by John 3:36, which might be taken to interpret 3:16–18, but I prefer to retain the language of judgment, which is more open to positive reconfiguration.

62. I take this description of divine nature to be a natural extension of the divine love both expressed in the giving of the Son for the salvation of the world (John 3:16) and descriptive of the bond between Father and Son (3:35; 5:20; 10:17; 14:31; 15:9–10; 17:20–26).

63. Bultmann, Theology of the New Testament, 2:38–39; Dodd, Interpretation of the Fourth Gospel, 208–11.

the world and people loved the darkness more than the light, for their works were evil."[64] Judgment is an inevitable consequence of the Light's coming in Jesus, not its purpose, and its occurrence corresponds with how people respond to the presence of the Light. Light illuminates, but by virtue of what it illuminates, it also divides. Judgment corresponds with that division based on a positive or negative response to the Light. "So," according to Stephen Travis, "in 3:16–21 John is saying that when people are confronted by Jesus, they divide themselves by their reaction to him."[65]

Rather different nuances regarding divine judgment emerge from John 5:19–30. In a passage emphasizing the Son's dependence on the Father, John 5:22 observes that the Father judges no one but rather has handed all judgment over to the Son. Within a Jewish context, this is a startling claim, and at one level it contradicts the earlier asseveration that God did not send the Son into the world to judge it. In view of the earlier passage, however, perhaps this saying may be taken to accentuate the earlier emphasis that judgment occurs in response to Jesus.[66] Since divine judgment is the inherent consequence of one's response to Jesus as Son of God and Light of the world, it is no longer to be understood as a divine act *in the same way* as raising the dead and giving life (cf. 5:21).

The contrast between life and judgment continues throughout this passage. John 5:24 reiterates 3:18a. One who hears the message of Jesus and believes the one who sent him has eternal life already and (thereby) escapes judgment. John 5:27 echoes 5:21 but also offers the rationale that the Father has granted the Son authority to exercise judgment because he is the Son of humanity. Here the evangelist seems to have conflated the idea of the Son sent from the Father with the Son of humanity who has descended from heaven. The Son sent from the Father, not any other figure, is the judging Son of humanity. There is a certain similarity between John 5:27 and 3:19 insofar as in each case a clarifying explanation of judgment is offered. In John 3:19 judgment is defined in terms of Light's coming into the world, whereas in 5:27 Jesus's identity as Son of humanity is the reason why divine authority to judge has been conferred upon him.

Remarkably, the reference to the judging Son of humanity in John 5:27 seems to provoke the articulation of a more traditional understanding of eschatological judgment. Whatever explains the presence of this more traditional expectation of end-time judgment following the general resurrection of the dead, it needs to be interpreted within the broader context of the Gospel as a whole.[67] Indeed, despite the difference in timing, "resurrection to life" awaits

64. Alternatively, "This (form of) judgment is because the light has come into the world. . . ."

65. Travis, *Christ and the Judgement*, 266; cf. Dodd, *Interpretation of the Fourth Gospel*, 210: "Men by their response to the manifestation of the light declare themselves, and so pronounce their own 'judgment.'"

66. See R. Brown, *According to John*, 1:345.

67. Other texts within the Fourth Gospel that reflect a nonrealized, future-oriented eschatology include John 6:39–40, 44, 54; 12:48; 14:2–3.

those whose lives are marked by doing good, similar to those who already enjoy life and have escaped judgment on the basis of belief in Jesus as Son of God. "Resurrection to judgment" is reserved for those who practice evil.

In a strictly logical schema, the substance of John 5:28–29 contradicts much of what the evangelist has thus far said about judgment and is incompatible with the similarly structured statement in 5:25. John 5:25 comprises a sober assurance that a time is coming—indeed, is now here—"when the dead will hear the voice of the Son of God and those who hear will [thereby] live." This seems to be a deliberate recasting into realized terms of a traditional future-oriented eschatological expectation, whereas John 5:28–29 reverts to the traditional expectation.

Despite the evangelist's emphasis on judgment already realized by virtue of one's response to divine disclosure in Jesus, to disallow a future dimension to divine judgment beyond the present would be to absolutize present experience, with all its ambiguity and ambivalence. Divine disclosure in the mission and message of Jesus may be definitive, but the human capacity to appropriate the meaning and significance of that revelation is limited and subject to all manner of self-deceptions. Eternal life may be something one is able to experience in the here and now, but not uninterruptedly.[68] In Bultmann's terms, "authentic existence" may be experienced fleetingly, but it is hardly a mode of life that anyone is capable of sustaining. By giving primacy to a realized form of eschatology, the evangelist expresses the conviction that the revelation in Jesus is ultimate and definitive. By retaining vestiges of a more traditional eschatology relating to a horizon beyond historical existence, he also expresses the realization that no matter how definitive divine disclosure in Jesus might be, its appropriation by human beings can only ever be partial, and its expression, even in the lives of believers, can only ever be feeble and faltering.

If this way of grappling with the evangelist's dialectical eschatology is insightful, the moral meaning of realized eschatology may be said to require a future-oriented perspective. Realized eschatology gives primacy to what is already fulfilled, in this case, the revelation of both God and humanity—to each other, but especially of God to humanity—in the person of Jesus. Realized eschatology is but the flip side of a coin that commemorates the definitiveness and determinativeness of the Logos-become-flesh. On the other hand, eschatology that is realized without remainder is susceptible to the temptation to sequester from divine judgment life in its historical particularity and ambiguity. Realized eschatology without a future horizon locks God into human perspectives about God. Paradoxically, a future-oriented

68. Compare O'Donnell, "Complementary Eschatologies," 763–64, who notes the obstacle posed to comprehending eternal life in wholly realized terms by "the difficulty [inability, I would say] of 'abiding' . . . over time in the beliefs and ethical norms that manifest such a life." O'Donnell draws on the helpful perspective of Carroll, "Present and Future in Fourth Gospel 'Eschatology,'" which is recast in Carroll et al., *Return of Jesus*, 77–92.

perspective is needed to safeguard the moral meaning and significance of realized eschatology.[69]

Although John 5:22, 27 depict the Father as relinquishing divine judgment to the Son, 5:30 has Jesus reasserting his dependence on the Father, as in 5:19, even with respect to judgment. "As I hear [from the Father], I judge," he asserts, "and my judgment is just because I do not seek my own will but rather the will of the one who sent me" (5:30). Just judgment by the Son is assured by virtue of the Son's concern to enact the Father's will.

While the theme of judgment is unnerving, divine judgment per se is neither theologically nor morally problematic. Strictly retributive, vindictive, or vengeful conceptions of divine judgment are problematic, however, both because they do violence to people's God-image and because they are morally corrosive. In the Gospel according to Matthew, there is a discrepancy between the peaceful character of Jesus's mission and ethic and the violence associated with the returning Son of humanity. Not so in the Fourth Gospel. In part, this is because the Johannine conception of judgment recasts the notion of recompense; divine judgment is but the ratification of self-discrimination provoked by encounter with Jesus as the definitive revelation of God. Seen from the perspective of revelation and the quality of life that it makes possible, unbelief is itself a form of judgment insofar as it entails cutting oneself off from life by rejecting the source of life. But even the remnants of future-oriented eschatological judgment are characterized in such a way as to cohere with the peaceable character of the mission and message of the Logos-become-flesh.

The Johannine reconfiguration of eschatological judgment, in both its realized and more traditional forms, serves to relativize vindictive and vengeful expressions of end-expectation as found, for example, in the Gospel according to Matthew. In its realized form, the Johannine conception of judgment as division provoked by Jesus shows how open divine judgment is to interpretation. In the Fourth Gospel, the theme of divine judgment is interpreted in relation to divine disclosure in the mission and message of Jesus. Moreover, it is interpreted in such a way as to cohere with the mission and message of the Logos-become-flesh. The same may be said with respect to future judgment in the Fourth Gospel. "Resurrection to judgment" in John 5:29 is not described in such a way as to presume on divine sovereignty. Indeed, in view of the form of judgment provoked by the Logos-become-flesh, one is entitled to leave the door open to an analogous form of future judgment. After all, "even as the Father raises and enlivens those who are dead, so also the Son enlivens those whom he wills" (John 5:21). Moreover, since the cross is also the means by which the world is judged and its ruler

---

69. I take the future-oriented eschatological hope of 1 John as confirmation that expressions of future-oriented eschatology in the Fourth Gospel are no less integral to its understanding of salvation (see 1 John 2:28; 3:2; 4:17). As in the Gospel, however, eternal life is a present possibility in 1 John 3:14–15; 5:11–13.

expelled (12:31), this mode of judgment—which is fully coherent with the incarnation because the cross is, in Painter's words, the symbol of incarnation—signals that divine judgment works in ways unimaginable to us. In a salutary way, this evangelist defers to divine determination regarding the form future judgment will take.

Ethical Effects

"If we had only the Fourth Gospel in the New Testament canon," according to Richard Hays, "it would be difficult indeed to base any specific Christian ethic on the teaching of Jesus."[70] This is because there is so little specific moral content to the instruction of Jesus in the Fourth Gospel, even when Jesus's disciples are exhorted to obey his commandments (John 14:15, 21; 15:10). But what of the well-known command of Jesus that his disciples love one another after the manner of his own love for them (13:34–35; 15:12–13; cf. 13:1)? Is there not sufficient moral content in this particular command?[71] The difficulty for many New Testament scholars is that the Johannine form of the love command is (allegedly) solely inward-looking, reflective of a starkly sectarian mentality. As Hays points out, "It is fashionable to derogate the Johannine exhortations to love within the community as sectarian retreats from the more universal call to love the neighbor, broadly defined as in Luke, or even the enemy, as in Matthew."[72]

When interpreting the Gospels, however, Hays contends that "narrative world" no less than explicit moral exhortation is ethically significant. Within the larger context of the narrative of the Fourth Gospel, he draws attention to the moral significance of texts that emphasize the close bond between Jesus and his disciples, including the commissioning texts in John 17:18 and 20:21, all of which intimate a discipleship of extending Jesus's own mission in and for the world (12:26). In this connection, Hays suggests, on the basis of John 14:12–14, that disciples of Jesus might well be expected to continue the miracle-working activity of Jesus.[73] Since the narrated signs of Jesus in the Fourth Gospel are invariably life-giving in some way, whether by enhancing,

---

70. Hays, *Moral Vision*, 138.

71. See Bultmann, *Theology of the New Testament*, 2:81: "Out of the love we have received arises the obligation to love: 'A new commandment I give you: to love each other as (καθώς) I love you, in order that you, too, should love each other' (13:34 Blt tr.)—in which καθώς means both 'as' and 'because' (i.e., it states both the manner and the cause of this love)." For Painter, the specific form of the love command in the Fourth Gospel provides the basis for the development of a καθώς ethic in 1 John. See Painter, *1, 2, and 3 John*, 152, 178, 265–72, 283–84.

72. Hays, *Moral Vision*, 145. This perception provides the rationale for much of Swartley's discussion of the Fourth Gospel in *Covenant of Peace*, chap. 10, titled "The Johannine Corpus: Conflictual Ethos and Alternative Community as Foundation for Peace" (276–303).

73. Hays, *Moral Vision*, 142–43.

sustaining, rescuing, or restoring life or well-being,[74] one might say that a crucial dimension of the mission of Jesus's disciples in the world is to continue
that life-enhancing, life-sustaining, life-rescuing, and life-restoring work of
Jesus. Such a mission must undoubtedly begin within the community of faith,
but inevitably it must also reach out beyond the boundaries of the Christian
community, especially if the narrated signs of Jesus are paradigmatic.

Hays also emphasizes the "enacted parable" of Jesus's action of washing
his disciples' feet. Coming as it does at the beginning of the second major
part of the Gospel, this incident demonstrates for disciples of Jesus what love
means in practice. This action of Jesus is explicitly exemplary (John 13:15),
but Hays also perceives the footwashing action of Jesus as prefiguring his
death, understood as a self-sacrificial laying down of life for others (15:13; cf.
10:17–18; 13:1).[75] Called as the disciples are to emulate Jesus's love expressed
as service and self-giving, it is difficult to construe their moral obligation as
restricted solely to the community of like-minded believers.[76]

Regarding the ethical implications of Johannine eschatology, Hays recognizes that in view of the present existential crisis (*krisis*) provoked by Jesus
as the incarnate Logos, the dynamic between eschatology and ethics in the
Fourth Gospel differs significantly from that in the other canonical Gospels.
The evangelist's emphasis on realized eschatology, life in its fullness already
available through faith in Jesus, makes for a different conception of moral
motivation. Hays explains:

> Future judgment no longer hangs over the community, as in Matthew, as a war-
> rant to motivate obedience in the present. Nor is the continuing history of the
> church to be understood, as in Luke, as a time in which the church carries out
> its patient mission of preparing a people for God, whose final judgment will
> establish cosmic justice. Least of all is the present time, as for Mark, a bleak
> time of keeping the faith and urgently longing for the return of the Son of Man.
> Rather, the community already lives in the fullness of eschatological life given
> by God to those who are in union with Jesus. . . .[77]
>   Both the warrants and norms for ethics are to be located almost exclusively
> in conformity to the person of Jesus. Future rewards and punishments play a
> minimal role in motivating ethical conduct; the thing that matters is living in
> the present in a way that authentically manifests the love of God in Christ.[78]

---

74. The narrated signs include John 2:1–11; 4:46–54; 5:1–9a; 6:1–14, 16–21; 9:1–9; 11:1–44.
Some would also include John 21:1–14 among the Johannine signs.

75. Hays, *Moral Vision*, 144–45.

76. Compare Pregeant's discussion of the Johannine love ethic in *Knowing Truth, Doing
Good*, 199–207, 214–15. Pregeant leans toward an inclusive interpretation of the Johannine love
ethic, but he appreciates that such a stance is an interpretation that gives priority to certain
textual data at the expense of other data. See also Burridge, *Imitating Jesus*, 325–30, 334–46.

77. Hays, *Moral Vision*, 150.

78. Ibid., 153.

Hays seems to differentiate sharply between the moral vision of the Fourth Gospel and that of Mark's Gospel, indeed, even more so than in relation to the Gospels of Matthew and Luke. But with respect to eschatological vengeance, both the Gospel according to Mark and the Fourth Gospel dissociate eschatology from divine vengeance. In both, the Christ-event is determinative for moral vision and conduct; in both, moral vision and eschatology are congruent. Like Mark's Gospel, then, the Gospel according to John is a canonical resource for relativizing end-time expectations at odds with the peace-oriented mission and message of Jesus.

This view is similar to that of D. Moody Smith. In "Ethics and the Interpretation of the Fourth Gospel,"[79] Smith responds to an earlier study by Wayne Meeks on "The Ethics of the Fourth Evangelist,"[80] in which Meeks effectively reduces the moral value of the Fourth Gospel to its sectarian, countercultural stance. For Meeks, "This Gospel does not provide moral instruction, . . . nor does its narrative directly model character to be emulated."[81] While largely in agreement with Meeks, Smith nevertheless finds more of moral value in the Fourth Gospel, especially in relation to the love command of John 13:34, which he regards as "capacious, capable of infinite expansion, so as to include all humanity."[82] He acknowledges the presence of an ethos of hostility within the Fourth Gospel but observes that despite this hostile ethos, violence against enemies is not endorsed. "Significantly," he writes, "with the disappearance of the apocalyptic in John, apocalyptic violence also disappears. There are no graphic portrayals of the destruction of enemies. The worst that is forecast is that they will remain or abide in darkness."[83] While I am in basic sympathy with Smith's observation about the absence of "apocalyptic violence" in the Fourth Gospel, I see this as a consequence not of the absence of apocalyptic but of this evangelist's reconceptualization of apocalyptic. In stark distinction from Matthew, this evangelist's narration of the story of Jesus in apocalyptic mode entails a reappraisal of eschatological vengeance in which end-time judgment is made to conform to the mode and manner of incarnation.

This is not the view of Adele Reinhartz, who has published extensively on the Fourth Gospel. In "Love, Hate, and Violence in the Gospel of John,"[84] she takes the Johannine form of the love command as her starting point to expose

---

79. Smith, "Ethics and the Fourth Gospel," 109–22.

80. Meeks, "Ethics of the Fourth Evangelist," 317–26.

81. Ibid., 322.

82. Smith, "Ethics and the Fourth Gospel," 111. On this view of the love command in the Fourth Gospel, Smith appeals to precedents in the work of Bultmann and Victor Paul Furnish. He is followed by Swartley, *Covenant of Peace*, 296–300. A balanced assessment is provided by Rensberger, "Love for One Another and Love for Enemies."

83. Smith, "Ethics and the Fourth Gospel," 112. And a little later: "The Johannine Jesus never endorses violence, but only prepares his followers to receive and endure it. Eschatologically, the end for those who reject the light is not violent destruction, but the silence of darkness" (113–14).

84. Reinhartz, "Love, Hate, and Violence."

this Gospel's role in the legacy of hatred and violence known as Western anti-Semitism. "Jesus' new commandment notwithstanding," she states, "the Gospel of Love has also been an instrument of hate, not once, not occasionally, but frequently and pervasively in the history of Jewish-Christian relations."[85] Moreover, she documents how the Fourth Gospel weaves a web of associations between those designated "the Jews" and such linguistic motifs as "darkness," "death," and "destruction" (John 2:19; 3:19; 8:24). Reinhartz acknowledges that such associations do not necessarily go back to Jesus, and she appreciates that Christian anti-Semitism belongs more to this Gospel's "history of influence" than to the evangelist's intention. "Nevertheless," according to Reinhartz, "the contradiction between the commandment to love and the incitement to hate not only belongs to later interpretations of the Gospel but is also inherent in the text itself."[86]

Reinhartz's study comprises two sections: first, a fairly extensive assessment of what she describes as the "vocabularies of love and hate"; and second, a much briefer section in which she outlines a proposed historical life-setting to explain the sharp antagonism depicted within the Gospel by the language of love and hate. For Reinhartz, "Love and hate are abstract nouns denoting emotions."[87] This is an overly restrictive definition of both love and hate. Especially with regard to the Johannine conception of love, love has less to do with how a person feels than with how one wills to behave toward another. The emotional dimension is not excluded, but it is not primary. In any case, Reinhartz correctly observes that "the Gospel of John defines love and hate with respect to a person's stance toward Jesus."[88]

Central to Reinhartz's analysis is the perception of three narrative levels within the Fourth Gospel: the historical or surface level concerned with Jesus in the early part of the first century CE; a second, ecclesiological level reflective of the experience of the Johannine community some decades later; and a third, "cosmological" level, which provides the metaphysical framework within which the story of Jesus is recounted and indeed interpreted. At each of these three levels, according to Reinhartz, an intractable enmity is established between the Jews and Jesus or those who align themselves with Jesus. In the first two levels, the (apparently) historical and the ecclesiological, this enmity, or "grammar of violence" motivated by hatred, takes this basic shape: the Jews hate Jesus and his followers and therefore perpetrate violence against them.

At the third, more complex cosmological level, however, this "grammar of violence" is reversed. Reinhartz's description of the Johannine "cosmological tale" is similar to, if not identical with, what has been described in this chapter as the evangelist's apocalyptic worldview. Here is Reinhartz's own description:

85. Ibid., 109.
86. Ibid., 110.
87. Ibid.
88. Ibid.

The cosmological tale has the cosmos—or the entire universe—as its setting, and eternity as its time frame. Its hero is the preexistent Word who becomes flesh and is sent into the world to bring salvation (1:1–18; 3:16). Its villain is the "ruler of this world" (14:30), "the evil one" (17:15), Satan (13:27), or the devil (8:44; 13:2). Its plot describes the origin of the hero in the divine realm, his descent into the world, his mission to humankind, his defeat of the "ruler of this world," and his return to the Father.[89]

Although I have argued that this apocalyptic perspective is compatible with a peace-oriented position, Reinhartz contends that the "cosmological tale" summarized above entails divine vengeance on those who rejected Jesus and harassed his followers, meaning the Jews. This viewpoint is often reiterated:

> In reading the cosmological and historical levels together . . . it is clear that the cosmological tale reverses the grammatical, and thereby also the theological relationships that are set out in the historical and ecclesiological tales. Furthermore, the actions and events in the historical and ecclesiological tales have repercussions in the cosmological tale. In the historical tale, the Jews kill Jesus. In the cosmological tale, Jesus/God condemn the Jews to death precisely because they strive to kill Jesus. . . .[90]
>
> Implicit in the expectation of condemnation is the notion of judgment. Just as the Jews have judged that Jesus deserves to die according to their law (19:7), so do God and Jesus judge that the Jews deserve eternal condemnation. . . .[91]
>
> The Jews' acts of persecution in the historical and ecclesiological tales take place on an earthly, physical plane. While it may seem that the Jews, on an earthly level, succeed in vanquishing their foe, their comeuppance in the fullness of time is divinely guaranteed. God's condemnation of the Jews may not be visible on an earthly level, but it has eternal consequences. . . .[92]
>
> But the cosmological tale goes beyond merely condemning the Jews. If in the ecclesiological tale the Jews expel believers from the synagogue (16:2), in the cosmological tale, God, through Jesus, expels Jews from the eternal covenant with him.[93]

Reading Reinhartz's review of the ramifications of the Fourth Gospel's cosmological level is a sobering experience. I read this Gospel differently, indeed, so differently that I fail to recognize the Fourth Evangelist in Reinhartz's reiterations of (alleged) divine condemnation of the Jews. Nevertheless, I accept that this Gospel can be—and more to the point, has been—read on Reinhartz's terms. I also recognize that on this matter, my reading reflects a hermeneutic of trust rather than a hermeneutic of suspicion, necessary as

89. Ibid., 114.
90. Ibid., 115.
91. Ibid., 115–16.
92. Ibid., 116.
93. Ibid.

the latter is. So long as my reading does not violate the text, perhaps it may contribute to a more ethically justifiable interpretation of the Fourth Gospel.

The differences between Reinhartz's reading and mine can best be seen in relation to two passages that Reinhartz cites to illustrate the complex relationships within the Fourth Gospel at the cosmological level. The first of these is John 3:18: "One who believes in him [the Son sent into the world] is not judged, but [one] who does not believe has already been judged because [that one] has not believed in the name of the only Son of God." Two principal differences separate my reading of this saying from Reinhartz's. First, her translation reveals that she interprets the language of judgment to signify condemnation, an interpretation that perceives judgment as fatal and final. Much depends on what conception of judgment one brings to the text. And second, Reinhartz maintains that the grammar of John 3:18 implies that "the agent of condemnation, though unspecified, is certainly divine."[94]

On both points, I demur. Reinhartz's reading of John 3:18 is feasible, but it fails to take into account the nuanced, dialectical, and indeed paradoxical understanding of judgment presented in the Fourth Gospel. For this evangelist, judgment is less a divine verdict than a division between persons as a consequence of self-discrimination in response to Jesus as divine disclosure. Interpreting judgment in John 3:18 as divine condemnation is possible,[95] but my own view is that the larger picture of judgment depicted dialectically within the Fourth Gospel makes divine condemnation an inadequate interpretation of judgment.

The second passage that Reinhartz cites to illustrate this Gospel's complex relationships at the cosmological level is John 3:36: "One who believes in the Son has eternal life; one who disobeys the Son will not see life, but rather God's anger remains on [that person]." For Reinhartz, the gist of this saying is "God (the subject) condemns those who do not believe (object)."[96]

John 3:36 echoes 3:18 and should therefore be understood along similar lines. The principal affirmation in John 3:36 appears in the first clause: for the one who believes in the Son, eternal life is a present reality. The second clause reinforces the first by identifying, in Johannine perspective, the inevitable consequence of one's disobeying the Son and thereby rejecting the life offered by the Son. Reinhartz may be correct to interpret "not seeing life" as "seeing death" and the anger of God as divine condemnation, but it is noteworthy that "the wrath of God" (ἡ ὀργὴ τοῦ θεοῦ, *hē orgē tou theou*) in John 3:36b occurs in the Fourth Gospel here and here alone. As a result, it seems prudent to interpret "divine anger" in John 3:36 within the broader horizon of the distinctively Johannine conception of judgment and especially in light

94. Ibid., 115.
95. On this point, Reinhartz is supported by Travis, *Christ and the Judgement*, 263–66.
96. Reinhartz, "Love, Hate, and Violence," 115.

of 3:18, which, as C. K. Barrett opines, is parallel in meaning.[97] As in the case of John 3:18, then, to interpret John 3:36 in terms of divine condemnation is to misconstrue the evangelist's nuanced conception of judgment.

Reading John 3:18 and 3:36 in light of the evangelist's dialectical understanding of judgment is especially important at the apocalyptic (or cosmological) level. As John 12:31–32 and 16:11 reveal, judgment of the world and its ruler occurs by means of Jesus's death by crucifixion. At the cosmological level, therefore, divine judgment takes the form of laying down one's own life (cf. John 10:17–18; 15:13) rather than taking life from another. Indeed, in the apocalyptic image of John 12:31–33, as already noted, there is a coincidence of divine judgment with Jesus's elevation from the earth—the paradoxical consequence and meaning of laying down his own life—and his drawing of *all* to himself. In the Fourth Gospel, *this* is the paradigm of divine judgment, but this apocalyptic perspective seems hidden from Reinhartz's view.

In the second and much briefer section of her study, Reinhartz presents a historical scenario to account for the "grammar of hate" she detects in the Fourth Gospel. She accepts that the Gospel reflects, to some extent, the life-setting of an early Christian community, but she contests the interpretive paradigm associated most closely with J. Louis Martyn,[98] according to which the Gospel reflects a situation in which Jewish-Christian believers had been expelled from the (local?) synagogue (see John 9:22; 12:42; 16:2). This interpretive paradigm has enabled scholars to explain anti-Jewish sentiment within the Gospel as a retaliatory response to the experience of exclusion and isolation. But Reinhartz finds this approach problematic for two reasons: "First, there is no external evidence to support the claim that Jews excluded any groups from the synagogue in the late first century. Second, to suggest that the Gospel's difficult language about the Jews is a justifiable response to the experience of persecution is to hold the Jews themselves responsible for its presence in the Gospel text."[99]

In support of her first contention, Reinhartz appeals to the "definitive critique" of Reuven Kimelman.[100] She might also have referred to the work of Stephen Katz and Daniel Boyarin.[101] But careful studies by William Horbury and Joel Marcus offer qualified support for Martyn's hypothesis.[102] Even Kimelman, as Marcus points out, considers it "safe to conclude that the Palestinian prayer against the *minim* was aimed at Jewish sectarians among

97. Barrett, *According to St John*, 227.
98. See Martyn, *History and Theology in the Fourth Gospel.*
99. Reinhartz, "Love, Hate, and Violence," 120.
100. Kimelman, *"Birkat Ha-Minim."*
101. Katz, "Separation of Judaism and Christianity"; Boyarin, "Justin Martyr Invents Judaism."
102. Horbury, "Benediction of the *Minim*"; Marcus, "Birkat Ha-Minim Revisited."

whom Jewish Christians figured prominently."[103] It would therefore seem that
Reinhartz's first objection is overstated. As for her second objection, there is
room here also for a more nuanced statement. The Fourth Gospel's vitriolic
language with respect to "the Jews" may be understandable as a response to
exclusion and harassment without being justifiable or defensible, especially
in a situation in which this Gospel is no longer the voice of a beleaguered
minority.

This particular instance of lack of nuance is reflective of a larger absence
of nuance in Reinhartz's essay. At no point does she point to textual data in
the Fourth Gospel that present Jews either neutrally or in a positive light.
An assessment that accepts the verbal vehemence of the Fourth Gospel as an
expression of intra-Jewish dispute is less likely to interpret "the Jews" as all
Jews for all time.

In any case, Reinhartz proffers an alternative explanation, which in her
view is suggested by the Fourth Gospel's cosmological level:

> Whatever the details of the historical relationship between Johannine Christians
> and the Jewish community, the former were likely profoundly disappointed
> at the overall lack of acceptance of their message among the Jews to whom
> the Gospel was first preached. As a minor Jewish sect in Roman Palestine in
> the late first century CE, Christians were powerless to act against the Jews on
> the historical plane. But Christians could take full cosmological vengeance by
> proclaiming Jews' exclusion from God's covenant and prophesying their future,
> eternal destruction.[104]

In other words, animosity toward "the Jews" was not a response to an experience of exclusion but rather an expression of frustration at Jews' poor
response to proclamation focused on Jesus as Messiah and Son of God. Rather
than a response of retaliation, it was a response of resentment. In Reinhartz's
analysis, the boot is on the other foot: Christian believers, not Jews, must take
responsibility for the denunciation of "the Jews" in the Fourth Gospel. With
this I am content. No exegesis and no interpretation can undo the legacy of
violence justified with reference to the negative depiction of "the Jews" in
the Fourth Gospel. As part of that taking of responsibility, however, those in
the Christian community must learn to desist from presuming to know what
shape divine judgment takes, especially as it pertains to those with convictions
other than their own. If Christian believers of the late first century did indeed
take "cosmological vengeance" against Jews who were unconvinced by their
witness to Jesus, neither the traditional story of Jesus nor the apocalyptic
interpretation of that story in the Fourth Gospel provided sufficient basis for
prophesying their eternal destruction or damnation.

103. Kimelman, "*Birkat Ha-Minim*," 232; Marcus, "Birkat Ha-Minim Revisited," 535.
104. Reinhartz, "Love, Hate, and Violence," 120–21.

The Peace Witness of the Fourth Gospel

In this chapter I have presented a case for regarding the Fourth Gospel as a nonviolent apocalypse. The evangelist clearly made use of apocalyptic motifs to interpret the mission (work) and message (words) of Jesus. No less clearly, however, he also reinterpreted apocalyptic motifs in light of his insight into the character of Jesus's works and words. Apocalyptic imagery and motifs no less than an apocalyptic worldview were drawn into the service of recounting the story of Jesus, but recounting the story of Jesus required a dramatic and indeed dialectical recasting of those traditional resources.

No interpretation of the Fourth Gospel that conflicts with the form, content, and purpose of the prologue is able to withstand scrutiny. While Painter is not responsible for my use of his work on the Fourth Gospel, his discussion of eschatological dimensions inherent to the prologue is critical to my understanding of it, especially in relation to the peace witness of the Gospel. Especially significant in this respect is Painter's description of the incarnation as the first stage of eschatological fulfillment and of Jesus's death by crucifixion as the symbol of the incarnation. To my mind, if Painter is correct that incarnation is the first stage of eschatological fulfillment, the defining character of that first stage is determinative for all successive stages, including end-time judgment no less than the vanquishing of evil by means of the cross. As for Luke, but in an even more pronounced way for the Fourth Evangelist, realized eschatology provides the pattern and norm for future eschatology.

Not everyone will see the peaceable implications that I perceive from comparing the prologue to the Fourth Gospel with the account of creation in Genesis 1:1–2:3. Compared with the *Enuma Elish*, however, the creation story in Genesis 1 bespeaks a fundamentally different understanding of God and God's relation to the created order. Read on its own, Genesis 1 describes a process of bringing order out of chaos or, perhaps better, of commanding chaos into order but without annihilating the chaotic forces themselves. Read in contrast to the *Enuma Elish*, that ordering of chaotic forces into something good and beautiful strikes me as a peaceful process, which might then be seen as the precursor to incarnation.

Such a view would stretch things too far if it were not for the role of the peace theme in the Gospel as a whole. For those who accept the prologue as a peace text, as I do, the threefold peace greeting on the lips of the crucified and risen Jesus (John 20:19, 21, 26) serves to enclose, with the prologue, the whole of Jesus's work as the Logos-become-flesh. For those who cannot accept the prologue as a peace text, the evangelist's explicit peace references (14:27; 16:33; 20:19, 21, 26) are nevertheless decisive for the second half of the Gospel: those before the Passion Narrative signal the subtext for Jesus's farewell to his disciples; two of them, John 14:27 and 20:21, relate the peace of Jesus to the gift of the Holy Spirit; and taken together, they enclose the evangelist's account of the suffering and violent death of Jesus, thereby signaling the character of divine response to human injustice and violence. Although the peace theme is not sounded often within the Fourth Gospel, both the narrative placement of references to peace and their thematic associations reveal how crucial peace is to the evangelist's theological and moral vision.

As in other respects, the evangelist's dialectical depiction of divine judgment coheres with a peaceful moral vision. Divine judgment is affirmed as both necessary and inevitable, but eschatological vengeance plays no part in the evangelist's conception of judgment. Crucially, the evangelist's interpretation of Jesus's crucifixion as his vanquishing of evil no less than his exaltation and glorification provides interpretive leverage for construing future judgment along lines that are theologically and morally congruent with divine love as manifested through incarnation and crucifixion. As a nonviolent apocalypse, the Fourth Gospel deconstructs anticipations of eschatological vengeance no less than it upholds an ethic centered on love. The love command is patterned on the love exemplified in the life of Jesus, which in its totality is an expression of God's love for the world and hence the basis for a peaceable hope.

7

Apocalypse of the Lamb

Reading Revelation in Peace Perspective

Tradition holds the Gospel according to John and the Revelation to John together, despite their evident differences. Although these two books were probably not written by the same person, there are enough commonalities between them to envisage that both emerged from the same stream of early Christian tradition. Perhaps surprisingly, I have come to regard both the Fourth Gospel and Revelation as nonviolent apocalypses: the Gospel is an apocalypse no less than Revelation, and Revelation entails a peaceful theology and ethic no less than the Gospel. Although the challenge with respect to the Fourth Gospel is to demonstrate its apocalyptic affinities, the challenge relating to Revelation is to show that it inculcates a theology and ethic of peace. After all, the morally disturbing prospect of divinely executed or authorized end-time vengeance seems especially evident in Revelation, in which violent imagery pervades the eschatological drama that John envisions. This chapter builds on a peace-oriented understanding of John's Lamb Christology and interprets the depiction of messianic judgment in Revelation 19:11–21 in light of the christologically renovated throne vision in Revelation 4–5. In so doing, it explores the nexus between Christology, moral vision, and eschatological vengeance, and it concludes with recommendations for reading Revelation in accordance with a hermeneutic of *shalom*.

The collection of authoritative Scriptures for Christians begins and ends with visions of *shalom* (harmonious wholeness). Taken together, the two visions in Genesis 1:1–2:3 and Revelation 21:1–22:5 witness to God's will and purpose for the created order. Creation neither emerges from violence nor is violence constitutive of it. If, for Christians, creation and restored creation mark the alpha and omega points of the biblical metanarrative, the mission of Jesus forms its normative midpoint. From a peace-oriented perspective, there is consonance and coherence between beginning, middle, and end of the canonical story, which attests to divine proneness to *shalom*. Conversely, however, the collection of peculiarly Christian Scriptures known as the New Testament begins and ends with books in which the imagery of eschatological vengeance features prominently. Both the Gospel according to Matthew and the Revelation to John apparently envisage God's creative purposes being realized through divinely authorized eschatological vengeance.

Is it possible for peaceful ends to be realized by violent means? "For God, all things are achievable," Jesus is remembered as teaching (Matt. 19:26; Mark 10:27; cf. Luke 18:27). In relation to God, however, the question of whether peaceful ends can be reached by violent means is less a matter of moral logic than of theology in the strict sense: human reasoning about God's "nature" and will for the world on the basis of scripturally mediated divine disclosure. In view of what is conveyed about God in the creation story in Genesis, in the vision of the new Jerusalem in Revelation, and in the story of Jesus in the canonical Gospels, might depictions of divine vengeance be aberrations deserving of deconstruction—or vital pieces of the puzzle concerning who God is and how God relates to the world? If the latter, the specifically Christian conception of God as One most fully revealed in the person, mission, and message of Jesus is jeopardized. If the former, however, what interpretive resources might there be to deconstruct, faithfully and legitimately, this dark aspect of the biblical depiction of God?

There are those who envisage a "nonviolent coming of God,"[1] but such an eschatological prospect is not generally associated with the Apocalypse of John, which has been lambasted for its violent imagery, its vindictive tone, and for some, its sub-Christian or morally dubious theology. Toward the end of the first of three essays that comprise *The Genealogy of Morals* (German, 1887), Friedrich Nietzsche punctuated his argument decrying the rancorous Jewish inversion of the aristocratic morality of triumphant self-affirmation (preeminently embodied by classical Rome) by describing Revelation as a "book of hatred," indeed, "the most rabid outburst of vindictiveness in all recorded history" (sec. 16).[2] Similarly negative appraisals have been expressed by biblical scholars. C. H. Dodd regarded the Apocalypse of John as the epitome of "futurist" eschatology reconstructed from pre-Christian Jewish sources

---

1. See, e.g., Douglass, *Nonviolent Coming of God*.
2. Despite his anti-Jewish invective, Nietzsche later expresses admiration and respect for the Old Testament, at least by comparison with the New. See section 22 of the third and final essay.

as the early church tried to make sense of the consummation's delay in the eschatological process proleptically fulfilled in Jesus's mission. Regarding Revelation, he wrote:

> With all the magnificence of its imagery and the splendour of its visions of the majesty of God and the world to come, we are bound to judge that in its conception of the character of God and His attitude to man the book falls below the level, not only of the teaching of Jesus, but of the best parts of the Old Testament. . . . The God of the Apocalypse can hardly be recognized as the Father of our Lord Jesus Christ, nor has the fierce Messiah, whose warriors ride in blood up to their horses' bridles, many traits that could recall Him of whom the primitive *kerygma* proclaimed that He went about doing good and healing all who were oppressed by the devil, because God was with Him.[3]

More recently, John J. Collins, widely acknowledged as one of the foremost interpreters of apocalyptic literature, has said this about Revelation: "The expectation of vengeance is . . . pivotal in the book of Revelation. The coming fall of Rome is heralded in gloating terms in chapter 18. In chapter 19, Christ appears from heaven as a warrior on a white horse, from whose mouth comes a sharp sword with which to strike down the nations, and who will tread the wine press of the fury of the wrath of God."[4]

In a similar vein, John Dominic Crossan has locked (s)words with John the prophet-seer, accusing him of betraying the vision of Jesus. Although Crossan's theological and moral vision is compelling, especially with respect to questions of justice and violence, his negative appraisal of the Revelation to John seems overly dependent on the book's history of effects and overlooks important dimensions of John's own theological and moral vision.

Crossan's Animus against the Revelation to John

In a study of "Divine Violence in the Christian Bible," this is how Crossan characterizes the Revelation to John: "That most consistently and relentlessly violent text in all the canonical literature of all the world's great religions."[5] Lest one attribute this to huffing hyperbole on Crossan's part, he reiterates this verdict later in the same study.[6] For people of Christian faith concerned about violence and its religious authorization, this is a damning indictment of a biblical book.

Crossan's study "Divine Violence in the Christian Bible" recognizes, as one must, that the Bible is replete with violence, some of it reflective of routine

3. Dodd, *Apostolic Preaching*, 40–41.
4. J. Collins, *Does the Bible Justify Violence?* 24.
5. Crossan, "Divine Violence in the Christian Bible," 209.
6. Ibid., 228.

human belligerence, but some of it purportedly perpetrated by God or apparently authorized by God and done on God's behalf. There is a contrary biblical strand, however, according to which violence is antithetical to God's will and way. Hence Crossan's question: "Is the God of the Christian Bible violent, nonviolent, or some transcendental combination of both violence and nonviolence to be mixed and matched according to one's religious tradition or theological taste?"[7] To address this question, he explores three major themes—justice, eschaton, and parousia. With respect to all three themes, he detects "a struggle of Gods, a clash between a nonviolent and a violent God."[8] This perception has moral implications: "If, from Genesis through Revelation, the God of the Christian Bible is both nonviolent *and* violent in resistance to evil, how do we Christians respond to that duality? Are we ourselves to be nonviolent, violent, or both, in our own resistance to evil?"[9]

It would be worthwhile to track Crossan's discussion in its entirety, but to keep the focus of this chapter fixed on the book of Revelation, I simply note my concurrence with his treatment of biblical justice and turn to his musings on the themes of eschaton and parousia. Those familiar with Crossan's tome *The Birth of Christianity* know that he has, for some time, made much of crucially different conceptions of the eschaton or, in Crossan-speak, "the Great Divine Cleanup of the World."[10] The basic distinction, for Crossan, is between violent and nonviolent eschatology, between cataclysm and restoration, between the Great Final Battle and the Great Final Feast.[11] The problem, as Crossan documents it, is that *both* visions of God's ultimate triumph over evil pepper the pages of Scripture. Are both visions equally compelling, theologically and morally, or one only? And if one only, which one? Crossan finally gets to that question and provides a satisfying criterion for answering it. First, however, he considers the theme of parousia, and it is here that one learns why he is so scathing in his assessment of the Revelation to John.

To comprehend fully Crossan's conception of both eschaton and parousia, one must come to grips with his relatively new emphasis on "collaborative eschatology," according to which the traditional notion of ultimate divine intervention is replaced by a process of divine-human collaboration.[12] Yet to pursue that here and now would again shift the focus from Revelation; in any case, according to Crossan, once eschaton is envisaged more as a process of divine-human collaboration than as a singular divine intervention, the question remains whether eschatological consummation will be violent or

7. Ibid., 209.

8. Ibid.

9. Ibid., 210.

10. See Crossan, *Birth of Christianity*, 257–89. For a brief discussion, see my introductory chapter (above).

11. Crossan, "Divine Violence in the Christian Bible," 221–22.

12. Ibid., 223. See also Crossan, "Jesus and Collaborative Eschatology."

nonviolent. This defining distinction persists, and Crossan contends that in the wake of Jesus's historical mission, two discordant depictions of eschatological consummation appear in the New Testament. The first is Paul's nonviolent picture of parousia, and the second is the violent vision one finds in Revelation.

In "Divine Violence in the Christian Bible," Crossan relies less on exegesis of texts than on exploration of alleged metaphorical models for Paul and John's visions of parousia. For Paul, according to Crossan, the defining image is of official imperial visitation to a subject city, when city dignitaries would go out to meet a visiting emperor (or delegate) and escort him and his entourage back into the city. On Paul's defining metaphorical model for the parousia, Crossan enjoys the concurrence of Tom Wright.[13] Both contend that, for Paul, the description of the Lord's imminent parousia in 1 Thessalonians 4:15–17 borrows from the widely familiar experience of imperial visitation. Both also maintain that the implication of this borrowing is that the Lord's return will result in a return to a restored earth, *not* rapture to heaven beyond the clouds. Upon meeting the Lord in the air, the Lord's people will escort their Lord whence they came.

There is much to be said for Crossan's contention that Paul's controlling metaphorical model for the parousia of Christ was the experience of imperial visitation, but I suspect that he overstates its alleged peaceable nature. Hosting the imperial presence may (at times) have been a privilege, but it came at a severe cost to the hosts and was premised on vengeance if due honor was not forthcoming. Crossan also makes more than can legitimately be argued from John's use of the Greek verb ἔρχομαι (*erchomai*, come) instead of Paul's *parousia* to refer to the return of Christ. Untenable to my mind is his inference from this difference in choice of vocabulary: "John's terminology does not reflect the nonviolent imperial visitation characteristic of that first-century Pax Romana."[14]

Beyond terminological differences between Paul and John, Crossan also argues that John's mandating metaphorical model for the future coming of Christ was, contrary to Paul, violent imperial visitation based on the Nero-redivivus legend. Although Nero committed suicide in the late-60s to avoid the shameful indignity of assassination, a superstition spread that he had escaped eastward of Rome and would presently return at the head of Parthian forces to rout Rome. Crossan shows that John is somewhat fixated on Nero, indeed, Nero as redivivus (Rev. 13:3, 12, 14; 17:8–11). That notorious numeral 666 of 13:18 almost certainly stands for Nero Caesar.

I now cite Crossan in extenso, as he offers an explanation for John's apparent fixation on Nero:

13. See Wright, *Surprised by Hope*, chap. 8.
14. Crossan, "Divine Violence in the Christian Bible," 227.

But why is John of Patmos so fascinated and focused not just on Nero as, say, the first great imperial persecutor of Christianity but on Nero precisely as Nero *redivivus*, precisely as the one who would return, as it were, from the dead to destroy the Roman Empire?

The answer is sad if not tragic. Rome will be destroyed imminently, announces John, but not by Nero *redivivus*. It will be destroyed by Christ *redivivus*. Not Nero backed by the Parthians but Christ backed by the angels will come—and come soon—to destroy Rome. In that transfer from Nero to Christ, the eschatological consummation retains all the violent imagery of imperial warfare. It is the counter-violence of Christ-as-Nero whose Coming will destroy the violence of the Roman Empire. That is the model and metaphor that controls the Revelation from Patmos.[15]

In short, John models the returning Christ on the Nero-redivivus legend, even to the point of attributing to the returning Christ the violence any Nero figure would need to vanquish Rome. And on one basic matter, Crossan's point must be granted. Whether or not John models the returning Christ on the Nero-redivivus legend,[16] there can be little dispute that, as Crossan puts it, "the eschatological consummation retains all the violent imagery of imperial warfare."

Crossan's study on "Divine Violence in the Christian Bible" reiterates central theses in his book *God and Empire*,[17] wherein he argues that the apostle Paul upheld Jesus's vision of divine peace through justice but that John the seer betrayed that vision by reverting to a vision of divine peace through violence. In *God and Empire*, however, Crossan's pursuit of this thesis is problematic, not only because of the way in which he contextualizes his discussion of Revelation but also by how relatively little space is devoted to that book itself. Fewer than one-third of the relevant chapter's forty-five pages focus on Revelation itself, and the chapter begins with as many pages given over to faith-inspired violence, violent rhetoric that prepares for religiously motivated violence, and fundamentalist Christian rapture theology. John may well have much to answer for with respect to the violent imagery deployed in his apocalyptic vision, but one wonders whether the reception history of Revelation has not jaundiced Crossan's own reading of the book. Moreover, as in Crossan's later study,

15. Ibid., 231.

16. For a full-scale investigation of the historical, cultural, and mythical backgrounds to this passage, see Thomas, *Revelation 19*. Thomas argues that John alludes to the Nero-redivivus legend no less than to the Old Testament motif of the divine warrior, albeit informed by both the tradition of Roman triumph and the Parthian image of the great king. This complex of allusions occurs within what Thomas describes as "a paradigm of counterclaim in Revelation 19" (147), by which he means that John presents the Rider of Rev. 19 as "counter-antitype," that is, the reality of which the Roman triumphator and Parthian king of kings are perverse pretenders (or antitypes). If I understand Thomas correctly, his conception of John's "paradigm of counterclaim" confirms Crossan's concerns regarding the "counter-violence of Christ-as-Nero" in Revelation.

17. Crossan, *God and Empire*.

John's apocalyptic vision is unfavorably compared to Paul's parousia vision, but here also buttressed by a discussion and positive assessment of the mini-apocalypse of Mark 13. In short, Crossan's reader is well and truly primed to perceive the Revelation to John as the violent antithesis to Jesus and Paul's visions of divine peace via justice.

Crossan's fundamental criticism of the Revelation to John is stated early and forcefully, not following an exegetical treatment of relevant texts but before any such exegesis:

> It is one thing to announce, as in Mark's Little Apocalypse, that there will be a spasmic paroxysm of *human* violence *before* the returning Christ. It is another thing to announce, as in John's Great Apocalypse, that there will be a spasmic paroxysm of *divine* violence *by* the returning Christ. The First Coming has Jesus on a donkey making a nonviolent demonstration. The Second Coming has Jesus on a war horse leading a violent attack.[18]

Crossan recognizes that the Lamb rather than the Rider on a warhorse is John's central christological image, but he asserts that the image of the Lamb-as-slaughtered in Revelation 5 refers solely to the first advent of Christ. Subsequently, at the Lamb's second coming, "the Slaughtered becomes the Slaughterer."[19] Moreover, according to Crossan, whereas Mark's Little Apocalypse (Mark 13) separates Rome's destruction of Jerusalem from Christ's anticipated second coming, John's Great Apocalypse envisages Rome's destruction as an integral part of Christ's return. "It is thus a double negation of Mark's warning not to confuse imperial violence *with* or *by* Christ's return."[20]

Crossan highlights two framing passages, Revelation 5 and 19, as decisive for his indictment against John's apocalyptic vision. For Crossan, the first appearance of the Lamb-as-slain in Revelation 5 is important primarily because it leads to describing what the Lamb's unsealing of the scroll of judgment unleashes upon the earth: the fantastic four horsemen of the Apocalypse, which Crossan associates with the sequence of conquest, war, famine, and pestilence (Rev. 6). In other words, the horsemen are precisely agents of the Lamb's judgment. "They do not simply happen as the last spasmic violence of civilization before the final transformation of the world. They are part of that transformation, and they are conducted by Christ."[21] Crossan is well aware that the four horsemen can be and have been interpreted differently, but such alternative interpretations are ignored. Moreover, the detail that the four horsemen are unleashed upon the earth by the Lamb's unsealing of the scroll is, in my view, interpreted too neatly and precisely within a causal schema.

18. Ibid., 217–18, emphasis original.
19. Ibid., 218.
20. Ibid., 223.
21. Ibid., 225.

Regarding the vision of the Rider on a white horse in Revelation 19, Crossan draws attention to the echo in 19:11 of the first horseman in 6:2. Intentional or not, he finds the echo "unfortunate," whereas things look differently if the first rider on a white horse in 6:2 is taken to symbolize Christ's proclaiming good news.[22] Like Crossan, I hold 19:11–21 to depict the returning, conquering Christ, but I construe the manner of that "conquering" differently. For Crossan, the militant mayhem of Revelation 19 is vengeful violence on the part of the Rider named Faithful and True, and the magnificence of Isaiah's vision of earth transformed, depicted as a feast in Isaiah 25, here morphs into a grotesque vision of vultures gorging themselves on victims of divine retribution. Little wonder that Crossan considers John to have betrayed Jesus's vision of divine rule, indeed, to have sinned against the Spirit.[23]

Crossan appreciates John's vision of a new heaven and a new earth, but he is appalled by how such a vision is (apparently) realized:

> It is hard to imagine a more magnificent consummation, but it will all be done by God and only after that terribly violent ethnic cleansing in the preceding chapters, with its climactic vulture-feast at Armageddon in 19:11–21. In conclusion, therefore, the Book of Revelation is the Christian Bible's last and thus far most successful attempt to subsume the radicality of God's nonviolence into the normalcy of civilization's violence. That is the vision of John of Patmos.[24]

Crossan's damning reading of Revelation gives one pause. It undoubtedly resonates with the perception of Revelation held by many. Crossan's view may seem grounded in a natural reading of Revelation, but it is not ultimately compelling. Conspicuously absent from Crossan's treatment of Revelation is engagement with a body of scholarship that envisages Revelation as open to interpretation compatible with a peace perspective. Also overlooked are features of John's apocalyptic vision that invite a peace-oriented reading of the book.

Interpreting John's Violent Imagery

Read from the perspective of its history of reception, Revelation has undoubtedly generated violence and vindictive vengeance.[25] According to Loren Johns, "The Apocalypse of John is arguably the most dangerous book in

22. For this early interpretation, see Rowland, "Imagining the Apocalypse." See also Finamore, "A Kinder, Gentler Apocalypse?" 207–17, who also offers a nongenerative reading of the remaining three horsemen.
23. Crossan, *God and Empire*, 227.
24. Ibid., 229–30.
25. See, e.g., Rowland, "Book of Revelation," 528–56. This is not to say that the violent imagery of John's Apocalypse *necessarily* inculcates a vengeful attitude or violent behavior.

the history of Christendom in terms of the history of its effects."[26] This is not simply a matter of reader response. One of the most evident features of John's Apocalypse is its grotesquely violent imagery. One thinks, for example, not only of the "second death," envisaged as a lake of seething fire and sulfur (20:14–15; 21:8), but also of the calamity and devastation accompanying the series of seven seal openings, trumpet blasts, and bowls of God's anger, or of the vision of the winepress of God's bloodletting wrath in 14:17–20, or of the feast of flesh following the victory of the Word of God in 19:11–21, which is especially disconcerting because it follows hard upon the beatitude of 19:9, "Blessed are those invited to the Lamb's marriage feast."[27] This may be one of the main reasons why Revelation has been either disparaged or neglected by so many down through the centuries or, on the other hand, embraced by Christians with a retributive-apocalyptic mind-set.[28]

Apart from the incongruity between a retributive-apocalyptic mentality and the historic mission of Jesus, at least as portrayed in the biblical Gospels, such a mind-set has morally corrosive ramifications, whether passively quietist or violently sinister. Even though violent texts *may* foster vengeful attitudes and violent behavior, my concern is with the theology of John rather than his ethical exhortation, which consistently advocates nonviolent perseverance on the part of believers. John nowhere calls on believers to use violence against opponents; in fact, in Revelation 13:10 he seems to reject violence out of hand—at least for believers: "If you are to be taken captive, into captivity you go; if you kill with the sword, with the sword you must be killed. Here is a call for the endurance and faith of the saints." As David Barr observes, "John does not call for violence but for endurance."[29] Likewise, commenting on interpretations of Revelation that have provoked violence, Ian Boxall retorts: "Yet it remains the case that not a single passage of the book bids its readers to take up arms or resort to violence against their fellow human beings. Despite the dominance of the language of warfare, battle and victory, vengeance is firmly placed in the hands of the Creator and Judge of the world."[30]

Here John seems to stand with Paul and the writer of the Letter to the Hebrews in restricting to God the entitlement to exact vengeance (Deut. 32:35; Rom. 12:19; Heb. 10:30). The picture John seems to paint is that once God's patience wears out, divine judgment is little different from the

26. Johns, *Lamb Christology*, 5, 186.
27. This is the fourth of seven unevenly distributed beatitudes in Revelation (1:3; 14:13; 16:15; 19:9; 20:6; 22:7, 14).
28. For a survey of various scholarly assessments of the significance of violence in Revelation, see Skaggs and Doyle, "Violence in the Apocalypse," 220–34.
29. Barr, "Doing Violence," 99.
30. Boxall, *Revelation: Vision and Insight*, 125.

violence of God's adversaries. It seems that God ultimately resorts to retributive violence to achieve the divine ends. If that is the case, however,
violence is finally determinative and "might makes right." Whether John
ever depicts the world's Creator and Judge actually exercising vengeance is
open to question, however.

In view of the violent imagery that pervades Revelation, is a peace-oriented
interpretation possible? There are reasons to think so. At crucial junctures in
the visionary drama that John relates, textual details in close but conflictual
relationship to one another create a level of dissonance that subverts the
text's surface imagery of violence. Moreover, this subversion of violence and
vengeance coheres with the Christology of Revelation, which in key respects
resonates with the historical mission of Jesus as that is displayed in the Gospel
narratives. Although certain texts in the Gospel accounts have been understood
to suggest otherwise, most Gospel scholars accept that Jesus's mission and
teaching were essentially nonviolent. Jesus applied nonviolent solutions to
the problems of his day, and he taught his disciples to emulate his example in
this respect. But is the nonviolent conception of Jesus's identity and mission
as presented in the Gospels replaced by a militant perspective in Revelation,
as Crossan contends?

Helpful in this connection is Mark Bredin's *Jesus, Revolutionary of Peace*, in
which he discusses alternative interpretations of Revelation with respect to violence and vengeance. He documents two basic positions on whether the portrayal
of Jesus in Revelation is significantly different from the nonviolent Jesus of the
Gospels. The dominant view, according to Bredin, is that Revelation is to be read
as a text that both anticipates and endorses divine vengeance. "Revelation, in this
perspective, does not call believers to take up arms. But it does call them to believe
that God will carry out his vengeful acts against their perceived oppressors."[31]
Such an interpretation reads with the grain of the text, taking the imagery of
eschatological vengeance at face value. Moreover, among representatives of this
interpretation such as Adela Yarbro Collins and Elisabeth Schüssler Fiorenza,
John's anticipation of divine vengeance serves to emphasize the present disparity
between justice and oppression and is, for that reason, justifiable.[32] Such a reading cannot be too easily relinquished. Any interpretation that dispenses with the
concern for divine vindication and restoration of those whose lives are marked
by suffering caused by injustice and oppression must be adjudged deficient.[33]

31. Bredin, *Jesus, Revolutionary of Peace*, 28.
32. So ibid., 27. But Fiorenza also calls for theological critique of John's violent rhetoric.
See, e.g., her "Words of Prophecy," esp. 19: "While one could argue, as I have done, that the
basic theological paradigm of the Apocalypse is not holy war and destruction but justice and
judgment, not prediction of certain events but exhortation and threat, it is nevertheless necessary to engage in theological ideology critique and to assess critically the violence proclaimed
by the Apocalypse in the name of G*d."
33. In this connection, see Rowland and Corner, *Liberating Exegesis*, 131–55.

Bredin associates an alternative, peace-oriented reading of Revelation with G. B. Caird,[34] William Klassen,[35] John Sweet,[36] Eugene Boring,[37] Wilfrid Harrington,[38] Richard Bauckham,[39] and Richard Hays.[40] For such scholars, and also for Loren Johns and Willard Swartley,[41] the figure of the Lamb is the hermeneutical key to interpreting the imagery of vindictive vengeance in Revelation. As Bredin summarizes: "The war metaphor is rebirthed in the light of suffering witness. Revelation offers another way of perceiving and resisting the world. It implores people to confront the dominant power[s], but in such a way that seeks their conversion rather than their destruction. Nonviolence is the essence of Revelation's understanding of God and his creation."[42]

This counterintuitive interpretation needs to be grounded in sound exegesis of Revelation. The primary point here is that, although not dominant, there is a relatively robust interpretive tradition of reading Revelation from a peace-oriented perspective. A brief overview of John's Christology followed by an attentive reading of two key texts, 4:1–5:14 and 19:11–21, confirms that this minority tradition cannot be written off lightly.

The Christology of Revelation

"Nowhere in the New Testament are christological perspectives more decisive than in the book of Revelation," according to Sarah Alexander Edwards.[43] But for Edwards, following in the footsteps of John Whealon,[44] John's christological perspectives serve the source-critical purpose of confirming that Revelation in its canonical form is the result of editorially embracing a (non-Christian) Jewish apocalyptic text (4:1–22:7) within Christian "parentheses" (1:1–3:22; 22:8–21). Even if one were to accept such a source-critical conclusion, it is difficult to maintain that John's Apocalypse has but a Christian "veneer." One need not doubt that Revelation is profoundly Jewish, but when considering a text from the late first century, that need not signify that Revelation is not also profoundly Christian. John may have been a more conservative Jewish Christian than Paul,[45]

34. Caird, *Commentary on the Revelation.*
35. Klassen, "Vengeance in the Apocalypse of John."
36. Sweet, *Revelation.*
37. Boring, "Theology of Revelation."
38. Harrington, *Revelation.*
39. Bauckham, *Climax of Prophecy*; idem, *Theology of Revelation.*
40. Hays, *Moral Vision.*
41. Johns, *Lamb Christology*, passim; Swartley, *Covenant of Peace*, 324–44.
42. Bredin, *Jesus, Revolutionary of Peace*, 34.
43. Edwards, "Christological Perspectives in Revelation," 139.
44. Whealon, "New Patches on an Old Garment."
45. On eating food offered to idols, Rev. 2:14–15, 20–22 suggests that John had stricter views than Paul.

but Jewish-*Christian* he surely was. This shuts the door on efforts to attribute expressions of vengeance within Revelation to a "reversion" to Judaism, historically a common explanation for the vindictive and vengeful tone of the book.[46]

The opening line of John's Apocalypse describes the book as a "revelation of Jesus Messiah," which can mean a revelation either *from* or *about* Jesus Messiah or, more likely, *both* from *and* about Jesus Messiah. If Revelation is no less about Jesus Messiah than it purports to be from him, this has a significant bearing on interpretation, insofar as it imposes certain interpretive constraints. An interpretation of Revelation that does not place *at its core* John's peculiar exposition of the identity and significance of Jesus can hardly comprise a faithful interpretation of Revelation.[47]

John's Christology is remarkably pluriform, as seen from the following descriptions. Revelation 1:5a describes Jesus as "the faithful witness, the firstborn of the dead, and the ruler of the kings of the earth." His atoning significance is signaled in the phrase "who freed us from our sins by his death" (1:5b), and his eschatological significance is signaled in the affirmation "He is coming with the clouds, and every eye will see him" (1:7a). At 1:13 and 14:14, John retrieves from Daniel 7:13 the image of "one like a person [son of humanity]" to conceptualize Jesus, who in addressing the angel of the church at Thyatira is also "the Son of God" (Rev. 2:18). In 1:17; 2:8; and 22:13, Jesus is "the first and the last," while in 1:18 he is "the living one" who has experienced death and now holds "the keys of Death and Hades." He is God's anointed (11:15; 12:10; 20:4, 6), "Lord of lords and King of kings" (17:14; 19:16), "Faithful and True" (19:11), and "the Word of God" (19:13).

An important dimension of John's understanding of Jesus is that much of what is said of God can also be said of Jesus. If God is the Alpha and Omega (Rev. 1:8; 21:6), so too is Jesus (22:13); if God is the beginning and the end (21:6), so too is Jesus (22:13; cf. 1:17); if God is enthroned, so too is Jesus (4:2–3; 5:6; 22:1). Praise of God (4:9–11) is paralleled by praise of Jesus (5:9–12), which culminates in 5:13–14 with praise and worship of *both* God and Jesus. God's wrath (14:10, 19; 15:1) is also paralleled by the wrath of the Lamb (6:16), although here it might be prudent to say that God's wrath parallels that of Jesus, since the wrath of the Lamb is mentioned first.[48] So, not only is John's Christology pluriform; it is also exalted.

---

46. See Klassen, "Vengeance in the Apocalypse," 302.

47. On the Christology of Revelation, see esp. Johns, *Lamb Christology*; yet also Bauckham, *Theology of Revelation*, 54–108; Bredin, *Jesus, Revolutionary of Peace*; Boring, "Narrative Christology in the Apocalypse"; Slater, *Christ and Community*; and Hoffmann, *Destroyer and the Lamb*.

48. In view of the argument of this chapter, readers may wonder how I interpret the wrath of the Lamb and of God. I take these expressions to refer to divine judgment so long as such judgment is construed along lines that cohere with divine disclosure in Jesus. If divine wrath is understood to express divine censure against sin or evil that is somehow purgative or restorative, rather than strictly retributive, this stands up to christological scrutiny.

As pluriform and exalted as John's Christology is, on multiple occasions Jesus is referred to as "Lamb," making this John's dominant or "most comprehensive"[49] christological image. Moreover, as Swartley observes, "'Lamb' is used 28 times in Revelation and is the only designation for Christ in the narrative plot other than 'Son of Man' in 14:14; other titles are used in the frames of the drama in chs. 1 and 22."[50] Paradoxically, the Lamb is one who triumphs in battle; however, it is precisely as the slain Lamb that the Lamb triumphs (5:6, 8–9, 12; 7:14; 12:11; 13:8). This paradox fits the dual emphasis on the Lamb's humiliation and exaltation. As Udo Schnelle explains:

> The foundation of Revelation's Christology is the saving act of God in Christ. This act establishes eschatological salvation and saves from the world's realm of power (cf. e.g., Rev. 1.5b, 6; 5.9–10; 7.15; 12.11). The distinctive christological dignity of Jesus is expressed in the title ἀρνίον (lamb, used 28x as a title in Rev.), which at one and the same time expresses Jesus' giving himself for his own and his exaltation as Lord (Rev. 5.6). The exaltation of the Lamb is based on his humiliation (cf. Rev. 5.9, 12); the firstborn of the dead (Rev. 1.5) is the slaughtered lamb. Jesus acts as God's authorized agent who in Rev. 5 is explicitly portrayed as being commissioned to accomplish God's plan of eschatological salvation.[51]

Schnelle's concluding observation is crucial. If it is as "slaughtered Lamb" that Jesus is God's authorized agent of eschatological salvation, this has a significant bearing on how the realization of the divine will and purpose should be understood. Crucial in this regard is the work of Johns, in which both the *origins* of the prophet-seer's Lamb Christology and *his own innovative use of it* are explored with a view to ascertaining its ethical force.[52] With Johns, Crossan, and others, I consider the Lamb-image to be John's central, controlling christological motif.[53] Significantly, John's first reference to the Lamb occurs in Revelation 5:6, within the heavenly vision recounted in chapters 4–5.

True Vision in Revelation 4–5

Revelation 4:1 marks a decisive transition in the book's structure. Following letters to seven churches in chapters 2–3, the scene changes from earth to

49. Slater, *Christ and Community*, 200.
50. Swartley, *Covenant of Peace*, 338.
51. Schnelle, *History and Theology*, 535.
52. Johns, *Lamb Christology*, passim. Also helpful in this respect is Bauckham, "Language of Warfare," who shows that although John repudiates "messianic militarism," he nevertheless employs militaristic imagery to symbolize nonmilitaristic victory over evil.
53. Johns is primarily concerned with the ethical implications of John's Lamb Christology; I am also concerned with the theological implications of this decisive christological image. Although Crossan accepts the Lamb-as-slain as John's central christological image, he does little to explore its meaning and significance.

heaven. John is invited to transgress the boundary between heaven and earth, with the promise that he will be shown what is to come. His translation into the heavenly sphere is described as a form of Spirit seizure, without mention of any journey of ascent. Thus the form of what follows is that of vision, perhaps recounting a recollected visionary experience.[54] More important, perhaps, is that the content of the opening scene of John's second vision (cf. the first in 1:10–20) is worship in the throne room of the Lord God "Almighty" (παντοκράτωρ, *pantokratōr*).[55] Here John perceives—and describes in symbol and imagery—what is ordinarily hidden from human perception.[56]

The central image in Revelation 4–5 is a throne surrounded by other thrones. The one seated on the central throne cannot be described precisely, but everything clearly centers on this figure, representing God. While John's vision may be of one enthroned in the heavenly court, it is nevertheless a profound challenge to the sovereignty of those who occupy earthly thrones.[57] Not the emperor, but the Creator God is sovereign over all; not the emperor, but the Creator God is entitled to adoration and worship. Worship serves to focus on primary things. When people via worship hymn God with adoration and praise, they acknowledge God as the only one worthy of such adoration and praise. But if God is the *only one worthy* of adoration and praise, other claims on human loyalty are false claims, as is the common assumption that those in power ultimately shape history and human destiny. Worship of God is a reminder that there can be no higher claim on human loyalty, a reminder that the scroll of history and the future is in God's hands, not in the hands of the powerful and the wealthy.

Since Revelation 4–5 is a vision of heavenly and thus authentic worship, this implies that the worship described is also a form of vision: a perception of reality shaped by faith in God as Creator and Redeemer. The vision described in these two chapters likely reflects features of worship from both the synagogue and the early Christian house church. Then as now, it was difficult to imagine that this world is in God's control; then as now, it was difficult to acknowledge God's sovereignty. As Elisabeth Schüssler Fiorenza discerns, "The central theological question of chapters 4–5 as well as of the whole book [of Revelation] is: Who is the true Lord of this world?"[58] If one were to answer this question solely on the basis of experience, one might say that the powerful, those with wealth and weapons, govern the world. That is not John's answer, however. His heavenly vision enables him to see things differently, to

---

54. See Boxall, *Revelation: Vision and Insight*, 30–36.

55. This divine designation occurs in Rev. 1:8; 4:8; 11:17; 15:3; 16:7, 14; 19:6, 15; 21:22. Boring, "Theology of Revelation," 259, points out that of the ten occurrences of this term in the New Testament, nine are in Revelation.

56. On what follows in this section, I acknowledge my indebtedness to Yoder, *Politics of Jesus*, 228–47; idem, "To Serve Our God and to Rule."

57. Compare Bauckham, *Theology of Revelation*, 35–39.

58. Fiorenza, *Revelation*, 58.

gain an alternative perspective on reality. "John's vision of heaven takes him deeper into reality, rather than removing him from it," as Boxall observes.[59] Precisely this alternative and more profound perspective on reality is crucial for a peace-oriented interpretation of theology and ethics in the Apocalypse.

For the interpreter, Revelation 4–5 is critically significant because the vision it recounts is what Boxall calls the "orienting vision" for the remainder of the narrative.[60] Or as Johns affirms, "The rhetorical fulcrum of the Apocalypse is the scene in heaven in chapters 4 and 5."[61] Later scenes, signaled by what is designated in 4:1 as "what must occur after these things," should be understood in ways compatible with the perspective of this heavenly vision.

A crucial feature of John's perspective-sharpening vision of worship in the heavenly throne room is its "bifurcated sense of reality," in which earthly and heavenly dimensions coexist as competing realities but in such a way that the heavenly sphere is conceived as both more real and ultimately more true and enduring than the earthly sphere.[62] Revelation 4 is recognizable as little different from traditional Jewish *merkabah* (throne-chariot) mysticism influenced by Ezekiel 1,[63] but Revelation 5 introduces into John's vision-account a distinctively christocentric dimension, in which the figure of the Lamb is praised alongside and in the same terms as the indescribable figure on the throne. For John, the Lamb is the key to God's way of working in the world, but that insight requires that one pass through a refining process that overturns one's preconceptions and assumptions about the way the world works. It requires, as Christopher Rowland suggests, something akin to a Nietzschean "revaluation of all values," a process of having one's assumptions about what is real and worthwhile challenged and inverted.[64]

John achieves this "revaluation" by means of a dramatic sequence of images: first, a scroll in the right hand of the enthroned one, clearly containing crucial information yet sealed with seven seals; second, the proclamation (as opposed to a simple query) whether anyone anywhere is worthy to break open the scroll and its mysteries; third, the realization that wherever one might think to look, there is no one worthy even to look upon the scroll, let alone open it, which causes John to weep disconsolately; then fourth, hope when John hears one of the twenty-four elders say that since the Lion of the tribe of Judah has "conquered" (νικάω, *nikaō*),[65] he is worthy to unseal the scroll (5:5); but fifth,

59. Boxall, *Revelation of Saint John*, 82.
60. Ibid., 79.
61. Johns, *Lamb Christology*, 158.
62. See Howard-Brook and Gwyther, *Unveiling Empire*, 120–35.
63. This is not to suggest that Rev. 4 is incidental or has no distinctively Christian elements. See Hurtado, "Revelation 4–5."
64. Rowland, "Book of Revelation," 605.
65. The verb νικάω occurs fifteen times in Revelation: seven times in Rev. 2–3 and eight times elsewhere (5:5; 6:2; 11:7; 12:11; 13:7; 15:2; 17:14; 21:7).

what John sees *in the place of the enthroned one* is a Lamb-as-slaughtered. Spatially speaking, this sequence of images begins and ends with one on the throne,[66] but in between the reader is ushered through all the dimensions of the created order only to learn that what needed to be found was not one worthy to unseal the scroll but rather a new perspective that enables one to perceive that the "conquering" normally associated with the image of a lion has *already* been accomplished, but in the *manner* of a lamb that submits to slaughter. The scope of John's artful innovation is breathtaking but all too often ignored or overlooked as readers rush forward to learn what is loosed from the unsealed scroll.

John's weeping ceases when he *hears* of "the Lion of the tribe of Judah, the Root of David" (cf. Gen. 49:9; Isa. 11:1, 10). Scholars quibble over what messianic associations in Jewish tradition best explain these specific images, but it is generally agreed that they evoke the image of a messianic warrior-king. What John *sees*, however, is a Lamb-as-slaughtered. Various interpretations have been offered to explain the rapid transfer of images from Lion of the tribe of Judah to Lamb-as-slaughtered.[67] One that is well known because it appears in an influential reference work is that by Adela Yarbro Collins. After posing the question whether the image of Jesus as divine warrior in Revelation 19 is transformed by the image of the Lamb in chapter 5 or vice versa, she writes:

> The character of the book as a whole, as well as the context of the image of the Lamb in chap. 5, suggests that the latter is the case [that is, the image of the Lamb is transformed by the image of Jesus as divine warrior]. The death of Christ is affirmed . . . as the event that freed believers from their sins (1:5b). In chap. 5, the image of the "lamb, standing as if slain" is immediately transformed by the description of the animal as having seven horns (v. 6). As is well known, the horn is a biblical and postbiblical image of military might and the horned ram is an image for great military leaders and for a warrior-messiah in the Dream Visions of Enoch (*1 Enoch* 85–90). The impression that the older Christian image of the sacrificial Lamb is being reinterpreted in Revelation is supported by the introduction of the figure as the "Lion of the tribe of Judah" (5:5).[68]

Adela Yarbro Collins interprets John's transformation of a nonviolent understanding of Jesus's identity and mission into a militant one as being a response to a threatening situation (or several perceived crises) in the life of the churches for which Revelation was written. In other words, in response to circumstances in which God's sovereignty seemed to be undermined by the way things were, John conceived of an alternative vision in which the rule of

66. See Knight, "Enthroned Christ of Revelation 5:6."
67. See Skaggs and Doyle, "Lion/Lamb in Revelation."
68. A. Collins, "Revelation, Book of," 705; cf. idem, "Book of Revelation," 400–401, where she differentiates between "the past metaphorical victory of Jesus and the future military victory of the risen Christ."

God and Jesus was reaffirmed, despite appearances to the contrary, and in which the faithful are ultimately rewarded and the unfaithful are condemned.

For Adela Yarbro Collins, John reinterpreted the peaceable mission of Jesus into a threatening prospect of eschatological vengeance to cope with present circumstances of suffering. The logic of her position is that traditional apocalyptic motifs are wholly determinative of John's meaning.[69] Whether they are determinative, however, or whether they are reworked and thereby provide the means whereby John *reinterpreted* traditional conceptions of divine agency is precisely the point at issue. An important aspect of Adela Yarbro Collins's position is her interpretation of the "seven horns" of Revelation 5:6 as signifying military prowess, a view also adopted by G. K. Beale,[70] among others. There is no reason to deny that the horn is symbolic of power, but again whether such an image *as used here by John* requires that it be understood as power associated with military prowess is open to question. An equally plausible interpretation is to read the "seven horns" *along with* the "seven eyes" as signifying the "seven spirits of God sent out into all the earth" (5:6), meaning God's irresistible but not necessarily militant agency in the world.[71]

One certainly needs to recognize stock apocalyptic motifs employed by John, such as the so-called "combat myth," but one also needs to attend to ways in which such motifs are subtly reworked to convey new insight. As Johns observes:

> If modern readers have never heard of an ancient combat myth, the Gestalt created by the act of reading the Apocalypse is more likely to emphasize the violence of the images. However, if the violent images are recognized as a standard part of the combat myth tradition, the reader will likely be more alert to the manner in which the combat myth is being reshaped and redefined in John's creative use of them.[72]

The shift of imagery from that of anticipated "Lion of the tribe of Judah," which is first *heard* about so as to evoke certain expectations in the reader's mind, to that of "Lamb-as-slaughtered" unsettles preexisting notions. When we look for the lion, our expectations are turned upside down by a Lamb; in turn, the honor accorded the Lamb turns our understanding of reality downside up. One way of expressing the conviction behind this clashing pair

---

69. Compare her critique of Boring, *Revelation*, in both "Eschatology in Revelation" and "Appreciating the Apocalypse," in which at various points her disagreement with Boring's allegedly "allegorical" and less-than-serious interpretation of John's violent imagery presumes John's retrieval, *but not renovation*, of traditional concepts, e.g., the allusion in Rev. 19:11–21 to the Word of God referred to in Wis. 18:15.

70. Beale, *Book of Revelation*, 352–55.

71. See Fiorenza, *Revelation*, 60; Aune, *Revelation 1–5*, 353–54.

72. Johns, *Lamb Christology*, 15.

of images is to say, with Bauckham and Denny Weaver,[73] that the lion symbolizes victory while the Lamb symbolizes the means or manner of victory. In other words, the Messiah of God accomplishes God's purposes for the world not by might but by suffering in solidarity with all that is broken, disfigured, crushed, humiliated, downtrodden. This is the heavenly perspective on the mission of Jesus, which led ultimately to the cross. Yet from the perspective of heaven, the cross was not a defeat but a victory worth celebrating. That God is on a throne does not signify that God's will for the world is best discerned and enacted by those on earthly thrones; indeed, the one deemed "worthy" is not on any kind of throne we are used to seeing but bears the marks of a cross.

The strange new song of Revelation 5:9–10, in which the same four creatures and twenty-four elders who had earlier praised the Lord of creation now praise the Lamb deemed worthy to open the scroll because it bears the marks of slaughter, signals something profound. It is precisely the scars of suffering that entitle the Lamb to open the sealed scroll in God's right hand. Whatever this scroll symbolizes, whether future judgment, the meaning of history, or something else altogether,[74] what matters most is that one who suffered is deemed worthy to break it open. If God the Creator is able to bring something meaningful and good out of the Lamb's suffering and death, that same God is able to bring something meaningful and good out of the suffering and woundedness of the world and those in it.

Steve Moyise,[75] in dialogue with James Resseguie,[76] contends that a literary difficulty for this particular interpretation is that elsewhere in Revelation it is usually what John *hears* that interprets or clarifies what he *sees* rather than vice versa, as in chapter 5. But the examples he cites (from Resseguie), as establishing the principle that in this book hearing generally interprets seeing, are not compelling instances of what John hears interpreting what he sees. By contrast, a Lamb's appearance when what John hears leads him to anticipate seeing a lion is a clear case of one image *supplanting* and thereby interpreting another.[77] As Johns observes, the juxtaposition of lion and Lamb is not sustained throughout John's Apocalypse; instead, the lion, once mentioned, is never actually seen and never actually (re)appears. For Johns, "This suggests

---

73. Bauckham, *Climax of Prophecy*, 179–85; Weaver, *Nonviolent Atonement*, 21, 33.

74. For Bauckham, *Theology of Revelation*, 80–88, the meaning of the scroll is that the faithful witness of believers, including death, is the means by which the nations of the world will turn to God, thereby establishing the reign of God over the world.

75. Moyise, "Does the Lion Lie Down with the Lamb?" esp. 188–89.

76. Resseguie, *Revelation Unsealed*.

77. Ibid., 33–37, the section cited by Moyise, does emphasize that what John hears generally interprets what he sees. In his introduction (7–10), however, Resseguie states that what John sees can also interpret what he hears. Beale in *Book of Revelation*, 353, contends that a common pattern within Revelation is that "visions are placed directly after heavenly sayings in order to interpret them."

that the images of the lion and the lamb were created specifically to address competing visions of how the messiah wields power."[78]

The Rider of Revelation 19:11–21

There is broad but not unanimous agreement that Revelation 19:11–21 is John's visionary account of the parousia, even though it differs in various respects from other early Christian depictions of the parousia.[79] Whether this passage portrays the parousia or a vision of messianic triumph by means of Jesus's death, as Barr argues,[80] is not ultimately decisive. The vision depicts definitive divine triumph over forces antagonistic to God. As elsewhere, John innovates to emphasize the ineluctability of divine "conquest" over the forces of evil, but one should not infer from the violent imagery that the mode of conquest is violent. Why not? The first point to make is that insofar as John's vision anticipates a future event, it is beyond the capacity of any human being to know precisely how events will play out. Related to this is the symbolic nature of this passage. As David Aune explains,

> The literary form of this unit is the *symbolic description*, which focuses on the *description*, *identity*, and *tasks* of the rider on the white horse. . . . The indicators of the *symbolic* nature of this description include the mention of the sharp sword that proceeds from his mouth (v. 15a) and the metaphorical interpretation of the wine that is pressed as "the fury of the wrath of God the Almighty" (v. 15c).[81]

Symbolic description within a visionary account of an anticipated event should not be pressed literally, which implies that the violent imagery of this passage may signify something altogether nonviolent.

Aune draws attention to numerous parallels between Revelation 19:11–16 and Jewish texts that portray God or God's Messiah as a warrior king.[82] There

---

78. Johns, *Lamb Christology*, 191. Moyise, "Does the Lion Lie Down with the Lamb?" 189, 193–94, contends that the Lion-Lamb juxtaposition requires a two-way dynamic of mutual interpretation, but he accepts that this juxtaposition of images *permits* a nonviolent interpretation.

79. Painter, "Johannine Literature," 559–62, displays multiple parallels between Revelation and the version of Jesus's apocalyptic discourse in Matt. 24. Revelation 19:11–16 is adjudged to be a transformation of the imagery of the Son of humanity's coming on the clouds of heaven with power and glory (Matt. 24:30; cf. Dan. 7:13).

80. Barr, "Lamb Who Looks Like a Dragon?" 215. See also McKelvey, "Millennium and the Second Coming," who challenges the view that Rev. 19:11–21 relates to the parousia on the grounds that this passage recapitulates other mythical battles recounted by John and is itself recapitulated in Rev. 20:7–10. However, his main concern seems to be to retrieve Rev. 19:11–21 from premillennialist interpretations in which Christ's second coming is associated with an escapist eschatology and is followed chronologically by a literal utopian millennium.

81. Aune, *Revelation 17–22*, 1047, emphasis original.

82. Ibid., 1048–52.

can be little doubt that such texts compose the principal literary and conceptual background to John's visionary description of the Rider on a white horse.[83] The vital question, however, is what John does with the image of the warrior king. Does he simply take over the imagery of divine warfare against antagonistic nations, or in taking it over does he also innovate?

The following details suggest that John's symbolic description utilizes imagery that signifies divine victory over opposing forces but without violent vengeance. First, the present tense of the verbs κρίνω and πολεμέω (*krinō*, judges/rules; *polemeō*, combats) in 19:11c suggests that these functions of the Christ-figure are integral to his characteristic manner of dealing with opposition to God. Aune designates the present tense of these particular verbs "the general or gnomic present, used to express customary actions and general truths."[84] Moreover, these "customary actions" are done "justly" or "rightly," perhaps even in a "right-setting" way (ἐν δικαιοσύνη, *en dikaiosynē*). Together, these considerations challenge the view that the returning Messiah will act in ways contrary to his customary demeanor. For John, there is no "division of labor" between the crucified Lamb and the Rider on a white horse, as Miroslav Volf asserts in *Exclusion and Embrace*.[85] Indeed, the detail that the Rider's garment is *already* blood-stained not only before the birds are called to gather for the feast of flesh but also well before antagonistic armies assemble to wage war against the Rider—not (*nota bene*) the other way around—intimates that it refers to his own death rather than to any violent death that he inflicts.[86] The means by which the Lamb conquers remain the means by which the Rider defeats all opposed to the purposes of God.

83. Thomas, *Revelation 19*, shows that Rev. 19:11–21 also alludes to significant non-Jewish traditions such as the Roman triumph and Parthian great king, but he accepts the primacy of Jewish divine-warrior traditions.

84. Aune, *Revelation 17–22*, 1053. In agreement on this point is Smalley, *The Revelation to John*, 488: "It is in general the case, the seer is saying, that the Messiah is right in his justice and his judgement."

85. Volf, *Exclusion and Embrace*, 275–306. Volf's two principal resources for advocating Christian nonviolence are the two christological images of the crucified Messiah and the Rider on a white horse in Rev. 19. For Volf, anticipation of the Rider's vengeance enables believers to renounce violence here and now.

86. Compare Johns, *Lamb Christology*, 184: "The rider approaches the battle dressed in a robe dipped in blood (19:13)—his own blood of witness/martyrdom. In keeping with the pivotal scene in Rev 5 and the message of the book as a whole . . . , the blood here is the blood of martyrdom. This contrasts with Isa 63:1–3, the source of this imagery, where the blood is the blood of the enemies of the divine warrior. John is, in fact, challenging the reader to look more carefully at his language and to reinterpret Isaiah 63 in the light of the Lamb." Carrell, in *Jesus and the Angels*, 199–200, summarizes the variety of explanations of the phrase βεβαμμένον αἵματι (*bebammenon haimati*, dipped in blood) and suggests that all are incorporated in this "multivalent image." Not all suggested interpretations are equally compelling, however. Slater, *Christ and Community*, 223–25, considers the most plausible interpretation to be that the blood on the Rider's robe is that of his enemies, seemingly because this reading fits a sociohistorical context in which Christians are suffering and will be helped to endure by anticipating divine retribution for their oppressors.

In view of Revelation's reception history, this point can hardly be overemphasized. Regarding 19:13a, Aune comments:

> The blood mentioned here is not primarily a metaphor for the atoning death of Christ . . . but rather a literal reference to the heavenly warrior whose garment is stained with the blood of those he has slain. . . . The imagery of a bloodstained divine warrior coming to destroy his enemies occurs in a number of texts in the OT and early Judaism (Exod 15; Deut 33; Judg 5; Hab 3; Isa 26:16–27:6; 59:15–20; 63:1–6; Zech 14:1–21 . . .), one of the oldest of which is Isa 63:1–3.[87]

Having said this, however, Aune continues by stating: "It was inevitable that this older image of God as the divine warrior with blood-soaked garments transposed into the Messiah as divine warrior would be understood as a reference to the death of Christ by both the author and his readers when placed in a Christian context."[88] Furthermore, in his summary explanation of the passage, Aune concludes: "The single apparent allusion to his [i.e., Jesus Christ's] redeeming death is his robe, which has been dipped in blood (see [Rev.] 1:5; 5:9; 7:14; 12:11), actually a Christian reading of a traditional conception of the divine warrior understood as the Messiah."[89]

In other words, John did not simply take over the motif of the divine warrior but, in doing so, subtly—*perhaps all too subtly!*—reworked the motif so as to convey that in view of the historic mission of Jesus Messiah, God's victory over antagonistic forces was no longer effected by inflicting violence but by suffering it. The symbolism of Revelation 19 is disturbing, but the reality to which the symbolism points is best interpreted in light of what is affirmed about the Lamb in chapter 5. No less than the messianic Lion of the tribe of Judah, the messianic Rider on a white horse is to be seen as symbolically affirming the potent efficaciousness of the Lamb's mode of overcoming evil and opposition to God.[90]

One might add that supposed battle scenes in Revelation are not literal battles. As Weaver points out, the battle in heaven in chapter 12 signifies the cosmic significance of the resurrection and/or ascension of Jesus, which is that through his death and vindication by God, evil's power is thwarted. As for the imagery of warfare in 19:11–21, Weaver contends that no literal battle is envisaged. He interprets the killing sword as the Word of God because it emanates from the Rider's mouth (cf. Eph. 6:17; Heb. 4:12):

87. Aune, *Revelation 17–22*, 1057.
88. Ibid.
89. Ibid., 1069.
90. Both Slater, *Christ and Community*, and Hoffmann, *Destroyer and the Lamb*, demonstrate that, whatever their origins, the christological images of the Lamb and the Rider on a white horse, together with the image of "one like a son of man," are integrally interrelated in Revelation. Revelation 17:14 and 19:16 confirm the identification of the Lamb with the Rider.

In Rev. 19:11–21, the beast and the kings and their armies are defeated not by violence and military might. They are undone—defeated—by the Word of God. This passage is another symbolic representation of the victory of the reign of God over the forces of evil that has already occurred with the death and resurrection of Jesus. It is by proclamation of the Word, not by armies and military might, that God's judgment occurs.[91]

Weaver's view is similar to that of Richard Hays: "We are to understand that the execution of God's judgment occurs through the proclamation of the Word. . . . Those who read the battle imagery of Revelation with a literalist bent fail to grasp the way in which the symbolic logic of the work as a whole dismantles the symbolism of violence."[92]

It is not simply that John's battle scenes are not to be taken literally. Here there is no battle, symbolic or otherwise. Birds are called to gather for the carrion of everything from kings to slaves, and the beast and kings of the earth muster their armies to combat the Rider and his entourage. But there is no description of battle, only the end result that the beast and false prophet are captured and thrown into the lake of fire while the rest are "slaughtered" by the sword emanating from the Rider's mouth and eaten by birds. The imagery is ghastly but not to be understood literally. As Aune confirms:

> To be slain by the sword that projected from the mouth of the warrior on the white steed certainly invites metaphorical interpretation; i.e., the "sword" must be the words spoken by the warrior (on the sword as a metaphor for the word of God, see Heb 4:12). . . . There is reason to suspect that the phrase τῇ ἐξελθούσῃ ἐκ τοῦ στόματος αὐτοῦ, "the [sword] projecting from his mouth," is a gloss intended to emphasize the metaphorical interpretation of the sword.[93]

Perhaps the best reason to interpret "the sword protruding from his mouth" metaphorically is that in the letter to the angel of the church in Pergamum, the One with the sharp twin-edged sword (Rev. 1:16; 2:12) threatens to "combat" the nefarious Nicolaitans with the sword of his mouth unless such pernicious persons are opposed (2:14–16). Apart from 19:11, in 2:16 is the only other occurrence of πολεμέω (polemeō, combat) used with John's Christ-figure as subject.[94] Since the "combat" envisaged in 2:16 can hardly be literal, this strengthens the case for interpreting 19:15, 21 metaphorically.

91. Weaver, *Nonviolent Atonement*, 34.
92. Hays, *Moral Vision*, 175; cf. Rowland, "Book of Revelation," 700. Citing Isa. 11:4; 2 Thess. 2:8; Rev. 2:12, 16; and 4 Ezra 13:9–11 alongside Rev. 19:15, 21, Rowland remarks: "All of these passages suggest that judgment in the context of an eschatological battle comes by means of the power of the Word of God rather than through force of arms. The effect is devastating, because it functions as a divine illocutionary act."
93. Aune, *Revelation 17–22*, 1067.
94. Klassen, "Vengeance in the Apocalypse," 305.

More might be written about this Rider on a white horse,[95] but enough has been said to counter the view that Revelation 19:11–21 unequivocally affirms divine vengeance. Not only the form of the passage but also grammatical and symbolic details within it encourage the interpreter whose perspective is focused on—*and by!*—the image of the Lamb to understand this vision as symbolizing God's nonviolent reclamation of the created order.

Christology, Eschatological Vengeance, and Moral Vision

Richard Hays's discussion of Revelation in *The Moral Vision of the New Testament* emphasizes how John's Lamb Christology and apocalyptic eschatology reinforce a moral vision in which faithful believers emulate the Lamb through nonviolent resistance to injustice and religiocultural accommodation. His discussion is compelling with respect to the vision of Christian morality portrayed in John's Apocalypse, even if he is perhaps too sanguine about "the way in which the symbolic logic of the work as a whole dismantles the symbolism of violence."[96] Revelation's history of reception suggests that even if this was John's intent, his violent symbolism has more often than not dismantled the symbolic logic of the narrative as a whole. One likely reason for this is that what is often understood to be John's theology overshadows his moral vision: people's perception of how Revelation envisages God's ultimate triumph over evil involves more overwhelming violence than the forces of evil can muster. Few dispute that John's explicit ethical exhortations disavow violence and vengeful retaliation. But his description of God or God's agents as inflicting violence to bring about the divine will has served to sanction *both* nonviolence and violence on the part of believers—nonviolence for those who expect that God will ultimately enact violent retribution, and violence for some who perceive themselves as acting on God's behalf. Thus how John's Christology impacts on his readers' conception of God and God's way of working in the world is at least as important as—if not more so than—his explicit ethical exhortations.

In this respect, Hays does not go far enough. He rightly affirms that John's moral vision proscribes human violence, but he indicates that this moral stance is grounded in the divine prerogative to exact vengeance. According to Hays, for example:

> A work that places the Lamb that was slaughtered at the center of its praise and worship can hardly be used to validate violence and coercion. God's ultimate judgment of the wicked is, to be sure, inexorable. Those who destroy the

95. On the reappearance in the new Jerusalem of "kings of the earth" (Rev. 21:24), despite their slaughter and consumption in Rev. 19:21, see Carroll, "Parousia in the Johannine Literature," 105. See also Bredin, *Jesus, Revolutionary of Peace*, 209–15, "Trampling the Wine Press."

96. Hays, *Moral Vision*, 175.

earth will be destroyed (11:18); those who have shed the blood of the saints and
prophets will find their own blood poured out on the earth. But these events
are in the hands of God; they do not constitute a program for human military
action. As a paradigm for the action of the faithful community, Jesus stands as
the faithful witness who conquers through suffering.[97]

The implication of these thoughts by Hays is that while human violence
cannot further God's will for the world, divine violence does. If so, so be it;
perhaps what God wills is good, as opposed to God's willing what is good. But
John, no less than other New Testament writers, goes further than to affirm
that Jesus and his way are to be emulated by Christian believers; rather, Jesus
and his way provide a window into the being and character of God. And on
this christological point, Crossan proffers this insight:

> We Christians are not primarily the People *of* the Book; we are primarily People
> *with* the Book. We are not fundamentally the People of the Inscribed Word of
> God; we are fundamentally the People of the Incarnate Word of God. If our faith
> demands a *sola* it is *sola incarnatio.* . . . Christ, as the incarnate revelation of the
> nonviolent God, is rule, norm, standard, and criterion even—or especially—of
> the Christian Bible itself. In other words, the nonviolence of the Incarnation
> negates the violence of the Apocalypse.[98]

In other words, if Jesus and his way offer insight into divine reality and
identity, one should not assume that God must ultimately resort to violence,
vengeance, or vindictive retribution to bring the divine will and purpose to
fruition. If within the fairly consistent New Testament portrayal of Jesus and
his way of responding to violence and injustice one catches a glimpse of the
very heart of God, that is surely greater warrant for eschewing violence here
and now than the anticipation that God will ultimately execute vengeance
on those who oppose the divine will. I concur with Hays that "the threat of
judgment as a warrant for obedience is implicitly present in Revelation (e.g.,
20:11–15),"[99] but without prejudging the form that divine judgment will take.
After all, we do not and cannot know how God might judge ultimately, but a
christologically conditioned religious epistemology leads to the view that divine
judgment is more likely to be restorative than strictly retributive.[100] Speaking of
the moral impetus to emulate the Lamb, Hays writes: "Those who follow him
[the Lamb] in persecution and death . . . are enacting *the will of God, who*

97. Ibid.
98. Crossan, "Divine Violence in the Christian Bible," 233, emphasis original.
99. Hays, *Moral Vision*, 180.
100. See C. Marshall, *Beyond Retribution*, 145–99. See also Phelan, "God, Judgment, and Non-
Violence," although he perhaps too easily accepts divine acquiescence to human recalcitrance.
Consideration of the restorative or transformative dimensions of divine justice and judgment
is absent from the otherwise fine study by Bauckham, "Judgment in the Book of Revelation."

has chosen to overcome evil precisely in and through righteous suffering, not in spite of it."[101] If thus in the Lamb and in the lives of those who faithfully follow the Lamb, why not thus ultimately?

Reading Revelation in Peace Perspective

One can hardly gainsay that the violent imagery that forms the warp and woof of Revelation's narrative fabric has had, and continues to have, a negative history of effects. Even those who consider that Revelation is susceptible of a peace-oriented interpretation are unable to deny the historical reality that Revelation has contributed to a violent God-image and fostered violent and vindictive behavior.

Although contentious, it is nevertheless reasonable to judge that John's visionary narrative is christocentric and cruciform, meaning that the Christ-event, albeit distilled almost to Pauline dimensions (cross, resurrection, and exaltation), is determinative for comprehending God's redemptive activity in the world, including the vanquishing of evil. As Patricia McDonald argues, the crucified Christ—portrayed as the slain Lamb—is central to Revelation in much the same way as for Paul and Mark.[102] As a result, John's christological portrait can be evaluated against the broad brushstrokes of Jesus's mission and message in the Gospels. When this is done with interpretive care, one finds that the Christology of Revelation is in step with the peaceable mission of Jesus, despite John's use of violent imagery. This implies that we cannot appeal to the Apocalypse of John in support of divinely authorized eschato-logical vengeance. The means by which the crucified Jesus "conquered" are the means by which God "conquers," *without remainder*.

If indeed the Christology of Revelation is in step with the peaceable mission of Jesus as displayed in the Gospels, this signifies that all associations of divine violence within John's Apocalypse are susceptible of intrascriptural critique. It is, of course, possible to respond to (apparent) eschatological vengeance in Revelation in a number of ways other than to affirm it. One might simply turn one's back on the book, ostracize it on the basis of a "hermeneutic of suspicion," deem it sub-Christian (as Dodd was wont to do), or turn to critical theorists for extrabiblical resources with which to deconstruct or subvert the image of God it (apparently) fosters. But only if what Ellen Davis terms an "inner-biblical" hermeneutic[103] is used to call into question theologically and morally problematic features of Revelation, while continuing to affirm its canonical status, will readers with a faith commitment combine charitable respect for John's visionary text with critical evaluation of its theological and moral difficulties.

101. Hays, *Moral Vision*, 179, emphasis added.
102. McDonald, "Lion as Slain Lamb," 31–32.
103. Davis, "Critical Traditioning."

Building on the pioneering work of Michael Fishbane, whose *Biblical Interpretation in Ancient Israel* demonstrates that biblical tradents often preserved authoritative tradition while at the same time adapting and reinterpreting it,[104] Davis infers that "faithful transmission of authoritative tradition must always be something more than rote repetition."[105] This process she describes as "critical traditioning," whereby preservation of tradition goes hand in hand with interpretive innovation. (Indeed, retention of tradition is at times contingent upon critical reformulation.) If this dynamism is discernible within Scripture, as it surely is, there is biblical precedent for an analogous hermeneutical strategy, which might be described as a twofold process of retrieval and renovation. Not only is this an intrascriptural dynamic, but the way in which it operates can be measured against the intrascriptural christological criterion of the Gospel portrayal of the mission and message of Jesus Messiah, the purported acting subject and content of the Revelation to John (1:1a).

In Revelation, John both retains and reworks, both adopts and adapts, apocalyptic motifs. Evidence of such "critical traditioning" is sufficient *on its own* to encourage readings attuned to possible interpretive innovation that subverts eschatological vengeance traditionally associated with apocalyptic texts. Such readings are further authorized, however, by their coherence with the intrascriptural christological criterion, which is both fitting and compelling because of John's appeal to the inner dynamic of the Jesus story: divine recovery of the created order by means of the Lamb's willingness to undergo slaughter rather than to inflict slaughter.

On the basis of John's own "critical traditioning" measured against the intrabiblical christological criterion that the way of Jesus is the way of God, one can faithfully read both with and against the grain of the text of Revelation. Reading with the grain of Revelation 4–5 encourages an against-the-grain reading of 19:11–21. In other words, 19:11–21 should be read in light of chapter 5, not vice versa (*contra* Adela Yarbro Collins). A reading of Revelation that ignores the book's narrative structure and "directionality" is likely to be a misreading. The gruesome details of John's symbolic account depicting the victory by the Rider on a white horse may serve to warn readers of the futility of opposing God's will and purpose, but they neither reflect on the character of God nor signal the means by which God's will and purpose for the created order are realized.

As noted near the beginning of this chapter, the Christian canon of Scripture begins and ends with visions of *shalom*, which witness to the Creator's will and purpose for creation as a whole.[106] The two visions that open and close

104. Fishbane, *Biblical Interpretation in Ancient Israel*.
105. Davis, "Critical Traditioning," 738.
106. This observation is also made by C. Marshall, "Violence of God and the Hermeneutics of Paul," 80–81. See also Sweet, *Revelation*, 13, 47, 51, who makes a similar point with respect to the structure of Revelation, pointing out that "the visions of destruction are bracketed by

the biblical canon are interpretive rather than empirical realities. They do not describe how any one of the human race has ever experienced life; rather, they express how life *should be* experienced. Protology and eschatology, first and last things, express the most deeply held convictions about the way things ought to be. In other words, depictions of first things give expression to what is of *primary* value; what is expressed about what *came first* indicates what *is first* in our perception of reality and system of values. Similarly, depictions of last things also give expression to what is of *primary* value; what is expressed about what *comes last* indicates what we believe and hope *to be lasting*.[107] When we read the opening and closing visions of the biblical story, therefore, we are as close as we can ever come to what is, for Christians, the way things should be. Both visions are construed as the result of divine agency: these visions of the way the world *should be* are attributed to God's will and purpose for the world and humanity.

Beginnings and endings are undoubtedly important for interpreting narratives. In the case of the biblical narrative, however, what is critical from a Christian theological perspective is that the two visions at the beginning and end of the canonical story cohere at the deepest level with the Jesus story in the Gospels, which for Christians forms the midpoint *and therefore the fulcrum and norm* of the larger story. As Crossan puts it, "The great and sweeping parabolic story of the Christian Bible is . . . an extraordinary or maybe even a unique one because its meaning is in the middle, its climax is in the center. That central core is Jesus of Nazareth who is confessed by faith as Christ the Lord."[108] Thus there is consonance and resonance between beginning, end, and middle of the canonical story, which attests to divine proneness to *shalom*. This in turn coheres with the central Christian affirmation about God: God *is* love, even deep down into the inner recesses of the mystery called Trinity.

Beginning, middle, and end of the biblical narrative thus stake out a *determinative canonical trajectory* against which other trajectories and perspectives may be scrutinized and judged. Or put differently, the canonical trajectory etched by tracing a theological-moral line from creation through Jesus to the restoration envisioned by John in his image of the new (or renovated) Jerusalem provides a big-picture, intrascriptural criterion for reading against the grain of specific Scriptures that depict God or God's agency in the world in

---

the overarching vision of God the Creator and Redeemer (4, 5), who makes all things new (21, 22)." On the basis of various levels of narrativity within Revelation, Boring's study "Narrative Christology in the Apocalypse" argues that the dramatic and often violent events associated with the breaking of the seven seals, the sounding of the seven trumpets, and the spilling of the seven bowls must be regarded as a "secondary play-within-a-play," which only makes proper sense when construed in relation to other, more determinative narrative levels, especially the implicit macronarrative or narrative world that stretches from creation to the eschaton and has the crucifixion of Jesus as its midpoint.

107. Compare McClendon, *Doctrine*, 96.
108. Crossan, "Divine Violence in the Christian Bible," 233.

contradictory terms.[109] Here I am in basic sympathy with Clinton McCann's notion of "The Hermeneutics of Grace."[110] Without denying the polyphony of Scripture, McCann detects a "single plot" through the Torah, Prophets, and Writings into the New Testament. The notion of a "*single* plot" in Scripture is unsustainable, in my judgment, but the trajectory staked out by the creation story in Genesis 1:1–2:3, in which the divine will is initially displayed; the Jesus story, in which the divine will is reaffirmed; and the vision of the new Jerusalem in Revelation 20–21, in which the divine will is ultimately realized—this trajectory is clearly enough etched to serve as a rule of orientation or intrabiblical canon for interpreting texts that speak in another voice.[111] In short, intimations of eschatological vengeance in Revelation (and elsewhere) should be read in accordance with a hermeneutic of *shalom*.

Throughout this chapter and indeed this book, I have tacitly appealed to an interpretive principle designated by Charles Cosgrove "the rule of moral-theological adjudication."[112] Analogous to the early church's *regula fidei*, or "rule of faith," as articulated by Irenaeus (*Adv. haer.* 1.10), and Augustine's interpretive rule of love (*Doctr. chr.* 1.84–85, 95–96; 3.54),[113] the rule of moral-theological adjudication proposes that in cases of interpretive ambiguity, "one may view Scripture as properly interpreted only where it is construed according to certain substantive principles, conceived as intrinsic to Scripture itself, taken as a whole."[114] Such an interpretive rule presupposes the authority of Scripture, but without granting that Scripture speaks with one clear voice throughout. In such a situation, the community of faith must inevitably interpret authoritative yet ambiguous texts, which implies that responsible interpretive choice is called for—and called forth—by those texts accepted as authoritative by the church.[115]

On broad canonical grounds, similar in certain respects to what Cosgrove identifies as an interpretive "rule of canonical structure,"[116] I submit that a

109. In certain respects, this proposal combines four of the six hermeneutical strategies for dealing with "morally dubious" scriptural passages discussed by E. Davies, "Morally Dubious Passages": canon-within-a-canon, holistic, paradigmatic, and reader-response approaches. See also idem, *Immoral Bible.*

110. McCann, "Hermeneutics of Grace."

111. This conception has affinities with the proposal of Hays, *Moral Vision*, 304, that metaphorical readings of New Testament texts should be "consonant with the fundamental plot of the biblical story as identified by the focal images of community, cross, and new creation." As far as canonical plotlines are concerned, however, one that stretches from creation to new creation via the cross seems stronger, no matter how important the church's role as interpretive community and constraint might be.

112. Cosgrove, *Appealing to Scripture*, 2–4, 154–80.

113. For a restatement of Augustine's interpretive rule of love, see Tannehill, "Freedom and Responsibility."

114. Cosgrove, *Appealing to Scripture*, 157.

115. Compare Tannehill, "Freedom and Responsibility," 275–76.

116. Cosgrove, *Appealing to Scripture*, 197.

hermeneutic of *shalom* should complement the church's earlier interpretive rules of faith and love.[117] Since the biblical record affirms that *shalom* derives from or is characteristic of divine creativity and therefore precedes human moral judgment, I prefer to speak of theological-moral, rather than moral-theological, interpretive adjudication. Christian moral vision and deliberation occurs within the context of, and in response to, what is affirmed to be the divine pattern of relating to humanity and the wider world. For people of Christian faith, that divine pattern is displayed decisively in the life story of Jesus of Nazareth and confirmed in the stories of creation and restored creation that bookend the canonical metanarrative. *Shalom* has intrabiblical theological sanction and, from the perspective of human flourishing, has more intrinsic moral meaning than violence ever could.

117. Compare Migliore, *Faith Seeking Understanding*, 60: "To the rule of faith and the rule of love, we should also add the rule of hope." So long as Migliore's proposed "rule of hope" is *shalom*-shaped, a peaceable hope, I concur.

Concluding Reflections

Having probed the writings of five early interpreters of the Jesus story, especially in relation to moral vision and end-expectation, it is time to draw together the principal conclusions reached in the preceding chapters. In my introductory chapter, I refer to a discrepancy at the heart of the New Testament—a discrepancy between the portrayal of the historic mission of Jesus in peaceable terms and expectations of end-time vengeance on the part of the returning Jesus. After investigating the relation between moral vision and eschatology in the Gospels, Acts, and Revelation, it is more difficult to speak so bluntly of a discrepancy inherent in the New Testament generally. A disturbing discrepancy is undoubtedly detectable in some texts, but in others the discrepancy is more apparent (or alleged) than actual. Indeed, of the six early Christian texts explored in this book, the Gospel according to Mark, the Gospel according to John, and the Acts of the Apostles articulate end-time expectations largely in keeping with Christian moral vision focused on the historic mission and message of Jesus. This conclusion may be unsurprising in relation to the Fourth Gospel, but it contravenes what is often asserted about Mark's Gospel and Acts.

Within each of the three parts of this book, texts have been paired together but for different reasons in each part. The Gospels according to Matthew and Mark share much narrative content, often conveyed using common vocabulary. There is a close relation between them, whether by virtue of the use of one by the other or, as I now think more likely, through common use of a shared source (Proto-Mark). Theologically, however, these two Gospels differ in a number of ways, not least with respect to end-expectation and hence moral vision. In part 1, these Gospels are coupled contrapuntally, primarily to protest the violent eschatology of one in light of the more ethical eschatology of the other, but also to signal that both are indispensable to Christian moral vision.

247

Matthew's eschatology and moral vision are not eclipsed by Mark's, even if I find the latter's more compelling.

Among the Gospel writers, Matthew's eschatology is evidently more vengeful and vindictive than that of his canonical counterparts. This is especially noticeable in a series of parables containing warnings of end-time retribution for a range of shortcomings. Matthew's retributive mind-set also colors the content of Jesus's explicit teaching on the eschaton. For example, both Matthew 16:27, with its explicit note of eschatological recompense, and 24:29–44, which presages universal mourning at the sign of the Son of humanity and compares the coming of the Son of humanity to the sudden calamity of the great flood—both texts heighten the theme of end-time vengeance relative to their contextual parallels in Mark and Luke. Even so, in Jesus's nonparabolic teaching, the note of eschatological vengeance is markedly more muted than in the series of Matthean parables containing warnings of end-time judgment. Within Matthew's Gospel, in other words, Jesus's nonparabolic instruction on judgment at the end of the age stands in less tension with Jesus's moral vision than do his parabolic warnings. So, not only is Matthew's violent eschatology out of kilter with the much less retributive eschatological outlooks of his canonical counterparts but also the vindictive tone of his parabolic warnings of end-time judgment is matched neither by Jesus's moral teaching nor by his nonparabolic eschatological instruction. Most important, however, Matthew's narrative of *Immanu-el* and his disavowal of violence, including transcendent violence (26:47–56), places an emphatic question mark against any expression of expected eschatological vengeance.

Protesting Matthew's relative emphasis on eschatological vengeance is important for at least two reasons. First and foremost, the Gospel according to Matthew was the darling of the church for centuries and profoundly influenced Christian expectation and imagination regarding end-time judgment. However important divine judgment may be for Christian theology and ethics, it is surely evident that Matthew's end-time expectations have had morally corrosive effects. And second, by virtue of Matthew's canonical placement as the first book in the New Testament, his end-time expectations have been reinforced by the tenor and tone of the last book of the Bible, the Revelation to John. Together, the Gospel according to Matthew and the Revelation to John enclose that part of the scriptural canon concerned with divine disclosure in and through Jesus of Nazareth. And together, these enclosing books have encouraged end-time expectations and accompanying moral dispositions in taut tension with the life story of Jesus that serves as their reason for being. As a result, readers are entitled to be taught to detect and to wrestle with the profound conflict between moral vision and eschatology inherent within these two books that bracket the New Testament.

Turning from Matthew's to Mark's Gospel is to enter narrative terrain that is both familiar and strange. Paradoxically, these two Gospels are sometimes closer when they differ than when they correspond closely in narrative order and wording. For example, there is nothing comparable to Matthew's Sermon on the Mount in Mark's Gospel. Indeed, Mark has only fleeting parallels to snatches of Jesus's inaugural sermon in Matthew's Gospel. Nevertheless, central dimensions of Mark's narrative, particularly his presentation of the moral stance of Jesus, approximate the moral vision expressed in Matthew 5. On the other hand, when recounting Jesus's future-oriented Son-of-humanity sayings, Matthew and Mark are in close concert, not only in terms of narrative sequence but also with respect to shared vocabulary. Despite their closeness in these respects, however, they convey rather different expectations regarding the manner and repercussions of the coming Son of humanity, although these differences should not be exaggerated. What deserves to be emphasized, especially in view of the contrary perspective promoted in certain quarters, is that Mark's eschatological expectations, while expressed in apocalyptic terms, are relatively peaceful. Especially when compared with Matthew's end-time expectations, most luridly expressed in parabolic form, Mark expresses a peaceable hope. Although there is within Matthew's Gospel a deep-seated discrepancy between moral vision and eschatology, in Mark's Gospel end-expectation largely coheres with moral vision centered on Jesus as Messiah.

Part 2 on the Lukan literature examines two texts by the same author. The Gospel according to Luke and the Acts of the Apostles reveal Luke to be the New Testament's evangelist of peace. In Jesus's mission Luke perceives "divine visitation" for the purpose of salvation, and the salvation associated with Jesus is *shalom*-shaped. Jesus's journey to Jerusalem and thence to God is not only his own way of peace but also, by virtue of his vindicating resurrection and ascension, God's peaceful way. Although the theme of peace is not as prominent in Acts as in Luke's Gospel, Acts 10:36 nevertheless makes clear that Jesus's mission in its entirety is a divine overture of peace.

Luke may be the evangelist of peace, but two features of his two-part narrative relating to divine judgment are difficult to reconcile with his evident concern to characterize the mission of Jesus as inherently peaceful. The first is the note of eschatological vengeance sounded from time to time within the Gospel by Jesus himself, and the second is Luke's view of Jerusalem's destruction as divine judgment. The first of these discordant motifs seems susceptible of satisfactory resolution, whereas the second motif appears intractable.

For Luke, the coming Son of humanity is the Son of humanity known in Jesus, whose historic mission is summed up as a divine announcement of peace. Most of what Luke records of Jesus's teaching regarding the future arrival of the Son of humanity is morally congruent with his characterization of Jesus's mission. Moreover, texts that associate the future arrival of the Son of humanity with end-time vengeance are enclosed within and hence relativized by nonretributive eschatological texts, Luke 12:35–40 and 21:25–36, which are wholly in keeping with the historic mission of Jesus. Somewhat surprisingly, in view of the relative fading of the peace theme in Acts, the end-time expectations of Luke 12:35–40 and 21:25–36 are reinforced by the predominantly restorative eschatology of Acts. On the whole, therefore, Luke's eschatological expectations largely cohere with his peaceful Christology and moral vision.

Strictly retributive eschatology in Luke's Gospel is most evident in the comparison between the anticipated day(s) of the Son of humanity and the biblical days of Noah and Lot. Even in these comparisons, however, the primary point seems to be the unanticipated interruption of the regular rhythm of life. Moreover, if one accepts that Luke 21 is the "programmatic doublet" of 17:22–37, one can say that the calamitous consequences seemingly associated with the day(s) of the Son of humanity are repressed rather than reinforced by the redemption associated with the coming Son of humanity in 21:27–28. Perhaps most significantly, Luke 17:22–37 occurs hard on the heels of 17:20–21, in which Jesus affirms the presence of divine reign in his own mission. This suggests that future-oriented eschatology is grounded in and shaped by realized eschatology, which is but another way of affirming that the historic mission of Jesus is the measure of end-time expectations centered on Jesus. Thus, although eschatological vengeance is a feature of Jesus's teaching in Luke's Gospel, it is neither dominant nor reinforced by other features in either the Gospel or Acts. Taken as a whole, the Lukan literature leans toward dissociating the eschaton from vengeance.

By contrast, Luke's apparent presentation of the destruction of Jerusalem as divine judgment threatens to undermine his biblical role as the evangelist of peace. Although other features of Luke's history of Christian origins agitate against anticipating eschatological vengeance, his conception of Jerusalem's destruction as "days of vengeance" not only reinforces the retributive dimension of his eschatological outlook but also provides the template for end-time judgment. I confess to feeling stymied by Luke's view of Jerusalem's destruction. All that seems possible to say, apart from the obvious point that Luke was a person of his time, is that this particular feature of his narrative is incongruent with his Christology of peace and peaceable moral ethos.

Part 3 investigates two texts, the Gospel according to John and the Revelation to John, that likely represent one particular stream of early Christianity. Although different with respect to genre and literary style, both the Fourth Gospel and Revelation are apocalyptic works in which traditional apocalyptic motifs are reconfigured to varying degrees to facilitate an interpretation of Jesus's identity and significance. Both the Fourth Evangelist and John the prophet-seer consider the death of Jesus on the cross as the means by which God has (already) triumphed over evil. In each case this insight has profound implications for envisaging eschatological judgment. For the evangelist, eschatological judgment is envisaged as occurring in consequence of one's response to divine disclosure in Jesus. This results in a portrayal of Jesus in which the prospect of eschatological vengeance is either absent or significantly muted, depending on how one interprets a small number of texts. In the case of John the prophet-seer, however, the imagery of eschatological vengeance is retained, resulting in a perplexing portrait of Jesus's role in relation to the eschaton. Although it is possible to read Revelation in peace perspective, to do so is an interpretive challenge.

The prologue to the Fourth Gospel is indispensable to the argument of this book. Taken as a whole, this prologue affirms Jesus's historic mission in its entirety as definitive divine disclosure, God's creative self-expression embodied in Jesus's life such that the particularities of this life compose nothing less than true exegesis of God (John 1:18). If that be granted, the shape of incarnation as discerned in the mode and manner of Jesus's historic mission is the touchstone for discerning God's will for—and way in—the world. It cannot be accidental that, among the five interpreters considered in this book, the evangelist who introduced the idea of incarnation into (Jewish-) Christian thought conceived of eschatological fulfillment in the most realized way. Moreover, if incarnation is accepted as the preliminary stage of eschatological fulfillment, that stage is determinative for all successive stages, including eschatological judgment. Whatever one expects of divine judgment at the eschaton should cohere, theologically and morally, with what Jesus has already revealed about God in his life, in his signs and teaching, in his death by crucifixion (understood as divine judgment of the antagonistic ruler of this world), and in his resurrection. As for Luke, so also for the Fourth Evangelist, realized eschatology is determinative for future eschatology.

Insofar as the prologue to the Fourth Gospel resonates with the creation story in Genesis 1, I read the Johannine prologue as a *shalom*-oriented text that serves to set the stage for, and to enclose, along with the threefold peace greeting of the resurrected Jesus (John 20:19, 21, 26), the entirety of Jesus's mission as the Logos-become-flesh. Even apart from the prologue, however, the pattern of the evangelist's references to peace, which cluster on either side of Jesus's suffering and violent death, bespeaks the peaceable manner in which God responds to human injustice and violence. This coheres with the evangelist's conception of Jesus's crucifixion as itself the means by which evil is vanquished. As a result, the evangelist's portrayal of Jesus's story in its totality provides the decisive interpretive criterion for construing eschatological judgment in line with divine love as revealed and expressed by incarnation, (succumbing to but also overcoming through) crucifixion, and resurrection.

The Revelation to John is replete with violent imagery, especially in relation to end-time judgment. This makes it difficult to read Revelation in peace perspective and helps to explain why many interpreters take the Apocalypse of John as a violent text, issuing from the vindictive expectation of eschatological vengeance. On reflection, as a result of both the reception history of Revelation down through the centuries and its decidedly ambivalent effect on Christian moral vision and imagination, one hesitates to endorse John's decision to make use of the violent imagery with which he seemed comfortable. On the other hand, the Apocalypse of John is presented as an apocalypse of the Lamb, whose own mode of defeating evil and injustice not only disavows violence but also exposes the impotence of violence to right wrongs. As with the Gospel writers, therefore, John's defining christological conviction destabilizes any apparent association between divine judgment and violence.

It is generally accepted that the image of the Lamb is John's controlling christological image, but not all interpreters permit this image to control their interpretation of the book. I follow in the footsteps of those who give priority to John's Lamb Christology, especially in view of the interpretive significance of the heavenly vision of Revelation 4–5, within which the figure of the Lamb is introduced. Both the narrative juncture at which the Lamb-image is introduced and the manner in which the Lamb is introduced lead to the conclusion that this christological image is decisive for interpreting divine action in and on behalf of the world. Displays of divine judgment that follow in the wake of the heavenly vision of chapters 4–5 should be read in accordance with this vision's unveiling of the Lamb as the means of divine agency.

When read in light of John's controlling christological Lamb-figure, the symbolic description of the Rider on a white horse in Revelation 19:11–21 can be read to signify the returning Messiah's vanquishing of evil by nonviolent means. Such a reading, though possible and in my view required, is not done with ease. Nor does such a reading rest easily, once proposed. Although I have marshaled various considerations in defense of such an interpretation, it is compelling only to the extent that it coheres with John's Lamb Christology. Even as I disagree with those who consider the Rider on a white horse as a symbol of eschatological vengeance, I appreciate that there are reasons for holding to such a view. Insofar as the Lamb-as-slain is a symbol of the reality and significance of the historic mission of Jesus, however, John's Lamb-image is determinative for discerning God's way of overcoming evil and righting wrong.

It is no small thing that John's Lamb Christology is in basic harmony with the Fourth Evangelist's notion of the incarnation of the divine Logos, whose symbol is the cross as an expression of both divine self-giving love and victory over the force(s) of evil. The same may be said for those variations on the theme of incarnation in the Gospels according to Matthew and Luke. Both Matthew's *Immanu-el* motif and that of "divine visitation" in Luke's Gospel attest to the character or moral shape of divine presence displayed in Jesus's life and mission, death and resurrection. While there is no specific motif comparable to incarnation in Mark's Gospel, nevertheless there is a basic congruence between the moral shape of incarnation in the Fourth Gospel and Mark's account of the mission of the serving, life-relinquishing Son of humanity. Thus one is able to detect a fundamental consistency in the various ways in which the Gospel writers and John interpreted the identity and significance of Jesus. For this reason, the christological criterion that the way of Jesus is the way of God is both central and decisive for each chapter in this book and for the argument of the book as a whole.

Read casually or carelessly alongside the Gospel according to Matthew, with which it brackets the New Testament, the Revelation to John may seem to anticipate eschatological vengeance and thereby inculcate a vindictive mind-set prone to violence. For this reason it is profoundly important that the Apocalypse of John not only concludes the New Testament but also includes the culminating vision of the new Jerusalem (Rev. 21–22). Together with the vision of creation in Genesis 1, the vision of the new Jerusalem serves to enclose the entire biblical narrative with visions of *shalom*. Moreover, these enclosing visions of how life should be experienced cohere with the messianic midpoint of the canonical story, thereby attesting to God's peace-proneness and providing a determinative canonical trajectory against which to assess scriptural texts that speak in a different voice or project a contradictory perspective. As a result, I advocate that a hermeneutic of *shalom* should complement the church's long-standing interpretive rules of faith and love, especially (but not only) in relation to texts of teleological terror.

In line with the *shalom*-oriented canonical trajectory traceable from creation to restored creation via the historic mission of Jesus, there is a series of texts that I have come to regard as *treasure texts*.[1] Matthew 13:44 records a parable unique to this Gospel: Jesus compares the reign of heaven with treasure of such value that it is worth selling all one has to possess it. In the parable, someone chances on treasure hidden in a field and buys the field to possess the treasure. The treasure makes the field valuable. Only to possess the treasure does the finder sell all to purchase the field. In an analogous way, I have come to regard certain texts within the Gospels, Acts, and Revelation as treasure texts, texts that by virtue of their luminousness add luster and value to the larger narratives within which they are embedded. Since all of these texts resonate with a hermeneutic of *shalom*, I see such texts as adding their cumulative weight to the larger argument of this book that end-expectation should be measured against the moral shape of the historic mission of Jesus narrated in the Gospels.

Among my list of treasure texts, the prologue to the Fourth Gospel takes pride of place. There the mission of Jesus in its totality is interpreted as the divine Logos-become-flesh, whose life displays God's character. The moral shape of Jesus's life and mission is not only exemplary but also revelatory. It comprises divine disclosure. The analogous motifs of *Immanu-el* and "divine visitation" in Matthew and Luke's Gospels reinforce the conviction that divine presence and power are to be interpreted christologically, not only historically but also eschatologically. Also comparable is the vision of the Lamb in Revelation 5. Together, these christological motifs and images combine to

---

1. For this basic idea I am indebted to Martin Luther and Thorwald Lorenzen.

cast serious doubt over eschatological expectations that do not conform to convictions concerning Jesus expressed by interpreting him as the Logos-become-flesh, *Immanu-el*, "divine visitation," or Lamb.

In Matthew's Gospel, the Sermon on the Mount is an obvious treasure text, but perhaps most precious of all is what is recalled of Jesus's teaching in Matthew 5. There the moral vision of Jesus—expressed in the Beatitudes and the so-called Antitheses that illustrate his conception of fulfillment—is the interpretive lamp on the lampstand, shedding its illuminating light far and wide. It is not always appreciated that the Beatitudes and what follows in Matthew 5 comprise Jesus's first words in public. In canonical perspective, this gives primacy to the counterintuitive moral vision presented in Matthew 5, which features meekness and mercy, justice and peace, fidelity and transparency, reconciliation, nonretaliation, and indiscriminate regard for others.

More than any other biblical text in its totality, I am inclined to view the whole of Mark's Gospel as the treasure text within the fourfold Gospel canon. Within this Gospel, as in no other, the moral vision shaped by Jesus's messianic mission, his heralding of God's good tidings in both his teaching and acts of compassion, his instruction on conduct congruent with divine reign, and his expectation of eschatological resolution—all these are in relative concord. The Gehenna-sayings in Mark 9:42–48 are perhaps an exception, but they read like hyperbolic warnings against jeopardizing one's own or another's entry into the reign of God. In context, moreover, the counsel of peace in Mark 9:50b reads like the antidote to the various forms of "scandal" that put entry into life at risk.

In Luke's Gospel, the Benedictus of Zechariah (1:68–79) is undoubtedly a treasure text because of its interweaving of central Lukan themes, including divine visitation, liberation, salvation, forgiveness, and peace. Another Lukan treasure text is the eschatological scenario sandwiched between two macarisms in Luke 12:35–40, encouraging readiness for the returning Son of humanity. Thus 12:35–40, especially alongside more retributive associations with the coming Son of humanity in 17:22–37, envisages a return of the Son of humanity closely in keeping with that selfsame Son of humanity's service-oriented mission (cf. 22:14–30). Here end-expectation is in concert with the historic mission of Jesus. If Luke 24:36 is original, the risen Jesus's peace greeting is one further treasure text within this Gospel, reinforcing the conviction that the peaceable way of Jesus is God's own way.

Even if the risen Jesus's peace greeting in Luke 24:36 is not textually certain, there is little doubt about the threefold peace greeting on the part of the risen Jesus in the Fourth Gospel (20:19, 21, 26). This cluster of peace greetings, together with the crucial themes with which it is associated in John 20, composes a treasure text in which peace is constitutive of the quality of life validated by resurrection. "Peace to you" already expresses divine judgment.

In the Acts of the Apostles, the programmatic ascension of Jesus in 1:9–11 has become for me a treasure text, not only because in Lukan perspective it is integrally related to Jesus's resurrection and the promised Holy Spirit but also because it can be understood as the parousia in reverse. This would be interpretive nonsense if the explicit eschatology of Acts were more retributive than restorative, but the reverse is the case. Although not a prominent theme in Acts, the eschatological proclamation of the early apostles is presented by Luke in relatively peaceful terms. This in turn strengthens my resolve to envisage the return of Jesus "in the same way" as his ascension and in the same "way of peace" as displayed in his historic mission, itself characterized by Acts 10:36—yet another, complementary treasure text—as a divine proclamation of peace to the children of Israel and beyond. Compared to Luke's Gospel, Acts apparently allows the theme of peace to fade. Nevertheless, the treasure texts of Acts 1:11 and 10:36, reinforced by the restoration eschatology of the book as whole, rights the balance.

If these various treasure texts were incidental to the narratives or canonical contexts in which they are found, their role within a hermeneutic of *shalom* would likewise be incidental and indeed trivial. To the contrary, however, each specific treasure text identified as such is decisive for the narrative or context within which it appears. The prologue to the Fourth Gospel is the interpretive key to the Gospel, and the motifs in other texts comparable to that of *incarnation* are likewise determinative for understanding Jesus's identity and significance. Matthew 5 is clearly decisive for Matthew's presentation of Jesus's mission and message as fulfilling Scripture. Something very like Mark's Gospel is the basis for the synoptic tradition and therefore determinative for the basic shape of the Jesus story. Taken alone, texts within Luke's Gospel identified as treasure texts might be less determinative than others, but they nevertheless cohere with Luke's peace emphasis and thereby reinforce Luke's status and stature as the evangelist of peace. The ascension is clearly programmatic for Acts, and Acts 10:36 comprises a distillation of Jesus's mission in its entirety as a divine overture of peace. Thus a series of treasure texts that feature *shalom* is central to conceiving the Jesus story and hence the normative midpoint of the biblical narrative as a whole. Texts that construe divine agency in and through Jesus differently find their role and meaning only in relation to the canonical trajectory that passes through the Jesus story from creation to the new Jerusalem. God, whose Logos beckoned creation into existence and in Jesus's mission as a whole proclaimed peace to Israel, thereby revealed Godself to be peace prone. Nothing short of a peaceable hope, such as one finds in the vision of the new Jerusalem, does justice to what the story of Jesus reveals about God's will and way in the world.

Bibliography

Adams, Edward. *The Stars Will Fall from Heaven: Cosmic Catastrophe in the New Testament and Its World.* London: T&T Clark, 2007.

Allison, Dale C., Jr. "Jesus and the Victory of Apocalyptic." In *Jesus and the Restoration of Israel: A Critical Assessment of N. T. Wright's "Jesus and the Victory of God,"* edited by Carey C. Newman, 126–41. Downers Grove, IL: InterVarsity, 1999.

———. *Jesus of Nazareth: Millenarian Prophet.* Minneapolis: Fortress, 1998.

———. "Matt. 23:39 = Luke 13:35b as a Conditional Prophecy." *Journal for the Study of the New Testament* 18 (1983): 75–84.

———. "Rejecting Violent Judgment: Luke 9:52–56 and Its Relatives." *Journal of Biblical Literature* 121 (2002): 459–78.

———. *Resurrecting Jesus: The Earliest Christian Tradition and Its Interpreters.* London: T&T Clark International, 2005.

———. *Studies in Matthew: Interpretation Past and Present.* Grand Rapids: Baker Academic, 2005.

Angel, Andrew. "Inquiring into an *Inclusio*—On Judgement and Love in Matthew." *Journal of Theological Studies* 60 (2009): 527–30.

Ashton, John. *Studying John: Approaches to the Fourth Gospel.* Oxford: Clarendon, 1994.

———. *Understanding the Fourth Gospel.* Oxford: Oxford University Press, 1991. 2nd ed., 2007.

Aune, David E. *Revelation 1–5.* Word Biblical Commentary 52A. Dallas: Word Books, 1997.

———. *Revelation 6–16.* Word Biblical Commentary 52B. Nashville: Thomas Nelson, 1998.

———. *Revelation 17–22.* Word Biblical Commentary 52C. Nashville: Thomas Nelson, 1998.

Baer, Heinrich von. *Der Heilige Geist in den Lukasschriften*. Stuttgart: Kohlhammer, 1926.

Balabanski, Vicky. *Eschatology in the Making: Mark, Matthew and the Didache*. Cambridge: Cambridge University Press, 1997.

———. "Mission in Matthew against the Horizon of Matthew 24." *New Testament Studies* 54 (2008): 161–75.

Barr, David L. "Doing Violence: Moral Issues in Reading John's Apocalypse." In *Reading the Book of Revelation: A Resource for Students*, edited by David L. Barr, 97–108. Atlanta: Society of Biblical Literature, 2003.

———. "The Lamb Who Looks Like a Dragon? Characterizing Jesus in John's Apocalypse." In *The Reality of Apocalypse: Rhetoric and Politics in the Book of Revelation*, edited by David L. Barr, 205–20. Atlanta: Society of Biblical Literature, 2006.

———. *Tales of the End: A Narrative Commentary on the Book of Revelation*. Santa Rosa, CA: Polebridge, 1998.

Barrett, C. K. *A Critical and Exegetical Commentary on the Acts of the Apostles*. 2 vols. International Critical Commentary. New York: T&T Clark, 1994–98.

———. *The Gospel according to St John: An Introduction with Commentary and Notes on the Greek Text*. 2nd ed. London: SPCK, 1978.

———. *New Testament Essays*. London: SPCK, 1972.

Barth, Gerhard. "Matthew's Understanding of the Law." In *Tradition and Interpretation in Matthew*, by Günther Bornkamm, Gerhard Barth, and H. J. Held, 58–164. Translated by Percy Scott. 2nd ed. London: SCM, 1982.

Bauckham, Richard. *The Climax of Prophecy: Studies on the Book of Revelation*. Edinburgh: T&T Clark, 1993.

———. "Judgment in the Book of Revelation." *Ex auditu* 20 (2004): 1–24.

———. "The Language of Warfare in the Book of Revelation." In *Compassionate Eschatology: The Future as Friend*, edited by Ted Grimsrud and Michael Hardin, 28–41. Eugene, OR: Cascade Books, 2011.

———. "The Restoration of Israel in Luke–Acts." In *Restoration: Old Testament, Jewish, and Christian Perspectives*, edited by James M. Scott, 435–87. Leiden: Brill, 2001.

———. *The Theology of the Book of Revelation*. Cambridge: Cambridge University Press, 1993.

Bayer, Hans F. "Christ-Centered Eschatology in Acts 3:17–26." In *Jesus of Nazareth: Lord and Christ*, edited by Joel B. Green and Max Turner, 236–50. Grand Rapids: Eerdmans, 1994.

Beale, G. K. *The Book of Revelation: A Commentary on the Greek Text*. New International Greek Testament Commentary. Grand Rapids: Eerdmans, 1999.

Beasley-Murray, George R. *Jesus and the Last Days: The Interpretation of the Olivet Discourse*. Peabody, MA: Hendrickson, 1993.

Bock, Darrell L. *Acts*. Baker Exegetical Commentary on the New Testament. Grand Rapids: Baker Academic, 2007.

———. *Luke 1:1–9:50*. Baker Exegetical Commentary on the New Testament. Grand Rapids: Baker, 1994.

———. *Luke 9:51–24:53*. Baker Exegetical Commentary on the New Testament. Grand Rapids: Baker, 1996.

Bolt, Peter G. *The Cross from a Distance: Atonement in Mark's Gospel*. Downers Grove, IL: InterVarsity, 2004.

Borgman, Paul. *The Way according to Luke: Hearing the Whole Story of Luke–Acts*. Grand Rapids: Eerdmans, 2006.

Boring, M. Eugene. "The Gospel of Matthew: Introduction, Commentary, and Reflections." In *The New Interpreter's Bible*, edited by Leander E. Keck et al., 8:87–505. Nashville: Abingdon, 1995.

———. "Narrative Christology in the Apocalypse." *Catholic Biblical Quarterly* 54 (1992): 702–23.

———. *Revelation*. Interpretation: A Bible Commentary for Teaching and Preaching. Louisville: John Knox, 1989.

———. "The Theology of Revelation: 'The Lord Our God the Almighty Reigns.'" *Interpretation* 40 (1986): 257–69.

Bornkamm, Günther. "End-Expectation and Church in Matthew." In *Tradition and Interpretation in Matthew*, by Günther Bornkamm, Gerhard Barth, and H. J. Held, 15–51. Translated by Percy Scott. 2nd ed. London: SCM, 1982.

Bovon, François. "The Child and the Beast: Fighting Violence in Ancient Christianity." *Harvard Theological Review* 92 (1999): 369–92.

———. *Luke 1: A Commentary on the Gospel of Luke 1:1–9:50*. Translated by Christine M. Thomas. Hermeneia. Minneapolis: Fortress, 2002.

———. *Luke the Theologian: Fifty-Five Years of Research (1950–2005)*. 2nd rev. ed. Waco: Baylor University Press, 2006.

Boxall, Ian. *Revelation: Vision and Insight*. London: SPCK, 2002.

———. *The Revelation of Saint John*. Black's New Testament Commentaries. London: A&C Black, 2006.

Boyarin, Daniel. "How Enoch Can Teach Us about Jesus." *Early Christianity* 2 (2011): 51–76.

———. "Justin Martyr Invents Judaism." *Church History* 70 (2001): 427–61.

Bredin, Mark. *Jesus, Revolutionary of Peace: A Nonviolent Christology in the Book of Revelation*. Waynesboro, GA: Paternoster, 2003.

Brett, Mark G. *Decolonizing God: The Bible in the Tides of Empire*. Sheffield: Sheffield Phoenix Press, 2008.

Bridge, Steven L. *"Where the Eagles Are Gathered": The Deliverance of the Elect in Lukan Eschatology.* New York: Sheffield Academic Press, 2003.

Brown, Jeannine K. "Creation's Renewal in the Gospel of John." *Catholic Biblical Quarterly* 72 (2010): 275–90.

Brown, Raymond E. *The Birth of the Messiah: A Commentary on the Infancy Narratives in Matthew and Luke.* New York: Doubleday, 1977.

———. *The Death of the Messiah: From Gethsemane to the Grave.* 2 vols., continuous pagination. Anchor Bible Reference Library. New York: Doubleday, 1994.

———. *The Gospel according to John: Introduction, Translation, and Notes.* 2 vols. Anchor Bible 29–29A. New York: Doubleday, 1966–70.

Brown, William P. *The Ethos of the Cosmos: The Genesis of Moral Imagination in the Bible.* Grand Rapids: Eerdmans, 1999.

Bruce, F. F. *The Book of the Acts.* Rev. ed. New International Commentary on the New Testament. Grand Rapids: Eerdmans, 1988.

———. "Eschatology in Acts." In *Eschatology and the New Testament: Essays in Honor of George Raymond Beasley-Murray*, edited by W. Hulitt Gloer, 51–63. Peabody, MA: Hendrickson, 1988.

Bryan, Christopher. *A Preface to Mark: Notes on the Gospel in Its Literary and Cultural Setting.* New York: Oxford University Press, 1993.

Bultmann, Rudolf. *Theology of the New Testament.* 2 vols. Translated by Kendrick Grobel. New York: Charles Scribner's Sons, 1951–55.

Burridge, Richard A. *Four Gospels, One Jesus? A Symbolic Reading.* 2nd ed. Grand Rapids: Eerdmans, 2005.

———. *Imitating Jesus: An Inclusive Approach to New Testament Ethics.* Grand Rapids: Eerdmans, 2007.

Byrne, Brendan. *The Hospitality of God: A Reading of Luke's Gospel.* Collegeville, MN: Liturgical Press, 2000.

Cadbury, H. J. "Acts and Eschatology." In *The Background of the New Testament and Its Eschatology*, edited by W. D. Davies and D. Daube, 300–321. Cambridge: Cambridge University Press, 1956.

Caird, G. B. *A Commentary on the Revelation of St. John the Divine.* London: A&C Black, 1966.

———. *Jesus and the Jewish Nation.* London: Athlone, 1965.

———. *The Language and Imagery of the Bible.* London: Duckworth, 1980.

Carrell, Peter R. *Jesus and the Angels: Angelology and the Christology of the Apocalypse of John.* Cambridge: Cambridge University Press, 1997.

Carroll, John T. "The Parousia of Jesus in the Johannine Literature." In *The Return of Jesus in Early Christianity*, by John T. Carroll, with Alexandra R.

Brown, Claudia J. Setzer, and Jeffrey S. Siker, 77–112. Peabody, MA: Hendrickson, 2000.

———. "The Parousia of Jesus in the Synoptic Gospels and Acts." In *The Return of Jesus in Early Christianity*, by John T. Carroll, with Alexandra R. Brown, Claudia J. Setzer, and Jeffrey S. Siker, 5–45. Peabody, MA: Hendrickson, 2000.

———. "Present and Future in Fourth Gospel 'Eschatology.'" *Biblical Theology Bulletin* 19, no. 2 (April 1989): 63–69.

———. *Response to the End of History: Eschatology and Situation in Luke–Acts*. SBL Dissertation Series 92. Atlanta: Scholars Press, 1988.

Carroll, John T., with Alexandra R. Brown, Claudia J. Setzer, and Jeffrey S. Siker. *The Return of Jesus in Early Christianity*. Peabody, MA: Hendrickson, 2000.

Carter, Warren. "Constructions of Violence and Identities in Matthew's Gospel." In *Violence in the New Testament*, edited by Shelly Matthews and E. Leigh Gibson, 81–108. New York: T&T Clark, 2005.

Chance, J. Bradley. *Jerusalem, the Temple, and the New Age in Luke–Acts*. Macon, GA: Mercer University Press, 1988.

Charette, Blaine. *The Theme of Recompense in Matthew's Gospel*. Sheffield: JSOT Press, 1992.

Collins, Adela Yarbro. "Appreciating the Apocalypse as a Whole." *Interpretation* 45 (1991): 187–89.

———. "The Book of Revelation." In *The Origins of Apocalypticism in Judaism and Christianity*, ed. John J. Collins, 384–414. Vol. 1 of *The Encyclopedia of Apocalypticism*. Edited by John J. Collins, Bernard McGinn, and Stephen J. Stein. New York: Continuum, 2000.

———. *Cosmology and Eschatology in Jewish and Christian Apocalypticism*. Leiden: Brill, 1996.

———. "Eschatology in the Book of Revelation." *Ex auditu* 6 (1990): 63–72.

———. *Mark: A Commentary*. Hermeneia. Minneapolis: Fortress, 2007.

———. "Revelation, Book of." In *The Anchor Bible Dictionary*, edited by David Noel Freedman et al., 5:694–708. New York: Doubleday, 1992.

Collins, Adela Yarbro, and John J. Collins. *King and Messiah as Son of God: Divine, Human, and Angelic Messianic Figures in Biblical and Related Literature*. Grand Rapids: Eerdmans, 2008.

Collins, John J. *The Apocalyptic Imagination: An Introduction to Jewish Apocalyptic Literature*. 2nd ed. Grand Rapids: Eerdmans, 1998.

———. *Does the Bible Justify Violence?* Minneapolis: Fortress, 2004.

———. "From Prophecy to Apocalypticism: The Expectation of the End." In *The Origins of Apocalypticism in Judaism and Christianity*, ed. John J. Collins,

129–61. Vol. 1 of *The Encyclopedia of Apocalypticism*. Edited by John J. Collins, Bernard McGinn, and Stephen J. Stein. New York: Continuum, 2000.

———. "Introduction: Towards the Morphology of a Genre." *Semeia* 14 (1979): 1–20.

———. *The Scepter and the Star: Messianism in Light of the Dead Sea Scrolls*. 2nd ed. Grand Rapids: Eerdmans, 2010.

Conzelmann, Hans. *Die Apostelgeschichte*. Tübingen: J. C. B. Mohr, 1963. ET, *Acts of the Apostles: A Commentary on the Acts of the Apostles*. Translated by James Limburg, A. Thomas Kraabel, and Donald Juel. Hermeneia. Philadelphia: Fortress, 1987.

———. *Die Mitte der Zeit: Studien zur Theologie des Lukas*. Tübingen: Mohr Siebeck, 1954. ET, *The Theology of St. Luke*. Translated by G. Buswell. London: Faber & Faber; New York: Harper & Brothers, 1960.

———. "Zur Lukasanalyse." *Zeitschrift für Theologie und Kirche* 49 (1952): 16–33.

Cooper, Ben. "Adaptive Eschatological Inference from the Gospel of Matthew." *Journal for the Study of the New Testament* 33 (2010): 59–80.

Cosgrove, Charles H. *Appealing to Scripture in Moral Debate: Five Hermeneutical Rules*. Grand Rapids: Eerdmans, 2002.

Crossan, John Dominic. *The Birth of Christianity: Discovering What Happened in the Years Immediately after the Execution of Jesus*. San Francisco: HarperOne, 1998.

———. "Divine Violence in the Christian Bible." In *The Bible and the American Future*, edited by Robert L. Jewett, with Wayne L. Alloway Jr. and John G. Lacy, 208–36. Eugene, OR: Cascade Books, 2009.

———. "Eschatology, Apocalypticism, and the Historical Jesus." In *Jesus Then and Now: Images of Jesus in History and Christology*, edited by Marvin Meyer and Charles Hughes, 91–112. Harrisburg, PA: Trinity Press International, 2001.

———. *God and Empire: Jesus against Rome, Then and Now*. San Francisco: HarperOne, 2007.

———. *The Historical Jesus: The Life of a Mediterranean Jewish Peasant*. San Francisco: HarperOne, 1991.

———. *In Parables: The Challenge of the Historical Jesus*. New York: Harper & Row, 1973.

———. "Jesus and the Challenge of Collaborative Eschatology." In *The Historical Jesus: Five Views*, edited by James K. Beilby and Paul Rhodes Eddy, 105–32. Downers Grove, IL: IVP Academic, 2009.

Culy, Martin M., and Mikeal C. Parsons. *Acts: A Handbook on the Greek Text*. Waco: Baylor University Press, 2003.

Davies, Eryl W. *The Immoral Bible: Approaches to Biblical Ethics*. New York: T&T Clark, 2010.

———. "The Morally Dubious Passages of the Hebrew Bible: An Examination of Some Proposed Solutions." *Currents in Biblical Research* 3 (2005): 197–228.

Davies, W. D., and Dale C. Allison. *A Critical and Exegetical Commentary on the Gospel according to Saint Matthew*. 3 vols. International Critical Commentary. Edinburgh: T&T Clark, 1988, 1990, 1997.

Davis, Ellen F. "Critical Traditioning: Seeking an Inner Biblical Hermeneutic." *Anglican Theological Review* 82 (2000): 733–51.

De Boer, Martinus C. "Jesus' Departure to the Father in John: Death or Resurrection?" In *Theology and Christology in the Fourth Gospel*, edited by G. van Belle, J. G. van der Watt, and P. Maritz, 1–19. Leuven: Uitgeverij Peeters; Leuven University Press, 2005.

Desjardins, Michel. *Peace, Violence and the New Testament*. Sheffield: Sheffield Academic Press, 1997.

Dodd, C. H. *The Apostolic Preaching and Its Developments*. London: Hodder & Stoughton, 1936.

———. "The Fall of Jerusalem and the 'Abomination of Desolation.'" In *More New Testament Studies*, 69–83. Manchester: Manchester University Press, 1968.

———. *The Interpretation of the Fourth Gospel*. Cambridge: Cambridge University Press, 1953.

Douglass, James W. *The Nonviolent Coming of God*. Maryknoll, NY: Orbis Books, 1991.

Dyer, Keith D. "Conflicting Contexts: Old Testament Reinterpretation and the Multi-ethnic Community in the Gospel of Mark." In *Prophecy and Passion: Essays in Honour of Athol Gill*, edited by David Neville, 190–208. Adelaide: Australian Theological Forum, 2002.

———. *The Prophecy on the Mount: Mark 13 and the Gathering of the New Community*. Bern: Peter Lang, 1998.

Edwards, Sarah Alexander. "Christological Perspectives in the Book of Revelation." In *Christological Perspectives: Essays in Honor of Harvey K. McArthur*, edited by Robert F. Berkey and Sarah A. Edwards, 139–54, 281–86. New York: Pilgrim, 1982.

Eusebius. *The Ecclesiastical History*. Translated by Kirsopp Lake. Vol. 1. Loeb Classical Library. New York: G. P. Putnam's Sons, 1926.

Evans, Christopher F. "The Central Section of Luke's Gospel." In *Studies in the Gospels*, edited by D. E. Nineham, 37–53. Oxford: Blackwell, 1955.

———. *Saint Luke*. Philadelphia: Trinity Press International, 1990.

Evans, Craig A. *Mark 8:27–16:20*. Word Biblical Commentary. Nashville: Thomas Nelson, 2001.

Finamore, Stephen. "A Kinder, Gentler Apocalypse? René Girard, the Book of Revelation, and the Bottomless Abyss of the Unforgettable Victim." In *Compassionate Eschatology: The Future as Friend*, edited by Ted Grimsrud and Michael Hardin, 196–217. Eugene, OR: Cascade Books, 2011.

Fiorenza, Elisabeth Schüssler. *Revelation: Vision of a Just World*. Minneapolis: Fortress, 1991.

———. "The Words of Prophecy: Reading the Apocalypse Theologically." In *Studies in the Book of Revelation*, edited by Steve Moyise, 1–19. New York: T&T Clark, 2001.

Fishbane, Michael. *Biblical Interpretation in Ancient Israel*. Oxford: Clarendon, 1985.

Fisk, Bruce N. "*See My Tears*: A Lament for Jerusalem (Luke 13:31–35; 19:41–44)." In *The Word Leaps the Gap: Essays on Scripture and Theology in Honor of Richard B. Hays*, edited by J. Ross Wagner, C. Kavin Rowe, and A. Katherine Grieb, 147–78. Grand Rapids: Eerdmans, 2008.

Fitzmyer, Joseph A. *The Acts of the Apostles: A New Translation with Introduction and Commentary*. Anchor Bible 31. New York: Doubleday, 1998.

———. *The Gospel according to Luke (I–IX): Introduction, Translation, and Notes*. Anchor Bible 28. Garden City, NY: Doubleday, 1981.

———. *The Gospel according to Luke (X–XXIV): Introduction, Translation, and Notes*. Anchor Bible 28A. Garden City, NY: Doubleday, 1985.

Flender, Helmut. *St. Luke: Theologian of Redemptive History*. Translated by R. H. and I. Fuller. London: SPCK, 1967.

Ford, Josephine Massyngbaerde. *My Enemy Is My Guest: Jesus and Violence in Luke*. Maryknoll, NY: Orbis Books, 1984.

France, Richard T. *The Gospel of Mark: A Commentary on the Greek Text*. New International Greek Testament Commentary. Grand Rapids: Eerdmans, 2002.

———. *The Gospel of Matthew*. New International Commentary on the New Testament. Grand Rapids: Eerdmans, 2007.

———. *Jesus and the Old Testament: His Application of Old Testament Passages to Himself and His Mission*. London: Tyndale, 1971.

Franklin, Eric. "The Ascension and the Eschatology of Luke–Acts." *Scottish Journal of Theology* 23 (1970): 191–200.

———. *Christ the Lord: A Study in the Purpose and Theology of Luke–Acts*. London: SPCK, 1975.

Galtung, Johan. "Cultural Violence." In *Violence and Its Alternatives: An Interdisciplinary Reader*, edited by Manfred Steger and Nancy Lind, 39–53. New York: St. Martin's Press, 1999.

Garland, David E. *Reading Matthew: A Literary and Theological Commentary.* Macon, GA: Smyth & Helwys, 2001.

Gathercole, Simon. "The Son of Man in Mark's Gospel." *Expository Times* 115 (2004): 366–72.

Gaventa, Beverly Roberts. *Acts.* Abingdon New Testament Commentary. Nashville: Abingdon, 2003.

Gibbs, Jeffrey A. *Jerusalem and Parousia: Jesus' Eschatological Discourse in Matthew's Gospel.* Saint Louis: Concordia Academic Press, 2000.

Grassi, Joseph. *Peace on Earth: Roots and Practices from Luke's Gospel.* Collegeville, MN: Liturgical Press, 2004.

Green, Joel B. *The Theology of the Gospel of Luke.* Cambridge: Cambridge University Press, 1995.

Gundry, Robert H. *Mark: A Commentary on His Apology for the Cross.* Grand Rapids: Eerdmans, 1993.

Haenchen, Ernst. *The Acts of the Apostles: A Commentary.* Translated by B. Noble and G. Shinn (supervised by H. Anderson) and revised by R. McL. Wilson. Oxford: Blackwell, 1971.

Harrington, Wilfrid J. *Revelation.* Sacra pagina. Collegeville, MN: Liturgical Press, 1993.

Hatina, Thomas R. *In Search of a Context: The Function of Scripture in Mark's Narrative.* New York: Sheffield Academic Press, 2002.

Hays, Richard B. *The Moral Vision of the New Testament—Community, Cross, New Creation: A Contemporary Introduction to New Testament Ethics.* San Francisco: HarperOne, 1996.

———. "'Why Do You Stand Looking Up toward Heaven?': New Testament Eschatology at the Turn of the Millennium." In *Theology and Eschatology at the Turn of the Millennium,* edited by James J. Buckley and L. Gregory Jones, 113–33. Oxford: Blackwell, 2001.

Hoffmann, Matthias Reinhard. *The Destroyer and the Lamb: The Relationship between Angelomorphic and Lamb Christology in the Book of Revelation.* Tübingen: Mohr Siebeck, 2005.

Holland, Scott. "The Gospel of Peace and the Violence of God." *CrossCurrents* 51 (2002): 470–83. Reprinted in *Seeking Cultures of Peace: A Peace Church Conversation,* edited by Fernando Enns, Scott Holland, and Ann K. Riggs, 132–46. Telford, PA: Cascadia, 2004.

Hood, Jason. "Matthew 23–25: The Extent of Jesus' Fifth Discourse." *Journal of Biblical Literature* 128 (2009): 527–43.

Hooker, Morna D. *A Commentary on the Gospel according to St Mark.* London: A&C Black, 1991.

———. *The Son of Man in Mark.* London: SPCK, 1967.

Horbury, William. "The Benediction of the *Minim* and Early Jewish-Christian Controversy." *Journal of Theological Studies* 33 (1982): 19–61.

Howard-Brook, Wes, and Anthony G. Gwyther. *Unveiling Empire: Reading Revelation Then and Now*. Maryknoll, NY: Orbis Books, 1999.

Hurtado, L. W. "Revelation 4–5 in the Light of Jewish Apocalyptic Analogies." *Journal for the Study of the New Testament* 25 (1985): 105–24.

Johns, Loren L. *The Lamb Christology of the Apocalypse of John: An Investigation into Its Origins and Rhetorical Force*. Tübingen: Mohr Siebeck, 2003.

Johnson, Luke Timothy. *The Acts of the Apostles*. Sacra pagina. Collegeville, MN: Liturgical Press, 1992.

———. *The Gospel of Luke*. Sacra pagina. Collegeville, MN: Liturgical Press, 1991.

———. "The Lukan Kingship Parable (Lk. 19:11–27)." *Novum Testamentum* 24 (1982): 139–59.

———. "The New Testament's Anti-Jewish Slander and the Conventions of Ancient Rhetoric." *Journal of Biblical Literature* 108 (1989): 419–41.

Justin. *The First Apology of Justin, the Martyr*. Edited and translated by Edward R. Hardy. In *Early Christian Fathers*, ed. Cyril C. Richardson et al., 225–89. Library of Christian Classics 1. London: SCM, 1953.

Käsemann, Ernst. "Sentences of Holy Law in the New Testament." In *New Testament Questions of Today*, 66–81. Translated by W. J. Montague. London: SCM, 1969.

Katz, Stephen. "Issues in the Separation of Judaism and Christianity after 70 CE: A Reconsideration." *Journal of Biblical Literature* 103 (1984): 43–76.

Keck, Leander E. *Paul and His Letters*. 2nd ed. Philadelphia: Fortress, 1988.

———. *Who Is Jesus? History in Perfect Tense*. Columbia: University of South Carolina Press, 2000.

Kimelman, Reuven. "*Birkat Ha-Minim* and the Lack of Evidence for an Anti-Christian Jewish Prayer in Late Antiquity." In *Aspects of Judaism in the Greco-Roman Period*, edited by E. P. Sanders, 226–44, 391–403. Vol. 2 of *Jewish and Christian Self-Definition*. Edited by E. P. Sanders et al. Philadelphia: Fortress, 1981.

Kinman, Brent. "Parousia, Jesus' 'A-Triumphal' Entry, and the Fate of Jerusalem (Luke 19:28–44)." *Journal of Biblical Literature* 118 (1999): 279–94.

Kitchen, Merrill. "Rereading the Parable of the Pounds: A Social and Narrative Analysis of Luke 19:11–28." In *Prophecy and Passion: Essays in Honour of Athol Gill*, edited by David Neville, 227–46. Adelaide: Australian Theological Forum, 2002.

Klassen, William. "Vengeance in the Apocalypse of John." *Catholic Biblical Quarterly* 28 (1966): 300–311.

Knight, J. "The Enthroned Christ of Revelation 5:6 and the Development of Christian Theology." In *Studies in the Book of Revelation*, edited by Steve Moyise, 43–50. New York: T&T Clark, 2001.

Koester, Craig R. *The Word of Life: A Theology of John's Gospel*. Grand Rapids: Eerdmans, 2008.

Kovacs, Judith L. "'Now Shall the Ruler of This World Be Driven Out': Jesus' Death as Cosmic Battle in John 12:20–36." *Journal of Biblical Literature* 114 (1995): 227–47.

Kupp, David D. *Matthew's Emmanuel: Divine Presence and God's People in the First Gospel*. Cambridge: Cambridge University Press, 1996.

Kysar, Robert. *John, the Maverick Gospel*. 3rd ed. Louisville: Westminster John Knox, 2007.

Lambrecht, Jan. "Q-Influence on Mark 8,34–9,1." In *LOGIA: Les paroles de Jesus—The Sayings of Jesus*, edited by J. Delobel, 277–304. Leuven: Uitgeverij Peeters; Leuven University Press, 1982.

Lee, Dorothy. *Transfiguration*. New York: Continuum, 2004.

Liew, Tat-Siong Benny. *Politics of Parousia: Reading Mark Inter(con)textually*. Leiden: Brill, 1999.

Lightfoot, R. H. *The Gospel Message of St Mark*. Oxford: Clarendon, 1950.

Loader, William. *The Christology of the Fourth Gospel: Structure and Issues*. Rev. ed. Frankfurt: Peter Lang, 1992.

Lorenzen, Thorwald. "Justice Anchored in Truth: A Theological Perspective on the Nature and Implementation of Justice." *International Journal of Public Theology* 3 (2009): 281–98.

Luz, Ulrich. *Matthew in History: Interpretation, Influence, and Effects*. Minneapolis: Fortress, 1994.

———. *Matthew 21–28: A Commentary*. Translated by James E. Crouch. Hermeneia. Minneapolis: Fortress, 2005.

Mack, Burton L. *A Myth of Innocence: Mark and Christian Origins*. Philadelphia: Fortress, 1988.

Malbon, Elizabeth Struthers. *Mark's Jesus: Characterization as Narrative Christology*. Waco: Baylor University Press, 2009.

Malina, Bruce J., and Richard L. Rohrbaugh. *Social-Science Commentary on the Synoptic Gospels*. 2nd ed. Minneapolis: Fortress, 2003.

Mann, C. S. *Mark: A New Translation with Introduction and Commentary*. Anchor Bible 27. Garden City, NY: Doubleday, 1986.

Marcus, Joel. "Birkat Ha-Minim Revisited." *New Testament Studies* 55 (2009): 523–51.

———. "Entering into the Kingly Power of God." *Journal of Biblical Literature* 107 (1988): 663–75.

———. "Mark—Interpreter of Paul." *New Testament Studies* 46 (2000): 473–87.

———. *Mark 1–8: A New Translation with Introduction and Commentary.* Anchor Bible 27. New York: Doubleday, 2000.

———. *Mark 8–16: A New Translation with Introduction and Commentary.* Anchor Yale Bible 27A. New Haven: Yale University Press, 2009.

———. *The Way of the Lord: Christological Exegesis of the Old Testament in the Gospel of Mark.* Louisville: Westminster John Knox, 1992.

Marguerat, Daniel. *Le jugement dans L'Évangile de Matthieu.* 2nd ed. Geneva: Labor et Fides, 1995.

Marshall, Christopher D. *Beyond Retribution: A New Testament Vision for Justice, Crime, and Punishment.* Grand Rapids: Eerdmans, 2001.

———. "The Violence of God and the Hermeneutics of Paul." In *The Work of Jesus Christ in Anabaptist Perspective,* edited by A. Epp Weaver and G. Biesecker-Mast, 74–105. Telford, PA: Cascadia, 2008.

Marshall, I. Howard. *The Gospel of Luke: A Commentary on the Greek Text.* New International Greek Testament Commentary. Exeter: Paternoster, 1978.

Martyn, J. Louis. *History and Theology in the Fourth Gospel.* 3rd ed. Louisville: Westminster John Knox, 2003.

Mason, Steve. *Josephus and the New Testament.* 2nd ed. Peabody, MA: Hendrickson, 2003.

Mauser, Ulrich. *The Gospel of Peace: A Scriptural Message for Today's World.* Louisville: Westminster John Knox, 1992.

McCann, J. Clinton. "The Hermeneutics of Grace." *Interpretation* 57 (2003): 5–15.

McClendon, James Wm., Jr. *Doctrine.* Vol. 2 of *Systematic Theology.* Nashville: Abingdon, 1994.

McDonald, Patricia M. "Lion as Slain Lamb: On Reading Revelation Recursively." *Horizons* 23 (1996): 29–47.

McKelvey, R. J. "The Millennium and the Second Coming." In *Studies in the Book of Revelation,* edited by Steve Moyise, 85–100. New York: T&T Clark, 2001.

McNicol, Allan J. *Jesus' Directions for the Future: A Source and Redaction-History Study of the Use of the Eschatological Traditions in Paul and in the Synoptic Accounts of Jesus' Last Eschatological Discourse.* Macon, GA: Mercer University Press, 1996.

Meeks, Wayne A. *Christ Is the Question.* Louisville: Westminster John Knox, 2006.

———. "The Ethics of the Fourth Evangelist." In *Exploring the Gospel of John: In Honor of D. Moody Smith,* edited by R. Alan Culpepper and C. Clifton Black, 317–26. Louisville: Westminster John Knox, 1996.

Mendham, Peter. "In the Green Wood: Jesus' Address to the Women of Jerusalem and the Destiny of Israel." *St. Mark's Review* 161 (Autumn 1995): 18–22.

Metzger, Bruce M. *A Textual Commentary on the Greek New Testament.* 2nd ed. Stuttgart: Deutsche Bibelgesellschaft, 1994.

Meyer, Ben F. *The Aims of Jesus.* London: SCM, 1979.

Migliore, Daniel L. *Faith Seeking Understanding: An Introduction to Christian Theology.* 2nd ed. Grand Rapids: Eerdmans, 2002.

Milbank, John. *Theology and Social Theory: Beyond Secular Reason.* Oxford: Blackwell, 1990.

Moessner, David P. "How Luke Writes." In *The Written Gospel*, edited by Markus Bockmuehl and Donald A. Hagner, 149–70. Cambridge: Cambridge University Press, 2005.

———. *Lord of the Banquet: The Literary and Theological Significance of the Lukan Travel Narrative.* Minneapolis: Fortress, 1989.

Moore, Richard K. *Rectification ("Justification") in Paul, in Historical Perspective and in the English Bible: God's Gift of Right Relationship.* Part 1, *Paul's Doctrine of Rectification.* Lewiston, NY: Edwin Mellen, 2002.

Moyise, Steve. "Does the Lion Lie Down with the Lamb?" In *Studies in the Book of Revelation*, edited by Steve Moyise, 181–94. New York: T&T Clark, 2001.

Myers, Ched. *Binding the Strong Man: A Political Reading of Mark's Story of Jesus.* Maryknoll, NY: Orbis Books, 1988.

Neville, David J. "Creation Reclaimed: Resurrection and Responsibility in Mark 15:40–16:8." In *Resurrection and Responsibility: Essays on Theology, Scripture, and Ethics in Honor of Thorwald Lorenzen*, edited by Keith D. Dyer and David J. Neville, 95–115. Eugene, OR: Pickwick Publications, 2009.

———. "Faithful, True, and Violent? Christology and 'Divine Vengeance' in the Revelation to John." In *Compassionate Eschatology: The Future as Friend*, edited by Ted Grimsrud and Michael Hardin, 56–84. Eugene, OR: Cascade Books, 2011.

———. "God's Presence and Power: Christology, Eschatology and 'Theodicy' in Mark's Crucifixion Narrative." In *Theodicy and Eschatology*, edited by Bruce Barber and David Neville, 19–41. Adelaide: ATF Press, 2005.

———. "Grace Elicits Correspondences: The Theologian as Peacemaker." In *Embracing Grace—The Theologian's Task: Essays in Honour of Graeme Garrett*, edited by Heather Thomson, 119–34. Canberra: Barton Books, 2009.

———. "Justice and Divine Judgement: Scriptural Perspectives for Public Theology." *International Journal of Public Theology* 3 (2009): 339–56.

————. "Moral Vision and Eschatology in Mark's Gospel: Coherence or Conflict?" *Journal of Biblical Literature* 127 (2008): 359–84.

————. "The Second Testament as a Covenant of Peace." *Biblical Theology Bulletin* 37, no. 1 (2007): 27–35.

————. "Toward a Teleology of Peace: Contesting Matthew's Violent Eschatology." *Journal for the Study of the New Testament* 30 (2007): 131–61.

————. "Violating Faith via Eschatological Violence: Reviewing Matthew's Eschatology." In *Validating Violence—Violating Faith? Religion, Scripture and Violence*, edited by William W. Emilsen and John T. Squires, 95–110. Adelaide: ATF Press, 2008.

Nicholson, Godfrey C. *Death as Departure: The Johannine Descent–Ascent Schema*. Chico, CA: Scholars Press, 1983.

Nickelsburg, George W. E. "Son of Man." In *The Anchor Bible Dictionary*, edited by David Noel Freedman et al., 6:137–50. New York: Doubleday, 1992.

Nickelsburg, George W. E., and James C. VanderKam. *1 Enoch: A New Translation*. Minneapolis: Fortress, 2004.

Nietzsche, Friedrich. *Zur Genealogie der Moral: Eine Streitschrift*. Leipzig: C. G. Naumann, 1887. ET, *The Birth of Tragedy and The Genealogy of Morals*. Translated by Francis Golffing. Garden City, NY: Doubleday Anchor Books, 1956.

O'Donnell, Tim. "Complementary Eschatologies in John 5:19–30." *Catholic Biblical Quarterly* 70 (2008): 750–65.

Painter, John. "Earth Made Whole: John's Rereading of Genesis." In *Word, Theology, and Community in John*, edited by John Painter, R. Alan Culpepper, and Fernando F. Segovia, 65–84. St. Louis: Chalice, 2002.

————. *1, 2, and 3 John*. Sacra pagina. Collegeville, MN: Liturgical Press, 2002.

————. "The Johannine Literature." In *Handbook to Exegesis of the New Testament*, edited by S. Porter, 555–90. Leiden: Brill, 1997.

————. "'The Light Shines in the Darkness . . .': Creation, Incarnation, and Resurrection in John." In *The Resurrection of Jesus in the Gospel of John*, edited by Craig R. Koester and Reimund Bieringer, 21–46. Tübingen: Mohr Siebeck, 2008.

————. "Monotheism and Dualism: John and Qumran." In *Theology and Christology in the Fourth Gospel*, edited by G. van Belle, J. G. van der Watt, and P. Maritz, 225–43. Leuven: Uitgeverij Peeters; Leuven University Press, 2005.

————. "The Point of John's Christology: Christology, Conflict and Community in John." In *Christology, Controversy and Community: New Testament Essays in Honour of David R. Catchpole*, edited by David G. Horrell and Christopher M. Tuckett, 231–52. Leiden: Brill, 2000.

———. *The Quest for the Messiah: The History, Literature and Theology of the Johannine Community*. Edinburgh: T&T Clark, 1991. 2nd ed., 1993.

———. "Rereading Genesis in the Prologue of John?" In *Neotestamentica et Philonica: Studies in Honor of Peder Borgen*, edited by David E. Aune, Torrey Seland, and Jerl Henning Ulrichsen, 179–201. Leiden: Brill, 2003.

———. "Theology, Eschatology and the Prologue of John." *Scottish Journal of Theology* 46 (1993): 27–42.

———. "Who Was James? Footprints as a Means of Identification." In *The Brother of Jesus: James the Just and His Mission*, edited by Bruce Chilton and Jacob Neusner, 10–65. Louisville: Westminster John Knox, 2001.

Parsons, Mikeal C. *The Departure of Jesus in Luke–Acts: The Ascension Narratives in Context*. Sheffield: JSOT Press, 1987.

———. *Luke: Storyteller, Interpreter, Evangelist*. Peabody, MA: Hendrickson, 2007.

———. "The Place of Jerusalem on the Lukan Landscape: An Exercise in Symbolic Cartography." In *Literary Studies in Luke–Acts: Essays in Honor of Joseph B. Tyson*, edited by Richard P. Thompson and Thomas E. Phillips, 155–71. Macon, GA: Mercer University Press, 1998.

Pervo, Richard I. *Acts: A Commentary*. Hermeneia. Minneapolis: Fortress, 2009.

Peterson, David G. *The Acts of the Apostles*. Grand Rapids: Eerdmans, 2009.

Phelan, John E. "God, Judgment, and Non-Violence." In *Compassionate Eschatology: The Future as Friend*, edited by Ted Grimsrud and Michael Hardin, 116–33. Eugene, OR: Cascade Books, 2011.

Pitre, Brant. *Jesus, the Tribulation, and the End of Exile: Restoration Eschatology and the Origin of the Atonement*. Grand Rapids: Baker Academic, 2005.

Pregeant, Russell. *Knowing Truth, Doing Good: Engaging New Testament Ethics*. Minneapolis: Fortress, 2008.

Pritchard, James B., ed. *Ancient Near Eastern Texts Relating to the Old Testament*. 3rd ed. Princeton: Princeton University Press, 1969.

Reid, Barbara E. "Violent Endings in Matthew's Parables and Christian Nonviolence." *Catholic Biblical Quarterly* 66 (2004): 237–55.

———. "Which God Is with Us?" *Interpretation* 64 (2010): 380–89.

Reinhartz, Adele. "Love, Hate, and Violence in the Gospel of John." In *Violence in the New Testament*, edited by Shelly Matthews and E. Leigh Gibson, 109–23. New York: T&T Clark, 2005.

Reiser, Marius. *Jesus and Judgment: The Eschatological Proclamation in Its Jewish Context*. Translated by Linda M. Maloney. Minneapolis: Fortress, 1997.

Rensberger, David. "Love for One Another and Love for Enemies in the Gospel of John." In *The Love of Enemy and Nonretaliation in the New Testament*, edited by Willard M. Swartley, 297–313. Louisville: Westminster John Knox, 1992.

Resseguie, James L. *Narrative Criticism of the New Testament: An Introduction*. Grand Rapids: Baker Academic, 2005.

———. *The Revelation of John: A Narrative Commentary*. Grand Rapids: Baker Academic, 2009.

———. *Revelation Unsealed: A Narrative Critical Approach to John's Apocalypse*. Leiden: Brill, 1998.

Rhoads, David. *Reading Mark: Engaging the Gospel*. Minneapolis: Fortress, 2004.

Riches, John K. *Conflicting Mythologies: Identity Formation in the Gospels of Mark and Matthew*. Edinburgh: T&T Clark, 2000.

———. *Jesus and the Transformation of Judaism*. London: Darton, Longman & Todd, 1980.

Ricoeur, Paul. *The Symbolism of Evil*. New York: Harper & Row, 1967.

Robinson, J. A. T. "The Most Primitive Christology of All." In *Twelve New Testament Studies*, 139–53. London: SCM, 1962.

Rowland, Christopher C. "The Book of Revelation: Introduction, Commentary, and Reflections." In *The New Interpreter's Bible*, edited by Leander E. Keck et al., 12:501–743. Nashville: Abingdon, 1998.

———. *Christian Origins: An Account of the Setting and Character of the Most Important Sect of Judaism*. 2nd ed. London: SPCK, 2002.

———. "Imagining the Apocalypse." *New Testament Studies* 51 (2005): 303–27.

———. *The Open Heaven: A Study of Apocalyptic in Judaism and Early Christianity*. New York: Crossroad, 1982.

Rowland, Christopher, and Mark Corner. *Liberating Exegesis: The Challenge of Liberation Theology to Biblical Studies*. London: SPCK, 1990.

Schaberg, Jane. "Mark 14.62: Early Christian Merkabah Imagery?" In *Apocalyptic and the New Testament: Essays in Honor of J. Louis Martyn*, edited by Joel Marcus and Marion L. Soards, 69–94. Sheffield: JSOT Press, 1989.

Schnelle, Udo. *The History and Theology of the New Testament Writings*. Translated by M. Eugene Boring. London: SCM, 1998.

———. *Theology of the New Testament*. Translated by M. Eugene Boring. Grand Rapids: Baker Academic, 2009.

Schrage, Wolfgang. *The Ethics of the New Testament*. Translated by David E. Green. Philadelphia: Fortress, 1988.

Senior, Donald. *The Passion of Jesus in the Gospel of Luke*. Collegeville, MN: Liturgical Press, 1989.

Sim, David C. "The Rise and Fall of the Gospel of Matthew." *Expository Times* 120 (2009): 478–85.

Skaggs, Rebecca, and Thomas Doyle. "Lion/Lamb in Revelation." *Currents in Biblical Research* 7 (2009): 362–75.

———. "Violence in the Apocalypse of John." *Currents in Biblical Research* 5 (2007): 220–34.

Slater, Thomas B. *Christ and Community: A Socio-Historical Study of the Christology of Revelation.* Sheffield: Sheffield Academic Press, 1999.

Smalley, Stephen S. *The Revelation to John: A Commentary on the Greek Text of the Apocalypse.* Downers Grove, IL: InterVarsity, 2005.

Smith, D. Moody. "Ethics and the Interpretation of the Fourth Gospel." In *Word, Theology, and Community in John*, edited by John Painter, R. Alan Culpepper, and Fernando F. Segovia, 109–22. St. Louis: Chalice, 2002.

———. *The Theology of the Gospel of John.* Cambridge: Cambridge University Press, 1995.

Snodgrass, Klyne R. *Stories with Intent: A Comprehensive Guide to the Parables of Jesus.* Grand Rapids: Eerdmans, 2008.

Soards, Marion L. *The Speeches in Acts: Their Content, Context, and Concerns.* Louisville: Westminster John Knox, 1994.

Sparks, Kenton L. "*Enūma Elish* and Priestly Mimesis: Elite Emulation in Nascent Judaism." *Journal of Biblical Literature* 126 (2007): 625–48.

Stanton, Graham N. *A Gospel for a New People: Studies in Matthew.* Louisville: Westminster John Knox, 1993.

———. "The Two Parousias of Christ: Justin Martyr and Matthew." In *From Jesus to John: Essays on Jesus and New Testament Christology in Honour of Marinus de Jonge*, edited by Martinus C. de Boer, 183–95. Sheffield: JSOT Press, 1993.

Swartley, Willard M. *Covenant of Peace: The Missing Peace in New Testament Theology and Ethics.* Grand Rapids: Eerdmans, 2006.

———. *Israel's Scripture Traditions and the Synoptic Gospels: Story Shaping Story.* Peabody, MA: Hendrickson, 1994.

———. "Politics and Peace (*Eirēnē*) in Luke's Gospel." In *Political Issues in Luke–Acts*, edited by Richard J. Cassidy and Philip J. Scharper, 18–37. Maryknoll, NY: Orbis Books, 1983.

———. "The Relation of Justice/Righteousness to *Shalom/Eirēnē*." *Ex auditu* 22 (2006): 29–53.

———. "War and Peace in the New Testament." In *Aufstieg und Niedergang der römishen Welt: Geschichte und Kultur Roms im Spiegel der neueren Forschung*, edited by Wolfgang Haase and Hildegard Temporini, part 2, *Principat* 26.3:2298–408. New York: de Gruyter, 1996.

Sweet, John. *Revelation*. London: SCM, 1979.

Tannehill, Robert C. "Freedom and Responsibility in Scripture Interpretation, with Application to Luke." In *Literary Studies in Luke–Acts: Essays in Honor of Joseph B. Tyson*, edited by Richard P. Thompson and Thomas E. Phillips, 265–78. Macon, GA: Mercer University Press, 1998.

———. *Luke*. Abingdon New Testament Commentary. Nashville: Abingdon, 1996.

———. *The Narrative Unity of Luke–Acts: A Literary Interpretation*. Vol. 1, *The Gospel according to Luke*. Vol. 2, *The Acts of the Apostles*. Philadelphia: Fortress, 1986–90.

———. *The Sword of His Mouth: Forceful and Imaginative Language in Synoptic Sayings*. Philadelphia: Fortress; Missoula, MT: Scholars Press, 1975.

Taylor, Vincent. *The Gospel according to St. Mark*. 2nd ed. London: Macmillan, 1966.

Theissen, Gerd. *Gospel Writing and Church Politics: A Socio-rhetorical Approach*. Hong Kong: Theology Division, Chung Chi College, 2001.

———. *A Theory of Primitive Christian Religion*. Translated by John Bowden. London: SCM, 1999.

Thomas, David Andrew. *Revelation 19 in Historical and Mythological Context*. New York: Peter Lang, 2008.

Tobin, Thomas H. "Logos." In *The Anchor Bible Dictionary*, edited by David Noel Freedman et al., 4:348–56. New York: Doubleday, 1992.

Travis, Stephen H. *Christ and the Judgement of God: The Limits of Divine Retribution in New Testament Thought*. Rev. ed. Milton Keynes: Paternoster; Peabody, MA: Hendrickson, 2009.

Trocmé, André. *Jesus and the Non-Violent Revolution*. Scottdale, PA: Herald Press, 1973.

Trompf, G. W. *Early Christian Historiography: Narratives of Retributive Justice*. New York: Continuum, 2000.

Tyson, Joseph B., ed. *Luke–Acts and the Jewish People: Eight Critical Perspectives*. Minneapolis: Augsburg, 1988.

Verhey, Allen. *The Great Reversal: Ethics and the New Testament*. Grand Rapids: Eerdmans, 1984.

Verheyden, Joseph. "Describing the Parousia: The Cosmic Phenomena in Mk 13,24–25." In *The Scriptures in the Gospels*, edited by Christopher M. Tuckett, 525–50. Leuven: Uitgeverij Peeters; Leuven University Press, 1997.

Volf, Miroslav. *Exclusion and Embrace: A Theological Exploration of Identity, Otherness, and Reconciliation*. Nashville: Abingdon, 1996.

Walker, Peter W. L. *Jesus and the Holy City: New Testament Perspectives on Jerusalem*. Grand Rapids: Eerdmans, 1996.

Wall, Robert W. "The Eschatologies of the Peace Movement." *Biblical Theology Bulletin* 15 (1985): 3–11.

Watts, Rikki E. *Isaiah's New Exodus in Mark*. Grand Rapids: Baker Academic, 2000.

Weaver, J. Denny. *The Nonviolent Atonement*. 2nd ed. Grand Rapids: Eerdmans, 2011.

Weiss, Johannes. *Jesus' Proclamation of the Kingdom of God*. Translated and edited by Richard H. Hiers and D. Larrimore Holland. Philadelphia: Fortress, 1971. Reprinted, Chico, CA: Scholars Press, 1985.

Wengst, Klaus. "Aspects of the Last Judgment in the Gospel according to Matthew." In *Eschatology in the Bible and in Jewish and Christian Tradition*, edited by H. G. Reventlow, 233–45. Sheffield: Sheffield Academic Press, 1997.

Whealon, John F. "New Patches on an Old Garment: The Book of Revelation." *Biblical Theology Bulletin* 11 (1981): 54–59.

Wilson, Alistair I. *When Will These Things Happen? A Study of Jesus as Judge in Matthew 21–25*. Waynesboro, GA: Paternoster, 2004.

Wink, Walter. *Engaging the Powers: Discernment and Resistance in a World of Domination*. Minneapolis: Fortress, 1992.

———. *The Human Being: Jesus and the Enigma of the Son of the Man*. Minneapolis: Fortress, 2002.

———. "'The Son of the Man' in the Gospel of John." In *Jesus in Johannine Tradition*, edited by Robert T. Fortna and Tom Thatcher, 117–23. Louisville: Westminster John Knox, 2001.

Witherington, Ben, III. *The Acts of the Apostles: A Socio-Rhetorical Commentary*. Grand Rapids: Eerdmans, 1998.

Wright, N. T. *Jesus and the Victory of God*. Vol. 2 of *Christian Origins and the Question of God*. Minneapolis: Fortress, 1996.

———. *Luke for Everyone*. 2nd ed. London: SPCK; Louisville: Westminster John Knox, 2004.

———. *The New Testament and the People of God*. Vol. 1 of *Christian Origins and the Question of God*. Minneapolis: Fortress, 1992.

———. *Surprised by Hope*. London: SPCK, 2007.

Yamasaki, Gary. "Shalom for Shepherds: An Audience-Oriented Critical Analysis of Luke 2:8–14." In *Beautiful upon the Mountains: Biblical Essays on Mission, Peace, and the Reign of God*, edited by Mary H. Shertz and Ivan Friesen, 145–60. Elkhart, IN: Institute for Mennonite Studies; Scottdale, PA: Herald Press, 2003.

Yinger, Kent L. *Paul, Judaism, and Judgment according to Deeds*. Cambridge: Cambridge University Press, 1999.

Yoder, John Howard. *The Politics of Jesus: Vicit Agnus Noster*. Grand Rapids: Eerdmans, 1972. 2nd ed., 1994.

———. "To Serve Our God and to Rule the World." In *The Royal Priesthood: Essays Ecclesiological and Ecumenical*, edited by Michael G. Cartwright, 127–40. Grand Rapids: Eerdmans, 1994.

York, John O. *The Last Shall Be First: The Rhetoric of Reversal in Luke*. Journal for the Study of the New Testament Supplement Series 46. Sheffield: JSOT Press, 1991.

Zehnle, Richard F. *Peter's Pentecost Discourse: Tradition and Lukan Reinterpretation in Peter's Speeches of Acts 2 and 3*. Nashville: Abingdon, 1971.

Subject Index

Scripture Index